A NEW DICTIONARY OF THE FRENCH REVOLUTION

RICHARD BALLARD

I.B. TAURIS

LONDON · NEW YORK

Published in 2012 by I.B.Tauris & Co Ltd
6 Salem Road, London W2 4BU
175 Fifth Avenue, New York NY 10010
www.ibtauris.com

Distributed in the United States and Canada Exclusively by Palgrave Macmillan
175 Fifth Avenue, New York NY 10010

ISBN: 978 1 84885 464 2 (HB)
       978 1 84885 465 9 (PB)

A full CIP record for this book is available from the British Library
A full CIP record is available from the Library of Congress

Library of Congress Catalog Card Number: available

Printed and bound in Great Britain by TJ International Ltd, Padstow, Cornwall

After reading History at Oxford University, Richard Ballard taught at Eton College, Wells Cathedral School, Haileybury and Westminster School. He has lived in the Charente-Maritime since 2003, where he has researched the French Revolution extensively and published articles on the subject. He is the author of *The Unseen Terror: The French Revolution in the Provinces* (I.B.Tauris, 2010).

To Mary

Contents

Preface   ix

Acknowledgements   xi

Maps   xii

A Chronology   xv

Entries A–Z   1

Reference Notes   391

Bibliography   411

General Index   417

Preface

The French Revolution fits the observation (often attributed to Winston Churchill) that history is 'one damned thing after another'. But if we have picked up a book like this, we admit to being interested in, and may even be fascinated by, what happened when the French nation fell into a melting pot and refashioned itself.

The idea of the French Revolution still conjures up the guillotine and knitting women watching aristocratic heads roll, or the Bastille being taken by a ferocious mob and the Terror. It can also suggest Liberty from arbitrary government and Equality before the law. In Abel Gance's 1929 film *Napoleon*, while the Thermidor coup to bring Robespierre down is in full cry, Saint-Just goes to the tribune to recount the positive achievements of the Revolution: 11,210 decrees passed, of which two-thirds were dedicated to humane causes.[1] As we look through the ten years that followed 1789, before it was arranged for a brashly competent general called Bonaparte to take the Revolution over, a sense of balance is often lacking. *A New Dictionary of the French Revolution* aims to help people who are beginning to find their way through the confused scenes of this drama with its huge number of players.

Many personalities and events have entries to themselves, with links indicated by means of bold text. Some entries about minor characters take more space than other more obviously important ones because they have been used to record general developments. Issues and personalities that do not rate an entry of their own, but are mentioned within larger topics, can be found by reference to the General Index.

There are many references in this book to writers about the French Revolution in the English-speaking world. A French lawyer once lent me his well-thumbed copies of all Claude Manceron's series called *Les Hommes de la liberté* published by Robert Laffont in the 1970s, with the comment, 'This is what *we* read about *our* Revolution.' So I have tried, during the compilation of this book, to refer to French commentators as well as to those who write in English. Albert Soboul had not finished editing his *Dictionnaire historique de la Révolution française* when he died in 1982, but it was completed for the Bicentenary in 1989 under the direction of Jean-René Suratteau and François Gendron (Paris, Quadrige/Presses Universitaires de France). The 2006 paperback edition is an unfailing and excellent source of factual information. As it has not been translated into English, the substantial number of references to it will make some of its contents accessible to those readers who may be unable to use it in its original language.

Another indispensable French reference book is *Dictionnaire Critique de La Révolution française*, edited by François Furet and Mona Ozouf (Paris, Flammarion, 1988). This has been translated by Arnold Goldhammer (London, The Belknap Press of Harvard University Press, 1989). My references to the book are from the French edition.

Where a relevant text appears on the Internet, I have given the URL. When I have found it appropriate, I have made suggestions for further reading in English in notes at the end of certain entries and at the end of the book as a bibliography to give a more extensive overview of the whole subject. Where I have made specific reference to sources in the text, I have provided the usual endnotes.

Richard Ballard,
Saint-Sorlin de Conac, 2012

Acknowledgements

Thanks are due to Guy and Henrietta Hopkins who made it possible for me to live in France in the first instance. Guy Hopkins also pointed me towards some of the musicians of the period. Claude and Dinah Teulet found and gave me a copy of *Dictionnaire des chansons de la Révolution* by Ginette and Georges Marty (Paris, Editions Tallandier, 1988). Cecilia Cussans provided me with the three volumes of the *Œuvres poétiques d'André de Chénier*, as well as the six volumes of a bound edition of Chateaubriand's *Mémoires d'outre-tombe* and complete editions of Michelet's *Histoire de France* and *Histoire de la Révolution française*. Andrew Brown and Anne Carman sent me in search of a rich vein of interest in Pierre-Joseph Redouté's work of botanical illustration. Members of a series of sixth forms in the 1990s asked questions and looked for answers.

Mary Critchley has given me constant encouragement and made time to discuss a great deal of what is contained in these pages.

I am grateful to Dr Lester Crook at I.B.Tauris for inviting me to undertake this project, and for the advice given by Joanna Godfrey. I also thank Paul Tompsett at Free Range for preparing the text for publication, and Merilyn Holme for editing my manuscript with such great perspicacity.

Flanders

Artois

Trois-Evêches

Picardy

Ile de France

Caen
Normandy

Paris

Champagne

Lorraine

Alsace

Brittany

Maine

Orléanais

Nantes
Saumurois

Anjou

Touraine

Franche-Comté

Poitou

Berry

Nivernais

Aunis

Bourbonnais

Burgundy

La Rochelle

Marche

Saintonge

Limousin

Auvergne

Lyonnais
Lyon

Grenoble
Dauphiné

Bordeaux

Guyenne and Gascony

Avignon
Languedoc

Provence

Marseille
Toulon

Comtat Venaissin

Roussillon

Béarn

Foix

0   150 km

0   100 mls

⌐·⌐ French frontier 1789

Boundaries of gouvernements
(military frontiers)

The Provinces of Old Regime France and Principal Towns

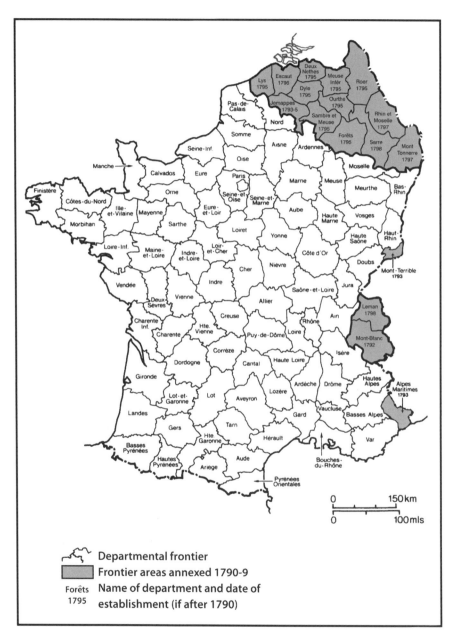

The New Departments of Revolutionary France

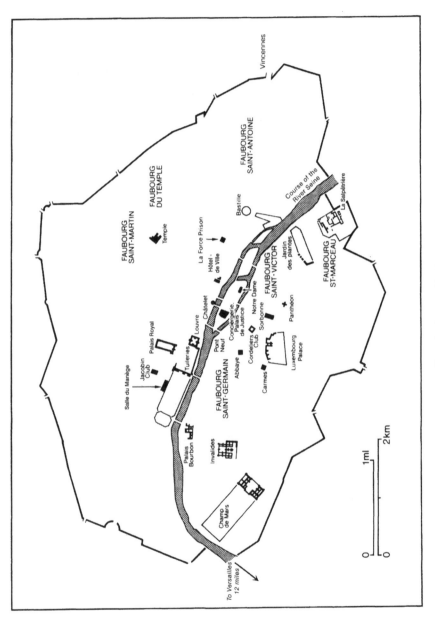

Revolutionary Paris

FAUBOURG SAINT-ANTOINE

FAUBOURG DU TEMPLE

FAUBOURG SAINT-MARTIN

Temple

La Force Prison

Hôtel de Ville

Bastille

Course of the River Seine

La Salpêtrière

Jardin des plantes

FAUBOURG SAINT-VICTOR

FAUBOURG ST-MARCEAU

Châtelet

Conciergerie
Palais de Justice

Notre Dame

Sorbonne

Panthéon

Palais Royal

Louvre

Pont Neuf

Cordeliers Club

Abbaye

Luxembourg Palace

Carmes

FAUBOURG SAINT-GERMAIN

Jacobin Club

Salle du Manège

Tuileries

Palais Bourbon

Invalides

Champ de Mars

To Versailles 12 miles

Vincennes

0   1ml

0   2km

A Chronology

1774
10 May   Louis XVI becomes King of France

1775
11 June   Louis XVI's Coronation at Reims

1776
22 October   Necker made Finance Minister

1778
6 February   Treaty of Alliance signed with American
                          revolutionaries

1781
19 May   Necker leaves government

1783   Treaty of Paris ends American War with no material
                          gain for France
3 November   Calonne becomes comptroller of the finances

1786
20 August   Calonne proposes reforms to Louis XVI

1787

22 February	Opening of the Assembly of Notables
8 April	Calonne dismissed
30 April	Loménie de Brienne becomes comptroller of the finances
25 May	Assembly of Notables ends
August	Paris and Bordeaux *parlements* exiled to Troyes and Libourne

1788

7 June	'Day of Tiles' in Grenoble
21 July	Vizille Assembly
26 August	Necker returns as comptroller of the finances Estates-General called for May 1789
September	*Parlements* of Paris and Bordeaux restored
October–December	Second Assembly of Notables
27 December	'Doubling the third'

1789

February–June	Elections in Provincial Assemblies for Estates-General
27 April	Reveillon Riots
5 May	Estates-General assemble at Versailles
17 June	Third estate declares itself the National Assembly
20 June	Tennis Court Oath
23 June	Royal Session
27 June	Union of Estates by Royal 'invitation'
2–9 July	Troops encircle Paris
11 July	Necker dismissed
12 July	Paris riots
14 July	Storming of the Bastille
15 July	Troops round Paris dispersed
16 July	Necker recalled to office
17 July	Louis XVI accepts the Revolution at the Hôtel de Ville in Paris

4 August	Spontaneous abolition of seigneurialism and church tithe in reaction to 'Great Fear'
26 August	Declaration of the Rights of Man and of the Citizen
10 September	Rejection of two houses for the national legislature
5–6 October	'October Days' in Versailles and Paris
19 October	Constituent Assembly in Archbishop of Paris's palace
2 November	Nationalization of church lands
6 November	Jacobin Club opens in the rue Saint-Honoré
19 December	First appearance of Assignat
24 December	All offices open to non-Catholics

1790

15 January	Creation of 83 departments to replace the provinces
21 January	Equality of capital punishment decreed
26 January	Decree that deputies may not occupy government ministries
13 February	Monastic vows abolished
30 April	Juries introduced
3 June	Slaves' revolt in Martinique
19 June	Abolition of hereditary titles of nobility
12 July	Civil Constitution of the Clergy
14 July	Festival of the Federation
16 August	Justices of the Peace instituted
4 September	Necker leaves for Switzerland
6 September	*Parlements* suppressed
9 October	Revolt of mulattoes in Saint-Domingue
27 November	Oath to Civil Constitution of the Clergy mandatory
30 December	Patents for inventions introduced

1791

28 February	'Day of the Daggers' at the Tuileries
2 April	Death of Mirabeau
4 May	Avignon and Comtat-Venaissin incorporated into France

20–1 June	The King's Flight to Varennes
	Emigration of the Comte de Provence
6 July	Padua Circular from Leopold II
11 July	Cordeliers petition for a republic
17 July	Massacre on the Champ de Mars
25 July	Treaty of Berlin between Austria and Prussia
30 July	Suppression of orders of knighthood
17 August	*Emigrés* ordered to return
27 August	Declaration of Pillnitz
8–13 September	Constitution presented to Louis XVI
14 September	Louis XVI takes oath to the constitution
1 October	Legislative Assembly opens
5 October	Famine in which farmers refuse to take *assignats* as payments
16 October	Louis XVI recalls his brothers
	By now 1,900 army officers are *émigrés*
12 November	Louis XVI refuses to sanction decrees against *émigrés*
17 November	Pétion elected mayor of Paris
22 November	Port au Prince burnt
29 November	Assembly demands that Louis XVI calls upon the princes of the Empire not to allow *émigrés* to assemble in their territory
14 December	Louis XVI ready to declare war on the princes if they do not comply with 29 November resolution
19 December	Louis XVI vetoes decrees about the refractory clergy
20 December	Notice to Trèves to disperse *émigrés*

1792

9 February	Sequestration of *émigrés'* property
1 March	Death of Emperor Leopold II
6 April	Suppression of convents
20 April	Declaration of War upon Francis II, King of Hungary and Bohemia
8 June	Decree about Paris camp for 20,000 *fédérés* vetoed by Louis XVI

12–13 June	Louis XVI dismisses Girondin ministers
20 June	Parisians invade Tuileries. King wears Phrygian bonnet
26 June	Formation of First Coalition against France
7 July	Francis II elected Emperor of Holy Roman Empire
11 July	*Patrie en danger* declared
28 July	Brunswick's declaration known about in Paris
30 July	Arrival of Marseillais in Paris
10 August	Storming of Tuileries Palace
	Royal family seeks refuge in National Assembly
11 August	Monarchy suspended
13 August	Royal family to Temple on Insurrectionary Commune's orders
14 August	Sale of *émigrés'* property
17 August	Tribunal for royalist survivors from Tuileries
18 August	Flight of Lafayette, after failing to persuade his army to restore constitutional monarchy
18–21 August	Foreign ambassadors leave Paris
28–29 August	Domiciliary visits organized to look for suspects
2–6 September	Massacre of royalists in Paris prisons
16 September	National treasury robbed of crown jewels
20 September	French victory at Valmy
21 September	National Convention opens
	Republic proclaimed
23 September	Conquest of Savoy starting with Chambery
28 September	Nice taken
29 September	Louis XVI separated from his family in Temple tower
8 October	Siege of Lille raised
9 October	Decree of immediate death for *émigrés* captured in arms
10 October	*Citoyen* and *Citoyenne* replace *Monsieur* and *Madame*
22 October	French territory free of allied armies
23 October	Returning French *émigrés* to be executed

6 November	French victory at Jemappes
7 November	Louis XVI's trial decreed
19 November	Convention offers 'aid and succour' to all nations desiring to overthrow their governments
26 November	Louis XVI's strongbox (*armoire de fer*) found
4 December	Decree of death for all proposing to restore monarchy
11 December	Louis XVI's trial begins
16 December	Decree banishes Bourbons except Temple prisoners and Duc d'Orléans
31 December	Great Britain refuses to recognize French ambassador

1793

14 January	End of Louis XVI's trial
15–20 January	Voting for sentence upon Louis XVI
20 January	Louis XVI notified of his death sentence
21 January	Louis XVI executed
24 January	Funeral of Le Peletier de Saint-Fargeau
28 January	Provence assumes regency for Louis XVII
31 January	Incorporation of Nice into France
1 February	War declared on Great Britain and Holland
24 February	Decree raising 300,000 men for the war
5 March	Colonies declared in state of siege
7 March	War declared on Spain
9 March	First representatives on mission sent out
9 March	First Coalition organized against France: Great Britain, Austria, Prussia, Holland, Spain, Portugal, Naples, Papal States, Sardinia
11 March	Revolutionary Tribunal set up
12 March	Paris Committee of Surveillance
15 March	Cholet taken by Vendéans
18 March	French defeat at Neerwinden
25 March	Committee of Public Safety set up
28 March	*Emigrés* banished for ever and their property confiscated
1 April	Dumouriez defects to Austrians

6 April	Duc d'Orléans arrested
	Representatives on mission sent to French armies
13 April	Marat arrested
14 April	Spain invades Roussillon
24 April	Marat acquitted
4 May	Price Maximum for corn and flour
16 May	Convention moves from Manège to Tuileries theatre
18 May	Girondins obtain decree for Committee of Thirty to look out for agitators
20 May	Forced loan imposed on rich people
29 May	Insurrection in Lyon
31 May–2 June	Exclusion of Girondins from Convention
5 June	Insurrection at Marseille and Caen
9 June	Protest of 79 deputies against exclusion of Girondins
10 June	Vendéans take Saumur
21–4 June	Insurrection at Saint-Domingue
26 June	Nantes attacked by Vendéans
13 June	Marat assassinated
26 June	Establishment of telegraphs
27 July	Robespierre takes seat in Committee of Public Safety
1 August	Marie-Antoinette taken to Conciergerie
8 August	Suppression of academies and literary societies
10 August	Constitution of 1793 adopted by communes
16 August	Institution of the 'Great Book of the Public Debt'
23 August	Law ordering implementation of Levée en masse
5 September	Journée at Convention
	Revolutionary Armies set up
8 September	French victory at Hondschoote
15 September	Siege of Lyon begins
17 September	Convention passes Law of Suspects
29 September	General Maximum on prices and wages
5 October	Revolutionary Calendar introduced
10 October	Lyon falls to Convention
	Government declared 'Revolutionary until peace'

16 October	Marie-Antoinette executed
	French victory at Wattignies
19 October	Defeat of Vendéans at Cholet
24 October	Embellishments of Revolutionary Calendar accepted
31 October	Girondins executed
6 November	Orléans (Philippe Egalité) executed
11 November	Sylvain Bailly executed
13 December	Vendéans defeated at Le Mans
20 December	Toulon retaken
23 December	Vendéans defeated at Savenay

1794

31 January	Drownings (*noyades*) at Nantes
4 February	Decree abolishing slavery in the colonies
24 March	Hébert executed
27 March	End of Revolutionary Armies
5 April	Danton, Desmoulins and others executed
24 April	Government ministries abolished
28 April	La Tour du Pin executed
1 June	Royal Navy victorious off Ushant (Glorious First of June) yet Caribbean grain convoy reaches Brest
8 June	Robespierre presides at Festival of Supreme Being
10 June	Convention passes Law of 22 prairial
26 June	France wins battle of Fleurus and expels Austria from Belgium
27–8 July	Thermidor *coup d'état* overthrows Robespierre
1 August	Thermidorean Convention repeals Law of 22 prairial
10 August	Restrictions placed on revolutionary tribunal
18 September	Abandonment of all state support for religious bodies
12 November	Paris Jacobin Club closed
8 December	Surviving Girondin deputies from 1793 purge restored to office
16 December	Carrier executed for terrorism

| 24 December | Thermidorean Convention abolishes General Maximum |
| 24 December | France invades Holland |

1795

20 January	French occupy Amsterdam
17 February	Charette signs Peace of La Jaunaye
2 March	Barère, Billaud-Varenne and Collot d'Herbois arrested
1–2 April	12–13 germinal rising
15 April	Prussia makes separate peace with France at Basle
20 April	Chouans sign peace treaty at La Prévalaye
4 May	'White Terror' outbreaks in Lyon
6 May	Execution of Fouquier-Tinville
16 May	France makes treaty with Batavian Republic
20–23 May	1–4 prairial rising
31 May	Thermidorean Convention abolishes Revolutionary Tribunal
8 June	Death in Temple prison of Louis XVII
24 June	Louis XVIII's uncompromising Declaration of Verona
27 June	Royal Navy lands *émigré* army at Quiberon
21 July	Hoche defeats *émigrés*
22 July	Spain makes separate peace at Basle
22 August	Constitution for the Directory approved along with Law of Two Thirds
1 October	Belgium annexed
5 October	Vendémiaire rising by royalists
26 October	Thermidorean Convention closes
2 November	Directory in operation
16 November	Pantheon Club formed

1796

19 February	Directory does away with *assignats*
25 February	Execution of Stofflet
27 February	Pantheon Club suppressed

2 March	Bonaparte given command of Army of Italy
18 March	*Assignats* replaced by territorial mandates
29 March	Execution of Charette
11 April	Bonaparte invades Italy
28 April	Piedmont makes peace
10 May	Bonaparte victor at Lodi
	Babeuf arrested
12 June	Invasion of Papal States
5 August	Alliance made with Spain
16 October	Great Britain makes overtures of peace
	Cispadine republic set up
15–18 October	Bonaparte victor at Arcole
15 December	Hoche sets out in support of United Irishmen

1797

6 January	Storms cause abandonment of Irish expedition
	Bonaparte victor at Rivoli
2 February	Fall of Mantua
4 February	Metal currency restored
14 February	Royal Navy victorious at Cape St Vincent
19 February	Treaty with Pope Pius VI
	Babeuf's trial begins at Vendôme
18 April	Leoben preliminaries of peace
15 May	French troops occupy Venetian Republic
27 May	Execution of Babeuf
29 June	Cisalpine Republic set up
25 July	Abolition of political associations
4 September	18 fructidor *coup d'état*
5 September	Carnot and Barthélémy off Directory
17 September	British peace overtures withdrawn
11 October	Royal Navy victorious at Camperdown
18 October	Peace of Campo Formio
28 November	Rastadt Conference begins

1798

15 February	Roman Republic instituted
21 February	France makes alliance with Cisalpine Republic
5 March	Directory approves Bonaparte's Egyptian expedition
11 May	Floréal *coup d'état*
19 May	Bonaparte leaves for Egypt
10 June	Bonaparte takes Malta
1 July	Bonaparte in Egypt
1 August	Nelson destroys French fleet at Aboukir Bay
5 September	Conscription enforced by Jourdan Law
25 November	Neapolitan force takes Rome

1799

23 January	French capture Naples
26 January	Parthenopean Republic set up
12 March	Austria declares war on France
10 April	Pope Pius VI captive in France
28 April	Suvarov in Milan
9 June	Sieyès replaces Reubell in Directory
18 June	Prairial *coup d'état*
12 July	Law of Hostages
5 August	Royalist rising in Toulouse area
22 August	Bonaparte leaves his army in Egypt
29 August	Pius VI dies at Valence
27 August	Anglo-Russian troops in Holland
9 October	Bonaparte back in France
16 October	Bonaparte in Paris
18 October	Anglo-Russian troops leave Holland
9–10 November	Bonaparte's Brumaire *coup d'état*
25 December	Consulate begins under the Constitution of Year VIII

A

Absolute Monarchy

The Term 'absolute monarchy' suggests that, in the old regime, the king ruled on the basis of being answerable only to God. There were certain features of monarchy which represented that idea, like the concentration of royal power at **Versailles**, and the authorization of the arrest of individuals by means of sealed letters (known as *lettres de cachet*) sent to prison governors. '*Absolutisme*' (a word recognized by the *Académie française* only in 1865[1]) is a caricature of seventeenth- and eighteenth-century realities in France. It was a matter of blood and inheritance, since the king personified the absolutist state, and was accountable to God for it. He was surrounded by ceremonial from his coronation to the etiquette at court. When he went to a town in the kingdom there was an *Entrée*, and his position at the head of a national hierarchy and judiciary was demonstrated.

But yet, even at his most imperious, Louis XIV, who devised the Bourbon monarchical system, could not rule without ministers or without having his edicts registered by the 13 *parlements* of the kingdom. The membership of the *conseil en haut* (upstairs council), which met next door to the king's bedroom at Versailles, could be changed but its advice could not be ignored. Louis XV worked within this framework, supporting his minister Choiseul in his plans for an unprecedented alliance with Austria in 1756, for example. He exiled the *parlements* at the end of his reign in what amounted to a *coup d'état*, but **Louis XVI** felt constrained to call them back at his accession in 1774. Customary law had always conditioned a monarch's decisions. In November 1787, the Duc d'**Orléans** asserted that raising government loans by the king in person in the Paris *parlement* (called a *lit de justice*) would not be legal. The king was in error when he replied that it would be legal 'because it is my will'. The charge against monarchy on the lips of revolutionaries was that it had become despotic, despite all the checks and balances. As Munro Price has said, 'The prime cause of the fall of the absolute monarchy was its failure to break free of the bonds of the social hierarchy and transform its basis of support.'[2] When **Calonne** had declared the extent of the monarchy's financial problems in 1786, the monarchy by itself was powerless to regenerate the nation. **Loménie de Brienne** had also failed to do so after Calonne's departure. Lamoignon's Plenary Court set up by the edicts of May 1788 to replace the *parlements* was a dead letter. Louis XVI had already agreed to the summoning of the **Estates-General**, but brought the date of its meeting forward from 1792 to May 1789. This was the first time the Crown admitted that it could not govern without some sort of representative assembly.[3] Then the government suspended payments on 8 August, which amounted to a partial bankruptcy, and Brienne resigned. **Necker** returned as the only politician the *rentiers* thought they could trust, and the king reluctantly accepted him. 'Absolutism had collapsed.'[4]

When we think of what changed and what did not in the French Revolution, centralized government was a feature of absolutism that persisted. Before the changes, the *intendants* (who could be called provincial governors) represented royal power in the provinces of France. From the seventeenth century onwards, Bourbon monarchs undermined the power of rural noble seigneurs and charters of town councils granted by earlier kings. And yet, in 1793–4, the new **administrative framework** of the One and Indivisible Republic, ruled by the **Mountain**, was even more rigidly centralized through **representatives on mission** responsible to the **Committee of Public Safety**. All **federalist** opposition was eliminated by means of official **Terror** and military action. If this was relaxed at all under the **Directory**, while the '**White Terror**' and *brigandage* were rife, the prefects in the Napoleonic Empire soon asserted it again.

Doyle, William, *Old Regime France* (Oxford: Oxford University Presss, 2001).

Active Citizens

'Active' citizens, designated in the decree of 29 October 1789, denoted men over 25 who paid tax each year equal to what a day-labourer would earn in three days. They would elect electors for the deputies in the **Legislative Assembly**. The electors chosen by the active citizens were qualified as such by paying a sum equal to ten days' wages for a labourer and being a proprietor of some kind.[5]

The deputies in the Legislative could be any active citizens. Originally the candidates for election were meant to be landowners who paid tax of a silver mark. This requirement was rescinded before the 1791 elections took place, but it was left to stand in most places because there was no time to change the electoral arrangements.

In comparison with the English electorate at the time, the number of active citizens was quite large, about two-thirds of the adult male population, that is 4.3 million.[6] They had the right to vote not only for electors, but all other officials, even constitutional bishops and parish priests, whether they were Catholics themselves or not. Those men whose income was below that of active citizens were called passive citizens. The **Declaration of the Rights of Man and of the Citizen** (used as a preamble to the 1791 constitution) gave them legal equality with everyone else, but no political equality. They could not vote for electors, but they were required to serve as soldiers when the *levée en masse* was ordered in 1793. **Army** service then qualified them to be active citizens.

When, after the overthrow of the **monarchy**, new elections were called for the **National Convention**, the distinction between active and passive citizens was abandoned and universal male suffrage was adopted for the only time in the revolutionary decade. The socialist historian and Third Republic politician Jean Jaurès called this decree 'the mass mobilisation of electors, preparing and announcing the mass mobilisation of soldiers'.[7]

Administrative Framework of France, 1790

The National **Constituent Assembly** rationalized the structure of the provinces of the old régime by a decree of 26 February 1790. They were replaced with 83 *départements* of more or less uniform size in which administrative centres (*chef-lieux*) could be reached in one day's travel.

(When papal **Avignon** and the Comtat-Venaissin were incorporated into France a little later, the Vaucluse became and remained Department 84.) These new areas were to be named after geographical features such as rivers or mountains.[8]

Then came sub-division into four or five districts, corresponding to the old *bailliages* or *sénéchaussées*. Departments and districts were ruled by elected directories whose function was to implement the decrees of central government – successively the **Constituent** and **Legislative Assemblies**, the **National Convention** and the **Directory**. The districts contained a number of *cantons* made up of a dozen or so *communes*, each of which was controlled by an elected mayor with a council and several notables. Large towns such as Paris, **Lyon** and **Marseille** were also called *communes*, and had their own structure by being divided into sections. These sections had primary assemblies which stayed in being to put pressure on the municipalities, especially in the capital itself and 'federalist' places such as Lyon in 1793.[9]

Alliance of Throne and Altar

Since 1516 when Francis I made his *Concordat* with the Papacy, French Catholic bishops had been appointed by the king and their choice approved by the pope. That meant dependence by the Church on the king, whose coronation oath included his undertaking to defend it. The Catholic bishops in Paris made Henry IV's coronation conditional upon his renunciation of his Protestant faith in 1598, and he agreed, with the famous words 'Paris is worth a Mass'. The partnership became exclusive. Louis XIV needed funds from the bishops of Languedoc for the Midi Canal to join the Atlantic to the Mediterranean. Their condition was that he should revoke Henry IV's Edict of Nantes and exclude the Protestants from France. In 1685 he complied.[10]

By the time of the Revolution, many great monastic foundations (and some small ones) had commendatory abbots who were appointed by the king for the sake of the revenues they paid to the individuals concerned – who did not need to be priests at all. When abbeys were abolished, church lands nationalized, and the **refractory clergy** exiled, the nostalgic alliance was of no use: **Louis XVI** was powerless to help them in spite of the putative delay afforded by his suspensive veto. The alliance was broken in 1790 by the subjection of the clergy to the authority of lay politicians in the **Civil Constitution of the Clergy** and the oath required in support of it.[11]

Amar, Jean-Pierre-André (1755–1816)

Amar was treasurer of Grenoble before the Revolution, a magistrate in the Dauphiné *parlement* and purchaser of an office which carried nobility. Even so, he became a radical member of the **Convention**, yet finished up as a devout mystic.[12] He remained in Grenoble until he was elected to the Convention, where he sat with the **Mountain** and voted vociferously for the king's death. As **representative on mission** in the Ain and Isère in 1793, he made a point of arresting as many as he could label as **counter-revolutionaries**. After the **Girondins** had been expelled from the Convention in June, he was put on the **Committee of General Security** (16 June 1793). He was implacable in his demands for the arrest of 41 **Girondins** and of their sympathizers.[13]

After the queen had been executed in October 1793, the Mountain took the opportunity to express its anti-feminist attitude. **Olympe de Gouges** was executed, and an attack was made on the Society of Revolutionary Republican Women (attached to the *enragés*) who had gained a decree from the Convention that all women must wear the **revolutionary cockade** and the **Phrygian bonnet**. Amar presented the report on the place of women in the Revolution to the Convention, on 1 November, reiterating the Jacobin line that women must bring up the republic's children and leave politics to men.[14]

Amar supported the indictment of the Hébertists, who had smeared him with being a rich banker, and the Dantonists. Yet he feared a Robespierrist dictatorship, and was irritated by the **Committee of Public Safety** setting up a police bureau because that was the brief of his own committee, and he supported the **Thermidor coup**.

He was accused of excesses in the **Terror**, but defended himself and his colleagues **Vadier**, **Billaud-Varenne** and **Collot**. **Merlin de Thionville** called him 'the vile instrument of kings who, to have his crimes under the old regime forgotten, wanted to appear more patriotic than the others'.[15] Amar was arrested after the **Germinal coup** and imprisoned, first in Ham Chateau and then in Sedan Citadel, but was released in the amnesty of 4 brumaire, year IV (26 October 1795). He regretted his part in the Thermidor coup and commented that the people did at least have bread in the time of **Robespierre**.[16] On flimsy evidence Amar was arrested and tried at Vendôme with **Babeuf**, but after an apology the charges were dropped. He was exiled from Paris as an amnestied terrorist and took no further part in politics, preferring to immerse himself in Swedenborgian mysticism for the rest of his life.[17]

Amis des Noirs, Société des

Since, like Britain and Spain, France had Caribbean colonies, French settlers there (known as *créoles*) and absentee proprietors of plantations were slave-owners. The prosperity of Bordeaux and La Rochelle depended upon the free labour of slaves, but many leaders of opinion in the eighteenth century had denounced the institution, such as Montesquieu, Diderot, **Voltaire**, Abbé Raynal and even the king's minister Turgot.[18] The 1788 founders of this abolitionist society included **Brissot**, **Condorcet** (who drew up the rules), **Lafayette**, **Mirabeau**, **Clavière** and **Carra**. As did the American Revolution, revolutionary France proclaimed universal liberty. The *Amis des Noirs* wanted this taken at face value.

French plantation owners saw the abolition of slavery through the same eyes as their American counterparts and opposed it through their meetings in the Club de l'Hôtel Massiac and in the Colonial Committee founded in March 1790 with the support of politicians such as **Barnave**. The *Amis* were a small but vociferous group and, like their British counterparts for whom Thomas Clarkson spoke, they stood for racial equality. In 1789, there were only about 150 members. With the **Estates-General**, membership reflected political life. Henri **Grégoire** became a member. Divisions appeared – the **Lameth** brothers would not associate with Brissot and his friends, but **Buzot** and **Vergniaud** joined when elected to the **Legislative**.[19] They had a journal called the *Patriote français*, which went with the periodicals of the **Social Circle**.

After the **Declaration of the Rights of Man and of the Citizen** was promulgated at the end of August, the Society took up the cause of the so-called 'people of colour' and worked for the end of the slave trade, as a feasible aim and a prelude to outright abolition.[20] In the debates in the

Legislative of 22 October and 30 November 1791, Brissot wanted to give rights to the mulattoes so as to help the colonists contain the slave revolt in **Saint-Domingue**. The Assembly, dominated by **Feuillants**, refused any abolition on 24 September and repulse the attacks by eloquent *Amis* such as Vergniaud. The best they could get was the decree of 28 March 1792, which gave political rights to 'free men of colour'. A further decree of 22 August brought 36 deputies – 18 from Saint-Domingue – into the Legislative Assembly. These passed into the Convention a few weeks later.

The *Amis* were dominant in the Convention's colonial committee. A decree of 4 February 1794 (16 pluviôse, year II) actually abolished slavery. However, after the exclusion of the Girondins from the Convention on 2 June, the *Amis des Noirs* had no real existence.[21] No further action was taken. Grégoire thought that abolition was premature in any case.

The **Thermidorean Convention** resorted to forced labour and requisitioned workers for the sugar harvest. The **Directory** maintained this legislation, although the Constitution of year III considered the colonies to be an integral part of metropolitan France. The *Amis des noirs* died with the **Girondins**, and First Consul **Bonaparte**'s Law of 10 May 1802 put the clock back to before the Revolution.[22]

Anti-Revolution

This term was suggested by Colin Lucas in 1984.[23] Anti-revolutionaries did not want the old regime brought back. They wanted a different kind of Revolution from the one that had developed since its hopeful outset. As even the minutes of the municipalities in small *communes* reflect, the Revolution soon went sour for many people who had supported it at first. The anti-revolutionaries did not want their bishops and priests to be subject to the oath to the **Civil Constitution of the Clergy** in 1790. They were not necessarily republicans. They looked to the king to deal with misgovernment since it was he who had invited the submission of their **statements of grievance** at the same time as the elections for the **Estates-General** in the spring of 1789. Disappointment with having to go to war or put down **federalist** rebellions by brutal means, at seeing young men compelled into the armies, even if they were given the status of '**active**' citizens when they did, all created an undertow of resentment which lasted all through the decade of the Revolution and was not withdrawn when **Bonaparte** took it over in 1799. 'Anti-revolutionary' could include constitutional monarchists as much as republicans who were not Jacobins. That the **Thermidor coup** was successful, and that the **Thermidorean Convention** was able to dismantle the **Terror**, adequately bears this out.

📖 Doyle, William, *Revolution and Counter-Revolution in France*, in *Officers, Nobles and Revolutionaries: Essays on Eighteenth-Century France* (London and Rio Grande: The Hambledon Press, 1995).

Army

From the outset, the revolutionaries were in fear of an attack from outside because of the challenge they had made to the established order in Europe. From 1791, **Brissot** and others saw a need for expansionism despite the early pronouncements of the **Constituent** that France would never be an aggressor. The **Pillnitz Declaration** and the one made by the Duke of **Brunswick** inflamed popular aggressiveness.[24] It was unavoidable, therefore, that Revolutionary France should be at war from April 1792 for the whole of its existence, followed by a Consulate and an Empire based upon military prowess.

The old-regime army was, of course, still in being, but was demoralized after July 1789 by so many desertions. It was soon apparent that there needed to be change from a system of recruiting soldiers on a provincial basis, and that the army would have to be as much identified with revolutionary politics as the rest of the nation.[25]

Under the old regime the officer corps was a noble preserve. The Ordinance made by War Minister Ségur in 1781 had denied officer status to anyone who did not have four quarterings on his coat of arms. This was meant deliberately to exclude those who had been ennobled recently. Commands were often venal offices, and wealth, not military skill or experience, led to them. There were objections to this system in the **statements of complaint** drawn up in early 1789. The army was inadequate for the purposes of the Revolution.[26]

Soldiers had become ready to desert and support insurgents. Mutinies were becoming more frequent, and there was the special example at **Nancy** in August 1790. Many officers were among the first of the *émigrés*. Between July 1791 (after the king's flight to **Varennes**) and December 1792, the army of the line lost a third of its officer corps either through resigning their commissions or through political emigration. **Dumouriez** and **Lafayette** were no more than the most conspicuous officers to desert.[27]

Reforms soon came about, with the abolition of cruel punishments, and the principle established that social origin was put aside in favour of merit for promotion of officers. There was to be no more dependence upon foreign mercenaries. The distinction between the line troops and the militia was removed. Regiments were not attached to provinces any longer since the army was to serve the Nation. The soldiers would become **'active' citizens** as long as there were such. These changes were partial. The most important was to improve the image of the serving soldiers. There were passionate appeals for volunteers in 1791 and 1792. 'To pour out one's blood for the *Patrie*' was a cliché often employed. The year 1791 was a good one for recruitment. The troops were engaged for only one campaigning season by the Legislative's decree of 28 December 1791, and they could return home to regulate their personal affairs. But when the war began, the arrival home of the wounded made the heroic image hard to create.

The line soldiers had skill, and the volunteers added enthusiasm. This was exploited in the Amalgamation Law of 21 February 1793, introduced by **Dubois-Crancy**, which was vociferously opposed by the **Girondins** because it meant that the volunteer soldiers were no longer controlled by their home departments. The law ended the army's duality: two battalions of volunteers were combined with one regular battalion to form a demibrigade. They would all qualify for the same rates of pay, the same discipline and the same uniform. Junior officers and NCOs would be elected by the troops from their number. This was delayed, but put into operation in the winter of 1793–4. A long and costly war could now be envisaged.[28]

In 1793, obligatory service was brought in. With 'the fatherland in danger' (*la patrie en danger*), there was a *levée* of 300,000 soldiers for the war against the kings of Europe in February 1793. The departments were made responsible for it, depending upon their population, but the communes had to raise the troops. All unmarried men and childless widowers between 18 and 40 were in a permanent state of liability for service. Lots were drawn, and if a 'black ticket' (*billet noir*) was drawn, a paid substitute could be found, which caused obvious resentment, especially in rural areas that were labour-intensive and because it favoured the well-off. There was also resentment that local officials were exempt. The enrolment of 1793 meant that the same soldiers were still serving in 1798. Between those dates, recruitment numbers varied.[29]

From 1793, the republican army was controlled by Lazare **Carnot**, a former engineer captain, as a member of the **Committee of Public Safety**. He was responsible for supplying the army and making it victorious against the **First Coalition**, earning the soubriquet 'Organizer of Victory'. Mass mobilization (*Levée en masse*) was decreed on 23 August 1793. The first clause makes the **Convention**'s intentions clear:

All Frenchmen are in permanent requisition. ... The young men shall go to battle; the married men shall forge weapons and transport provisions; the women shall make tents and clothing and shall serve in the hospitals; the children shall tear [old sheets] into shreds (*feront la charpie*); the elderly men in public squares shall enliven the warriors [by] teaching hatred of kings and the unity of the Republic.[30]

The practice of paying substitutes was forbidden. At the same time, the Amalgamation decreed in February was implemented. This scheme was intended to produce 750,000 men. In 1799, the **Jourdan** law brought in annual conscription, the origins of the armies of the Empire. In the revolutionary decade, service never became a sacred obligation or a rite of passage for young men as it would under the Empire.

Officers were the experienced old-regime NCOs (*sous-officiers*) and political loyalty became the essential for promoting them. Generals were government nominees. **Saint-Just** commented: 'The right to choose generals belongs to the whole community', so the choice belonged to the nation's deputies. The army was enormous by comparison with the old regime which had two armies in the Seven Years War (1756–63) of only 99,000 and 24,000. In 1795, there were half a million troops serving, and 326,000 by the end of 1798.[31]

In the winter of 1793–4, new tactics were made official: there was to be rapid movement and the wings of an army were meant to encircle the enemy force to break its ranks from behind – the *Tactique de masse*. The Committee of Public Safety set all this out in an instruction on 8 October 1793.[32] A new type of professionalism was emerging, overlaid with a political factor. The Committee of Public Safety was most interventionist, with **representatives on mission** attached to all the armies, as in the departments. They were actually present at battles: Saint-Just at **Fleurus**, **Barras** and **Fréron** at the retaking of **Toulon** and **Jean-Bon Saint-André** at the naval battle off Ushant on 1 June 1794. **Custine** and **Houchard** were tried and executed for not obeying instructions. The representatives had gained their military experience during the debates at the **Jacobins** and in the Convention.[33]

The political education of the soldiers was carried out by distributing newspapers: the Army of the North circulated **Hébert**'s *Le Père Duchesne*. There were cells of Hébertistes and *enragés* in garrison towns, such as Lille and Cambrai. Under the **Directory**, the armies and garrisons became places of refuge for former Jacobins once the clubs were closed.[34]

Pay often arrived late, and farmers and lodging-house keepers refused to take *assignats*. Uniforms, boots and weapons were often deficient. Even so, a new integrated structure for the army had been created with a real connection between soldiers and citizens.[35] The army that went to **Italy** with Bonaparte was very different from Dumouriez's troops at **Valmy**.[36]

 Blaufarb, Rafe, *The French Army, 1750–1820: Careers, Talent, Merit* (Manchester: Manchester University Press, 2002).

Forrest, Alan, *Soldiers of the French Revolution* (Durham, NC and London: Duke University Press, 1990).

Art and Artists in the Revolution

During the revolutionary decade, pictorial art was characterized by the representation of contemporary events or of allegories that had represented the ethos of the new order.[37]

In the *Tennis Court Oath*, **David** meant to recapture the enthusiasm of the occasion by his multiplicity of portraits, but he could not complete it because events were far from static. His main revolutionary work is a series of republican martyr's memorials: *Death of Le Peletier de Saint Fargeau* (non-extant), *Death of Marat* and *Death of Bara*.

Artists were encouraged by the **Convention** and the **Directory** to produce propagandist works and many complied. Gérard began *The Tenth of August 1792*, a work of modest size, depicting the king and his family behind the reporter's table in the national assembly while the monarchy is being suspended with shouts and gestures. Vincent painted *The Heroine of Saint-Milhier* in which a republican household is being defended from Vendéan traitors (this became a popular print in various versions). The pictures for the occasion were necessarily not on a large scale taking years, but done quickly, and often not finished. There were plenty of portraits to go with the cult of prominent men, many of them now in *Musées des Beaux-arts* dotted around the country.

After **Thermidor**, allegorical works were looked for. David's *The Sabine Women* is a symbol of national reconciliation. This work and others like it represent a return to formal style and expression, and these were not hurried or for any particular circumstance. Even so, Tonino-Lebrun's *The Death of Caius Gracchus* is an obvious homage to **Babeuf** (the artist himself was accused with others of conspiring to stab First Consul Bonaparte at the Opera in October 1800[38]). Guérin welcomed the returning *émigrés* with his *Marcus Sextus*.[39] **Gros** emerged as a portraitist.

When **Bonaparte's** Army of Italy was winning campaigns and creating sister republics, a great deal of Renaissance art made its way to Paris. A debate began in and out of the Councils of Elders and of 500 of how to make use of all these pictures and pieces of sculpture to the best advantage for victorious France. These works had a civic and an educative function. François de Neufchâteau, for some time a Director, thought that the cradle of liberty ought to be where the world's masterpieces should be kept. The Louvre in Paris had been declared the National Museum by the **Legislative Assembly** in September 1792, and opened to the public a year later. On 27 and 28 July 1798, a convoy brought the Italian works for hanging there.[40] But this art was **national property**, to be kept in churches, monasteries and *châteaux* which were now museums. Inventories of pictures and sculptures were drawn up by the Commission of Monuments so that they could be sent on loan to provincial galleries. Pierre-Louis Roederer claimed that these works of art were the prizes of the French army and therefore the property of all Frenchmen. Pictures in *beaux-arts* galleries, statues in the streets and on the façades of public buildings, ought to be available in all urban centres, not Paris exclusively.

Kohl, Hubertus and Rolf Reichardt, *Visualizing the Revolution: Politics and Pictorial Arts in Late Eighteenth-Century France* (London: Reaktion Books, 2008).

Artois, Charles-Philippe, Comte d' (1757–1836), King Charles X (1824–30)

Artois was the third son of the Dauphin Louis-Ferdinand, born after Louis-Auguste (**Louis XVI**) and Louis Stanislas (Louis XVIII). He became Charles X on Louis XVIII's death in 1824.

Artois represented the decadence of the court at Versailles in the popular mind. He bet the queen a thousand livres that he could complete a splendid pavilion before the court came back to Versailles from Fontainebleau for the winter. He had the Bagatelle built in four weeks (and a day) and won the bet.[41] He had helped topple **Necker** on 11 July 1789 and was regarded as an instigator of the supposed attempt to starve Paris into submission by military coercion in July 1789. So he left France as soon as the **Bastille** had fallen to go to his wife's home in Turin, capital of Savoy. **Calonne** and the Prince of Condé joined him. They made Turin a focus for *émigrés*.

He settled in Koblenz, in the territory of his uncle, the Archbishop of Trier, in June 1791. Once back from **Varennes**, Louis XVI wrote to Artois to ask him to desist from plotting **counter-revolution**. **Provence** emigrated at the same time as the king's flight to **Varennes**, and joined Artois in Koblenz. They organized the Army of the Princes after the second emigration, when many noble officers who had been elected for the Second Estate to the **Estates-General** were excluded from standing for election to the **Legislative**. This army took part in the Prussian invasion in 1792 and was defeated with **Brunswick** at **Valmy** in September. After this disaster, Artois and Provence went to Hamm in Westphalia, as guests of the King of Prussia, kept by grants of money from him and from Catherine II of Russia.[42]

Artois hoped for British support, although Pitt was equivocal because France had supported the Americans. In January 1793, Pitt considered that it was more important to win battles against the Republic than to restore the Bourbons. Artois wanted to be taken to the **Vendée** to obtain a grand role. When it did not happen, he went to Russia where Catherine II gave him 6,000 livres a week and fêted him. Persuaded of a British change of heart, he sailed to Hull on a Russian frigate loaded with Catherine's money to pay an army for the Vendée. The British made him leave or be arrested for debt in England. He had hopes in the Midi, if he could not reach western France, since the British were in **Toulon**. But he returned to the Vendéan idea. He hoped to go with Lord Moira who intended to support **La Rochejaquelein** in December, but was not allowed to.[43] He returned to Russia and was back at Hamm in early 1794, still looking for British help, whereas Provence, as regent for **Louis XVII**, looked to Spain and had his secret agency in Paris. Artois had used up all the Russian money and went to Rotterdam in the summer until the French arrived there, then to Bremen, and back to Britain, although there were some vicissitudes involving his gambling debts.[44] He settled in Holyrood House in Edinburgh as George III's guest, and at 72 South Audley Street in London. Perpetrators of the **White Terror** after July 1794 were in contact with him.

Artois might have been in the ships that disastrously landed a force of *émigrés* on the **Quiberon** peninsula in June 1795. In fact he never came closer than the Ile d'Yeu and soon went away again. Evidence was found for this in the Duc d'Aumale's archive at Chantilly.[45]

Mansell, Philip, *Louis XVIII* (London: John Murray, 2005).

Assembly of Notables, (1787)

Calonne gambled on calling an Assembly of Notables to meet on 22 February 1787 to carry through his reform package and by-pass the *parlement* of Paris. Such an assembly had met for the last time in 1626. He hoped to woo public opinion to his side through this archaic body of 144 handpicked nominees. He revealed the annual deficit of 112 million livres to people who remembered **Necker**'s claim only five years before, in wartime, that there was a surplus of 10 millions, although a reliable recent historian has asserted that the truth of Calonne's claim has yet to be shown.[46] The Assembly's response was to say that he had not given enough detail and to suspect that these figures were false. Calonne had been regarded with antagonism by the *parlements* ever since he had written a speech for Louis XV in 1766 in what was called the 'Flagellation Session' (*séance de flagellation*) to deny that they had any independent authority.[47]

Calonne had arranged for seven committees, each chaired by a Prince of the Blood. Only **Artois** gained him support. Archbishop **Loménie de Brienne** expressed concern over loss of church rights in the reform package. The Notables said that the proposed provincial assemblies would either be too democratic or, since they were to be controlled by royal intendants, too despotic. Both sword and robe nobility objected to the new tax to be collected in kind at harvest time payable by all landowners. They said it was unconstitutional. **Lafayette** floated the idea, and received support for it, that the **Estates-General** would be the only body competent to deal with these issues.

Finding a solution was becoming more urgent since Calonne could not create the credit to attract short-term loans. He claimed that the king was endorsing his measures and drew up a notice to be read in all parish churches on 7 April (Palm Sunday). He also said that the notables had obstructed his reforms to protect their own privileges, but they ostensibly had not. They in turn made sure that any implication on Calonne's part that they had approved of tax increases or, more important, opposed equality in taxation, was deleted from the record of events, and used public information leaks to do so.[48] The king dismissed Calonne immediately. His successor, the queen's nominee, Loménie de Brienne, tried to gain acceptance for modified reforms, but the Assembly still refused to accept the important changes and was dispersed. The failure of the Assembly produced a remarkable change in the king. He became depressed, obsessed with his hunting, apathetic. **Mercy-Argentau** reported all this to Emperor Joseph II, saying that the king had wept in the queen's apartments about the situation.[49]

The assembled notables were as alert to public opinion as Calonne. During the work of the bureaux, they had found themselves opposed to him and, by implication, to the king. Newspapers, letters and contemporary diaries show that the reading (and read to) public were looking to the Assembly for some solutions. In return, the notables ignored the rules of secrecy and let their ideas and opinions leak into newspapers and correspondence.[50]

It was important that 'the Notables were fashioning an image of themselves as spokesmen for and defenders of the public'.[51] They were the precursors of what the **Constituent Assembly** would turn out to be. The nobles, high ecclesiastics and mayors present were finding that there was common ground in opposition to the Bourbon monarchical system and were not subservient in the face of it. Moreover, they were becoming representatives of a new understanding of what constituted the nation. Perhaps we ought to say, as Vivien Gruder does, that the revolution starts here.[52]

Assignats

The French crown deficit reached 112 million livres in 1786, according to **Calonne**, which represented a quarter of the year's likely income. **Louis XVI** and his ministers failed to reduce it before 1789. Once the National **Constituent Assembly** was in being, a drastic solution was found. Bishop **Talleyrand** of Autun took up a proposal already canvassed beforehand that the nation should take over the lands of the Catholic Church in France as national property, valued at 2.1 billion livres, upon which annual interest was 70 million or so, and sell them to restore national solvency. The decision was made on 17 March 1790. In April, however, Talleyrand inveighed against *assignats*, and repeated his objections when more were to be printed in the autumn. He rightly predicted that printing money would be disastrous when gold was scarce.[53]

To facilitate this sale, the state had issued 400 livres of treasury bills (*assignats*) at 3 per cent interest, with **national property** (*biens nationaux*) being the guarantee of payment to enable purchases. Wealthy townsmen living at a distance and neighbours in the countryside bought the bonds, and used the certificates to purchase abbey lands or buildings. This had aroused great interest among people with disposable capital by September, so a new issue of 800 million *assignats* was made for sums as small as 50 livres with no interest to be paid.[54] This was caused by the fact that there was also a scarcity of specie because people were hoarding their coin, the nobles who usually spent a great deal were leaving France, short-term crop failure meant that grain had to be imported and paid for and there was a balance of payments deficit.[55] Peasant farmers were keeping grain from the market, workers were not receiving wages and taxes were not being paid. By September, when **Necker** finally left the government having no further contribution to make after, six months earlier, predicting a deficit of 294 millions,[56] *assignats* were acceptable as paper money with no interest and the rate at which they lost their value against coin was alarming for everybody.[57]

It was not until February 1797 that the **Directory** forbade the use of *assignats*, ordered the breaking of presses used for printing them, and returned to metal currency. National solvency had been restored by then because of the taxes paid in territories conquered by the republican armies.

Aulard, François-Victor-Alphonse (1849–1928)

It has been pointed out that nineteenth-century historians of the Revolution were rarely professors or even specialists. Louis Blanc was a journalist, Adolphe Thiers a politician and Lamartine an author and poet, for example. They were all curious about the French Revolution. The history of the Revolution sustained itself because it was still working itself out. For this reason the Sorbonne did not teach it. As a subject, it was too 'volcanic' to be able to be mastered by the university.[58]

Then, in 1885, the Paris municipal council, with its leftist majority, decided that the time was right to set up a course in French Revolution Studies. The Ministry of Education chose the Faculty of Letters for this and put Aulard, who had written a study of parliamentary eloquence during the Revolution, in charge of it. He presented his first course in March 1887.[59] His post was changed into a professorial chair at the Sorbonne four years later. Other universities followed the example of Paris, either to agree with or oppose its judgements, as **Mathiez** was to do in 1908.[60]

Aulard was born into a Charentais bourgeois family who were loyal republicans. In the 1870s, he was following a career as literary historian.

He had written about the Italian patriot poet Giacomo Leopardi, and had finished the first volume of his study of the orators of the Revolution. He was close in outlook to anti-clerical freemasonry. He wanted to foster cumulative knowledge of what happened in the revolutionary years in the hands of specialists, rather than any further philosophical interpretation. His aim was erudition and 'scientific' writing about 'what happened'. The central documents for him were the **Declaration of the Rights of Man and of the Citizen** and the Constitution of 1793, drawn up by the **Convention** but not adopted because of the war. He was not interested in the '**Days**', but in the debates of the Assemblies and the Convention, not in insurrections but in institutions. He studied public opinion, democratic elections, political parties and parliamentary majorities.[61]

Aulard found it problematic that the men of 1789 made the Declaration of the Rights of Man but then set up suffrage based upon tax qualifications, and that those of 1793 decreed universal male suffrage, but set up dictatorship by **Terror**.[62] The republic outlined in the 1793 constitution expressed loyalty to the Revolution of 1789. Its descent into terrorism and dictatorship can only be explained by the circumstances of the need for public security. In practice, what was built as revolutionary government in 1793–4 was a regime of circumstance. It was a provisional construction, unfinished business. Some elements in it, such as controlled economy (the **Maximum**) or an egalitarian utopia, looked forward to nineteenth-century socialist ideologies. So, in the eyes of the historian of the republican synthesis writing in the Third Republic, 1793 has an important function in the revolutionary saga, and can be justified inasmuch as it was both unpredictable and necessary.[63]

The personification of Aulard's republican synthesis is neither **Mirabeau** nor **Robespierre**, but **Danton**. This idea came from Auguste Comte, the positivist philosopher, who applauded a provisional dictatorship in the 'naked authority' of Danton as a prelude to government by experts. So the Revolution was but the beginning of a drama in which the decisive scene took place nearly a century later when the Republicans emerged victorious after the debacle of the Second Empire and the Paris Commune. In **Furet**'s words, the historian is taken unawares by the retrospective analogy in which 'the Revolution emerges flattened, tamed and domesticated by the

Third Republic'. Aulard's conclusion was that the Revolution could not do everything, but it began everything.[64]

Aulard's pupil Albert Mathiez could not agree about Danton's place. Danton was venal, opportunistic and had to be replaced by Robespierre, the incorruptible incarnation of a merciless conflict without compassion in the service of the people. Mathiez will turn up in this book in his place …

📖 Furet, François, *Academic History of the Revolution*, in François Furet and Mona Ozouf, (eds), *A Critical Dictionary of the French Revolution*, trans. Goldhammer, Arthur (London: The Belknap Press of Harvard University Press, 1989), pp. 881ff. References here are to the French edition.

'Austrian Committee'

Rumours of the existence of an 'Austrian Committee' were developed in the radical press, starting with Camille **Desmoulins** in 1790, and repeated by J.-L. **Carra** in July 1792. It was supposed to meet in the **Tuileries** at the instigation of Queen **Marie-Antoinette** to try and foil the further development of the Revolution, to encourage the *émigrés* in the Army of the Princes at Koblenz and to make contact with foreign powers hostile to France.[65] Its members were supposed to include the Princesse de **Lamballe** who returned from England in mid-1791 to represent the queen on the committee, and any courtiers who had not yet gone into exile.[66]

The idea seized the popular imagination and rumour and reality were mixed in what was spread about. It came out of an atavistic dislike of Austria dating from before the diplomatic revolution of 1756. The disasters of the Seven Years War (1756–63) were blamed on it, and Desmoulins and his associates were known to favour a rapprochement between France and Prussia. The queen, of course, was identified with this dislike, and was called *l'Autrichienne* as soon as she came to France in 1770. The activities of **Mercy-Argentau**, the Austrian ambassador, the missions of the Baron de **Breteuil** and **Mallet du Pan** to European courts, coded messages sent to Vienna about **Dumouriez**'s strategy towards Liège and in Savoy, all undoubtedly real, fanned the flames of this 'committee' idea after the king's flight to **Varennes**. It came to represent fear of a court conspiracy leading to **counter-revolution** when the Habsburg Emperor made his declaration of **Pillnitz**.[67]

After war had been declared in April 1792, there seemed to be more evidence. There was a real suspicion that the allies were being informed of French troop movements. Treason by Dumouriez and then **Lafayette** seemed to clinch the argument. Carra said he had obtained his information from deputies such as **Basire, Chabot** and **Merlin de Thionville**, members of the Assembly's Committee of Research. He denounced Foreign Minister Montmorin and Navy Minister **Bertrand de Moleville** for leading the Austrian Committee in the *Annales patriotiques*. They sued for defamation and won their case. But the Assembly stood by the inviolability of the deputies, and declared a decree of accusation against their judge. The Minister of Justice, Duranthon, tried to assert that the king was making a denunciation against the calumnies himself. This action was considered unconstitutional. Gensonné and **Brissot** made speeches on 23 May repeating the accusations. This went to increase fear of obsession with royal (and royalist) treason. The knowledge that some court papers had been burnt in the potteries at Sèvres was taken as proof of inculpation. Ultimately, when the **Brunswick** declaration was made known in Paris on 3 August, the patriots were sure that there had been collusion with the invaders.[68]

The existence of such a committee was called 'chimerical' by the ex-Navy Minister Bertrand de Moleville, who was supposed to be a member of it,[69] but a great number of revolutionaries believed that this committee was the governing force in French foreign policy at the Tuileries court while the monarchy lasted.

Avignon

Avignon in 1789 was one of the five or six larger towns in the Mediterranean Midi, with a population of 28,000. Since the Middle Ages, it had been a papal dependency, along with the Comtat Venaissin whose capital was Carpentras. Both together were ruled by a papal vice-legate. Avignon was stagnating to a certain extent in the eighteenth century, but it had a commercial life manufacturing silk and maintained itself as a centre for printing. It had, therefore, developed a sizeable **bourgeoisie**. Avignon looked towards France whereas the Comtat looked more towards the Papal States. Both places, before and after annexation by France in 1791, were among the 'hotspots' of the Revolution in the south.[70]

Lower Provence had experienced the '**Great Fear**' in July 1789. Avignon created its militia in the face of it, as did most places, and this revealed a shift of opinion open to French influence. Vice-Legate Casoni ordered a **statement of complaint** to be drawn up in Avignon and the Comtat but, when a deputy called Bouche presented a motion in the **Constituent** to annexe them, they reasserted their loyalty to the papacy. In February 1790, however, popular demonstrations led to the resignation of the town council and the patriot Lescuyer proposed an administration along the new French lines, with Avignon and the Comtat as no longer separate entities. The vice-legate made concessions which led to the setting up of a municipality under moderate patriots. They had abolished corporal punishment (the *strappado*) and the Holy Inquisition. The pope intervened on 21 April 1790 to revoke all their innovations, so tension increased between patriots and nobles and clergy. A series of violent outbreaks followed, provoked by the papal party, which led to a vote for union with France. The Abbé **Maury** persuaded the Constituent Assembly to adopt a policy of 'wait-and-see'.

Avignon and Carpentras then began an armed conflict. An Avignonais 'patriot army' was recruited, led by a Chevalier Patrice, with Duprat, Minveille and Jourdan (who was called 'Head-Cutter' because he claimed to have cut off Governor Delaunay's head after the **Bastille** was taken) as his lieutenants. In January 1791, they failed in two attacks on Carpentras. The suggestion of a federation made by Avignon was refused by the papal party in Carpentras, who regarded its army, now led by Jourdan, as brigands.

In the Constituent in the autumn, **Robespierre** argued for a speedy annexation: 'The cause of Avignon … is that of Liberty,'[71] and a decision was at last made. Avignon was to be in the Bouches du Rhône and the Comtat in the Drôme. There was a moderate patriot municipality in Avignon upheld by a **Jacobin Club** with a vociferous 'papist' opposition. Mediators from Paris permitted the continuation of '*Coupe-Têtes*' Jourdan's army, who pushed out the moderates, set up an extremist council and confiscated church property, including bells, for coin and weapons. There was a counter-revolutionary rising on 16 October 1791 leading to an uproar in the Cordeliers church (where there was a miraculous image appearing to weep for the extremists' crimes). This finished with the murder of patriot Lescuyer.[72] Jourdan arrested 60 or so of his opponents, and he authorized their collective killing by Lescuyer's son and his adolescent friends. The bodies were thrown into the *Tour de la Glacière* at the *Palais des papes* through a hole specially made in the wall.[73] The perpetrators of this atrocity became known as *Glacièristes*.

This event had national repercussions. Deputies in the **Legislative** spoke of exemplary punishment. The moderates won the municipal elections in December 1791, but the perpetrators of the massacre were amnestied in April 1792 and the *Glacièristes* won the July election, making Duprat the mayor. Avignon was in the hands of extreme patriots in 1793 at the time when the **federalist** revolts broke out in other southern cities against similar administrations. They remained loyal to the Convention, but the Marseillais federalists marched up the Rhône and pushed them out. Then, after being defeated by General Carteaux, they returned and did it again. There were then new imprisonments and massacres. On 25 July the patriots returned again to power in Avignon. The Convention definitively decreed the setting up of the Vaucluse Department (84 then as now) and Avignon was its capital (*chef-lieu*).

The year 1794 was marked by the presence of a series of **representatives on mission**, one of whom was Maignet, '*robespierriste pur et dur*' (a pure and hard-line Robespierrist).[74] He made 47 federalist victims – and there were 70 more in Orange. '*Coupe-têtes*' Jourdan was denounced to the **revolutionary tribunal** and guillotined on 27 May 1794.

After **Thermidor**, Maignet was recalled to Paris. There was more revenge, and outbreaks of **'white terror'**, dealt with by Stanislas **Fréron**. Under the **Directory**, Avignon was once more a Jacobin centre. But it was a fragile equilibrium, and there was more 'white terror' at the **restoration of the monarchy** in 1814.

B

Babeuf, François-Nöel (1760–97)

Babeuf is often regarded as an early proponent of pre-Marxist communism in Paris. However, the Marxist historian Georges Lefebvre summarized Babeuf's aims as more concerned with distribution than production since, in his scheme, the peasant would work his own fields but bring the harvest to a common storehouse. Babeuf's ideas remained utopian. Most of his associates were not advocates of communism but simply bourgeois democrats acting together with a few members of the former **Convention** who wanted to regain power.[1]

His father had been a soldier but had become a salt-pan guard, employed by the farmers-general. At 12 years old he had to work on the construction of the Picardy Canal but after that he worked for a feudal notary and learned land surveying in Roye, near Amiens. He had his own business there, in difficult circumstances. He wrote several tracts on land management, but also read Jean-Jacques **Rousseau** and Sébastien **Mercier**. When **national property** was for sale in 1790, he thought that his land-sharing ideas could be put into practice. He subordinated property ownership to the right of people to work their own land. He fumed over the unequal division of land holdings. In October 1789 he published his *Cadastre perpétuel* (perpetual land-register) that he had worked on since 1787 to present ideas on equal taxation, public assistance for the poor and education for all, regretting the impossibility of land-sharing.[2]

In Paris during the events of July 1789, he protested at the murders of Foulon and **Bertier** and began to work in journalism. He went home to Picardy and edited a local paper. He drew up several petitions to the **Constituent Assembly**, which raised the Picardy peasantry, and received prison sentences in Paris and Roye lasting until April 1791. Nevertheless he was elected a delegate to the electoral assembly of the Somme at the time of the elections to the Convention, and was made a departmental official. In January 1793, he fled to Paris after being implicated in a fraud case, and worked with a sansculotte leader, Fournier 'l'Américain', then in the Paris office for food supply. He found himself condemned to 20 years in irons, but had to serve only eight months.[3]

After **Thermidor**, he edited a journal in Paris which soon turned into his *Tribune of the People*. He was very anti-Jacobin, denouncing **Carrier** for his excesses at Nantes. He distanced himself from the **Thermidorean Convention** when he saw constitutional liberties fading in December 1794. He called himself Gracchus at this point, and joined the radical Electoral Club to sharpen up its initiatives. For this he was arrested on 7 February 1795, and transferred to Arras for six months in prison. He spent the time in intense reading and exchanges with other political prisoners, working out his programme for the 'Conspiracy of Equals'. Commerce should be banned, agricultural and artisanal production should be shared, and there should be equal distribution in times of scarcity. Brought back to Paris, he was released on the day after the **Vendémiaire coup** to take up the *Tribune of the People* again.

The paper had some success and created a loyal following. He published his ideas on 30 November. Many former **Jacobins – Amar** was one – and **sansculottes** allied with him, appreciating his calls for revolt against the **Directory** more than his programme for change. When a vituperative issue of the *Tribune* was read out in the **Pantheon Club**, the Directory closed it down. Repression united the radicals. On 30 March 1796, Babeuf's followers constituted a Secret Directory of Public Safety, as a hierarchical and disciplined group with a network of agents. General Rossignol was to lead an insurrection on 1 May. Other celebrities included Robert **Lindet**, Drouet, the 'hero of **Varennes**', Laignelot, a former Conventionnel, and the Italian radical **Buonarroti**. When the Directory decreed the death penalty for defending the 1793 Constitution on 10 May, Babeuf and his associates were arrested. Drouet was a deputy in the Council of 500, and the constitution said that, as such, he had to be tried in the high court at Vendôme. It was in the Directory's interest to try them all away from Paris.

It was a long trial, lasting from 20 February to 25 May 1797. Babeuf and one other were condemned to death, executed after both attempted suicide on 26 May. Seven were deported and 56 were acquitted, including Lindet and Drouet (whose escape was not prevented).[4]

 Birchall, Ian H., *The Spectre of Babeuf* (Basingstoke: Macmillan, 1997).

Bailliage

This was the term used in northern parts of France before the Revolution for an administrative district. In the south, the term *sénéchaussée* was used instead. The larger *bailliages* or *sénéchaussées* were taken as the units for an assembly from which deputies of all three estates would be elected to the **Estates-General**: two each for the **clergy** and **nobility** and four for the **Third Estate**, since the latter's representation had been doubled on this occasion.[5]

All bishops and beneficed clergy (*curés*) had the right to be present at the assembly. Heads of monasteries sent a representative, and so did abbesses. If a nobleman held lands in more than one of these districts, he had the right to be represented in all the assemblies concerned. Noblewomen who held lands in their own right appointed male representatives in the assemblies. The qualifications to elect a delegate to the assembly for the Third Estate were to be male, over 21 and on a register of tax-payers. The delegate these electors chose had to be wealthy enough to have several days free to attend the assembly.

Broadly speaking, the district (a sub-division of a *département*), divided into *cantons* comprising a dozen or so *communes*, replaced the *bailliages* and *sénéchaussées* in 1790.

Bailly, Jean-Sylvain (1736–93)

Bailly was a liberal caught up in a world of extremists. In the early stages of the Revolution he was one of its most powerful leaders. He was at the head of the list of Parisian deputies elected for the **Third Estate**, and temporary president of the National **Constituent Assembly** set up on 17 June. He presided over the **Tennis Court Oath** as portrayed in **David's** monumental, unfinished painting of the occasion.

Bailly's father was the keeper of the royal art collection housed in the Louvre, and he was given an excellent education. After trying to develop literary tastes, he chose natural science and gained a national reputation as an astronomer. His monumental *Histoire de l'Astronomie* in six volumes gained him his place in the *Académie française* in 1783, and in the *Académie des inscriptions* in 1785.

In May 1789, he was the president of the electoral district of Paris in which he lived, and drew up its **statement of complaint**. He was elected first deputy of the Third Estate of Paris at the **Estates-General**. He was president of the National Assembly on 17 June, and on 20 June was the first to take the oath in the Tennis Court – he stands with hand raised in David's painting. On 23 June, he famously uttered the reply to Dreux-Brézé's question whether he had heard the king's order to disperse: 'I believe that the assembled nation is not able to receive such an order.'[6]

Paris had never had a mayor before, and Bailly was its first, in office from July 1789 to November 1791. It was from his hand that **Louis XVI** received the tricolour cockade in the city three days after the fall of the **Bastille**, and the king confirmed his appointment as mayor. He developed new institutions for the government of Paris, but it was noticed that his attitude towards them was elitist. Other influences were also at work, however. **Danton**, **Brissot**, **Marat** and other activists had more democratic plans for the city. For them, the setting up of the 48 **Paris Sections** to replace the 60 districts was ideal, with the Commune at the Hôtel de Ville as a partner with, or even subservient to, them. Bailly, on the other hand, opted for a strong mayoralty, and was antagonistic towards the **sansculottes**.

In August 1790, Bailly beat Danton in the mayoral elections by 12,550 votes to 1,460. However, nearly a year later, after the king was brought back from his flight to **Varennes**, the **Cordeliers Club** and others organized a petition for a republic to be signed on the altar on the Champ de Mars that had been used for the celebration of the anniversary of the fall of the Bastille. It was widely believed that Bailly declared martial law by flying a red flag and, although **Lafayette** brought up his National Guard, the petitioners would not disperse. The troops fired. Fifty unarmed people fell dead. This event quickly became known as the massacre of the Champ de Mars and Bailly was blamed for it. Donald Sutherland's 2003 appraisal, however, categorically denies that Bailly declared martial law, and attributes the massacre to the National Guardsmen panicking.[7]

Bailly retired from being mayor in November 1791 and found a rural retreat near Nantes to write his memoirs. His democratizing opponents assumed posts of responsibility with the overthrow of the monarchy and the establishment of the Republic. They authorized Bailly's arrest as a suspect at Melun on 10 September 1793, and the **Committee of General Security** ordered his removal to Paris to be imprisoned in La Force and then in the **Conciergerie**. He was a witness at **Marie-Antoinette's** trial and his own began on 10 November, after he was charged with having 'stifled the voice of the people'. He pleaded that he was obeying orders of the **Constituent Assembly** in declaring martial law, but he was condemned to death after a day, and went to the scaffold, exceptionally set up on the Champ de Mars itself, on 12 November.[8]

Bara, Joseph (1779–93)

When the churches had been closed, the priests removed and the example of the lives of the church's saints suppressed, republican leaders found there was a lack of role models. A boy soldier called Joseph Bara, aged 13, had been killed in battle at Jallais in the **Vendée** in December 1793. He was taken up by **Robespierre** as an example for good republicans to follow. This was repeated all over the country. A specific example comes from La Rochelle, immediately south of the Vendée, from where much of the retribution against the rebels was controlled.

At the meeting of the popular society (**Jacobin Club**) in the town on 2 April 1794, Bonnin, its president, made a speech about Bara and told his story:

> He had charged at the enemy with the cavalry; the brigands had seized him and tried to make him shout, '*Vive la Religion. Vive le Roi!*' but he would not. He cried out '*Vive la République!*' instead and they killed him … [9]

Bonnin made him into a cult figure who would watch over his listeners' words and actions as a republican replacement saint. The Third Republic reinforced this by commissioning a huge canvas of Bara's death for the salon of 1883 from J.C. Weerts, in which the boy in his uniform is about to be bayoneted among the blown horses of the cavalry charge, as opposed to **David**'s contemporary image of a virtually hermaphrodite nude left to die.

Barère (de Vieuzac), Bertrand (1755–1841)

The most eloquent of the second rank revolutionaries, Barère became the spokesman in the Convention of the ideas thrashed out in the **Committee of Public Safety** of which he was a member. He was nicknamed 'the Anacreon of the guillotine' – Anacreon was an ancient Greek lyric poet. Until the king's flight to **Varennes**, he was a centrist, even a moderate, but his position subsequently hardened and, until the fall of **Robespierre**, he was generally in support of the republic of virtue.[10]

Before the Revolution, Barère had moved to Toulouse from Tarbes, where he had an inherited right to a position as a judge, and made a name for himself by his brilliance in the law court. He was elected as a deputy for Bigorre in the Pyrenees in the **Estates-General**. He maintained his links in the south, and was said to have bent the strict rules imposed by the Convention in favour of his local supporters.

Barère supported the **Terror** reluctantly, persuaded that it was the only defence against infiltration by agents in British pay. He was, like Henri **Grégoire**, a fervid supporter of French being the language of the nation. He saw Breton as 'the language of **federalism** and superstition' by means of which aristocrats and churchmen could turn the populace into counter-revolutionaries, as he maintained had happened in the **Vendée**. He helped create the myth of the 'One and Indivisible Republic'. Even so, he had tried to act as a conciliator when the **Girondins** were expelled from the Convention in June 1793.

Barère was not wholehearted in support of the **Maximum**, and wanted it modified 'since commerce must be healed'. Yet he voted for the king's immediate execution and regarded the queen as 'the cause of all the woes of France'. He was a political trimmer. It was said that on the morning of the fall of Robespierre he had two speeches in his pocket, one to use if Robespierre beat off his detractors, and the other for if he failed. As it was, his own speech in the Convention after **Tallien**'s denunciation of Robespierre was bland.

After **Thermidor**, he was arrested as a terrorist with **Collot d'Herbois**, **Billaud-Varenne** and **Vadier**. Like them, he was condemned to deportation to Guiana (the 'dry guillotine'). He escaped at the port and lay low in Bordeaux until re-emerging to support **Bonaparte** after **Brumaire**. In the Empire he was employed to write propaganda. He was exiled by Louis XVIII in 1816 as a regicide and for supporting Napoleon's 100 Days.

Barère returned to France from Belgium in 1830 and was *persona grata* with King Louis-Philippe, spending his last years in affable retirement back at Tarbes.

Barnave, Antoine (1761–93)

Barnave was a moderate in the Revolution. He and his associates Alexander de **Lameth** and Adrien **Duport** (known as the 'triumvirs' – so much of the Revolution referred back to the ancient Roman republic) were in favour of a second chamber for the legislature on the British model, ministers appointed from among the deputies, and a suspensive veto for the king. This innovation would complete the Revolution and implement the **Declaration of the Rights of Man and of the Citizen** agreed in August 1789.

Barnave was a Protestant lawyer from **Grenoble**. After the 'Day of Tiles' there on 7 June 1788 (when residents threw tiles down on royal troops in support of their suspended *parlement*), he associated with the judge **Mounier** to demand constitutional change. They wanted a revised version of Bourbon monarchy, stripped of absolute power, as a guarantee of stable government. Both men were elected to the **Estates-General**, the arrangements for which broadly reflected nationally what had been proposed in their town.

Barnave's prominence increased after the king's return from **Varennes**. He had been sent from the **Constituent Assembly** to accompany the king and queen back to Paris, and sat in their coach with them the whole way. He discussed future possibilities with them, and persuaded them to accept the fiction that they had been abducted by counter-revolutionaries. Later, he negotiated with the queen for the abandonment of armed **counter-revolution**, for the return of the king's brothers, **Provence** and **Artois**, to France, and for persuading the queen's brother, the Emperor, to withdraw support from the noble *émigrés*. In return, the king would retain the right to have overall command of his own army and to appoint the French ambassadors abroad. 'The weak point ... was a faithless king.'[11] He swore the oath to the new constitution in order to buy time, was disappointed in the Emperor's **Pillnitz Declaration**, and hoped to be able to dominate a humiliated nation with other monarchs' help. The king's duplicity (although short of treason) was matched by the queen's, who asked for her family's intervention and sent them military secrets when the war came.

Between the king's return and the opening of the new **Legislative Assembly** in October, Barnave and the other triumvirs brought 346 members of the **Jacobin Club** to the **Feuillants'** Chapel near the **Tuileries** in use as a replacement for the one at Versailles. From the new political club they formed there they canvassed their proposals: a new kind of monarchy for a new idea of the nation. When he saw that his ideas were not going to be acceptable in an increasingly republican political context, especially considering the desire for war of Brissot and his friends, Barnave went home to Grenoble.[12]

Barnave was arrested in August 1792 after the overthrow of the monarchy. He was in prison until he went to the scaffold in November 1793. A republic whose government was 'revolutionary until peace' had no room for constitutional monarchists whose expressed aim was to conclude the Revolution.

Barras, Jean-Nicolas-Paul-François, Vicomte de (1755–1835)

Barras personifies the sleazy, hedonistic nature of the **Directory**, the years between the fall of **Robespierre** and the seizure of power by General **Bonaparte**. Five men dressed in costumes designed by **David** living in luxury apartments in the **Luxembourg Palace** (reconverted from a prison) had collective power during a period of political sleight of hand, financial corruption and sexual scandal. Barras was the only permanent Director, keeping himself in power by means of a succession of manipulative *coups d'état* and then succumbing to one. The other Directors came and went around him. As Colin Jones has said, 'the republic of vice seemed to have succeeded the Republic of Virtue'.[13]

Barras was born into the Provençal nobility and took up a military career, serving in support of Tipu Sultan in the second Anglo-Mysore War against the British in India. He resigned his commission in 1783. When the Revolution came, he offered himself for administrative posts, and was elected to office in the Var and then at Orléans. In 1792, he became an army commissioner and then a deputy for the Var in the **Convention**. As such, he voted for the king's death, and was away from Paris as a **representative on mission**, suppressing the federalists at **Marseille** and at **Toulon** after Admiral Hood had left. He became acquainted with Bonaparte at Toulon, and their association persisted until Bonaparte became First Consul.

Barras was among Robespierre's opponents at **Thermidor**. He was in command of military forces in Paris, and sent **National Guard** units from the richer sections of the city to arrest him and the others in the Hôtel de Ville. Rising to greater prominence in the **Thermidorean Convention** he was in a position to order Bonaparte to disperse a royalist attack on the **Tuileries** from outside the Church of Saint-Roch on 5 October 1795 (**13 vendémiaire**), from which the event takes its name. With the adoption of the 1795 Constitution, Barras was elected to the Council of 500 and thence became one of the five Directors.

Among Barras's many mistresses were Thérèse **Tallien** and Rose (Joséphine) **Beauharnais**. He helped to facilitate the marriage of the latter to Bonaparte, and her 'dowry' was his appointment as general commanding the Army of Italy. Having Bonaparte out of sight gave the Directory some sort of security until the 1797 partial elections, after which the *coup d'état* of 18 **fructidor, year V** was necessary against royalists and surviving **Girondins**. Through his deputy, Augereau, Bonaparte saved the Directory again by arresting the opponents of the Republic. Barras also survived the **Prairial coup** on 18 June 1799, which replaced two other directors, leaving him in control.

Barras raised very little resistance to Bonaparte's **Brumaire coup**. **Talleyrand** and Admiral **Bruix** persuaded Barras that the other four directors had resigned, and that another royalist threat was putting the *Patrie* in danger. Barras agreed to retire to his Château Grosbois in great luxury. He was kept virtually under house arrest on Bonaparte's orders. He was exiled then, first to Brussels and then to Rome. In 1810, he was interned in Montpelier. He accommodated himself to the **Restoration of the Monarchy**, despite being a **regicide**, and lived on into the July Monarchy.

Basire, Claude (1764–94)

After spending the first years of the Revolution in local Burgundian politics, Basire became a deputy for the Côte d'Or in the **Legislative** and a member of the **Jacobin Club** (he had his fortnight as its president in February 1792). For a time he was a **Feuillant**, but soon became a radical and vehemently denounced the 'Austrian Committee'. He was allied politically with **Chabot** and **Merlin de Thionville**, a 'Cordelier trio'.[14]

He was involved in the scandal that erupted around his mistress, the feminist Etta **Palm**, who was deported on suspicion of being a Prussian spy. At the time of the invasion of the **Tuileries** on 20 June 1792, he was in favour of deposing **Louis XVI**. When the **National Convention** opened, however, he wanted more discussion before the monarchy was definitively abolished. Nevertheless, he sat with the **Mountain**, and voted for the king's death.

Basire was in favour of the exclusion of the **Girondins**, but he opposed the official **Terror** from his place on the **Committee of General Security**. He also expressed a fear that the kind of subversion that had occurred in the centres of **federalist** risings (**Lyon**, **Toulon**, **Marseille**) was about to happen in the **Paris Sections**.

When Chabot was arraigned for fraud in the **Company of the Indies** scandal, he implicated Basire, who was brought before the **Revolutionary Tribunal** and executed with the **Dantonists**, Chabot himself and the Frey brothers on 5 April 1794.

Basle, Treaties of (1795)

After **Brunswick**'s defeat at **Valmy**, Prussia played little part in the war against France. The principal Prussian minister, Comte Hertzberg, led a faction at Frederick William II's court that did not favour such policy. There was no hurry for a conclusion, but a peace, independent of the First Coalition, was signed by Barthélémy and Prince Hardenberg in Basle on 5 April 1795.[15]

Despite the early disparagement **Brissot** gave them, the Spaniards had crossed the Pyrenees into Roussillon, beaten a French army at Mas d'Eau, and then taken over a great deal of territory. This put them in a good position to make their separate peace with the Republic in Basle on 4 July, concluded by Barthélémy and Yriarte. France withdrew from occupied Spain, and Spain ceded the eastern half of **Saint-Domingue** to France. Spain withdrew from the coalition and undertook to make Portugal and Naples do the same. This meant that Austria was the only effective opponent of France left in the land war. Additionally, by a secret clause, the Republic agreed to free **Louis XVI**'s daughter from the Temple prison.[16]

The next time France and Spain went to war, they would be on the same side.

Bastille, Taking of the

When the king and the National **Constituent Assembly** at **Versailles** seemed to be ineffective in controlling the drastic increase in grain prices in July 1789, predominantly foreign troops in French service were ordered to encircle the capital, apparently to dismantle the revolutionary changes so far achieved there. Mayor **Bailly** organized the raising of a bourgeois militia to quell any rioting, but shops selling firearms were looted and cannon were taken from Les Invalides.

The popular financial controller, **Necker**, was dismissed by **Louis XVI** on 11 July when he protested about the troop concentrations (although his letter of dismissal was vaguely worded). Grain prices peaked on 14 July. Two days beforehand, **Camille Desmoulins** had incited the crowd in the gardens of the **Palais-Royal** to take gunpowder from the ancient Bastille fortress which towered above the **faubourg Saint-Antoine** as a symbol of royal despotism. Its governor, de Launay, was indecisive, and some royal troops deserted to help the citizens take the fortress. The gunpowder was seized, the seven remaining prisoners held there were freed, and the governor's corpse was soon afterwards beheaded with a pocket knife. Another official, de Flesselles, was similarly treated and their two heads were carried around on pikes. The 662 people on a list supplied by Maillard who had taken the fortress were honoured with the status of *Vainqueurs de la Bastille*.[17]

In response to the taking of the Bastille, the king reinstated Necker and came to Paris himself as early as 17 July to receive, in public, a red, white and blue **revolutionary cockade** for his hat from Mayor Bailly, appearing to have acquiesced in the limitations on his power. This event was greeted all over the nation as an occasion for rejoicing.

Georges Lefebvre, *1789*, trans. R.R. Palmer, *The Coming of the French Revolution*, (Princeton University Press, Bicentennial Edition, 1989), Chapter 7, 'The Paris Revolution of July 14', pp. 110–28.

Batavian Republic

The Batavian Republic was founded on 19 January 1795 and lasted until Napoleon I turned it into a kingdom for his brother Louis in 1805. It was the result of a popular revolution, but only with French support, which made it a 'sister republic'. Previously, the Dutch Republic was a confederation of states. Now it was unified like France but maintained by popular support. The constitution was established by a *coup d'état*, but it was thoroughly democratic, and the Dutch maintained a considerable measure of independence.[18]

The unsuccessful revolution in Holland had aroused interest in France in the 1780s. There were plenty of links between the two countries. A Francophile bourgeoisie in Holland was in favour of throwing over the remains of feudalism along with the *stadthouder*, William V of Orange, who had the support of small enterprises, mariners and the Calvinist church establishment. William V kept the upper hand and 40,000 patriots fled to France, to live in Gravelines and Saint-Omer and Paris itself. Many wanted a unified, democratic republic. Baroness Daelders gained support from **Marat** and **Robespierre**. The idea of a Batavian republic existed before the French conquest. After **Dumouriez** had been repulsed at Neerwinden in March 1793, the Dutch patriot clubs had time to form themselves in reaction to the support given to William V by the British.

When Belgium had been retaken, General Daendels (born in Holland, but a member of the French army) incited a rising, and French troops entered the Low Counties on 27 December 1794. William V left for England. The Dutch patriots met at The Hague on 26 January 1795 and took over the provincial assemblies and the Estates-General. **Reubell** and

Sieyès were sent from Paris and signed the Treaty of The Hague on 16 May. They imposed a large war indemnity on the Dutch, and took Flanders into Belgium. They ordered the maintenance of a garrison at Flessingue, a war fleet and an army of 25,000 men. It was soon realized that Dutch riches were illusory.

The Batavian republic wanted autonomy. A Convention elected by universal suffrage met in March 1796 to devise a constitution little favourable to the radical Francophiles. It was rejected by a referendum, with 80 per cent against, in August 1797. When another Convention was elected, the **Directory** had organized the **Fructidor coup** on 4 September, and the French felt strong enough to intervene to support the Dutch radicals. Generals Joubert and Daendels organized a coup on 22 January 1798. The democrats ousted the moderates, organized the country into departments, and drew up a constitution based on the French unadopted one of 1793. The anti-Jacobin campaign in France in spring 1798 lost them confidence, and they had to accept an electorate based on tax levels and institutions like the French ones of 1795: a legislative power in two councils, and an executive council of state with five members. This was affirmed by a 93 per cent referendum on 23 April. The radicals lost power in June, and tried to return with General Brune's help, but the **Brumaire** coup in France prevented it.

The sister-republic had co-operated with France. Although the Batavian fleet lost the battle of Camperdown (11 October 1797) to the British, the Batavians repulsed another British offensive on their own in August 1799.

Beauharnais, Marie-Josèphe-Rose (Joséphine) (1764–1813)

Rose Tascher de La Pagerie was from a prominent *Créole* family in Martinique, the daughter of a naval officer. She came to Paris in 1779 to marry Alexandre, Marquis de Beauharnais, a general, with whom she had two children: Eugène was the future viceroy of Italy, and Hortense married Louis Bonaparte, King of Holland, and became Napoleon III's mother. The Beauharnais were both imprisoned as aristocrats in the **Terror** and the General was executed. Rose made friends with Thérèse **Cabarrus** and was, like her, **Barras's** mistress. Barras introduced her to **Bonaparte** whom she married just before he left in command of the Army of Italy in 1796, and was his consort when he crowned himself Emperor of the French in 1804.

Bonaparte adopted her children, but divorced her in 1809 so as to have a son of his own by the Austrian Archduchess, Marie-Louise (eerily related to **Marie-Antoinette**).

📖 Bruce, Evangeline, *Napoleon and Josephine: An Improbable Marriage* (London: Weidenfeld & Nicolson, 1995).

Beaumarchais, Pierre-Augustin Caron de (1732–99)

Beaumarchais is best known as the author of the play, *The Marriage of Figaro*, which was accepted by the censor in 1781, but angrily banned as subversive by **Louis XVI** in person after he had heard Figaro's Act V monologue at a private reading with the comment: 'We would have to demolish the **Bastille** before putting on a play like this. … This man makes fun of everything he ought to respect in a government.' In June 1783, the play was put on in the *Salle des Menus-Plaisirs* at **Versailles** (where the **Estates-General** were to convene six years later). A great crowd of the quality was queueing up to see it but, before it could start, a duke arrived with a *lettre de cachet* from the king to cancel it. The reaction was 'so intense that never before the fall of the throne were the words *oppression* and *tyrannie* articulated with such passion and vehemence'.[19] The ban was lifted in 1784 (by a 'weak tyrant'[20]), and nobles enjoyed seeing themselves the object of satire. Beaumarchais had spent a great deal of money and energy on getting himself ennobled. Mozart's opera appeared in 1786 with the more explicit political statements omitted. **Danton**'s comment was: 'Figaro killed the nobility.' **Bonaparte** observed: '*The Marriage of Figaro* was the Revolution already in action.'[21]

In 1784, Beaumarchais was imprisoned on Louis XVI's orders for lampooning members of the royal family in a journal. He was sent to the Lazare prison, not the Bastille – insulting treatment compared with the gilded confinement given to the Cardinal de Rohan for the **Diamond Necklace Affair** soon afterwards.[22]

Beaumarchais could turn his hand to anything. He made watches, taught music, bought arms for the Americans, tried to buy some for the Republic, preserved the corpus of **Voltaire**'s writings, travelled in Spain, whence came Figaro and Comte Almaviva, and tried to improve the Paris water supply. He went to Holland to buy arms for the Republic, but was listed as an *émigré* while he was there. His name was not taken from the list until 1796 when he returned to Paris to live out his days quietly.

 Blanning, T.W.C., *The Culture of Power and the Power of Culture: Old Regime Europe 1660–1789* (Oxford: Oxford University Press, 2003), pp. 432–5.

Belgium

The Brabant Revolution had ousted Emperor Joseph II from the Austrian Netherlands in October 1789 and set up the United States of Belgium, which included the prince-bishopric of Liège. But the new Emperor Leopold II and Frederick William of Prussia concluded the Convention of Reichenbach on 27 July 1790, in which Prussia agreed not to help the revolutionaries.[23] Austrian troops retook Brussels and Liège on 11 January 1791.

Leopold II had learned discretion as ruler of Tuscany. He released political prisoners and sanctioned moderate reforms. The old regime was restored entirely in Liège. After **Dumouriez**'s victory over the Austrians at **Jemappes** on 6 November 1792, the occupying force wanted the Brussels lawyer Vonck's party to act more quickly than it did, and on 15 December a decree abolished privileges and called assemblies to unite Belgium with France. The Liègois were more enthusiastic than the Flemings. Dumouriez was defeated at Neerwinden on 18 March 1793 and defected to the Austrians. This left the Belgian revolutionaries to act in their own way until the summer of 1794, when **Pichegru** and **Jourdan** retook Ypres and Charleroi and defeated the Austrians at **Fleurus**. By the end of July they were in possession of Anvers and Liège as well. There was a reaction from conservative Belgians. French commissioners raised levels of taxation, requisitions and exports of grain coal and metal ore to benefit France.

In August 1795, Belgium was divided into nine departments administered as part of metropolitan France. This reduced the tension somewhat, as Belgium seemed less exploited, and the union was voted into being on 1 October 1795, recognized by Austria after the preliminaries of Leoben, and confirmed by the **treaty of Campo Formio**, 18 October 1797. After that there was a similar movement to the right as there was in

France itself. New laws and the sale of church land accelerated to meet the threat.

A civil war was provoked by conscription laws, and the 'Belgian Vendée' began, which needed 3,500 troops and took from October to December 1798 to crush. The **Directory**'s religious policy intensified the rebellion. Opposition was united by the prohibition of public worship and the oath of hatred for royalty. Nine hundred priests were arrested, and half of them deported. Belgian priests arrived on the Ile d'Oléron as prisoners. Nobles' land was also nationalized for sale. Not until well into the Consulate was co-operation restored.[24]

Bernadotte, Jean-Baptiste-Jules (1763–1844)

Bernadotte was a lawyer's son from Pau and a sergeant in the army before the Revolution. By 1818, he had become King of Sweden. He was a commissioned officer in 1791, and was in campaigns on the Rhine and in Flanders, a brigadier at the battle of **Fleurus** in June 1794, and a general from the time he went to Italy under **Bonaparte**'s command. He was made ambassador to Vienna at the time of the breakdown of the **Rastadt Conference** in 1798.

The Directory trusted him because of his extreme republicanism and, when the **War of the Second Coalition** began, he had a command on the Rhine until **Jourdan** was repulsed at Stockach. He was war minister from July until September 1799 and was rewarded for not opposing Bonaparte's **Brumaire** *coup d'état*.

The main part of his career was during the Empire. He annoyed Napoleon who dismissed him after the Walcheren Expedition in 1809, although he had been a marshal since 1804. He was invited to become the heir to the throne of Sweden in August 1810 and, as such, brought Sweden into the Sixth Coalition against France. He was King of Sweden from 1818 to his death.[25]

Bernard, André-Antoine, 'de Saintes' (1751–1819)

Bernard 'de Saintes' served his apprenticeship as a revolutionary in Saintes, the *chef-lieu* of the Charente-Inférieure in the south-west, as a lawyer and freemason who carved his own way in local administration. Not elected to the **Estates-General** and beaten by his rival Garnier to the office of mayor, he seized the colonelcy of the Saintes **National Guard**, and was elected to the **Legislative Assembly** and the **Convention**. He took his place with his fellow **Jacobins** as a member of the **Mountain**, and expressed his vote for the king's death in dramatic language.

As **representative on mission** in eastern France and Burgundy he exceeded the demands of the Republic, being responsible for a judicial murder in Dijon. His language and actions against **federalists** and churchmen were harsh and uncompromising. He brought Montbéliard back into France, but his conduct there was excessive too, even to the extent of taking out the coffins of former rulers from the castle crypt and emptying them on the road so that the metal could be melted down for cash and cannon.

He was in Paris at the time of **Robespierre**'s fall, but was protected from sharing his fate because he was a member of the **Committee of General Security**. However, he was put in prison along with the painter **David** who made a pen and ink sketch of him. He was amnestied with others like him in October 1795. Returning to Saintes, where he had acquired a good deal of church property, he held legal office during the Empire. He was exiled in 1816 as a **regicide**, and was shipwrecked on Madeira, where he died after three years.

Ballard, Richard, *The Unseen Terror: The French Revolution in the Provinces* (London and New York: I.B.Tauris, 2010), pp. 43–57.

Bertier de Sauvigny, Louis-Bénigne-François (1737–89)

As soon as the **Bastille** had been taken on 14 July 1789, there were four murders carried out by the Parisian crowd. First, of the Marquis de Launay, the governor of the Bastille, whose head was hacked off and paraded around that evening, then of Jacques de Flesselles, the chief magistrate (*prévôt des marchands*) of Paris, who had tried to delay the handing over of weapons to attack the fortress, and then, on 22 July, of Bertier de Sauvigny, the *intendant* of the Ile de France, and of Joseph Foulon de Doué. This was the basis of Simon Schama's assertion in his bicentenary chronicle that the **Terror** was 'merely 1789 with a higher body count'.[26]

Bertier had been lieutenant to his father, the *intendant* of the generality of Paris at the time of **Louis XVI**'s accession and the 'flour war' of 1775. He was reprimanded for his severity during that time of scarcity but, nevertheless, was himself appointed *intendant* in 1776. While the **Assembly of Notables** was in session, he caused resentment by reorganizing the way his generality was taxed.

When Paris was being surrounded by troops in summer 1789, many of whom were foreign mercenaries, Bertier was ordered to find provisions for them at the same time as the price of grain peaked, which provoked the seizure of the Bastille. Originating in the Duc d'**Orléans**'s circle at the **Palais-Royal**, rumours spread that he was keeping grain from reaching the city with the intention of starving the occupants into obedience to the court at **Versailles**. He was on his way to join **Artois** and other *émigrés* when he was captured at Compiègne, and brought to the place de Grève in front of the Paris Hôtel de Ville. Joseph Foulon, Bertier's father-in-law, had previously suggested that hungry people should eat grass and had been appointed a government minister when **Breteuil** replaced **Necker**. Bertier was made to watch Foulon's severed head dragged over the cobbles with its mouth full of grass in revenge. Then they lynched him.

One of the more moderate revolutionaries, Antoine **Barnave**, trying to justify such horror, asked, 'What was it that made their blood so pure? (*Ce sang, était-il donc si pur?*)'[27]

Bertrand de Moleville, Antoine-François, Marquis de (1744–1818)

Bertrand tried to accommodate the crown with the Revolution and brought five years' experience as intendant of Brittany to being minister for the navy and the colonies to the constitutional monarchy. **Brissot** and others mounted a press campaign against him until he was denounced in the **Legislative Assembly** and resigned his ministry. He remained in the king's circle in the **Tuileries Palace** and was supposed to be a member of the so-called '**Austrian Committee**' in the last year of the monarchy. He even discussed with the king a plan for him to escape immediately before the Tuileries Palace was invaded on the orders of the **Insurrectionary Commune** on 10 August 1792. He went to England, where his memoirs were published in English. They contain some valuable information about the way the court co-existed with the **Legislative Assembly** and a full (if biased) account of the flight to **Varennes**.

Bertrand de Moleville (Marquis de), Antoine-François, *Private memoirs relative to the last year of the reign of Lewis the Sixteenth, late king of France, Volume 2* (London: A. Strahan, 1797), available online at http://books.google.com/.

Billaud-Varenne, Jacques-Nicolas (1756–1819)

'Either the Revolution will triumph or we will all die.'[28] Billaud-Varenne's utterance is a key to understanding the **Terror**. The organizers of the Terror were responsible for the death of **Louis XVI** and they were facing the possibility of defeat by and reprisals from the kings of Europe. There is a desperate element in the Terror. Even when the Republic gained its military victories, there was always the internal enemy to overcome: the royalist conspirator – whether absolutist or constitutionalist – financed by the British.

Billaud-Varenne was brought up in La Rochelle, the son of a magistrate in the Paris *parlement*. He had come to his radical conclusions well before the Revolution began. He had been a teacher with the Oratorian order, and had tried to be a dramatist, but went to Paris to be a lawyer associated with the *parlement*. He also wrote long, quasi-philosophical books. He eventually found the best outlet for his single-mindedness as a politician of the **Mountain**.

Billaud-Varenne was one of the earliest to demand a republic. He was a member of the **Insurrectionary Commune** and made a deputy commissioner of the **Paris Sections** as the events of the overthrow of the monarchy unravelled. He was suspected of complicity in planning the assault on the Abbaye Prison in the **September Massacres**.

He was elected as a deputy for Paris in the **Convention** and voted for the king's death 'within 24 hours'. He anticipated the **revolutionary calendar** by claiming that time had begun again and that everything must be dated subsequent to Year I of the French Republic. He helped to organize the expulsion of the **Girondins** on 2 June 1793. In close association with **Collot d'Herbois** in the **Committee of Public Safety**, he expressed terrorist views and spoke in favour of deporting foreigners, arresting suspects, forcibly taxing the wealthy, and the creation of the 'revolutionary army'. He demanded the queen's execution in October, and took part in the attacks on **Hébert** and **Danton** in March and April 1794.

Like **Tallien** and **Fouché**, Billaud-Varenne sensed **Robespierre**'s antagonism and joined the attack on him on **8 thermidor**.[29] His previous close association with Robespierre then caught up with him and he was arrested, along with Collot d'Herbois and **Barère**. They were deported to Guiana (except Barère who escaped). Billaud-Varenne refused the amnesty offered under the Consulate and stayed in Guiana until 1816. He moved to New York and then to a farm he bought in Haiti (formerly **Saint-Domingue**), where he died.[30]

Boissy d'Anglas, François-Antoine de (1756–1828)

The career of Boissy d'Anglas from 1789 until the restoration of the monarchy was that of a constitutional royalist. He had previously been a lawyer attached to the Paris *parlement* and was elected for the **Third Estate** to the **Estates-General**. He was instrumental in turning the Third Estate at **Versailles** into the National Assembly on 17 June 1789. His speeches commended the taking of the **Bastille**. At this stage, he spoke against royalist conspiracies in the south.

As a member of the **National Convention**, he took a seat in the Marsh (the centre benches where the uncommitted deputies sat). At the king's trial, he voted for imprisonment until deportation. He was not pursued after the **Jacobins** excluded his **Girondin** associates from the Convention on 2 June 1793 and was in favour of the official Terror in its early stages. Nevertheless, he joined **Robespierre**'s opponents at **Thermidor**. In the **Thermidorean Convention** he was put on the **Committee of Public Safety** with responsibility for the Paris food supply in a time of scarcity. They called him '*Boissy-Famine*' because he refused to have the **Maximum** re-adopted. He was actually presenting his report when the rioters of 1 prairial (20 May 1795) broke into the Convention to demand 'bread and the Constitution of 1793'. They were carrying the head of the murdered deputy Jean Féraud on a pike. Boissy stopped speaking, stood still to salute it, and began again when the demonstrators withdrew.[31]

Boissy was a member of the Committee of Eleven who drew up the constitution for the **Directory**, expressing the need to prevent both tyranny and anarchy (a word now used for Jacobinism), for which he was praised by royalists. He stood for order, and approved of voters being qualified by the amount of tax they paid, rejecting all theories of equality. 'The property of the rich must always be guaranteed,' he said.[32] When he was elected (under the **Law of Two-Thirds**) to the Council of 500, he did not deny being a royalist since he was a leading member of the **Clichy Club**. He wanted freedom for the right-wing press, for returned *émigrés* and for the **refractory clergy**. After the **Fructidor coup** the Directory excluded him and he stayed in England until after Bonaparte's **Brumaire coup**.

By 1805 Boissy was a Senator in the Empire, and voted for Napoleon to abdicate in 1814, which meant he was acceptable as a peer of France at the first **restoration of the monarchy**. He turned back to Napoleon in the Hundred Days, which made him unacceptable to Louis XVIII, but only for a while. He spent his last years in cultural pursuits.

Bonald, Louis-Gabriel-Ambroise, Vicomte de (1754–1840)

Bonald was among the principal defenders of **counter-revolution** and the **restoration of the monarchy**, a 'prophet of the past' in the eyes of constitutionalists and republicans. He was among the *émigrés* of 1791, and spent his exile in Switzerland. Bonald was a prolific writer, even at that stage, and the long book he wrote about political and religious power was condemned in his absence by the **Directory** in 1796. It was called the *Theory of Political and Religious Power*. 'Its geometrical method claimed to elucidate the axioms of a political and religious anthropology: man's sociability, the potential of the divine plan in the earthly city, rationality of and necessity for social organization of security.' For him 'the philosophy of the **Enlightenment** writers and the revolutionaries had dissolved the social body. ... Democracy was no more than the anarchy of individualists, and liberalism a doctrine of the atomization of society.' He himself commented, 'Wherever all men of necessity want to dominate with equal wills and unequal forces, it is essential that one man only dominate or all destroy themselves.' So only a Catholic king could give form to (*constituer*) a people and put a brake on the centrifugal forces that threaten its identity.[33]

Bonald returned to France during the Consulate and edited the *Mercure* with **Chateaubriand**. During the Empire he accepted a post associated with the Imperial University in 1808. When the Bourbon monarchy was restored, he was on the Council of Public Instruction, and elected to the National Assembly, one of the 'Ultra' royalists. He was a Minister of State and then a Peer of France. His literary output gained him a place in the French Academy. When the former Comte d'**Artois** inherited the throne as Charles X in 1824, he was emotionally at home. He was very much in favour of the act introduced in 1825, which made blasphemy punishable by death. He argued for an infallible church and an absolutist state: the '**alliance of throne and altar**'. After the 1830 Revolution he withdrew from public life.

📖 Devlin, Roger F., *Bonald's Theory of the Nobility, The Occidental Quarterly Online*, available online at: http://www.toqonline.com/2009/12/bonalds-theory-of-the-nobility/.

Bonaparte, Napoleon (1769–1821), First Consul (1799–1804), Emperor Napoleon I (1804–1814/5)

Bonaparte's significance in the decade of the Revolution ranged from being the **Jacobin** artillery officer who made the retaking of **Toulon** possible in December 1793, through assisting the **Directory** to take power in October 1795 and exporting the Revolution to Italy in 1796, to seizing power for himself as First Consul in November 1799.

Bonaparte was born in Corsica, where his lawyer father was noble enough to qualify him for a place at the military school at Brienne. After the Ecole Militaire in Paris, he specialized in artillery, and joined the **Jacobin Club** while stationed in Valence. He hovered between Corsica and France after his father's death in 1785, and was actually in Paris in 1792 for the '**Day' of 10 August 1792**, expressing republican opinions. He was stationed at Valence in 1793, and was in command of artillery during the retaking of **Marseille**. Then he was ordered to the siege of Toulon by **representatives on mission Saliceti** and Gasparin. He set himself against General Carteaux, asking for an artillery attack on the town before any infantry action. This was accepted by Dugommier, Carteaux's replacement.

General Teil, who had commanded Bonaparte before, bombarded the town before the attack and this persuaded Admiral Hood and his Anglo-Spanish fleet to leave. Augustin **Robespierre**, also a representative on mission, gained Bonaparte's promotion to the rank of brigadier at the age of 24. General Dugommier told the war minister: 'Reward that young man because, if his services are not recognized, he will promote himself.'[34]

Bonaparte was artillery commander with the Army of Italy, but he was denounced by Saliceti as a Robespierrist and brought back to be imprisoned at Antibes in August 1794. He was released after nine days. He kept his rank but had no employment until **Carnot** put him in charge of the new Mapping Office. He wanted to go to Turkey, where officers were being invited to reorganize the army, but he was refused permission. He in turn refused to serve in the **Vendée**, and lost his rank. **Barras**, commanding the army of the interior, gave it back to him and made use of him and his cannon in central Paris to quash the royalists during the **Vendémiaire** **coup**.[35] After his marriage to Joséphine **Beauharnais** in March 1796, he was given command of the Italian campaign, and won spectacular victories for the Republic, culminating at Rivoli.

Bonaparte then turned to politics, setting up the **Cisalpine** and Cispadine Republics, imposing the preliminary peace of Leoben and then the treaty of **Campo Formio** on the Austrians. His next appointment was to an army to invade England in October 1797, but he turned his attention eastwards. With foreign minister **Talleyrand**'s political support,[36] he landed in **Egypt** in 1798 and was successful at the Battle of the Pyramids, but lost his fleet to Admiral Nelson at Aboukir Bay (the Battle of the Nile). He advanced into Syria as far as Acre and returned to Egypt. He became aware of the French loss of his own Italian gains. Leaving his army with Kléber, he returned to Paris via Fréjus in October 1799 in time for his **Brumaire** *coup* *d'état* on 9–10 November, in which he adapted the plans previously made for it by Talleyrand, **Sieyès** and **Fouché**.

Asprey, Robert, *The Rise and Fall of Napoleon Bonaparte*, 2 vols (London: Little Brown, 2000, 2001).

McLynn, Frank, *Napoleon* (London: Jonathan Cape, 1997).

Schom, Alan, *Napoleon Bonaparte* (New York: HarperCollins, 1997).

Bouchotte, Jean-Baptiste Noël (1754–1840)

Bouchotte was chosen as War Minister while the **Terror** gathered momentum in April 1793. His ministry is remarkable for the close association between the **army** and **sansculotte** principles which he called 'the popular system'. He worked closely with Lazare **Carnot**, through whom he had the complete support of the **Committee of Public Safety**. **Hébert**'s *Le Père Duchesne* was circulated among the troops to politicize them.

Bouchotte had been in the army since 1769, but could not rise beyond his 1789 rank of captain in the old regime. He was temporary commander of the fortress at Cambrai in 1792 and had to control two mutinies. After **Dumouriez**'s defection, he successfully defended Cambrai. He was promoted to colonel in January 1793, and became minister of war in April. The **Girondins** attacked him immediately and wanted General Beauharnais (the future empress's first husband) to replace him. After the removal of the Girondins on 2 June and, with the support of **Robespierre** at the **Committee of Public Safety** after 27 July 1793, he was able to 'sansculotticize' his ministry[37] during the time that ministries remained (they were suppressed in April 1794). He had the assistance of other sansculotte supporters such as **Pache**, **Ronsin** and **Vincent** as administrators, after purging those who were already there. He replaced many of the ministry staff with nominees from the **Paris Sections**, even if not many of them had the necessary experience to be civil servants. In Year II, he had a staff of 1,800. He was not able to solve equipment problems for the army, and his enemies made much of it. Nevertheless, with the support of **representatives on mission** from the **Mountain**, the armies were able to retake the initiative and win victories, such as at **Fleurus** in June 1794, though he had no say in the conduct of operations. He was severe with deserters, but was regarded by the troops as supportive towards them. He made a point of communicating news from Paris, including the unadopted, extremely democratic, 1793 Constitution. 'The army became a school of Jacobinism.'[38]

In April 1794, the Committee of Public Safety took over all ministerial functions, and Bouchotte returned to active service. He was arrested as a suspect in June 1794 – Hébert had gone to the scaffold in March – and sent to the fortress of Ham, but was amnestied with others prominent in the **Terror** in 1795. He supported **Bonaparte's** **Brumaire coup** but was never promoted beyond colonel. The best Bonaparte would do for him was provide him with a general's pension on which he retired. He lived quietly near Metz for the rest of his 86 years.

Bouillé, François-Claude-Amour, Marquis de (1739–1800)

Bouillé is remembered best, perhaps, for being the royalist general who failed to link up with **Louis XVI** at Saint-Ménéhoude during his flight to **Varennes** in June 1791.

He had served in the Seven Years' War and in the American War of Independence. On his return, he held governorships in eastern provinces of France. He did not accommodate himself to the Revolution and was responsible for the severe punishment of the mutineers at Metz and **Nancy** in August 1790.[39] Despite this, he was commander-in-chief of the Armies in the eastern provinces of France in the same year.

The plan agreed between the king and queen, **Fersen** and Bouillé for June 1791 was that the royal family would escape from the **Tuileries** and make their way to Montmédy on the eastern frontier. The delays in the king's journey meant that the planned rendezvous was not achieved, though Bouillé had assembled his troops as arranged.[40]

After the king and queen had been brought ignominiously back to Paris, Bouillé's letter to the **Constituent** from exile assuming responsibility for the king's evasion allowed the fiction to be sustained that the king had been abducted.[41] The letter was read out from the tribune on 30 June: It said that the king had let himself be persuaded to leave Paris for Montmédy where he would call a new legislative assembly, act as mediator between the foreign powers and the French people to prevent an invasion, and to order the state on the basis of the *cahiers de doléance* (**statements of grievance**) received in May 1789. Bouillé asserted his own responsibility: 'I arranged it all, controlled it all, gave orders for it all; it is against me that your bloody fury should be directed. I knew the roads; I would have led the foreign armies myself.' Bouillé was then regarded as 'the one who led this family astray (*Le séducteur de cette famille*)' in the pamphlets that appeared.[42]

Bouillé was present at Emperor Leopold II's coronation in Prague in September. Then he joined the Army of the Princes, and served with the Duke of York. He died in England seven years later.[43]

Bourgeoisie

The word '*bourgeois*' was used to designate someone who lived in a town and carried on a business there, as opposed to a *paysan* who lived in and off the countryside. But eighteenth-century bourgeois society had ceased to be static. Its late eighteenth-century characteristic was dynamic, upward mobility. If a bourgeois could afford to sell his commercial business on, buy government stock and live 'nobly' as a *rentier*, then it was not unlikely that the next step would be to buy an office from the crown that would, after a generation or so, turn the purchaser into a nobleman. This could be a financial office, or a royal secretaryship. Moreover, his son could marry a nobleman's daughter, inherit her father's title and live off landed income. The wealthy bourgeois would also want to have land of his own. Together with the nobility, 2.75 million people made up the dominant classes out of a population approaching 28 million at the outset of the Revolution. Their characteristics were 'soft hands, formal clothing, servants, effortless literacy, and incomes and possessions far beyond the dreams of the average Frenchman or woman'.[44]

The special place of non-commercial bourgeoisie was in the legal profession. To obtain an office as a royal advocate (*avocat du roi*) was the primary aim of many who qualified as lawyers. They pleaded cases in one of the thirteen *parlements* whose main function, after the registration of royal edicts, was to be higher courts of law. These lawyers also acted as land agents for the nobility or the higher clergy. They certainly had administrative experience even if they were no more than 'obscure provincial advocates, stewards of petty local jurisdictions, country attornies … and the whole train of the ministers of municipal litigation' about whom Edmund **Burke** was so dismissive in his *Reflections*.[45] Listed in this dictionary are a good many qualified lawyers who took upon themselves the new profession of elected politician in 1789. Men of law made up more than two-thirds of the Third Estate deputies in the **Estates-General**, and about half of the deputies in the **National Convention**.[46]A quarter of the deputies in the Estates-General were old-regime holders of offices which they, their fathers or their grandfathers had bought. Their numbers fell to only an eighth in the two councils of the **Directory**. For the most part, antagonism against the **nobility** was limited, and there was a great deal of co-operation between the two orders. There were ways round the prohibition against noblemen engaging in commerce. The honours for wealth amongst ship owners in La Rochelle, for example, were evenly shared between nobles and bourgeois who lived in the up-market Saint-Barthélémy quarter between the Gran'rive and the place d'Armes.[47] There were plenty of noblemen who were finding alternative 'crops' of metal ore and coal under their land.[48] The 'rise' of the bourgeoisie can be considered historically without any ideological preconception of intended class struggle. The real struggle for both orders was against the designs of the monarchy through its provincial *intendants* to deprive both groups of political authority.

Doyle, William, *The Origins of the French Revolution,* 3rd edn (Oxford: Oxford University Press, 1999), chap. 10.

Breteuil, Louis Charles Auguste le Tonnelier, Baron de (1730–1807)

In the early part of the Revolution, Breteuil was the replacement for **Necker** on 12 July 1789, then recognized as prime minister in exile, an organizer from exile of the king's flight to **Varennes** and, ultimately, after the death of **Louis XVII**, a lonely figure disliked by **Louis XVI**'s brothers.

He was a soldier in the first two years of the Seven Years' War, but became a diplomat in 1758. He was ambassador in turn at Cologne, Saint Petersburg, Stockholm, Naples and Vienna. When he returned he was appointed Minister of the King's Household, which included responsibility for policing Paris. Intellectuals liked him because he interpreted the censorship laws with moderation. During the **Diamond Necklace Affair** he supported the queen[49] and she was grateful. He did not get on with **Calonne**. Breteuil resigned on 24 July 1788 and left Versailles.

The courtiers around the queen and **Artois** contacted Breteuil to ask him to return as first minister after they had got rid of Necker on 11

July 1789.[50] Artois hurried the plan and it misfired into the ineffective 'ministry of a hundred hours' until, after the **Bastille** had fallen, Necker was recalled.

Breteuil went at first to Switzerland. Though Artois favoured Calonne as minister in exile – he joined him in Turin – the queen gained Breteuil's official appointment as such. Louis XVI gave him authority to represent him in the royal courts of Europe in November 1790. The tensions he encountered at **Versailles** re-emerged in exile.

He shared in the organization of the flight to Varennes through his contact with Gustavus III of Sweden. He was in touch with the Emperor Francis II and Frederick William II of Prussia before and after the **declaration of war**. He was involved in a plan to disrupt the French economy with counterfeit *assignats* in December 1792. His disputes with the princes continued after the execution of the king and queen, and he withdrew from their world altogether to live quietly in Hamburg.

First Consul Bonaparte allowed Breteuil's return in 1802, and he was one of the old nobility who were prepared to accept the new conditions of the Empire.

Price, Munro, *The Fall of the French Monarchy: Louis XVI, Marie-Antoinette and the Baron de Breteuil* (London: Macmillan, 2002).

Brissot, Jacques-Pierre (1754–93)

Brissot was a leading light in the **Girondin** faction, excluded from the **Convention** by the **Mountain** with the aid of the **sansculotte** sections of Paris in June 1793. His associates provided the ministers for **Louis XVI** after his return from **Varennes** in June 1791, while constitutional monarchy was still a possibility. When the Republic was declared, the Brissotins (as they were first called) were opposed by the **Jacobins**, who excluded them from the Convention within six months of the king's execution.

Brissot came from Chartres, where his father was a caterer and landowner in the Beauce, and moved early to Paris. After his marriage, he moved to London and wrote theoretical law books heavily influenced by Jean-Jacques **Rousseau**, one of which he dedicated to **Voltaire** who accepted it. He was also associated with **Mercier**, **Condorcet**, **Sieyès** and the banker **Clavière**.[51] He took up journalism and, back in Paris, was put in the **Bastille** for four months for criticizing the French establishment. On his return to London, he met British anti-slavery activists. A visit to the United States in 1788 had great influence on his ideas.

Once more in Paris, he founded the *Société des Amis des Noirs* and was its president in 1790 and 1791. He was active in Parisian politics at the outbreak of the Revolution, even being presented with the keys to the Bastille as it was being demolished. He spoke often at the **Jacobin Club**, and was a deputy in the **Legislative Assembly** and then the **Convention**. When Emperor Leopold II and Frederick William II of Prussia made their Declaration of **Pillnitz** in August 1791, threatening military intervention should the French king and queen be harmed, Brissot was a member of the foreign affairs committee. There were for him great advantages in a defensive war against the rulers of Austria and Prussia and the *émigrés* and, possibly, *rapprochement* with Great Britain.[52] It would force the king to declare his real intentions and export the benefits of the Revolution to other victims of despotism, thereby uniting the nation. He was influential in declaring war against the Habsburg monarchy, claiming that the Revolution would not be secure unless the foreign threat to it had been defeated in war.

At the time of Louis XVI's trial, the Girondins proposed a national referendum on whether he should be executed or not were he to be found guilty of crimes against the Nation. The Jacobins (also called the **Mountain**, because of their high seats to the left of the tribunal in the Convention) overruled this. They orchestrated the group's forced exclusion from the Convention on 2 June 1793, and their subsequent pursuit and execution.

Brissot escaped and was arrested without a passport. **Desmoulins** vocalized the manufactured charges against him. Robespierre's faction had the rules of the **revolutionary tribunal** changed on 29 October so that the prosecutor **Fouquier-Tinville** could have the Girondins declared guilty if the jury's consciences were satisfied that there was moral certainty of guilt after three days. They were.

Brissot, **Vergniaud** and 19 others went to the scaffold on 31 October, a fortnight after Queen **Marie-Antoinette**.

Bruix, Etienne-Eustache (1759–1805)

Bruix was a naval lieutenant in 1789. He had served in the American War of Independence and then been responsible for making charts of the coast of **Saint-Domingue**. He was promoted to captain in January 1793, but was dismissed ten months later by the **Jacobin** government because he had noble connections. He used his enforced inactivity to write a report on provisioning the navy solely from French territory which was read and approved of by **Bonaparte**. After the fall of the Jacobins at **Thermidor**, he was reinstated as a captain. He was adjutant to Admiral Morard de Galles who commanded the fleet that took **Hoche** to Ireland. Hoche took note of Bruix and, as a result, he was promoted to rear-admiral in May 1797.

For fifteen months, from April 1798 to July 1799, Bruix was Navy Minister. He took personal command of the fleet that went from Brest to try without success to re-provision **Bonaparte's** army in **Egypt** after the loss of its fleet to Nelson in Aboukir Bay in August 1798. He avoided the British squadrons cruising off Brest and sailed with his 25 vessels to assist General **Masséna**, besieged in Genoa, and then returned to Brest ('Bruix's Cruise'[53]). Then he gave up his navy minister's portfolio. By autumn in 1799, he was a vice-admiral and privy to the secret of the **Brumaire** *coup d'état*. First Consul Bonaparte made him a full admiral in 1801 and put him on the *conseil d'état* (National Council) in 1802. After the failure of the Peace of Amiens, he was appointed commander of the fleet at Boulogne in anticipation of an invasion of England. He died of natural causes in 1805.

Brumaire *coup d'état*

On 9–10 November 1799 (18–19 brumaire in the **revolutionary calendar**), influential opponents of **Barras**, tired of the ineffectiveness of French war policy against the **Second Coalition**, overthrew the **Directory**. The principal plotters were **Sieyès** (himself a Director at that time), **Talleyrand** and **Fouché**. They made Bonaparte effective head of state after admiring his earlier victories in Italy and representing the setbacks of his recent expedition in **Egypt** as propaganda victories. He had left his Egyptian army in Kléber's hands, and was back in France a month before the coup.

Bonaparte did not go along with Sieyès's plans for a constitution any more than the framers of the Directory had in 1795. He wanted three consuls to draw up a new constitution with the aid of a parliamentary commission from both legislative councils. The coup took two days. On 9 November, the Council of Elders met in the early hours to take a vote on moving the councils to Saint-Cloud in fear of an anarchist plot. Bonaparte was in charge of their move. The Council of 500, under Lucien Bonaparte's presidency, met at 11 and agreed to move next day. Bonaparte and some troops met Sieyès and Roger Ducos at the **Tuileries Palace**. Barras had agreed to resign and go to his Grosbois estate. The other Directors, Gohier and Moulin, were guarded in their **Luxembourg Palace** apartments. A public argument staged between Bonaparte and Barras's secretary took place in the Tuileries gardens. Bonaparte asserted himself: '… I left you peace and I find war! I left you conquests, and the enemy is crossing our frontiers …' [54]

More determined opposition showed itself at Saint Cloud on the day after, when the Council of 500, despite all Lucien Bonaparte's efforts, insisted upon a roll-call vote about loyalty to the existing constitution of the Directory. At the same time, the Council of Elders began to discuss the election of new Directors. Bonaparte himself then began a campaign speech as if to his troops, and there were cries of 'Outlaw!' in response as the 500 milled around him. He was rescued by Lucien on horseback, who ordered the troops to chase out 'seditious' elected deputies, and Generals Leclerc and Murat complied.

Then the Elders obeyed Sieyès and, before dinner, replaced the Directory with a three-man commission – Sieyès himself, Roger Ducos and Bonaparte. Lucien wanted to legalize what had happened and had the deputies rounded up from restaurants to take a vote. When a hundred of them were present, they voted that there should be three Consuls and two legislative commissions from the Councils. The First Consul established himself in December with two different colleagues, **Cambacérès** and Lebrun, and set up three bodies to cancel each other out: a Senate, a Tribunate and a Legislative Body. Then he claimed that the aims of the Revolution had been met.

On the surface, it looks as though there was no continuity between the Directory and the authoritarianism that had just been imposed. However, a study of 498 high officials in the new Consulate just after the coup found that 77 per cent of them had been deputies in the time of the Directory, and 83 per cent since 1789. What was significant was the elimination of the left. The property-based elite had come to support a unitary authority which Bonaparte increasingly represented as he made himself Consul for life and then Emperor in 1804. The republican forms were kept, but many republicans were disenchanted with their own achievements since 1792.[55]

The most recent long study of the Brumaire coup in French is that of Patrice Gueniffey, and its conclusion is worth quoting, especially in relation to the carnage that the Empire was to bring to the whole of Europe. *Coups d'état* are 'certainly a more economical solution and less costly in human lives than a revolution and, *a fortiori* [a term beloved of French people], a civil war. We could say, in most cases, a lesser evil.' [56]

The *Brumaire* entry in Albert Soboul's *Dictionnaire historique de la Révolution française* concludes with an anecdote to illustrate the fact that Bonaparte had gained everything. A woman who could not read asked what was in the text of the constitution of Year VIII printed on a poster. Someone replied, 'Bonaparte is there' (*Il y a Bonaparte*).[57]

Gildea, Robert, *Children of the Revolution, The French 1799–1914* (Cambridge, MA: Harvard University Press, 2008), pp. 19–31.

Hunt, Lynn, *Politics, Culture and Class in the French Revolution* (London, Berkeley and Los Angeles: University of California Press, 2004), Conclusion.

Neely, Sylvia, *A Concise History of the French Revolution* (Lanham, MD and Plymouth: Rowman & Littlefield, 2008), pp. 243–8.

Schom, Alan, *Napoleon Bonaparte* (New York: HarperCollins, 1997), chaps 12 and 13.

Brunswick, Charles William Ferdinand, Duke of (1735–1806)

The Duke of Brunswick was Field Marshal of the Prussian Army in 1792 when France had declared war on the Holy Roman Empire, of which Prussia was a subordinate state to Austria. Brunswick's full title was Duke of Brunswick-Wolfenbüttel, hereditary ruler of another contributory state of the Empire.

He had been contacted by Axel **Fersen**, who told him about the danger **Louis XVI** and **Marie-Antoinette** found themselves in. Brunswick was arranging his dispositions from his headquarters at Koblenz with Prussian forces and the Army of the Princes. An old-school general officer, veteran of the Seven Years' War, he took his time to deploy his force meticulously, and could not move quickly in response to Fersen's pleas. Under additional pressure from the Prince of Condé at Koblenz, and against his better judgement, he issued his 'Brunswick Manifesto' (actually written by *émigrés*), which reached Paris on 28 July 1792. This document was meant to intimidate, and threatened dire reprisals for resisting invasion. **National Guardsmen** captured with weapons would be punished as rebels against their king. Civilians defending their homes and property would see their houses razed and they would be dealt with 'according to the rules of war'. Parisians were regarded as responsible for the protection of the royal family. The invaders would exact 'exemplary and forever memorable vengeance by delivering the city of Paris to a military execution'[58] if the king, the queen, the *dauphin* or the princess-royal were harmed.

It made Republicans naturally more determined to resist when the manifesto was made public in Paris on 3 August. **Pétion**, as mayor of Paris, in the name of 47 **Paris Sections**, demanded the end of the Bourbon dynasty. The Gravilliers section, one of the poorest in the capital, saw the manifesto as proof that Louis XVI was at the centre of a conspiracy in which foreign tyrants, *émigrés*, counter-revolutionary generals and corrupt politicians were joined. They said that if the Assembly did not act to save the *Patrie*, they would do it by themselves. The sections were more convinced of corruption when a roll-call vote in the Legislative on 8 August refused to put **Lafayette** on trial.[59] The **Insurrectionary Commune**, quickly formed on the night of 9 August, organized the **'Day' of 10 August** before an attempt at getting the king and queen away to Rouen financed by **Necker** and others could happen. Brunswick began his advance and took Verdun and Longwy, but the Republic turned the tide of invasion at **Valmy**. By that time, the royal family was imprisoned in the Temple.

@ The text of the Manifesto is available at:
http://history.hanover.edu/texts/bruns.htm.

Buonarroti, Philippe (Filippo) (1761–1837)

Buonarroti provides a link between the revolutionary decade in France and agitation in Piedmont in the Mazzinian phase of the Italian

Risorgimento. He was associated with **Babeuf** and was the chronicler of his movement.

Buonarroti was born into a noble family in Pisa, and read jurisprudence at the university there. He was a subversive while a student and edited a radical newspaper. When the French Revolution began, he went to Corsica, where he edited another paper in support of it. He joined a **Jacobin Club**, and associated with the Bonaparte family. He was driven out of Corsica and went home to Tuscany where he spent time in prison, but was able to become a **freemason**.

He moved to Paris in 1793 and then to Nice, where he organized other radical Italians. He was given French citizenship in May 1793, and continued to rally Italians who supported revolution on the French model. Back in Paris after **Robespierre**'s fall, he was imprisoned as a Jacobin. A fellow prisoner was Gracchus Babeuf and he aligned himself with his Conspiracy of Equals. He was arrested again by orders of the **Directory** in May 1796, put on trial at Vendôme with the *Babeuvistes* and imprisoned in February 1797 in the fortress at Cherbourg. He received an indulgence from Lucien Bonaparte in April 1800 to be a schoolmaster on the Ile d'Oléron on the west coast. He left France until 1830, but remained a supporter of radical movements for the rest of his life.[60]

Burke, Edmund (1729–97)

The first reaction to the fall of the **Bastille** on the part of the Whig opposition in Great Britain was typically that of Charles James Fox: 'How much the greatest event it is that ever happened in the world – and how much the best!'[61]

Burke was a Whig in opposition too, but made a more sombre response after further developments. His *Reflections on the Revolution in France* appeared after the decree on the **Civil Constitution of the Clergy**. Burke became at once vituperative and prophetic. He asserted that 'obscure provincial advocates' and 'stewards of petty local jurisdictions' were dominating the National Assembly instead of the 'natural landed interest' of France.[62] Already, French society was beginning to be destabilized. Property was at risk as shown by the confiscation of church lands, and the introduction of the *assignat* was 'fraudulent'. He presumed that an intention to do away with Christianity altogether was behind all this.

The English Revolution of 1688, recently commemorated by the Revolution Society in London, had been the rediscovery of traditional values. The French had discarded their principles altogether in favour of risky new ones. France would inevitably descend into civil war and anarchy that could only be resolved by the arrival of a general who would assert 'the true spirit of command'.

Early in 1791, Thomas **Paine** replied equally forcefully to Burke in his *Rights of Man*. Burke had 'pitied the plumage, but forgot the dying bird'[63] in his praise for the old order, and not seen the real suffering beneath it. Burke had observed the Revolution from the objectivity of distance: Paine had been involved in America, and would soon be a subjective participant in Parisian events, even the **Terror**. These points of view could not be reconciled.

Burke, Edmund, *Reflections on the Revolution in France*, ed., with Introduction, L.G. Mitchell (Oxford: Oxford University Press, repr. 2009).

Goodwin, Albert, *The Friends of Liberty: The English Democratic Movement in the Age of the French Revolution* (London: Hutchinson, 1979), chap. 4.

Buzot, François-Nicolas-Léonard (1760–94)

Buzot was prominent among the **Girondins**, and Manon **Roland**'s lover at the critical time of the group's exclusion from the **Convention** in June 1793.

He had been a lawyer at Evreux, then a deputy in the **Estates-General** and the **Constituent**, supporting the nationalization of church lands. During the **Legislative**, he was elected president of the criminal tribunal in the department of the Eure. He remained in correspondence with Madame Roland and **Pétion**. The food scarcity of the winter 1791–2 was acute in the Eure and he had to pass judgements on rioters and tax-evaders. He had to maintain the law on free circulation of grain and against demonstrations, but his rulings were more lenient than the general level of repression in other regions. He had a real social conscience with regard to riots. Besides, he considered that the Revolution would be endangered by outright conflict between the **bourgeoisie** and the people at a time when the foreign war was about to begin. In relation to the royal veto and the invasion of the **Tuileries** on 20 June, Buzot was in favour of the removal of the king. After the **'Day' of 10 August**, he campaigned determinedly for his election to the Convention, which occurred on 3 September.[64]

Back in national politics as a deputy in the **Convention**, Buzot was again associated with the Girondins under Manon Roland's influence. He took on the aggressive Jean-Paul **Marat** and wanted a **National Guard** battalion from outside Paris to protect the Convention against **Hanriot's** Paris **sansculottes**.[65]

Buzot voted for **Louis XVI's** execution, but for it to be suspended, and with the appeal to the people his Girondin associates wanted. All the Bourbon family, including the Duc d'**Orléans**, should be exiled as well. He was not lenient towards royalists, being in favour of the death sentence for all who wanted a return to monarchy and *in absentia* upon *émigrés* who did not return to France.[66] He voted against Marat being put on trial, but wanted his expulsion from the Convention. He was opposed to the setting up of the **Committee of Public Safety** and the **Revolutionary Tribunal**. As a Girondin, he proposed the division of Paris into four autonomous municipalities to break its excessive influence on national politics.[67] He was excluded and condemned with the other Girondins on 2 June 1793, but escaped, first home to Evreux, and then to Caen to help organize an unsuccessful **federalist** rising in the Calvados. He was declared an outlaw by the Convention and after the defeat of the rising at Pacy-sur-Eure on 13 July he made his way to the Gironde. The **Jacobins** ordered his house in Evreux to be destroyed in reprisal. He hid at Saint-Emilion long enough to compile his memoirs in which he declared himself for federalism in American style, but denied that the Girondins had ever elaborated such a scheme. The revolt beginning in the departments was against a minority in the Convention limiting its power as a whole.[68] Knowing he was being searched for, he committed suicide along with Pétion and Barbaroux.

C

Cabarrus, Jeanne-Marie-Ignace (Thérèse) (1773–1835)

Better known in the Revolution as Thérèse Tallien, Cabarrus was ennobled by her first marriage, experienced the whole gamut of the Revolution, and then returned to the nobility.

Born of Franco-Spanish parents in Madrid, Cabarrus was convent-educated in France and a student in the painter Isabey's studio. She had an arranged marriage to the Marquis de Fontenay, a member of the Paris *parlement*, and was presented at **Versailles**. Fontenay emigrated in 1793[1] and she used the new law to divorce him.

She was living with her brothers in Bordeaux when she was arrested as an aristocrat and taken to the Fort du Hâ. She had met Jean-Lambert **Tallien** at Elisabeth **Vigée Lebrun**'s studio and, when he was **representative on mission** in Bordeaux, he rescued and married her.[2] She gained the release of many prisoners, such as Lucie de **La Tour du Pin**, though she was later accused of taking bribes from those she saved.[3]

Back in Paris, Cabarrus was arrested, but saved from the **revolutionary tribunal** by Tallien's part in the **Thermidor coup**. She became a close friend of the future empress, Joséphine de **Beauharnais**, which had important consequences after they had both become mistress to Paul **Barras**. Living in her thatched cottage off the Champs Elysée,[4] she became the leader of ancient Greek-style fashion during the **Directory**, associated with **Bonaparte**'s rising star and with the '**golden youth**'.

She divorced Tallien in 1802, protected by the wealthy speculator in the Empire, G.-J. Ouvrard, and then married the Prince de Chimay in 1805.[5] She lived at Chimay in Belgium until her death.

Caen in Rebellion (1793)

In north-western France, as in Bordeaux, **Lyon**, **Marseille** and **Toulon**, there was resistance to a take-over of the municipality by local **Jacobins** and plans to overthrow the Parisian **Mountain** as well. The rebellion in Caen was a serious affair, enough to be called '**federalist**' by its Jacobin enemies. The municipality there raised objections to the **Convention** on 31 May 1793 as the action against the **Girondins** was coming to a head in Paris. **Prieur de la Côte d'Or**, on a mission to inspect coastal defences, was put in prison in Caen.

The town declared itself in a state of insurrection on 9 June when **Buzot**, **Pétion** and other Girondin deputies arrived there. This was part of a grand design by all the federalists to march inwards on Paris and overthrow Jacobin 'anarchy'. General Wimpffen was asked to head a force to attack Paris.[6] He had been a noble deputy in the Estates-General and was a crypto-royalist in British pay. On paper, the force to be raised was 3,000 strong; 2,500 of them paraded in Caen on 7 July drawn from 6 departments (Charlotte **Corday** had watched the parade in Caen, and then decided to carry out her attack on **Marat**). This force left Caen on 8 July and reached Evreux in four days. However, confronted by republican troops at Brécourt, it fled back home. The Mountain reacted to this rising with unusual clemency.

Calonne's Plans for Financial Reform (1786–7)

As the king's Controller-General of the Finances, Charles-Alexandre de Calonne (1734–1802) denied the assertion of public opinion that court extravagance had created the financial crisis which his immediate predecessors had failed to solve. The deficit was so large (he claimed it was 112 million livres in 1786) because of four years of naval involvement in the American War of Independence (1778–83) when Jacques **Necker**, then finance minister, had covered costs by continually raising fresh loans and declared a surplus of 10 million livres in 1781.

Calonne informed the king on 17 August 1786 that finding new revenue was the only way to avoid national bankruptcy, and made the state of the finances publicly known. He argued that, since the current 5 per cent tax (known as a *vingtième*) was about to expire, new crown finance was essential, but not in taxes as such because they would be politically dangerous. Since 1776, the government had borrowed 1.25 billion livres, so servicing the debt would take 50 million a year by 1790, and there were short-term loans of 280 millions.[7] He persuaded the king to summon an **Assembly of Notables** consisting of 144 personal nominees of the king, drawn from the most distinguished nobility, bishops and government officials in order to by-pass the *parlements* (only 2 were not nobles), relying on their patriotism. Its agenda would be the regeneration of the state's entire administrative system. He proposed his scheme to this assembly, whereby all landowners, without any exemptions, would pay a land tax in produce rather than money before the harvest was sold, the amount being agreed in provincial assemblies of which most landowners would be members, regardless of status. Internal customs dues would be abolished to help the circulation of grain in times of local scarcity and stimulate the growth of industry. Instead of work-service for repairing roads and bridges, cash payments would be made.

These were the new ideas of the **Physiocrats** with their scientific approach to agriculture, to be implemented by co-ordinating the finances of all branches of government, with Calonne himself emerging as a prime minister. The assembly met between February and May 1787, agreed to most of Calonne's reforms, but demanded to inspect the relevant financial records for themselves. Calonne tried to appeal to public opinion by means of a notice to be read in all parish churches on Palm Sunday 1787, claiming that the notables were unwilling to pay their share of taxation. Public opinion sided with the notables, and Calonne was dismissed on 8 April, with the Assembly limping on under his successor **Loménie de Brienne** until May. The Revolution began with the king's decision to dispense with Calonne's services. Calonne himself was prosecuted by the Paris *parlement* and fled to England in August 1787.

Hardman, John, *Louis XVI* (New Haven, CT and London: Yale, 1993), chap. 5.

Cambacérès, Jean-Jacques-Régis de (1758–1824)

During the revolutionary decade, Cambacérès was a second-rank figure who worked behind the scenes on the details of legislation that were issued in profusion, being a lawyer from Montpelier. This stood him in good stead for his work on the Civil Code during the Empire. He was chosen as a stand-by deputy for the **nobility** in Montpelier for the **Estates-General**, but there was no place for him as the Second Estate was not 'doubled' as the third had been. He was, however, elected to the **National Convention** as a deputy for the Hérault, in 1793, and associated with the moderates of the Plain.

When Cambacérès was sent to the king in the Temple to tell him it had been decreed that he could choose his own defence counsel, he called him Louis Capet and the king replied that it would be better if he called him Louis, his baptismal name, of which he could still be proud. Cambacérès voted for the king's guilt, but for a suspended sentence. He had a low profile in the Convention during the **Terror**, serving only on the Committee of General Defence until it was replaced by the **Committee of Public Safety**. He supported **Robespierre** against **Hébert**'s de-Christianization, and did not approve of **Danton**. He did not support the Law of 22 prairial that set up the 'Great Terror'. In the **Thermidorean Convention**, he was on the Committee of Public Safety for a short time.

Cambacérès was elected to the Council of 500 in the Directory, but a compromising letter found in his papers led opponents to think he was a royalist, despite what was being said about his possible involvement in the mystery of **Louis XVII**'s death, so he was never a minister, except for a few months as Minister of Justice immediately before the **Brumaire coup**. He was second Consul from December 1799 and was prominent in the Empire.[8]

Campo Formio, Treaty of, 18 October 1797

This treaty was based on the preliminaries signed by General **Bonaparte** at Leoben in April 1797, ending a war with Austria that had lasted five years. It was signed by Bonaparte for the **Directory** and Cobenzl for the Austrians at the castle of Passariano near Udine, but it takes its name from the little village where their meetings had begun.

Austria accepted French occupation of the Ionian Islands, recognized the existence of the **Cisalpine** and **Ligurian** republics, thus abandoning any claim over Lombardy, and agreeing to France's occupation of the left bank of the Rhine which would now be her natural frontier. The Austrian

Netherlands (**Belgium**) would be yielded to France after compensation to German princes. Austria would keep control of the Dalmatian coast and take over the former territory of the Republic of **Venice**, conquered by Bonaparte in May.

There were disputes around this agreement, largely concerned with German territories, which were left for a conference to be called at **Rastadt** in November, which was to last for two and a half years.

The Directors were not satisfied with what France acquired by the treaty. Nor was Bonaparte, but he defended it as expedient: it was too late in the year to begin a new military campaign, and it might provide the opportunity to come to an agreement with Britain, although peace talks at Lille had wound up with no result a few weeks before.[9]

Carnot, Lazare (1753–1823)

Carnot is well known as 'the organizer of victory' against the **First Coalition** and the struggle against **Federalists**. A member of the **National Convention**, he was appointed to the **Committee of Public Safety** on 14 August 1793, as its military specialist, working closely with War Minister **Bouchotte**.

Carnot was a Burgundian, born in a substantial house in the centre of Nolay in the Côte d'Or. His father was a notary who arranged for his education at Autun, and then at Mezières Military Engineering School. Carnot came to admire the skill and military principles of Sébastien Vauban, the builder of forts and organizer of defence and attack for Louis XIV. His book about Vauban made him known. He always considered Vauban as his teacher.[10] Commissioned in the Prince of Condé's engineer regiment, he was given time for his scientific studies, but was still a captain six years later in 1789. That was the rank beyond which non-noble officers (the French word for commoners is *roturiers*) could not be promoted. He had also been prevented from marrying Ursule de Bouillet by her noble family. He was even imprisoned at Béthune by a *lettre de cachet* at their behest from April to May 1789. Such injustice inevitably rankled. In 1791, he married Sophie Dupont instead.[11]

Elected to the **Legislative Assembly** and then the **National Convention** for the Pas-de-Calais, he sat with the **Mountain** and joined the **Jacobin**

Club where he was respected as a technician rather than as a political figure. He was a **representative on mission** in Bayonne, responsible for the defence of the border with Spain and in other places while the king was on trial, but he was back in Paris to vote in favour of his execution.

Carnot made contributions to Jacobin plans for national education, progressive taxation and poor relief, but in external relations he was more of a **Girondin**, supporting the idea of the Rhine, the Alps and the Pyrenees as natural frontiers. He was on mission in the Nord and Pas-de-Calais departments in March 1793 when the raising of 300,000 soldiers on a national scale was ordered, and was instrumental in defeating General **Dumouriez**'s design for an armed march on Paris.

Once appointed to the Committee of Public Safety, Carnot had a crucial role in French military success, along with **Lindet** and **Prieur de la Côte d'Or**, organizing supplies and making full use of volunteers and regulars alike under the *Amalgame* Law. He took charge in person of some half brigades of the Army of the North at the time of General **Jourdan**'s victory at Wattignies on 16 October 1793, after which he revived Vauban's master-plan for operations in north-eastern France, developing the fortresses as points of assembly and departure both for attack and defence. He was associated with the **Terror**, but opposed Robespierre at **Thermidor**. He prepared opinion in the armies for the news of the fall of **Robespierre**, severely criticizing him as a traitor who used the disguise of virtue to cover his personal ambitions. Carnot became a suspect himself but, when it appeared he was to be denounced in the Convention, one of the deputies shouted that no one should dare to harm the man who had organized the victories of the Republic's armies. He was included in the amnesty voted by the **Thermidorean Convention** 'for deeds relative to the Revolution' on 26 October 1795.

Elected to the Council of Elders, Carnot became one of the initial Directors in November 1795 when Sieyès refused to serve.[12] He was prominent in the Directory's action against Gracchus **Babeuf** and against the 21st Dragoons' camp at Grenelle, where some radicals of the Left tried to subvert the troops but were met with a fusillade and the execution of 30 prisoners including former deputies of the **Mountain** in the Convention.

Carnot was warned about General Augereau's decision to arrest him as a crypto-royalist in the **Fructidor coup**, and made his escape to Geneva and then Germany, to take up his scientific pursuits again. He returned to France after the **Brumaire coup**. First Consul Bonaparte gave him the War Ministry for a short time in 1800, but he preferred to be a private citizen. Nevertheless, he was Minister of the Interior during Napoleon's 100 Days and, on Louis XVIII's second restoration, exiled himself to Prussia for the rest of his life.[13]

 Palmer, R.R., *Twelve Who Ruled: The Year of the Terror in the French Revolution* (University Park, PA: Princeton University Press, Bicentennial Edition, 1989). Online at: http://www.history.mcs.st-and.ac.uk/Biographies/Carnot.html.

Carra, Jean-Louis (1742–93)

Carra was well known nationally as a contributor to Diderot's Encyclopaedia and a radical journalist. He was a founder member of the *Société des **Amis des Noirs***. His *Annales Patriotiques* had a circulation of 8,000 and was read by many in the provincial Jacobin Clubs as a principal source of information about the Assemblies and then the **Convention**, along with letters sent to clubs by their own deputies.

Carra orchestrated a violent polemic against Finance Minister **Calonne** in the '**pre-revolution**'. He was elected to the Convention by eight departments (Robespierre was elected by only two), and was **representative on mission** to the Charente-Inférieure at the outset of the **Vendée rebellion** – a participant in the undisciplined retreat of a scratch force of **National Guard** sent north from La Rochelle in the first military encounter with the rebels on 19 March 1793 under General Marcé.

Carra was not trusted by the **Jacobins** on account of a wild suggestion he made of offering the throne of France either to the Duke of **Brunswick** or to the Duke of York. Yet, as he told the constitutional monarchist, Regnaud de Saint-Jean-d'Angély when he denounced him as a member of a putative 'Austrian Committee' in 1792, the Jacobins were paying his journalist's fees. After the overthrow of the monarchy, he was usually found in the amorphous fringes of the **Girondins** while the Jacobins accused him of having a part in the **September Massacres**. It was for his links to the Girondins that he went to the scaffold on 31 October 1793.[14]

Carrier, Jean-Baptiste (1756–94)

Carrier was responsible for some of the severest reprisals against the enemies of the Republic, especially in Nantes against the rebels of the **Vendée**. Even though many **representatives on mission** were amnestied at the closure of the **Thermidorean Convention**, he was not.

Carrier had a Jesuit education at Aurillac in the Auvergne, and worked in a law firm in Paris before he went home as a qualified lawyer to join the **National Guard** and the local Jacobin Club. He was elected to the **National Convention**, and joined both the **Cordeliers** and the **Jacobins** in Paris. With **Danton**, he proposed the **Revolutionary Tribunal**. He was sent on mission in Flanders. He voted for the king's death and was enthusiastic for the expulsion of the **Girondins**.

More missions followed, first to Normandy and then to Nantes where he established a revolutionary tribunal for the suppression of the Vendée rebels, many of whom were prisoners in the town. His Marat Legion was set up to deal with them in summary fashion without a trial. Firing squads and the guillotine were not adequate for him, and he organized the *noyades* in the River Loire, sinking boats full of prisoners, with the added atrocity of the 'republican marriages' (perhaps exaggerated by counter-revolutionary historians) in which couples were tied together naked to be drowned or run through with sabres. His claim was that 3,000 rebels perished in this *torrent révolutionnaire*.[15]

Carrier was recalled by the Convention in February 1794, and joined **Robespierre**'s opponents in the **Thermidor coup**. He was brought before the revolutionary tribunal himself soon afterwards and guillotined on 16 November.

Cathelineau, Jacques (1759–93)

Cathelineau is unexpected as the first overall commander of the Military **Vendée**. He was well known in Anjou as a pedlar,[16] though we could elevate that to 'travelling salesman' if it were not for his stock-in-trade being contraband. He was known to have a strong physique and he was a very pious Catholic. The peasants who followed him called him 'the saint of Anjou'. The preaching of the 'good priests' who risked death to return from exile in Jersey and England to minister in the woods to their former parishioners inspired him to be a leader of the rebellion. With his force of tenant farmers and smugglers, he took the château at Gallais, captured the cannon which became known as 'The Missionary' and took several towns including Cholet, in March 1793, right at the outset of the rebellion. His troops' actions against republican officials brought down reprisals from the 'Blues' but more men rallied to him, so that he could make common cause with Nicolas **Stofflet** and Gigot **d'Elbée** to take Beaupreau, Fontenay and Saumur.

Cathelineau was put in overall command of the Royal and Catholic Army, which tried to take Nantes. He took on the Republicans under General Canclaux and went into the town. He was killed there. The next overall commander was d'Elbée.

Certificates of Civism

From November 1791, committees of surveillance were set up in each administrative unit of France, the membership of which was to be taken from reliable supporters of the Revolution. One of their tasks was to issue certificates of civism so that opponents could be recognized by not having one. They were the equivalent of an identity card. In the absence of photographs, they contained a full description of the bearer, and all the details about him that could prevent the document being used by anyone else. A typical example was one given to a former monk who had taken the oath to the constitution in the rural canton of Port d'Envaux in the Charente-Inférieure:

> Voisin, Urbain-Jacques-François-Marie, is forty years old, five feet tall, with a round and full face, chestnut hair and eyebrows, brown eyes, a well-formed nose, a long forehead, and a round chin. He lives in the commune of Plassay.[17]

The certificate would be duplicated in the register of the authority that issued it for future reference.

Chabot, François (1756–94)

Before the Revolution, the implacably anti-royalist Chabot had been a Capuchin friar at Rodez, whose licence to preach was revoked in 1788 after a dispute with church authority and he responded with a pamphlet entitled *The Origins and Destination of what the church calls its property* (*L'Origine et destination des biens soi-disant ecclésiastiques*). He became a leading light in the **Jacobin Club** at Blois and, when the Abbé **Grégoire** became the constitutional bishop, he made Chabot his episcopal vicar. He was elected as the fourth deputy for the Loir and Cher in the **Legislative Assembly**. His next move was to join the Parisian Jacobins and sit with the **Mountain**.[18]

Chabot was one of the first to circulate the rumour of an '**Austrian Committee**' in May 1792, and kept popular fervour alive with declamations against the court and **Lafayette** in the **Paris Sections** to bring about the overthrow of the monarchy on 10 August. He was implicated in the **September Massacres** and acted as a go-between, bringing information from the Abbaye to the Assembly with obvious satisfaction. He showed that he was a 'vehement'[19] republican once he was elected to the **Convention** and an 'unrelenting denouncer'[20] while on the **Committee of General Security**. He attracted attention to himself by his manner of dress, with a shirt open-necked to show his chest. An English commentator in 1799 said of him that he vied with **Marat** for 'precedency in filthiness.'[21] He voted for the king's death. On mission in the Tarn and Aveyron in March 1793 he made forceful attacks on all moderates and suspects that he found. His vehemence was particularly focused on the exclusion of the **Girondins** in early June: 'The people will remain on their feet until these selfish people have kissed the dust of the **sansculottes**,' he said.[22] He was savage towards Charlotte **Corday** at her trial in July. David Andress calls him 'the unsavoury ex-monk' for the way he set out to humiliate her.[23]

Chabot took up the cudgels for the *enragé* faction – **Roux** and **Varlet** – and claimed to support their economic proposals. This led **Hébert** to denounce him, in turn, as a 'perfidious little monk' and he was removed from the Committee of General Security on 14 September after attracting scandal by marrying the sister of the Austrian bankers, the Frey brothers, who had set her up with a rich dowry. He was booed in the Jacobins, and went to **Robespierre** to denounce 'a clique of foreign bankers who were planning counter-revolution', claiming that he had joined with them only to take them more easily by surprise.[24]

He was compromised when other speculators were prosecuted, but exerted himself against the **refractory clergy** and, in a speech for which he was applauded, refused to take his salary as an episcopal vicar. Nevertheless, he was arrested for fraud in the **Company of the Indies**. He unsuccessfully tried to poison himself in the **Conciergerie**. Tried before the **Revolutionary Tribunal** with the **Dantonists**, he was guillotined with the Frey brothers on 27 April 1794.

Chalier, Marie Joseph (1747–93)

Joseph Chalier is known in the Revolution for having been the Jacobin leader in **Lyon** arrested by the moderates and executed by them.

He had been a Dominican novice, a teacher and then a commercial traveller for a Lyon silk firm. He was in Paris as a participant in the storming of the **Bastille** and wrote articles for **Prudhomme's** newspaper *Les Révolutions de Paris*. He went back to Lyon, which was by then radicalized through its section clubs that were controlled by a central club (a 'section' is what the English call a 'ward' in a city or town). He was a municipal official from November 1790, as well as a member of the inspectorate of commerce and industry and a judge in the commercial tribunal. He organized domiciliary visits in the Jacobin interest that led to his suspension from office and arrest after only a month. He went to Paris to justify himself.

The suspension of the monarchy in August 1792 allowed **Girondins** close to **Roland** to take over the departmental directory of the Rhône et Loire at the same time as Chalier returned to Lyon, where the Hôtel de Ville was also Girondin. He had his own supporters, called the 'Chaliers', and raised the city's **sansculottes** in support of a radical programme of changes. He proposed the abolition of the private grain trade and state control of flour mills and the food supply, together with a minimum wage for the silk workers.

When the municipal elections came round in November 1792, Chalier seized control of the central club and some of the electoral assemblies.

However, Chalier was beaten by his moderate opponent, Nivière-Chol, to the post of mayor. Several 'Chaliers' gained seats on the council and he was elected as president of the district judicature which he set about transforming into a **revolutionary tribunal**.

Chalier played the part of a local **Marat** in the style of his speeches, and his supporters pushed the city council into taking measures towards economic control. On 6 February 1793, the central club organized a secret meeting which decided to hold a revolutionary event (*journée*) aimed at taking over the Hôtel de Ville and putting the Girondins on trial. Nivière-Chol resigned to provoke a crisis and was immediately re-elected on 18 February with 80 per cent of the votes. However, a good number of those voting were royalists, and he resigned again. This rightist take-over alarmed the Paris Jacobins, who sent three inspectors, Rovère, Legendre and **Basire**. On 8 March, they contrived the replacement of Nivière-Chol by Chalier's associate, A.-M. Bertrand.

The Chaliers established a committee of public safety for the Rhône et Loire, and tried to raise a revolutionary army. But the Girondins took over the sectional assemblies, gaining control of 22 **surveillance committees** and 14 section clubs. The measures taken by the Chaliers had been ineffective in the economic crisis and they had raised taxes to support a **revolutionary army**. So, on 29 May 1793, 23 of the 32 sections marched on the Hôtel de Ville, suspended Chalier's council, and arrested his faction. A new provisional council drove out the Jacobin inspectors from Paris.

Chalier was executed in Lyon on 17 July (a terribly bungled job because the guillotine blade had to drop three times before the executioner used a knife).[25] It was these events that made the **Convention** decree the siege of insurrectionary Lyon. Chalier became a martyr for the Republic alongside **Le Peletier de Saint-Fargeau** and **Marat**.[26]

Charette de la Contrie, François-Athanase (1763–96)

Charette was one of the leaders of the **Vendéan rebellion** which began soon after the overthrow of the **monarchy** and the exile of the **refractory clergy**. There was no great social difference in the Military Vendée between the *hobereaux* **nobles** and their tenants as elsewhere in France, and a former naval officer, the Chevalier François-Athanase Charette, squire of Fonteclose near Nantes, was soon to be persuaded to assume command.[27]

Charette was in Nantes when Republican troops besieged it in June 1793 and he fought in several actions against the 'blues'. After a dispute with other rebel leaders, he led guerilla actions from the Poitevin *Marais* (wetlands), keeping clear of Turreau's '**infernal columns**' in February 1794. The **Thermidorean Convention** offered an amnesty. He saw no alternative but to accept the Convention of La Jaunaye on 17 February 1795 after six days of negotiation. It gave the Vendéans freedom to practise the Catholic religion, exemption from republican military service while keeping their weapons and restitution of destroyed or damaged property but, of course, it could not give them back the monarchy.

Sympathizers elsewhere and other Vendéans found Charette's acceptance difficult to believe and did not trust the Republicans. However, secret dispatches to England show that he only accepted the convention out of desperation. When *émigrés* were landed at **Quiberon**, northwards in the Morbihan, five months later, he took up arms again in support of Louis XVIII. He was captured and later shot on the orders of General **Hoche**. 'Look where these beggarly English have brought me!' he said as he came before the firing squad.[28]

Chateaubriand, François-René, Vicomte de (1768–1848)

Chateaubriand was among the earlier chroniclers of the Revolution, with his *Mémoires d'outre-tombe* (Memoirs from beyond the Grave), which is a personal account of the private and public events of his life.

His father had, as was customary with poorer Breton nobles, 'put his nobility to sleep' so as to restore his wealth by commerce, and then bought back into his family the château at Combourg where François-René grew up.[29] He decided upon a military career – as a nobleman he could have gone further than the rank of captain which he achieved in 1788 at the age of 20. He came instead to Paris in search of a literary career with André **Chénier** and Jean-François La Harpe as companions.

In 1791, Chateaubriand left France and travelled in the United States. He returned after a year but soon went to Koblenz as a noble *émigré* to join the Army of the Princes. He was wounded at the siege of Thionville and then moved, first, to Jersey and then to England. He stayed in London and, for a while, in Bungay. He rediscovered his Catholic faith during his exile.

He returned to France under the amnesty offered by First Consul **Bonaparte** in 1800. His main periods of public office were during the **restoration monarchy**, when he was ambassador to London and Berlin, and Foreign Minister at the time of the war to reimpose Ferdinand VII in his Spanish kingdom in 1824.

Chateaubriand began his *Mémoires* in 1809. He allowed them to be read to a select few at a *salon* in 1834, and reports of them circulated in the press, but he would not permit their publication, although he was living impecuniously and out of office during the Orleanist monarchy. In the age of railway speculation, wealthy friends made his memoirs the object of investment, and raised funds with them as capital for publication when he had died, so that he could live on the interest as a ***rentier***. He was indignant when a newspaper editor offered to bring them out in serial form, and they were published only after his death, as he intended.[30] He died during another revolution which toppled the Orleanist monarchy in 1848. He is buried by the sea at his birth-place, Saint-Malo in Brittany.

Chaumette, Pierre-Gaspard (Anexagoras) (1763–94)

Chaumette was one of the leaders of the de-Christianizing faction and was instrumental in the Festival of Reason held in Notre Dame Cathedral on 10 November 1793, bringing the actress, Madame **Momoro**, who played the goddess, into the **Convention** afterwards. He was prominent in the **Insurrectionary Commune** and close to **Hébert**, a member of a group called the '*exagérés*'.

Before the Revolution, Chaumette had scientific interests and trained as a doctor. He was a **Freemason**. He joined the **Jacobins** and allied with the **sansculottes**. He was an active journalist and, as a member of the **Cordeliers** was one of the first to sign the anti-monarchical petition on 17 July 1791. He was a militant member of the assembly of the *Théâtre-française* Section, who elected him to the Insurrectionary Commune at the overthrow of the **monarchy**. He was accused of having responsibility for the **September Massacres** but had did not become procurator of the Commune until later.[31]

He was re-elected to the Commune in December, and concerned himself with recruiting volunteer soldiers. He was strongly in favour of the king's execution in January 1793, expressing a strange emphasis on the event having economic results. Chaumette supported the sansculottes' **'Day' of 5 September** and the setting up of **Revolutionary Armies** to search and punish hoarders of grain in the countryside of the Ile de France, as well as other measures such as the **Maximum**, which the Jacobins accepted only reluctantly as a compromise three weeks later.

In support of de-Christianization, Chaumette abandoned the names Pierre-Gaspard in favour of Anaxagoras, a philosopher in ancient Athens who was condemned for speaking against established religion. In support of the One and Indivisible Republic, he helped initiate the exclusion of the **Girondins** from the Convention between 31 May and 2 June. He was vociferous for the **Terror**, not associated closely with **Roux**'s *Enragés*, but equally vituperative in his demands. He was arrested with the Hébertists, imprisoned in the **Luxembourg**, sent to the **Revolutionary Tribunal** and executed on 13 April, three weeks after the rest of them.

Chénier, André (1762–94)

Chénier was a poet who associated himself with the Revolution as a constitutional monarchist (*monarchien*), but went to the scaffold for alleged crimes against the nation in the closing days of the official **Terror**.

He was born in Istanbul, where his father was in business, and spent his infancy in Morocco. His translations of classical verse at school back in France were noticed with approval. After a very short time as an army officer in Strasbourg, he enjoyed *salon* life in Paris and became acquainted with the painter J.-L. **David**. He was restless in England from 1787 to 1790 as private secretary to the French ambassador, the Chevalier de La Luzerne. On his return, he joined the **Feuillants Club** as a convinced constitutional monarchist.

The day after the Feuillant ministry fell, on 15 March 1792, the mutineers from **Nancy** were freed from the galleys, so the Jacobins, principally **Robespierre** and **Collot d'Herbois**, organized a festival for them on 15 April, approved by the **Constituent Assembly**. This drew a savagely ironic 'hymn' from Chénier, published in the *Journal de Paris*, which included the couplet 'Forty murderers, beloved of Robespierre, are coming to present themselves at our altars' (*Quarante meurtriers, chéris de Robespierre, vont s'élever sur nos autels*),[32] and also referred to Collot by name. Moreover, he assisted **Malherbes** over the drawing up of the king's defence in preparation for his trial in December 1792.

Chénier's brother Marie-Joseph was a **Jacobin**, a deputy for the Seine et Oise in the **National Convention** and wrote a different kind of verse, in support of the Republic. His were the words of the Hymns to Reason and to the **Supreme Being**, for the celebration of the retaking of **Toulon**, and of the famous Parting Song (*Chanson de Départ*) which **Méhul** set to music. André, on the other hand, when Charlotte **Corday** 'executed' **Marat**, wrote a poem praising her because 'one villain less is rampaging in the mud' (*Un scélerat de moins rampe dans cette fange*).

André Chénier lay low for a year at a friend's house in Versailles after the king's death, but was arrested in mistake for someone else whom he was visiting at Passy on 7 March 1794. He was detained as a suspect in the **Luxembourg Palace** and then the Saint-Lazare prison for nearly five months. The anti-republican poems he wrote were smuggled out to his father tied up in his washing.[33]

His execution took place on 8 July 1794 – two days before **Robespierre**'s – after which his reputation grew. His poems were soon in the public domain. **Chateaubriand** quoted them in his works.

Cholet, Battle of (17 October 1793)

This battle, a set-back for the **Vendéans**, was fought in the early stages of their Catholic and Royalist rebellion. Their commander Louis d'**Elbée** was wounded and executed afterwards. Generals Kléber and Haxo were in command of the republican forces. Other republicans present were two **representatives on mission**, Antoine **Merlin de Thionville** and Jean-Baptiste **Carrier**, and the general, Louis Turreau, who was later responsible for the '**infernal columns**'.

The Vendéans under **d'Elbée**, **La Rochejaquelein** and **Stofflet** attacked Cholet and were defeated in a complicated engagement, although they fought in columns like regulars. They then moved to Saint-Florent-le-

Vieil in order to cross the Loire, hoping to find a port to make contact with the Royal Navy.

Cholet was to be retaken for a short time and set on fire by Stofflet in March 1794. When the Revolution was over, half the town's population had gone, having either fled or been killed in the war, and its commercial life was practically ruined.[34]

Chouans

North of the Loire, in Brittany, there was a movement parallel with the **Vendée** rebellion known as *Chouannerie*. It was less organized, more spontaneous, and lasted more than a decade. It had its early stirrings in 1791 when it was discovered that rents to the urban purchasers of **national property** were larger than the amount that used to be paid in tithe. There was a rising against the revolutionaries in Lorient who were pressurizing the Bishop of Vannes to take the Oath to the **Civil Constitution**, and another against the **bourgeoisie** of Quimper. As in the Vendée, the major protest was against recruitment for the war declared in 1792. However, the republican garrisons in Brittany were stronger and the rebellion was soon controlled. Brittany did not become a **federalist** area.

News of Turreau's '**infernal columns**' in the Vendée sparked the real outbreaks of *Chouannerie* in February 1794, with attacks on 'intruded' constitutional priests and buyers of church lands. At first their leaders were all commoners (*roturiers*), often of humbler origin, but then Joseph-Geneviève de **Puisaye**, a nobleman from Mortagne-au-Perche who had been a captain in the old-regime army, became overall commander of these independent bands. After **Thermidor**, the Republican government became more conciliatory, **Hoche** offered an amnesty on 1 December 1794, but explained that, although he could restore the free practice of religion, the monarchy could not be restored.

Puisaye claimed that he had a 'Catholic and Royal Army' of 30,000 behind him when he negotiated in London, despite the republican change of policy. He impressed Pitt, and the debacle on the **Quiberon** peninsula in June–July 1795 was the outcome. Puisaye survived and stayed for a time in France, but he was replaced as overall leader by Georges Cadoudal, himself a Breton, who brought his Chouans to fight alongside Puisaye and Hervilly. Like Puisaye, he went into hiding after Hoche's reprisals.

In the autumn, Chouan bands made new attacks on republicans. Three thousand of them attacked Le Mans on 14 October. For the next three years, the Chouans carried on their guerilla activities but, after **Brumaire**, they gradually made peace with the Consulate. Cadoudal continued his activities against **Bonaparte**'s government, even though Bonaparte's Concordat with Pius VII had restored the Catholic Church. He tried to assassinate First Consul Bonaparte in 1800, and again in 1804. **Fouché**'s police caught him and he was executed.[35]

Cisalpine Republic

Bonaparte conquered most Austrian possessions in northern Italy, Parma, Modena and the northern Papal States, and entered Milan, capital of Lombardy, on 12 May 1796. The French occupation was finalized by the Treaty of Bologna on 24 June. **Carnot** and **Reubell** wanted to retain these acquisitions as bargaining counters with Austria to make the Rhine the natural frontier of the Republic. Bonaparte, however, consolidated his gains by organizing a Lombard republic. The Directors gave him a free hand in the Papal States south of the Po which Carnot called 'the throne of foolishness' (*le trône de la sottise*).

At a conference in Bologna, Italian sympathizers (patriots) from Modena and Emilia set up the Cispadane republic. Ferrara and Ravenna joined it. They all confirmed the Cispadane republic at the end of 1796 with a constitution approved by Bonaparte. The Cispadane was the first 'sister-republic' in Italy (the first of all was the Batavian). There was no intention on the part of the Directors or of Bonaparte to unify northern Italy.

Meanwhile in Lombardy there were disagreements between the two French commissioners, **Saliceti** and Garrau, the military commander, and the local patriots. Bonaparte played them off against each other. A series of demonstrations demanded that Lombardy should be an independent republic. It seemed to have come into existence, but Bonaparte had other ideas.

In Paris the dispute between the Directors and the Councils gathered momentum in spring 1797. The Directors needed the help of the 'Italian' general and could not but support Bonaparte. The result was that on 29 June the Cisalpine Republic came into being, comprising Lombardy, the Cispadane republic, the Valtelline and part of mainland **Venice**. A constitution was adopted. Bonaparte appointed the state officials himself, claiming he had the French Directors' authority. This provided a model for the later constitutions of the **Helvetic** and the **Roman Republics**.

The Cisalpine, like its French sister, was governed by means of *coups d'état* (four in seven months). The deputies sued for a treaty of alliance with France, and France, after initial reluctance from the deputies and threats from General Berthier, gained an annual contribution of 18 million francs and a 40,000-strong army under French command. Berthier's replacement, when he went to Egypt with Bonaparte, was Brune, and after disputes between **Barras** and **La Révellière-Lépeaux** over who should represent French interests in Milan, Brune was retained as military commander and the ambassador was **Fouché**. Both of them were Barras's candidates. Then Fouché was replaced by Revaud, and Joubert succeeded Brune. The sister republic was moribund, subject to the self-aggrandizement of military and civil governors from France.

Then it was all swept away by the forces of the Second Coalition. In the spring of 1799, the Russians invaded, the French were defeated, the Austrians returned. The Italians in the Cisalpine Republic's government were arrested, and some were executed. The same archbishop who celebrated a *Te Deum* for Bonaparte on 13 May 1796 did the same again for Suvarov on 30 April 1799.

After that came the **Brumaire coup** in November and, on 2 June 1800, Bonaparte's victory at Marengo ...[36]

Civil Constitution of the Clergy

One of the decisions made on the bizarre **Night of 4 August 1789** in the National Assembly at **Versailles** was to abolish the tithe, almost the only source of income for the Catholic parish clergy in France. This was the basis of a decree passed on 12 July 1790, which **Louis XVI** reluctantly accepted on 22 July.

It has been pointed out that every revolutionary change made by the **Constituent** – equal taxes, the end of seigneurialism, equality of opportunity, suppression of venal offices, removal of tariffs on inland rivers and so on – had its origin in the **statements of complaint** drawn up in the villages before the deputies were elected. But there was never any mention of nationalizing church lands or the church itself. This was an example of the deputies inventing policy as they went along.[37] There was a majority who asserted that the Assembly had the right as a sovereign body to make laws binding on the church and, after they had done so, the bishops and other opponents of the measure withdrew from taking part. The benches on the right were often nearly empty. But not many on the left took part in the debate either, apart from a small group of patriot clergy, lay theologians and canon law specialists, many of whom were **Jansenists**. Louis-Simon Martineau was an eloquent if sarcastic spokesman for the ecclesiastical committee, but the assembly's big guns, like **Mirabeau**, **Barnave** and **Maury**, were silent. Most deputies were not interested in the measure that would cause not only church, but national, schism and strife.[38] Yet if, to use today's idiom, the taxpayers' money was used for paying the clergy, the state's representatives should have power over them in their view.

The Catholic bishops and parish clergy were to be regarded as civil servants (*fonctionnaires*) by the sovereign nation and to be paid a salary accordingly. A decree of 28 October 1790 abolished all orders of monks and nuns unless they could show that they were involved in education or hospitals or poor relief, though the writing was on the wall for them too. These arrangements were made without referring to **Pope Pius VI** until after they had all been done.

On 27 November 1790, another decree ruled that, in return for their state salaries (1,200 livres a year was the offer), the clergy had to take an oath to maintain the Civil Constitution of the Clergy, or be regarded as having resigned their livings. Traditionalist bishops loyal to the pope refused to take the oath and forbade their clergy to accept this new status. They became known as **refractories** or non-jurors. Those who took the oath were called constitutionals, and were installed, after election by the **active citizens** (whether or not the electors were Catholics), in the parishes and bishoprics left vacant by the expelled refractories, even in the smallest communes. They were backed up by republican officials.

78

Out of the 300 clergy actually sitting in the Constituent, only 109 took the oath. The 136 bishoprics of the old regime were soon afterwards replaced by 83 in the new order because each department became a diocese as well. Only seven old-regime bishops took the oath – conspicuous among them were **Loménie de Brienne** and **Talleyrand**. These few immediately consecrated priests who were elected as constitutional bishops, being qualified by having been parish priests (*curés*) for 15 years, in spring 1791.

When the pope's rejection of these measures was known about, after 13 April 1791 (Pius VI took his time), some priests withdrew their oath. Many had taken it with convoluted reservations in any case. In the final count, between 52 and 55 per cent of the clergy on a national scale took the oath: that is, 28,000 of them.[39] When the papal nuncio had left France, the Constituent returned to the question of annexing the papal enclave of **Avignon**.

The importance of this act by the sovereign National Assembly was that it polarized opinion in France between the supporters of change (including those who went along with it without any enthusiasm) and its opponents. As Donald Sutherland has observed,

> Whatever else it was, the Civil Constitution of the Clergy was also a kind of plebiscite for and against a Church that was associated with the Revolution, a church that was expected to proselytise for it and to keep order for it. In other words, to reject the Revolution was to reject the rule of the citizen-lawyers who had come to power in the elections of 1790.[40]

Those who stood by their **refractory clergy** regarded their constitutional replacements as intruders (especially in places like the **Vendée** and Brittany) and became counter-revolutionary monarchists. The constitutional clergy's supporters usually became republicans when the time came. The king, with great reluctance, accepted these changes on 26 December 1790.[41]

The constitutional *curés* were to be the 'first line of defence against fanaticism',[42] and the fanatics were the refractory clergy and those who supported them. But, by the summer of 1793, it seemed that the front line was giving way. It has been pointed out that **Fouché** became so decidedly a de-Christianizer after he had helped to organize the defence of Nantes against the Catholic and Royal army of the Vendée.[43] The constitutional church was deemed by the **Hébert**s and the Fouchés to have failed in its main purpose and the regime had to find another front line: for them, de-Christianization would serve as such and would be worth all the energy they put into it.

Aston, Nigel, *Religion and Revolution in France, 1780–1804* (Basingstoke: Macmillan, 2000), chaps 6 and 7 and pt III.

Tackett, Timothy, *Religion, Revolution and Regional Culture in Eighteenth-Century France* (University Park, PA: Princeton University Press, 1986).

Clavière, Etienne (1735–93)

Clavière's family was originally from Dauphiné but, as Protestants, they had moved to Geneva. Etienne married a wealthy cousin from Marseille in 1758. He represented his father's cloth works all over Europe. Influenced by **Rousseau**, he opposed the Genevan aristocracy, and was prominent in the Genevan revolution of 1782. When French military intervention overthrew it, he fled to Neuchâtel, where he met **Brissot** and **Mirabeau**. He moved to Ireland, took British nationality and started a clock factory which failed. He lived in Paris from 1784 and became involved in profitable financial business, encouraged by **Calonne**'s government borrowing. He rivalled **Necker** as a banker, bringing out polemical pamphlets against other bankers over the signatures of Mirabeau and Brissot. He founded the first French life assurance company in 1787, and was involved in speculations about bringing fresh water to Paris by canals and steam pumps, against which **Beaumarchais** wrote invective on behalf of the Paris water company.

With Brissot, Clavière wrote about the United States of America as a model for France's future, proposing the abolition of **absolute monarchy**, privileges and commercial monopolies. Together they founded a Franco-American Society but, when Brissot returned from visiting America in 1788, they saw a better future in the coming **Estates-General**. From 1789 onwards, Clavière's ambition was to replace **Necker** as finance minister. He remained attached to Mirabeau.

He devised a theory for using the *assignat* as paper money, issued in small denominations, whereas **Talleyrand**'s scheme was based on a simple treasury bond to enable land purchases. Clavière planned a financial revolution to go with the political one. After Mirabeau's death and the king's flight to **Varennes**, he allied openly with the **Girondins** as their financial spokesman during the **Legislative**. He saw the war as a way of relaunching French external commerce. **Roland** invited him to be finance minister on 23 March 1793, but all he could do in wartime was organize day-to-day finance. On 13 June, the king dismissed the Roland ministry after their criticisms of his use of his suspensive veto, but they were reappointed after 10 August. Any initiatives were stopped then because of **Danton**'s presence as a minister and the furore that surrounded the **September Massacres**. War resulted in the inflation of the *assignat* which Clavière could not prevent. The king's execution and hostilities with Britain prevented the closer co-operation with British business that he wanted. He tried to recover the debt owed to France by the United States.

He took part in the Girondin offensive against domination by Paris. At their exclusion from the **Convention** on 2 June he was put under house arrest, and sent to the **Conciergerie** on 6 September. He was not on trial with the others. He prepared his defence but committed suicide on 8 December 1793, knowing he was to be charged and who was on the jury.

It was not until the Empire that Clavière's projects of unified metallic money, the Bank of France and life insurance were taken up.[44]

Clergy, The First Estate in 1789

The Catholic bishops and clergy in France before the Revolution still had a respected position in society, despite the erosion of their influence by attacks on them by writers such as **Voltaire**, and an increasing indifference towards what they stood for. The presence of a great many priests, monks and nuns in town and country alike meant that the church had a visible presence, generally deferred to by the rest of the population, although increasingly criticized for worldliness.

The **statements of complaint** (*cahiers de doléance*) often criticized the great wealth of monasteries and convents, because their small numbers made monks and nuns incapable of keeping the vows of their orders and allowed them a life of considerable comfort compared with most country curés who lived on very small incomes. These latter were often close to their parishioners, and helped in the drawing up of the *cahiers*. The tithe, which was meant to support them, often went to augment the enormous incomes of the diocesan bishops who were for the most part nobles. The income of some abbeys sometimes went to reward a lay courtier appointed by the crown who would be known as a commendatory abbot.

The clergy were privileged in the sense that they decided for themselves, in assemblies at regular intervals, how much tax they would pay the king as a 'free gift' (*don gratuit*). Nevertheless, there were some churchmen, such as Archbishop Boisgelin[45] of Aix-en-Provence, who wanted, as early as the **Assembly of Notables** of 1787, to change the way the Church was taxed, even as far as removing its financial privilege.

At the provincial assemblies in spring 1789 all the clergy had a vote to elect their two deputies from each district (*sénéchaussée* or **bailliage**) for the **Estates-General**. In some cases, they elected their bishop, as at Autun in Burgundy, where **Talleyrand** favoured the Revolution and survived, and Saintes in the Saintonge, where Bishop de La Rochefoucauld did not, after three years meeting his end in the **September Massacres**.

McManners, John, *Church and Society in Eighteenth-Century France*, vol. 2 (Oxford: Oxford University Press, 1998), chap. 49.

Clichy Club (Clichyens)

The *Club de Clichy* was formed in the aftermath of the fall of **Robespierre** on 9 **thermidor** (28 July 1794). It met in the Hôtel Bertin in the wealthy western Parisian suburb of Clichy. Its members were rightist republicans, some of whom had been deputies in the **Convention** now released from prison, and constitutional monarchists (*monarchiens* with similar ideas to the earlier *Feuillants*). François-Antoine de **Boissy d'Anglas** and General Charles **Pichegru** were among their leaders. Supporters included Pierre Paul Royer-Collard and General Willot (who had recently turned a blind eye towards **White Terror** outbreaks in the south-east). The **Jacobin Club** had been closed at the same time and the Right seemed to be in the ascendant during the First **Directory**. Their programme was to turn out the Directors, remove restraints from returned *émigrés* and **refractory clergy**, and to restrict any resurgence of **Terror**, which they designated as 'anarchy'. There was a certain similarity of purpose between them and Directors **Carnot** and Letourneur. Their significant gain was when Balthazar-François Barthélémy was made a Director. Nevertheless, there was embarrassment when some monarchists supported a revival of absolutism while Louis XVIII (formerly **Provence**) remained in his Declaration of Verona phase, and while 'white terror' raged unrestricted in the south-east. These were nicknamed 'White Jacobins'.

In September 1797, there was the anti-royalist **Fructidor coup**.[46] Pichegru was arrested, the Clichy Club was closed and the salons closely scrutinized. There were several deportations. The chief means by which the Directors maintained themselves in power was by successive coups, until they were overthrown by one organized on behalf of General Bonaparte in November 1799 by **Talleyrand**, the Directory's foreign minister, **Sieyès**, himself a Director since the preceding May, and **Fouché**, police minister since July. **Brumaire** meant the suppression of monarchist revival for 15 years.

Clootz, Jean-Baptiste (Anarcharsis) (1755–94)

Clootz called himself 'the orator of the human race' and was called 'a violent **Cordelier**' by others since he was an eccentric proponent of extreme republicanism.

He was born near Cleves into a Dutch family, whose wealth was derived from East Indian commerce, and he had arrived in Paris at the age of 21 to associate with *philosophes* of the **Enlightenment**. He claimed to be a Prussian baron. When the Revolution began, he was an ardent pamphleteer in its cause and joined in the 'Days' of **October 1789**. His speeches at the **Jacobins** were verbose and often incomprehensible. **Brissot** accused him of being a spy for the King of Prussia. Before the **Festival of the Federation** to be held on the Champ de Mars on the first anniversary of the taking of the **Bastille**, he appeared at the head of a deputation of foreigners to point out that the festival was not just for the French but for the whole of the human race.[47] He marched with them and then delivered a bombastic speech on the abolition of hereditary titles.[48]

When war had been declared in April 1792, he made a speech lasting two hours at the bar of the **Legislative**, abusively to denounce every king he could apply his tongue to. He also wrote to the Assembly to say that he had invented 'a moral wildfire' which he would let the deputies have to use against their enemies. He presented a book to the Assembly in which he said that the aim of the war should be to make the whole of Europe into departments of France that should send representatives to Paris. England would become 'the department of the Thames'.

Clootz co-operated with **Chabot** over the **sansculotte** invasion of the **Tuileries** on 20 June 1792. After the king had been overthrown, he went to the bar of the Assembly again to offer to raise a battalion of Prussians called the 'Vandal Legion' to march with the *fédérés* to expel the (real Prussian) invaders. Along with Thomas **Paine** he had French citizenship conferred upon him after some generous payments for war expenses. He had a stake in the Revolution from having purchased 450,000 livres worth of **national property**. He was vociferous in favour of the **September Massacres** even at Manon **Roland**'s supper table.

Elected to the **Convention** for the Oise, he sat with the **Mountain** and supported the ousting of the **Girondins**. He joined **Hébert's** de-Christianizing movement and persuaded Archbishop **Gobel** to renounce the Catholic faith.

Robespierre attacked him for atheism. He was excluded from the **Jacobin Club** on 12 December 1793 and from the Convention when it decreed that foreigners were no longer acceptable as deputies.[49] He was arrested on 28 December, imprisoned in the **Luxembourg Palace** and brought before the **Revolutionary Tribunal** with the Hébertists. He was guillotined with them on 24 March 1794.

Collot d'Herbois, Jean-Marie (1749–96)

Collot-d'Herbois is best known for his role as **Fouché's** colleague in the suppression of **Lyon** after the federalist insurrection there in November 1793. He and **Billaud-Varenne** were closely associated as radicals in the

Paris **Jacobin Club** and in the **Insurrectionary Commune** of August 1792. Both men were Paris deputies in the **National Convention**, and appointed on the same day to the **Committee of Public Safety** as representatives of the radical left.

Collot was born in Paris to an artisan jeweller's family and his grandfather ran a brewery. He was fascinated by marionettes, but it is not known why he took up an itinerant actor/playwright's career, involving civic exclusion in the old regime, at the age of 17. This took him to Bordeaux in 1772, and Lyon in 1787, where he was a theatre manager (it is said he received bad notices there), and added 'd'Herbois' to his name. He came back to Paris in 1789, already full of revolutionary ideas, to use his presentation skills in public events. His play *The Patriot Family, or the Federation* was put on at the **Palais-Royal** in 1790. By 1791, he was a public figure. The Jacobins held a competition for a presentation to popularize the new constitution in the countryside. Collot won, with his immensely successful *Almanac of Father Gerard*, out of 42 entries. His resulting popularity meant that he had the political clout as a Jacobin to gain the release of the 41 soldiers of the Swiss Châteauvieux Regiment who had been sent to the galleys at Brest after the 1790 **Nancy Mutiny** on 31 December, and to organize a celebratory festival for them in Paris on 15 April 1792.[50]

Collot was a member of the **Insurrectionary Commune** set up on the eve of the overthrow of the monarchy, and was elected as a deputy for Paris in the **National Convention**. Sitting with the **Mountain**, he voted for the king's death without delay and hounded the **Girondins** after their expulsion in June 1793. While a member of the **Committee of Public Safety**, he was **representative on mission** to several places. Then he was sent to Lyon with Fouché where he shared responsibility for the harshness of the republican reassertion. In November 1793, he produced his *Instruction*, often taken by historians as the manifesto of the **Terror**. He argued that anything was permissible in pursuit of the Revolution's aims and there was need, now, for what he called 'total revolution'.[51] If perfect equality could not be obtained by goodwill, then it had to be done by force. This justified for Collot the whole range of notions from 'suspects', through forced loans on the rich and de-Christianization, to the **Maximum on**

Prices and Wages. The Committee recalled him to the capital to answer for his excesses, but the popular reaction to an assassination attempt on him in May 1794 reassured him.

On 9 **thermidor**, Collot was president of the Convention. He had recognized himself in the general denunciation that **Robespierre** had made and would not allow him to speak in his defence, aggressively drowning his words by ringing his bell. He was, nevertheless, accused of supporting Robespierre but was declared innocent. A second denunciation in March 1795, however, led to him and Billaud-Varenne being sentenced to deportation to Guiana for their terrorist excesses. His death took place in Cayenne, the colony's capital, less than a year later – rumoured to have been caused by downing a bottle of rum in one go.

Committee of General Security

This committee was set up by the **National Convention** as one of its earliest acts on 2 October 1792, with vaguely defined police and counter-espionage powers. It developed out of similar bodies that existed at the time of the **Constituent** and **Legislative** Assemblies. It was to have 30 members, half being replaced by other *conventionnels* in elections every 2 months.

In the first place, the members were largely from the **Mountain** but, after an election in January 1793, the **Girondins** were in a majority on the committee. '**Roland** drew up the list,' asserted **Marat**.[52] The **Jacobin Le Peletier Saint-Fargeau** was assassinated on 20 January and the Mountain blamed the Girondins for not providing better security. Membership was then reduced to 12, and elections produced only one Girondin.

With the exclusion of the Girondins in June 1793 and the official **Terror** beginning, the Committee's task was more recognizable. When the Convention decreed the **Law of Suspects** on 17 September, surveillance was the responsibility of this Committee. One of its Jacobin members was Jean-Pierre-André **Amar**, a lawyer from **Grenoble**, who reported the whereabouts of the Girondins who had hidden in October, and the scandal in the **Company of the Indies**. In spring 1794 Amar also contributed to the indictment of the Hébertists and Dantonists.

It clashed with the **Committee of Public Safety** in April over the setting up of a separate police bureau, since police matters were its own responsibility. In the run-up to **Thermidor**, the Committee of General Security manipulated the affair of the fanatic Catherine **Théot** who claimed a messianic role for **Robespierre**. The members disliked the festival of the **Supreme Being**. Only one member, **Le Bas**, was condemned in the Thermidor Coup because he himself chose to die with Robespierre and **Saint-Just**.

After Thermidor, the Law on Revolutionary Government recognized three powerful committees, those of Public Safety and General Security and the Legislation Committee. The Committee of General Security oversaw the release of political prisoners. On 11 March 1795, policing was put wholly back into the hands of General Security. From April 1795 onwards, the new constitution of the **Directory** did not have executive committees as they had existed under the Convention.

Committee of Public Safety

The Committee of Public Safety had its origin in the Committee of General Defence proposed by a **Girondin** called Kersaint at the beginning of 1793, which developed, after the defeat and defection of **Dumouriez** at Neerwinden, into a Commission of Public Safety on 25 March. This was restyled as the Committee of Public Safety on 6 April with **Danton** as a member. After the Girondins had been excluded from the **National Convention** in June 1793 and hounded to their deaths in the name of the One and Indivisible Republic, the Convention itself had become a lopsided Jacobin preserve and accepted Danton's proposal that it should delegate its functions to its committees, especially to this one. On 27 July 1793, Maximilien **Robespierre** replaced Danton and became its ideologist. He remained in place until he and other members were overthrown at **Thermidor** exactly a year later.

The importance of the committee to revolutionary government is registered by the increasing number of staff it employed: 67 in frimaire (November 1793) and 418 in prairial year II (May 1794). This was a sign of an 'undeniable bureaucratization'.[53] Systematic information gathering and decision making for a nation at war needed such numbers on the staff.

The committee's task was foreign policy, the conduct of the war against the powers of the **First Coalition**, and of the civil war against centres of **federalism**. It had 12 members who met in what had been **Louis XVI**'s private office in the **Tuileries Palace**, usually at night after the Convention sittings had finished, often in an atmosphere of intense crisis. There was rarely a full meeting because nearly all the members became **representatives on mission** for long periods. **Couthon** went to Lyon and began its destruction after the federalist revolt. **Collot d'Herbois** went to Clermont-Ferrand before he went to Lyon, Jean-Bon **Saint-André** and **Prieur de la Marne** were in charge of navy affairs at Brest at the time of the battle the British called 'The Glorious First of June', and ensured the arrival of a vital grain convoy from the Caribbean which helped the Revolution survive in a time of scarcity. Lazare **Carnot** remained in the office to receive reports and make decisions about military supply, receiving the soubriquet 'the organizer of victory', though even he went on mission to **Jourdan**'s Army of the North. Robespierre did not go on mission but developed his role as self-appointed ideologist for the government which was to be 'revolutionary until victory'. He was backed up by **Saint-Just**, away on mission for a time, but also a mouthpiece of the committee in the Convention and responsible for introducing the **Law of Ventôse** in the spring of 1794 for the redistribution of *émigrés'* property to proved republicans in need. The committee itself was not dismantled at Thermidor, but reconstituted to remain an essential part of the Convention's bureaucracy until it gave way to the Directory under the Constitution of year III.

Representatives on mission were answerable to the Convention via this committee. Its brief was extended to economic policy. It devised the **Maximum on Prices and Wages**. Through the advice given by the committee to the National Convention, **Terror** became official.

Palmer, R.R., *Twelve Who Ruled: The Year of the Terror in the French Revolution* (University Park, PA: Princeton University Press, Bicentennial Edition, 1989).

Committee of Thirty (1789)

Early in 1789 there seemed to be some central body directing criticism of the king's ministers while elections for the **Estates-General** were being held in the *bailliages*. Georges Lefèbvre suggested it was the 'Committee of Thirty' which met in Adrien **Duport**'s house as part of the 'aristocratic revolt' and as part of the formation of a patriot party.[54] Membership may have included the Duc de Larochfoucauld-Liancourt, **Lafayette**, **Condorcet**, the Duc d'Aiguillon, **Sieyès**, **Mirabeau** and **Talleyrand**. Donald Sutherland claims that 50 out of 55 members that can be identified were nobles, almost all from old **nobility**. They resented **Louis XVI**'s preference for new nobles in the royal administration as intendants, and they all despised the queen for depriving their families of privileges and sinecures at court. They were nobles with a grudge, and this was the basis of their revolt.[55]

The committee proposed titles for pamphlets, and sent their agents with model **statements of grievances** to provincial centres. Wealthier members financed these concerns. They were covering similar ground to the Duc d'**Orléans**, but neither they nor the duke could detract from the initiative being taken by individual members of the **Third Estate** in their own localities. Bishops canvassed their diocesan clergy to have themselves elected, and small-town lawyers jockeyed for one of the four places available to them. Some nobles offered themselves to several provincial assemblies before they were elected.

Company of the Indies

This company was set up by **Calonne** in 1785 to try to bring in revenue to help the royal finances; he gave it the monopoly of trade east of the Cape of Good Hope and sole use of the quays at the port of Lorient. The company was suppressed in April 1790 by decree of the **Constituent Assembly** when privileges were abolished.

When it came to be formally wound up over a period of months in 1792–3, there was a corruption scandal, with large sums of money sticking to speculators' hands. **Fabre d'Eglantine**, the embellisher of the **Revolutionary Calendar**, who had already been implicated in speculation over army contracts, was involved in this. He was associated with **Danton**. At the latter's trial before the **Revolutionary Tribunal**, **Fouquier-Tinville** made the scandal an issue, and Fabre was executed with the Dantonists in April 1794. **Chabot** had already been arraigned for speculation with the Hébertists in March. **Robespierre** could see both factions against him involved in it.[56] **Amar** was heavily involved in the scandal, but managed to avoid the consequences.

Conciergerie

The Conciergerie prison stands on the bank of the Ile de la Cité in Paris opposite the Louvre and the Tuileries and by the side of the Palais de Justice where the **Revolutionary Tribunal** sat in the months of the **Terror**. It was called the ante-chamber to the guillotine. Suspects were sent to other prisons during the **Terror** before they went to the Tribunal for hearing and judgement. The great hall was divided up into little cubicles which served as cells, and the revolutionary tribunal was very near them. The prosecutor, **Fouquier-Tinville**, had his offices in the towers on the river front.[57] During and after their trials the accused were kept in the Conciergerie, until the carts took those who were found guilty to the scaffold. Visitors to the rooms in the Conciergerie nowadays need to be very insensitive not to feel the spirit of desperation there …

Condorcet de Caritat, Marie Jean Antoine Nicolas, Marquis de (1743–94)

Condorcet brought the ideas of the **Enlightenment** into the first five years of revolutionary change. By 1789, he was a well-established figure in the worlds of philosophy and mathematics. He had been a member of the Académie royale des sciences for 30 years and was recognized as a scientist in Europe and the United States. The main influences on him as a young man were the encyclopaedist d'Alembert and **Louis XVI**'s first Controller of the Finances, Jacques Turgot (whose biography he wrote). The latter made him inspector-general of the Paris Mint in 1774.

Public office widened his interests. He joined the *Société des **Amis des Noirs*** and was one of the rare supporters of the rights of women in the Revolution as a member of the **Social Circle**. Despite Turgot's dismissal, Condorcet remained at the Mint until 1792.

Before the Revolution, Condorcet became interested in the way voting processes might operate in a democracy at the same time as working on the differential and integral calculus. He also took up **Voltaire**'s antagonism towards the Church, despite (or because of) his early Jesuit education.

He was elected to the **Legislative Assembly** in 1791 as one of the Paris deputies. His design for secular state education was taken seriously. While preserving his independence, he favoured the **Girondins** over the **Jacobins** in the final months of the **Legislative**, and in the **Convention** as a member of the constitutional committee.

Although he regarded the establishment of a republic as a mark of progress, Condorcet opposed the king's execution. When his turn came to vote in the roll-call election, he said 'I have no voice'. On the question whether the king's execution should be suspended, he abstained.[58] Automatically he became a traitor in the eyes of the Jacobins. He went into hiding in the face of a warrant they issued for his arrest in October 1793, and remained in a safe house in Paris (writing a book about human intelligence) until 25 March 1794. He was arrested while leaving Paris and was found dead in his prison cell, perhaps given poison by a friend, or murdered. The official verdict was that he had suffered a heart attack.

Constituent Assembly

Challenged by the deputies of the **Third Estate** swearing their **Tennis-Court Oath** on 27 June 1789, Louis XVI 'invited' the **nobility** – and the **clergy** who had not already done so – to join them in a united assembly. At the end of the month, the deputies elected to the **Estates-General** in the spring – for the three orders separately – assumed the new name of the National Constituent Assembly and continued their sessions together. Deputies such as Pierre-Louis de La Rochefoucauld-Bayers, bishop of Saintes and a future victim of the **September Massacres**, did all they could to oppose revolutionary decrees.

In the July Crisis, it was not the fall of the **Bastille** as such that mattered in the Constituent Assembly, but the king's coming to it on 15 July before he went to Paris. He accepted the Assembly's existence and authority and, although they had debated during the short time between knowing he was coming and his arrival whether to applaud him or not, their greetings were rapturous after he had made his announcement that he vowed to work with them for the salvation of France.[59]

During the **October days**, the Constituent endured the market women's invasion of their meeting hall and heard the demands of Citizen Maillard for bread and the punishment of those who had insulted the **revolutionary cockade**. Soon afterwards, the deputies followed the king from **Versailles** to Paris.[60] After that, they held their meetings in the archbishop of Paris's palace and then moved to the former riding school (*Manège*) by the **Tuileries Palace**. The various ministries took over prestigious premises in the capital and took on staffs of functionaries (civil servants).

After the decree devised by Maximilien **Robespierre** which excluded all members of the Constituent from offering themselves for election to the **Legislative Assembly** in October 1791, new elections were necessary. First estate deputies (clergy and bishops) had no separate elections, though some former nobles (titles of nobility had been abolished) and a few constitutional clergymen, like the Abbé **Grégoire**, were re-elected. A good many noble deputies left France to become *émigrés*, but others went back to the country to live as quietly as they felt able. Some military officers, who refused the oath to the Nation after the king's flight to **Varennes**, went to join the Army of the Princes at Koblenz with the intention of restoring the old regime, and others went to England, where they were not so keen on being mobilized, but suffered defeat and massacre by General **Hoche** after being landed on the **Quiberon** peninsula in 1795.

Tackett, Timothy, *Becoming a Revolutionary* (University Park, PA: Princeton University Press, 2006), pt 2.

Corday d'Armont, Marie-Anne Charlotte de (1768–93)

Charlotte Corday assassinated Jean-Paul **Marat** and **David** painted one of the most potent images of the French Revolution.

Corday had been brought up in Normandy where her father was a seigneur. Two of her brothers were *émigrés*. She was well educated at the *Abbaye aux Dames* in **Caen** where she stayed on after her schooling. With like-minded **Girondin** sympathizers in the town, she was fearful of civil war between **federalists** and the Paris **Jacobins** after the expulsion of **Brissot**, **Vergniaud**, **Buzot** and others from the **National Convention** on 2 June 1793. After their arrival in Caen, she met them and admired their courage.[61] She regarded Marat as primarily responsible for the **September**

Massacres in the preceding year, and targeted him in the hope of ending the **Terror**.

In July 1793, she left Caen for Paris, booked into a hotel, and bought a kitchen knife. She discovered that Marat no longer attended the National Convention because of his acute skin condition, soothed only by medicinal baths. She wrote an explanation of her intended action, and found where Marat lived. On the pretext of denouncing the **Girondins** in Caen, she was let in to his apartment where she began giving him the names on her list while he wrote them down, resting his paper on a board over his bath tub. Then she expertly stabbed him and he quickly died.

'I killed one man to save a hundred thousand,' she said at her trial before the **Revolutionary Tribunal**. She was condemned to death wearing the red shirt the old regime reserved for parricides and went to the scaffold on 17 July 1793.

Cordeliers Club

'The Society of the Friends of the Rights of Man and the Citizen' was the club's actual title and it appeared in the first half of 1790. It held its meetings at first in the refectory of the Cordeliers Convent, situated on the left bank in the centre of the city in the Théâtre-française Section. Its subscriptions were much more affordable than in the bourgeois **Jacobins**, and artisans like the butcher Louis **Legendre** were members, though it was dominated by the pragmatic lawyer **Danton**. Women and 'passive' citizens were members. **Chaumette, Desmoulins, Hébert, Marat, Momoro, Vincent** and other radicals were also prominent Cordeliers.[62] In May 1791, the club was ejected from the convent by the Paris Commune and met for the rest of its existence, until March 1794, at the Hôtel de Genlis in the rue Dauphine.

The club saw its role as the chief critic of all government action and all decrees of the assemblies and the Convention that might assail the Rights of Man. Albert **Mathiez** called it 'a group for action and combat'. Fraternal clubs were founded in its likeness in the provinces, and Marat's *Ami du peuple* was its journal of communication. From the spring of 1791 onwards, the club took the initiative in the movement towards replacing the monarchy with a republic. After the king had been brought back from **Varennes** in June 1791, the Cordeliers feared that the political gains already made were under threat from counter-revolutionaries. They organized the signing of a republican petition at the altar of the Federation in the Champ de Mars. This event ended with 50 deaths when the **National Guard** panicked after two men found hiding under the altar for dubious purposes had been lynched (they had carpenter's tools and had made holes in the steps so as to look up women's skirts as they came to sign the petition. One of them had a wooden leg and was easy to catch). **Bailly** and **Lafayette** were accused of ordering the shooting.

For a while, the club lost its momentum – it was 'effectively neutered' in Sutherland's phrase[63] – especially with Danton prudently withdrawing to England for a while. It recovered its position at the heart of the fraternal societies, however, in 1792. It played a major part in drawing the *fédérés* to Paris against the king's veto and in organizing the **'Day' of 10 August**. Its role was consolidated even more firmly in the winter of 1792–3 when the Jacobins made their onslaught on the *enragés*, **Roux**, **Varlet** and **Leclerc**. Hébert's *Le Père Duchesne* joined Marat's *Ami du Peuple* in publicizing the issues that the Cordeliers wanted to emphasize.

During the three days when the **Girondins** were being excluded from the Convention (31 May–2 June 1793), the Cordeliers came into their own as a rallying point for all the radical institutions: the **sansculottes** under **Hanriot**, the war ministry where Vincent was active, the Paris Commune, and the popular societies under the Jacobin banner. The Cordeliers did not agree with Varlet and other extremists who wanted to institute direct democracy through strengthening control over the deputies in the **Convention** by their primary electors, but they did favour the setting-up of central committees to co-ordinate the popular societies. The **'Day' of 5 September** was a decisive turning point. The Jacobins accepted the compromise of the revolutionary armies to attack hoarders of grain, and **Terror** had been made the order of the day.

Then, in reprisal, **Robespierre** attacked the Cordeliers in the Jacobin Club and **Billaud-Varenne** did the same in the Convention a fortnight later. This led to Vincent being arrested, and the Jacobin **representatives on mission** repressed Cordelier sympathizers in the provinces. By this means, the Cordeliers were reduced once more to a local Parisian club by the beginning of 1794. In February and March the Jacobins supported **Saint-Just**'s **Ventôse decrees** for the redistribution of *émigrés*' property to deserving republicans, and so stole the Cordeliers' thunder. Hébert's arrest and execution in March meant that the Cordeliers Club had lost its political clout.

Counter-revolution

This term was coined by revolutionaries themselves because they expected their opponents to push in a contrary direction against their early achievements and restore the old regime. By the end of the **Constituent Assembly** in 1791, those who were identified as such were using the term about themselves, for example, the *émigrés* in the Army of the Princes. The **Terror** aimed at the elimination of those counter-revolutionaries who were still in France before they could gain enough power to assert themselves openly. The **Jacobins**, despite the confident utterances of **Robespierre** and **Saint-Just**, knew how precarious their position was as a minority government. The plots of the *émigrés* in Savoy, where **Artois** had his Turin Committee, were explicitly made for '*une contre-révolution*'.[64] Similar activity went on in Koblenz under the Prince of Condé, and later in Verona when **Provence** was there. The **Vendée** rebellion, the **Chouan** risings in Brittany, and the '**White Terror**' in the Rhône Valley in early 1795 were also counter-revolutionary. Refractory Catholic bishops, like de Coucy of La Rochelle who was still running his diocese secretly from Pamplona, and **refractory clergy** ministering to their former congregations from forest hide-outs after returning from exile in Jersey, were counter-revolutionary too.

The king and queen had their own secret counter-revolutionary agenda, starting at least as early as their move to Paris on 6 October 1789, when **Louis XVI** sent the letter to his Bourbon cousin, Charles IV of Spain, which he had prepared some time before, to express his objections to what had happened. They bought **Mirabeau**'s services in 1790 and, possibly, those of **Danton**. The queen's relations, successive Habsburg Emperors, had too many involvements of their own to do more at first than make declarations. There may have been an '**Austrian Committee**' in the **Tuileries**, and the queen was accused with good reason of giving away

French military information to Emperor Francis. They certainly could not look towards George III of England who still resented the help given by Louis XVI to the American revolutionaries.[65]

Yet there was much more opposition to the Jacobins than this, which made the Terror necessary if they were not to lose their predominance in the Nation. In his Preface to his 1985 study of Revolution and Counterrevolution (*sic*), Donald Sutherland made this pertinent assertion:

> The history of the entire period can be understood as the struggles against a counterrevolution that was not so much aristocratic as massive, extensive, durable and popular. This theme explains why the revolutionaries violated their own ideal of the rule of law with scarcely a qualm. It helps explain the early recourse to repression, the foreign war (undertaken paradoxically to cope with the interior enemy), the Terror, the failure of constitutional government between 1794 and 1797 and the necessity of a dictatorship in 1799–1801.[66]

In his later work, Professor Sutherland has elaborated this to say that the counter-revolution had a strategy in place almost from the outset, 'a mix of foreign intervention combined with internal conspiracy and insurrection,' which would work eventually in 1815. Coalitions of the **bourgeoisie** were forming, people like former tax-assessors, church officials, and those with business interests in places like **Lyon**, together with artisanal craftsmen and **peasants** loyal to the Church, who looked for support from the former privileged orders, which was not forthcoming.[67]

Doyle, William, *Revolution and Counter-Revolution in France*, in *Officers, Nobles and Revolutionaries, Essays on Eighteenth Century France* (London and Rio Grande: The Hambledon Press, 1995).

Couthon, Georges-Auguste (1755–94)

Georges Couthon was from Puy-de-Dôme in the south-central France, where he was a lawyer, **freemason** and local government official. He came to Paris in 1791 as an elected deputy to the **Legislative Assembly**, rising above the limitations imposed on him by paralysis in his legs which took hold in 1788. Until the king's flight to **Varennes**, however, he was a loyal monarchist. After it, he rejected the **Feuillant** position, remained in the **Jacobin Club** and sat with the **Mountain** in the Convention. He voted for the king's death, but shared **Robespierre**'s deistic views as opposed to the de-Christianization being pressed in the Nation by **Hébert** and others. He had supported the abolition of feudal dues on the **night of 4 August 1789** and opposed the tenants having to buy their indemnity from payments to the landlords by a subsequent decree, so he voted in the Convention for the removal of feudal dues altogether, for the order to burn all title deeds on 17 July 1793 and for the decree of 20 August 1793 against all feudal privileges, such as the maintenance of fortified places.

Couthon also voted for the **Girondins**' expulsion from the Convention. Elected to the **Committee of Public Safety** at the same time as their exclusion (June 1793), he was sent to **Lyon** during the military action against the federalists there. His previous missions had been remarkable for their moderation. He raised a large force from Puy-de-Dôme to support the defeat of the rebellion in Lyon, and then replaced **Dubois-Crancy** as **representative on mission** in the town itself, where he was received with Jacobin acclamations and restored their municipality. He put the rebels on trial. The Convention wanted to raze Lyon to the ground. Couthon obediently started the process in the richest quarter of the town, but did not press the destruction with any vigour and returned to Paris. The real repression began in Lyon after he had been replaced in late November by **Collot d'Herbois** and **Fouché**.

Nevertheless, Couthon helped Robespierre to obtain the execution of **Hébert** and his faction, and then of **Danton** and his. He shared responsibility for the Law of 22 prairial, year II (10 June 1794) which took away the right of defence counsel or even witnesses from people accused before the **revolutionary tribunal**. His fervent support for the **Terror** was expressed in his utterance made on 17 July 1794: 'The **National Convention** is sublime at this moment; it is vomiting from its breast everything impure.'[68]

Ten days later, Couthon was arrested as a Robespierrist on 9 **thermidor** and, during the second arrest in the Hôtel de Ville, propelled his wheelchair down a flight of stairs, receiving severe injuries. His execution in the morning was a drawn-out affair because of the difficulty of arranging his paralysed legs in the guillotine.

 Palmer, R.R., *Twelve Who Ruled: The Year of the Terror in the French Revolution* (University Park, PA: Princeton University Press, Bicentennial Edition, 1989).

Custine, Adam Philippe, Comte de (1740–93)

Custine was an old-regime army officer who served in the Seven Years' War and the American War of Independence. He was in command of **Toulon** as a brigadier in 1789, but left to be elected to the **Estates-General** by the nobles of his native Metz. Ineligible for the **Legislative**, he rejoined the army in October 1791. Commanding the Army of the Vosges, he took Speyer, Worms, Mainz and Frankfurt between September and October 1792.

In the territories he occupied, Custine ruled by proclamation, raising substantial taxes on the nobles. Very soon, however, he was forced out of Frankfurt and back across the Rhine to Landau. He blamed the war ministry and General Kellermann's jealousy for this setback. He even went as far as to write to the Convention that the Republic could only be saved by a dictator, and that this dictator could only be a general. When he was accused of treason, **Robespierre** defended him and the **Committee of Public Safety** appointed him to command the Army of the North but he continued to maintain a political stance independent of the government. However, this was at the time of **Bouchotte**'s 'sansculottization' of the war ministry, and its secretary, **Vincent**, prepared evidence that Custine was a traitor to the Republic. Vincent and **Hébert** approached **Marat** to have Custine denounced in the *Ami du Peuple*. Hébert wanted to inherit Marat's place as *Montagnard* publicist after his murder, and gave the evidence against Custine to the Committee of Public Safety. Custine was called back to Paris to face the **revolutionary tribunal** on a charge of conspiring with the enemy. This time, no one defended him and he went to the scaffold on 27 August 1793. 'Military power was now no more than a lever held by the civil power.'[69]

D

Danton, Georges-Jacques (1759–94)

'Audacity, always audacity, then more audacity' (*audace* is the more forceful French word), was Danton's war cry before the French military victory at **Valmy** on 20 September 1792. It was typical of the utterances of this larger-than-life figure lionized by the crowd. In contrast to the fastidious and incorruptible **Robespierre**, Danton was ebullient and twice married, besides being rumoured to have accepted corrupt payment for favours during his rise to prominence in Parisian and national politics. Born in the Champagne province, educated by Oratorians, he moved to Paris to be a lawyer's clerk. He took his qualifying examinations in Reims (easier there than in Paris), borrowed from his future father-in-law to buy a potentially lucrative practice, married and became influential in the Cordeliers district on the left bank.

Danton was a founder member of the **Cordeliers Club**, open to working men for a few pence, while, at the same time, joining the bourgeois **Jacobins**. He accepted a place in the coterie of the Duc d'**Orléans**, and was a vehement opponent of Mayor **Bailly** and General **Lafayette**. He was elected to the Directory of the Seine Department, along with **Mirabeau**, **Sieyès** and **Talleyrand**, nominally superior to the Commune dominated by his antagonists. After the king's flight to **Varennes** in June 1791, he instigated the Cordeliers' petition against royalty to be signed by the patriots on the altar of the previous year's Festival of the Federation on the Champ de Mars, at which the **National Guard** panicked[1] and fired into the crowd, killing 50 people. Horrified by this massacre, Danton went to

London for six weeks until the Assembly decided not to proceed with the prosecution of the authors of the petition. His brief meeting with Charles James Fox, leader of the opposition in Great Britain, was of little value. During his stay, British attitudes were conditioned by the 'Church and King' riots in Birmingham in reaction to the events in Paris.

On his return, Danton held legal office as an assistant procurator of the Paris Commune. He and **Pétion** remained in place when the **Insurrectionary Commune** took over on the night of 9/10 August 1792, and he was active in organizing the violent overthrow of the monarchy on 10 August 1792. He was elected Minister of Justice immediately afterwards, and turned a blind eye, Madame **Roland** said, to the **September Massacres**. Historian Albert **Mathiez**, writing in 1922, gave evidence for her assertion from the later recollections of the young Duc de Chartres, heir to the Duc d'Orléans, uttered when he had become King Louis Philippe I (1830–48). When Chartres came back to Paris to report the republican army's victory at **Jemappes**, he complained to Danton about the massacres, and Danton replied by telling him not to become involved in that question, because it could cause him serious problems. He went on to say that, when the male population of Paris had gone to the eastern frontier, the royalist detainees would have burst out of the prisons, waited for the foreigners to arrive and then massacred the soldiers' families. He said he wanted the young soldiers to reach the Champagne country 'covered in blood' to assure him that they would be faithful to the Revolution – 'I wanted to put a river of blood between them and the *émigrés*.'[2] This amounted to an admission by Danton that he had been involved in bringing the massacres about. He had a pragmatic turn of mind and an intuitive political instinct which **Robespierre**, ever the revolutionary ideologist, never acquired.

As one of the deputies for Paris in the **National Convention**, Danton voted for the king's death without delay, despite the rumours that Foreign Minister Montmorin had been paying him large sums from the civil list to promote the king's interest. He devised the rules for the **Revolutionary Tribunal** in the **Terror**, and was a founder member of the **Committee of Public Safety**. Nevertheless, he did not join with Robespierre in the ejection of the Girondins from the Convention.

Robespierre and **Saint-Just** charged Danton with 'indulgence' towards **counter-revolutionaries**, with wanting to soften the effect of the Terror and negotiate an end to the war with the kings of Europe. A rigged trial resulted in his execution, along with **Desmoulins** and others, on 5 April 1794. According to **Michelet**, as the tumbrel passed Robespierre's shuttered lodgings on the rue Saint-Honoré, Danton's voice could be heard amid the shouts of the crowd, 'Robespierre's next! Robespierre comes after me!' (*J'entraîne Robespierre, Robespierre me suit!*).[3] Whether Robespierre heard him or not, **Thermidor** was only weeks away.

 Hampson, Norman, *Danton* (Oxford: Basil Blackwell, 1974).

Lawday, David, *The Giant of the French Revolution: Danton, A Life* (New York: Grove Press, 2009), together with *He Roared*, Hilary Mantel's extensive review of Lawday in *The London Review of Books*, vol. 31, no. 15 (6 August 2009): pp. 3–6, online at: http://www.lrb.co.uk/v31/n15/hilary-mantel/he-roared.

Ozouf, Mona, *Danton*, in François Furet and Mona Ozouf (eds), *A Critical Dictionary of the French Revolution,* trans. Arthur Goldhammer (London: The Belknap Press of Harvard University Press, 1989), *ad loc.*

Mantel, Hilary, *A Place of Greater Safety* (London: Viking, 1992; Fourth Estate, 2010). Novel.

Wajda, Andrzej, *Danton,* Franco-Polish film, 1983.

David, Jacques-Louis (1748–1825)

As a **Jacobin** and a close associate of Maximilien **Robespierre**, David was commissioned to stage-manage celebratory events in Paris, the most conspicuous being the festival of the **Supreme Being** in June 1794, with its artificial mountain and the figure of Wisdom emerging from within the burnt statue of Atheism. All this was despite his previous association with the court and **Louis XVI** having given him the privilege of a studio in the **Tuileries**.

David had been a pupil of François Boucher, famous for his portrait of Madame de Pompadour. He won the *Prix de Rome*, giving him five years in Italy where he visited the newly discovered ruins of Pompeii. By the time he returned to Paris in 1779, his style was set firm. His *Oath of the Horatii*, exhibited in the 1785 salon, expressed values of the

Enlightenment and alluded to **Rousseau**'s *Social Contract*. David gives a theatrical representation of the young men expressing a virile readiness to pour out their blood for the *patrie*, victory or death, forgetting themselves in the face of their duty, contrasted with the sensitive femininity 'which cannot face death and lets itself be subjected to horror at the prospect'.[4] Donald Sutherland has pointed out that this represented a flowering of popular resentment against the power of women at court, from Louis XV's apparent subservience to Madame de Pompadour and, worse, Madame du Barry, and then, worse still, Queen **Marie-Antoinette**'s reputation for overspending the revenues of Louis XVI's household.[5] This underlines a great deal of the **Jacobin** misogyny to be expressed in the Revolutionary years by the likes of Robespierre and **Amar**.

David associated himself with the Revolution from its outset. The Jacobin Club commissioned a large, monumental painting of the **Tennis Court Oath** of 20 June 1789. It exists as a collection of portraits of the deputies involved. He found it impossible to take it beyond the stage of a meticulous ink and wash drawing for the salon of 1791 because the personalities prominent in political life tended not to remain in office for any length of time. Nevertheless, he became close to Robespierre and the Jacobins when he organized the festival for the restitution of the soldiers sent to the galleys at Brest for their part in the 1790 **Nancy Mutiny** on 15 April 1791. **Danton** and **Marat** helped him in his candidature for the **National Convention** and he was, along with them, a deputy for Paris.

David voted in the Convention for the execution of Louis XVI in January 1793. He produced a posthumous, monumental portrait of **Le Peletier**, who had been assassinated by a royal bodyguard for voting as he had. Marat, another friend of David's, was assassinated on 13 July by Charlotte **Corday**, a Girondin sympathizer from Caen. David produced his *Death of Marat* very quickly. The painting is often compared to Michelangelo's *Pieta*: the Republic was a religion in itself. David organized Marat's progress to the Pantheon as a great public spectacle. Another icon of the revolution is David's little sketch of the reduced figure of the queen on her way to execution after her show trial in October 1793.

He designed uniforms for state officials, and even made suggestions as to what patriots should adopt as their normal dress.

David was a member of the **Committee of General Security** and was involved in the **Terror**, signing death warrants. He was arrested himself in the aftermath of Robespierre's fall in July 1794, and imprisoned for nearly a year in his old school, the College of Four Nations. While there, he produced exquisite ink and wash drawings of Jacobin colleagues such as **Bernard de Saintes** and Jean Bon **Saint-André**, who were his fellow prisoners, on roundels of paper. He was amnestied 'for deeds relative to the Revolution' on the last day the Convention sat. His large painting called *The Intervention of the Sabine Women*, which took from 1795 to 1798 to complete, was intended to illustrate national reconciliation.

He supported General Bonaparte's **Brumaire coup**, and he was appointed First Painter of the Empire. He exiled himself to Brussels in 1815.

Blanning, T.C.W., *The Culture of Power and the Power of Culture: Old Regime Europe 1660–1789* (Oxford: Oxford University Press, 2002), pp. 435ff.

'Day' of 20 June 1792

The king's **Feuillant** ministers were subject to a virulent press campaign, largely directed by **Brissot**.[6] They were replaced by Brissot's political friends, **Roland** at the interior, **Clavière** at Finance, Servan at the War Ministry and General **Dumouriez** at Foreign Affairs. The war was not the short conflict which those who supported it wanted. Defeats at Mons and Tournai were taken as treason, the result of conspiracies, not only by **Marat** but all the prominent politicians. The Brissotins fed rumours of an '**Austrian Committee**' at the king's court, and of the queen inciting action against the patriots; they made use of the desire for revenge these rumours sparked off.[7]

The **sansculottes** in the **Paris Sections** were becoming overtly political. The **Girondin** government increased pressure on any **refractory clergy** who were denounced by 20 people to leave the country (27 May), and the king's bodyguard was to be replaced by the Paris **National Guard**. Twenty thousand *fédéré* National Guards were to be encamped outside Paris. **Louis XVI** used his suspensive veto on these laws (which should have prevented their enforcement for six years). Roland protested (Madame Roland wrote the letter he read to the king). The king dismissed him and his colleagues. The sansculottes in the sections helped by the **Cordeliers** planned an armed demonstration for the anniversary of the **Tennis Court Oath** and the Flight to **Varennes** (more or less) on 20 June 1792.[8]

A crowd of sansculottes, armed with pikes and sabres decorated with tricolour ribbons and carrying placards threatening the queen, presented petitions to the Assembly, and then forced an entry to the **Tuileries Palace**. They caught the king alone in one room while the queen and the dauphin were in another, the queen having decided not to put the king at further risk by her unpopularity in the capital. The king was required to put on a **Phrygian bonnet** and to drink a toast to the Nation. He did both with grace and dignity, and with none of the awkwardness he had shown on other public occasions, such as when he declared war on 20 April. Eventually, after four hours,[9] a group of deputies arrived, Mayor **Pétion** among them ('What took you so long?' the king asked him), and the crowd was persuaded to withdraw. This was a prelude to the events of 10 August, when the **Insurrectionary Commune** organized the major violence which brought the monarchy to an end.

When **Lafayette**, on 28 June, tried to use the National Guards against everyone he thought might be involved in the demonstration, Marat's predictions of a military dictatorship seemed to be coming true. Lafayette caused offence not only to the sansculottes and the Cordeliers, but to the Jacobins who had held aloof on 20 June, the Paris Sections that were considered bourgeois, and to the king and queen who would have nothing to do with his escape plans for them.[10]

'Day' of 10 August 1792

The context of the 'second French Revolution' was the emergency proclaimed on 11 July in the Legislative Assembly that the 'fatherland was in danger' (*la patrie en danger*). The 1792 Festival of Federation in 14 July saw the arrival of **National Guardsmen** from **Marseille**, ignoring the king's veto, to camp around Paris. They had all served since 1790, had *certificats de civisme*, and were, many of them, professed **Jacobins**.[11] **Louis XVI** came to the festival, but it was not like that of 1790.

Brunswick's declaration was known about in Paris on 2 August,[12] and it was suspected that the king had foreknowledge of it, in spite of his criticisms of the *émigrés* in the Army of the Princes. On 3 August, Mayor **Pétion** in the name of the sections petitioned the Assembly for the end of the monarchy and the calling of a **national convention**. The **Girondins** began secret negotiations with the king to preserve his throne. On 6 August, a rally on the Champ de Mars called for the **Legislative** to impeach Lafayette. There was a petition from the sections for the Legislative to depose the king or they would do it themselves. The Legislative refused to impeach Lafayette on 8 August. The sections no longer trusted the Assembly.[13]

On 9 August, 47 of the 48 sections into which the administration of Paris had been divided, dominated by **sansculottes**, sent three representatives each to replace the administrative body at the Hôtel de Ville with the **Insurrectionary Commune**. This new body organized the armed invasion of the **Tuileries** for the following day. The attack began early in the morning. Louis XVI, with **Marie-Antoinette** and the royal children, sought refuge in the Legislative Assembly itself. While they sat in the reporters' box, the monarchy was suspended. Four hundred sansculottes attacking the Tuileries lost their lives, as did many of the Swiss royal guards who were resolutely defending the palace and who had no orders to do otherwise although the king had left it.

The Insurrectionary Commune kept the royal family prisoners in the tower at the Temple, built by the Knights Templar and last owned by the king's brother, **Artois**. The king was put on trial for treason against the Nation, with each deputy having to come to the tribunal for a roll-call vote in person for or against the king's guilt. Louis was executed on 21 January 1793. The Queen followed him to the scaffold after her trial in October, and **Louis XVII** was kept confined in the Temple until his death.

The immediate results of the terrible day were soon seen. The Legislative was freed from the veto on the deportation of the **refractory clergy** (the order for it was given on 26 August). Primary assemblies were to meet to elect a **national convention** by universal suffrage. The patriot ministers returned: **Roland**, **Clavière** and Servan with the addition of **Danton** as justice minister, since he could control the sections. A spin-off was that there were not enough priests left to register births, marriages and deaths in their vestries, so the communes took over what became called the civil state (*état civil*). The declaration of the Republic could wait until the Convention met. The fatherland was still in danger.

📖 Hardman, John, *Louis XVI* (New Haven and London: Yale University Press, 1993). Price, Munro, *The Fall of the French Monarchy: Louis XVI, Marie-Antoinette and the Baron de Breteuil* (London: Macmillan, 2002).

'Day' of 5 September 1793

With **federalist** civil strife increasing, the confusions of government in Paris needed to be resolved. As news was arriving of The British Admiral Hood's taking over **Toulon** in return for a declaration in favour of **Louis XVII**, a new 2 June (when the **sansculottes** helped remove the **Girondins** from the **National Convention**) was being prepared. On 5 September, armed members of the **Paris Sections'** assemblies surrounded the Convention while **Pache** and **Chaumette** made several demands in their name. They wanted a **Revolutionary Army** raised from the sansculottes themselves, organized and armed in military fashion to scour the countryside to find grain and punish hoarders with their portable **guillotine**.[14] They wanted a General **Maximum** on grain and fodder, the arrest of suspects, and the purging of the members of the revolutionary committees. The Convention accepted all these propositions and made **Terror** 'the order of the day' (in **Barère's** words). All through the rest of the month, measures were taken in response to pressure from the sansculottes, setting up the machinery for the Terror and for strict economic control. **Billaud-Varenne** and **Collot d'Herbois**, two known supporters of **Hébert**, were co-opted on to the **Committee of Public Safety**.

But the Convention preserved its own powers. The *enragé* leaders **Roux** and **Varlet** were arrested. The section assemblies wanted to be in perpetual session, but they were limited to two meetings per week (and paid less in the allowances compensating them for loss of work). From then on, the **Insurrectionary Commune**, the sections, the **Cordeliers** and the fraternal clubs would be under the control of the Convention through the **Committee of Public Safety**. 'In the short term, this was the end of pressure from the streets.'[15] The Cordeliers Club, where **Vincent** and the staff of the war ministry were increasingly important, tried again in February and March 1794 to promote another 'day' on the basis of the high price of food and its scarcity. On 4 March, at the Cordeliers, a veil was thrown over the Rights of Man displayed behind the president's chair. Chaumette and Pache did not support the rising so it did not work. The leading Cordeliers were arrested on the night of 13–14 March, and Hébert, Vincent, **Ronsin**, **Momoro** and, later, Chaumette went before the revolutionary tribunal and were executed. The Paris Commune was to be Robespierrist and no more than a post office for the Convention. It was so powerless that, on 27 July 1794, **Hanriot** could do nothing to protect **Robespierre**, **Couthon** and **Saint-Just**. **Barras** and the more prosperous sections called the shots now.[16] The sansculottes had become regarded as 'drinkers of blood (*buveurs de sang*)'.[17]

The machinery for the Terror was finalized in the **Law of 14 frimaire** (4 December 1793), on a motion from Billaud-Varenne. All state bodies and officials, including **representatives on mission**, were responsible to the Committee of Public Safety (Ministers as such would disappear in April 1794) which was from now on to appoint generals and members of the other committees. It was responsible for public order, the conduct of the war, and supplying foodstuffs, horse fodder and war *materiel*. With the *patrie* in danger, this was no time for the separation of powers.

Declaration of the Rights of Man and of the Citizen

The **night of 4 August 1789** at **Versailles** was astonishing. Great noble landowners, alarmed by the spate of destruction of the châteaux belonging to some of them during the days of the **Great Fear**, vied with each other to see how much of their privilege could be abolished. Then the National **Constituent Assembly** took three weeks to embody what had been decided in the form of laws and this Declaration was promulgated 'By Order of the King' on 26 August. Images reproducing its clauses gave it status in the popular mind as if it were replacing the Law of Moses. It certainly reflected the American Declaration of Independence from 4 July 1776, largely written by Thomas Jefferson, who was present in person at Versailles as the official representative of the United States of America. Its fundamental assertion was that men – no mention of women – had been born free and had equal rights, and this cut at the roots of both **absolute monarchy** and seigneurial superiority.

There was to be freedom of speech, of the press, of religion, and to do anything which did not impinge upon the liberty of others. The Declaration established the rule of law and the principle that sovereignty resides in the Nation (i.e. not in any absolute monarch). It asserted Jean-Jacques **Rousseau**'s principle that law is the embodiment of the general will. 'Men are born free and remain free and equal in rights' is a statement about liberty in deliberate contrast with the opening of his *Social Contract* which says that 'men are born free and are everywhere in chains'.

The issues were not clear-cut as the deputies debated what should be put into the declaration in its final form as a preamble to the constitution they were supposed to be drawing up. It takes its place in the rift between 'patriots' and conservatives that was already showing at the early stage in the backlash to the euphoria of the night of 4 August.[18] The deputies from all three orders seemed reluctant to discuss the principles involved, shying away from what they called 'metaphysics'.

That all this was in the air even before it was made law is proved by its tenets being asserted in the **statement of complaint** drawn up by a man who owned a serge-manufacturing business in the south-western town of Jonzac. He was a Protestant merchant-philosopher called Joseph-Augustin Bourrilhon, who had devoured works of the **Enlightenment**, and on whom his Protestant upbringing sat lightly. Although he was in commerce, the greater part of his income came from his investments in the French colonies.[19] That such principles were held so far from the intellectual salons of Paris is fascinating evidence of the genuinely national character of the desire for change and readiness to accept it when it came about.

Sutherland, Donald, *The French Revolution and Empire: The Quest for a Civic Order* (Oxford: Blackwell, 2003), pp. 72–4.

A translation of the text can be found online at:
http://www.historyguide.org/intellect/declaration.html.

Declaration of War, 20 April 1792

Once the deputies in the **Legislative Assembly** had seen that they could act successfully to expel the **refractory clergy**, they turned their attention to the noble *émigrés* serving with the Army of the Princes. On 29 November 1791, they put pressure on the king to demand their expulsion by the Rhineland prince-bishops of Mainz and Trier. **Louis XVI** hoped privately that a rejected ultimatum would bring his brother-in-law Leopold II, who had issued the deceptive **Pillnitz Declaration**, into a war that would rescue him.

An ultimatum was given to the Archbishop-Elector of Trier on 14 December. **Brissot** and the **Girondins** formed a war party in the Legislative Assembly. **Robespierre** opposed them in the **Jacobins**, fearing the outcome to be a military dictatorship under **Lafayette** if the French were victorious, or the dismantling of the Revolution if they were not. **Narbonne** raised an army of 150,000. Several radicals such as **Clootz** joined the war party. Trier and Mainz ordered the *émigrés* out of their territory and, although the cause of war seemed to have been removed, Brissot and his associates still wanted it.

In Vienna, it was thought that a re-run of Pillnitz would succeed, so news reached Paris on 31 December that Leopold was threatening invasion if the French carried out their threats against the prince-bishops. Brissot favoured pre-emptive action, and charged the *émigrés* with treason against the Nation. On 25 January 1792, the Legislative voted their agreement that Leopold, by his arrangements with Prussia and Russia and states in the Empire, had violated the 1756 treaty with France. They demanded that Leopold should renounce all agreements detrimental to France by 1 March 1792.[20] They pressed **Louis XVI** to support this demand, but he already had (in his own way).

On 7 February, Leopold II made a formal pact with Prussia against French aggression. He died on 1 March, leaving the thrones of Hungary and Bohemia to his son, Francis I, not yet chosen by the prince-electors of the Holy Roman Empire as Emperor Francis II. Louis XVI dismissed his ministers on 10 March. Brissot's Girondin nominees replaced them. **Roland** became Interior Minister, **Clavière** took finance and their fellow traveller General **Dumouriez** became foreign minister. 'The court in desperation had also begun seeing war as the only chance of salvation; the country, faced with defeat and foreign invasion, would turn to its king to save it.[21] When the Austrian army mobilized in mid-April, Louis XVI, with the support of all but seven deputies in the Legislative, declared war on Francis as King of Hungary and Bohemia on 20 April.

📖 Blanning, T.C.W., *The Origins of the French Revolutionary Wars* (London and New York: Longman, 1986), chap. 4.

@ The text of the declaration can be found online at:
http://personal.ashland.edu/~jmoser1/declarationofwar.htm.

Desmoulins, Camille (1754–94)

Camille Desmoulins was a precocious journalist aged 26 in 1789. He had been at the Lycée Louis le Grand two years behind Maximilien **Robespierre** who did all he could to protect him from his own indiscretions as events unfurled. He was always called by his first name by those associated with him, suggesting that they did not believe in his maturity.[22] His speech was limited by an acute stutter, yet it was his peroration in the **Palais-Royal** gardens on July 12 that endorsed the popular spirit leading to the storming of the **Bastille** two days later.

Desmoulins's journalistic outlook from then onwards was very incisive, as editor of the *Révolutions de France et de Brabant*. In August 1790, when he was attacked by the Second Estate deputy, Baron Malouet, in the **Constituent Assembly** as an 'incendiary pamphleteer', it was Robespierre who defended him, but there were many others who admired what he wrote. He was a member of the **Cordeliers** and of the **Jacobins**. In September 1790, he spoke the funeral oration in the Jacobins for Elisée Loustalot, a fellow journalist who had exulted in the violent deaths of **Bertier** and **Foulon** on 22 July 1789. When he married Lucille Duplessis, Robespierre was their witness and, in due time, their son's godfather. He gave up his newspaper after the failed republican petition that led to the massacre of the Champ de Mars in July 1791.

When **Brissot** remonstrated with him about his favouring the continuance of gaming houses, Desmoulins accused Brissot of corruption

and advocating republicanism prematurely, and then became an outspoken opponent of all the **Girondins** during the debate that led to the **declaration of war** in April 1792, siding with Robespierre and **Danton** in their objection to it. When the war had started, along with **Fréron** he tried to found another newspaper, *La Tribune des Patriotes*, which produced only four issues in April and May. He also became the target of several cartoons in the royalist press.

After the pronouncement that the fatherland was in danger (*la patrie en danger*), he made a speech before the Paris Commune, '*On the situation of the Capital*', which the Jacobins had printed and circulated. In it he lambasted rich *rentiers*, claiming that they feared the egalitarian **sansculottes** and would welcome the Austrians in preference to the Jacobins. He added that 'one day of anarchy would achieve more than four years of the national assembly …'

Desmoulins took an active part in the **'Day' of 10 August**, and Danton gave him a place with him in the ministry of justice. He saved his old teacher, the Abbé Bérardier, who was in the Abbaye prison, from the **September Massacres**. Under Danton's patronage, he was elected sixth out of the 24 deputies for Paris in the **National Convention**. He left the ministry when Danton did. He was usually silent in the Convention, but spoke out against the Girondin desire for a referendum on the king's execution. Robespierre published his speech. He also produced a furious diatribe against the Girondins in May 1793, accusing them of conspiracy against the republic and demanding that they be 'spewed out of the Convention'.

He pressed for the reorganization of the **Committee of Public Safety**, considering the failure of the Republic to gain supremacy in the **Vendée**. He supported General Dillon, under suspicion of a conspiracy to help the king's family to escape from the Temple. Abandoned by his friends, he said that because he had been denied the right to speak, he would go back to his writing desk. He had been refused the posts on mission that he asked for. When the remaining Girondins were executed in October, he was remorseful. He then attacked Hébertist extremism. In December 1793, he began to attack all the sansculotte leaders, claiming that the **Terror** had violated liberty.[23]

He brought out a newspaper called *Le Vieux Cordelier*, with Robespierre's acquiescence. This extolled the virtues of the Revolution before Terror became a bureaucratic necessity. The third issue hid behind quotations from Tacitus about corruption in ancient Rome to criticize contemporary Terrorist developments as being counter-productive. Robespierre withdrew his protection.[24]

Desmoulins was brought before **Fouquier-Tinville** at the **revolutionary tribunal** and executed along with Danton on 6 April 1794 for his 'indulgent' views towards the enemies of the Republic. He was one of the few victims of the guillotine who went to his end breaking down in tears. His wife was arraigned for association with General Dillon in a conspiracy in prison. She was executed a week after Camille.

📖 Mantel, Hilary, *A Place of Greater Safety* (London: Penguin, 1993). Novel.

Palmer, R.R., *Twelve Who Ruled: The Year of the Terror in the French Revolution* (University Park, PA: Princeton University Press, Bicentennial Edition, 1989). Online at: http://www.nndb.com/people/480/000097189/

Diamond Necklace Affair (1784–6)

Napoleon saw this incident and the resultant legal process as the beginning of the French Revolution since it brought discredit to the monarchy and the church in France in equal measure, and the fervent republican Jules **Michelet** gave it two chapters in the final volume of his 1866 *History of France*.[25]

The queen was innocently implicated in a dubious transaction[26] which intensified her reputation for extravagance at a time when the national deficit of 112 million livres was becoming public knowledge for the first time. The court jewellers had made a *rivière* of diamonds worth 1.6 million livres in hopes that Louis XV would buy it for Madame du Barry. The jewellers still had it and tried to sell it to **Marie-Antoinette**, who had learnt by the 1780s that she must curb her lavish spending and in any case disliked its blowsy style.

Cardinal de Rohan, Archbishop of Strasbourg and the king's Grand Almoner, became the current focus for popular conviction that the Church was decadent. The cardinal wanted to return to the queen's favour which he had forfeited after his hapless tenure of the French Embassy in Vienna. An adventuress called Jeanne de La Motte, who knew Rohan to be gullible, paid an 'actress' from the **Palais-Royal** to impersonate the queen in a secret meeting with Rohan in a **Versailles** garden by night. What the actress was told to say convinced Rohan that the queen would buy the necklace indirectly if he and two others were to pay for it first. Jeanne de La Motte obtained the necklace but, before it could be given to the queen, it was broken up and spirited away to London for sale. Soon afterwards, La Motte was living in some opulence at Bar-le-Duc in Burgundy.

The jewellers presented their bill to Marie-Antoinette, provoking additional scandal in Paris, where it was known that the king had already handed over 15 million livres to buy the palace of Saint-Cloud from the Duc d'**Orléans** for her. The king agreed 'with amazing ineptitude' to place Rohan under gilded arrest in the care of the governor of the **Bastille**, 'thus allowing the affair to gain maximum publicity'.[27] At his trial before the magistrates of the Paris *Parlement*, Rohan was acquitted by 26 votes to 23, which was a humiliation for the king.

Although exiled from Versailles to his distant abbey of Chaise-Dieu in the Auvergne, the cardinal was fêted by anti-monarchical citizens in the capital before he left.

 Hardman, John, *Louis XVI* (New Haven and London: Yale University Press, 1993).

Directory (1795–9) – Constitution of Year III

After the **Germinal Rising** of 1 and 2 April 1795, the so-called **Thermidorean Convention** appointed a commission of eleven made up of moderate republicans and constitutional royalists to devise the Constitution of Year III, aiming for a stable new form of government to provide effective leadership in the war. Prussia and Spain had made peace by July 1795 in the **Treaties of Basle**, but peace negotiations with Great Britain were to fail and Austrian hostility remained. Nevertheless, while all sorts of people were beginning to murmur that things were better under the king, the methods of **Terror** had been dismantled and suspects released from the prisons. The commission of eleven was obsessed with the need to prevent a dictatorship of any kind.[28]

Under the new constitution there were to be five Directors acting collectively as executive heads of state, one being replaced every year. Lots would be drawn each year to decide which one would leave.[29] Jacques-Louis **David** designed impressively bizarre costumes for them, and the **Luxembourg Palace**, no longer required as a prison, was turned into separate apartments for each of them. They were to have a guard of honour. Despite all the trappings of collective power, however, they were allowed no right to suspend laws and no initiative in making them. Their authority consisted in supplementing laws with regulations, having surveillance over local government, and appointing general officers, diplomats, taxation officials, colonial administrators, and police chiefs. The period 1795 to 1799 is usually considered as divided between the First Directory, from 2 November 1795 until the anti-royalist **Fructidor** *coup d'état* on 4 September 1797, and the Second, from then on until the **Brumaire** *coup d'état* which brought **Bonaparte** to power as First Consul on 9 to 10 November 1799.

The legislative was to be in the form of two elected councils. There was one 'of Five Hundred', in which the deputies were to be at least 30 years old, and another 'of Elders (*Anciens*)', who were to be at least 40 and either married men or widowers (more costumes from J.-L. David). This was something like the bi-cameral legislature the *monarchiens* had wanted in 1791. The Elders were to meet in the *Salle des Machines* in the Tuileries Palace, and the 500 in the old riding school (*Manège*). The two chambers would serve as a republican form of the former royal veto. To enforce lengthier consideration of laws, three successive readings at least ten days apart from each other were thought necessary. A supplementary law said that two-thirds of the members of the Councils would be from the existing **National Convention**, which paid respect to deputies' experience, as was not done in 1791. Subsequently, a third of both councils would be replaced each year. The Directors were to be elected by the Elders after nomination by the 500. They could not be criticized by the Councils, and they would not be able to attend meetings of either assembly nor to order their dissolution.

Universal male suffrage (even though it was a two-stage process), which had elected the National Convention in 1792, was abandoned. The new electorate of 1795 comprised only 6 million '**active citizens**' out of a total population of 28 million. They, in turn, elected the 30,000 higher tax-paying citizens who chose the members of the two councils. In the national referendum to endorse this constitution, 941,853 were in favour, 41,892 against, but most of the rest abstained. The National Convention under Jacobin control had abolished ministries to give the **Committee of Public Safety** overall control of government machinery in April 1794, and the Directory's constitution re-established them. **Talleyrand**, back in France from the United States, was chosen as foreign minister.

Rather than 'men are born free and of equal rights' as was said in 1789, the preamble of the new constitution asserted that 'equality consists in having one law for all' in order to maintain a man's 'right to enjoy and dispose of his property, income, and the fruit of his labour'. A property qualification became a condition of Liberty and Equality. The French historian Michel Pertué asserted in 1989[30] that the Directory was a revolutionary government in appearance, but it did not have enough of a social basis to allow it any permanence, nor was it supple enough to allow for any self-transformation.

Several generals were operating almost independently, and it was feared that any one of them might seize power and establish a military dictatorship. Bonaparte emerged under the protection of the former Vicomte de **Barras**, the only one of the Directors who was to be in office permanently. Barras, who owed his position to Bonaparte's military defeat of the royalist challenge in the **Vendémiaire** *coup d'état*, chose him as the commander of the Army of Italy, and when he had won a series of spectacular victories he demonstrated political *savoir-faire* before proposing his **Egyptian expedition** in 1798. As soon as Bonaparte had left France, it was seen that the Directory was, after all, a very inadequate instrument for command of total war. Talleyrand, **Sieyès** and **Fouché** decided to end the Directory by plotting to bring a general to power by the **Brumaire** *coup d'état*.

Neely, Sylvia, *A Concise History of the French Revolution* (Lanham, MD and Plymouth: Rowman & Littlefield, 2008), pp. 236–48.

@ The text of the 1795 constitution can be found online at: http://chnm.gmu.edu/revolution/d/450/.

Dubois-Crancé, Edmond Louis Alexis (1747–1814)

Dubois-Crancé was a soldier during the old regime and brought his military skills to the service of the Revolution, uniting them with his leftist politics.

He was a **Third Estate** deputy in the **Estates-General** in 1789, and was elected secretary of the **Jacobin Club**. As early as December 1790, he urged conscription as the best means of providing an **army** for the Nation: 'I maintain as a principle that in France each citizen ought to be a soldier and each soldier ought to be a citizen, or we shall never have a constitution.'[31] His suggestion was rejected in favour of volunteers and, besides, the **Constituent Assembly** had committed itself to peace. Because he was not eligible for the **Legislative Assembly**, he returned to the army and became an adjutant-general. His interest in politics remained and he was elected for three departments in the **National Convention**, choosing to be a deputy for the Ardennes. He was **representative on mission** with the Army of the Midi. He voted for the king's execution.

Soon after the king's execution, he served his fortnight as president of the Convention, and brought in the *Amalgame* Law on 21 February. By means of this, the volunteer soldiers were to be amalgamated with the regulars from before the Revolution. The volunteers would no longer be controlled by their home departments, but were integrated into the national force. The Convention did not enforce this law immediately, but it was the first step towards an institutional recasting of the army of the republic.[32] In March 1793, Dubois-Crancé was elected to the new Committee of General Defence, which was the precursor of the **Committee of Public Safety** set up in April. His principle of conscription was implemented in the mass mobilization (*levée en masse*) decreed on 23 August 1793.

Barère did not trust Dubois-Crancé and had him made representative on mission to Kellermann's Army of the Alps. This brought him into combat with the insurrection in **Lyon**. **Couthon** and other Jacobins accused him of treating the Republic's enemies indulgently. The Committee of Public Safety ordered his arrest on 12 October 1793. He was cleared of the charge in only a week. He returned to his place on the war committee, and then he was in charge of the *amalgame* in the Army of the West. The ceremonies of amalgamation, over which he presided, had a religious quality, bonding the former royal soldiers, the volunteers, the conscripts and the civilian population together. In conflict with the **Chouans**, he was present at every battle: at Nantes in February 1794, at Rennes in March and at Brest in June.

Back in Paris he faced accusations from Barère and **Robespierre** of being a counter-revolutionary. He responded and the arranged debate was postponed until 10 thermidor (28 July), but the agenda became crowded. He was a **Thermidorean** in outlook, and served on the war committee again, dealing with further amalgamations, and then alongside **Carnot** on the Committee of Public Safety.

Dubois-Crancé became a member of the Council of 500 under the Directory, and was Inspector of the Army of the Rhine. As Minister of War for several weeks before **Bonaparte's Brumaire coup**, he undertook the setting-up of light infantry units. He served neither in the Consulate nor the Empire. [33]

Dugué, Perrine (1777–96)

Perrine Dugué was called 'the saint with tricolour wings'. She became a republican martyr in an area of the Mayenne department where there were republican villages and hamlets surrounded with countryside dominated by **Chouans**. She lived near Thorigné-en-Charnie with her parents, two brothers and a sister, in constant danger. Chouans joined with the **Vendéans** as they crossed the Loire and went to Granville in 1793, and then came back to live off the country. The republican communities protected themselves against their incursions, backed up by General **Westermann**'s troops. Another village to the north of Thorigné, Saint-Suzanne, mounted a reprisal against them, and the Dugué brothers were in the fighting. This situation persisted for years. Perrine, aged 17, was herself a fervent republican, and had been subject to Chouan threats, which she ignored.

On 22 March 1796, Perrine wanted to go to Saint-Suzanne market with her neighbours. She shrugged off parental objections and set out. Three Chouans stopped her on the way, frightened her companions off, abused and tortured her, and left her tied to a tree to die. There was no pursuit of her assailants because the republican authorities could not make the laws respected. Her reputation as a republican martyr soon spread in the neighbouring departments. Her mother put a box by her grave under the tree where she was found, and 'pilgrims' came there and filled it with money offerings. People claimed that miracles of healing were available there.

On 6 thermidor, year V (the Dugués would have used the revolutionary calendar for 25 July 1797), Perrine's relations were summoned to the civil tribunal of the Mayenne to account for the offerings which had been meant for the poor. The situation was saved by Citizen Dagoreau, who gave some of his land for a chapel to be built for 'Saint Perrine'. When it had been built, Perrine's body was transferred there at night for fear of the Chouans, and buried before the altar. The Chapel was filled with patriotic emblems and tricolour flags, but there were also rosaries and *ex voto* plaques. Perrine had become one of 'the guardian geniuses of the people', in **Saint-Just**'s phrase. She was 'a martyr for Liberty'. Here was traditional religion in republican guise, despite the fact that the republicans' deadly enemies were Catholic royalists.[34]

Dumouriez, Charles-François du Périer (1739–1823)

Dumouriez was well established as a soldier and diplomat before the Revolution, welcomed it when it came, associated himself with the **Girondins** and then defected to the allies, remaining in support of French constitutional royalists for the rest of his life.

He was educated at the Lycée Louis-le-Grand, then served in the Seven Years War, retiring as a captain with the Order of Saint-Louis. In the army again soon as a lieutenant-colonel, he joined Louis XV's secret service. In 1770, he organized Polish militia against the Russians, but on his return he was imprisoned in the **Bastille** because he had criticized the court in his letters. He was not freed until the accession of **Louis XVI**, who appointed him commandant at Cherbourg for 10 years. According to one of his pre-revolutionary contemporaries, the war minister Montbarey, Dumouriez was good at intrigue, and 'not motivated by anything beyond his own interests or of those to whom he was attached at the moment'.[35]

He was in the entourage of **Lafayette** at the start of the Revolution. He actually received a **certificate of civism** from **Robespierre**, but he was closer to the Girondins. During his brief time as foreign minister, in March 1792, he tried to drive a wedge between the Austrians and Prussians before the war began. He returned to his military rank in June and was commanding the Army of the Centre by 20 September for the battle of **Valmy**, where **Westermann**'s artillery triumphed, and then was victorious himself at **Jemappes** on 6 November. He occupied **Belgium** and was preparing an attack on Holland. Back in Paris in January 1793, he was criticized by the **Jacobins** when he tried to save Louis XVI from execution, yet castigated the **Convention** for not supplying his army well enough for their advance.

When the Austrians counter-attacked successfully at Neerwinden on 18 March 1793, Dumouriez began negotiations with them, and they agreed to turn their backs while he tried to lead a march on Paris to overthrow the Jacobins and re-establish the monarchy in the person of young **Louis XVII**, for whom he was to propose himself as regent. The Convention, warned of this, sent General Beurnonville, the war minister, to stop him. Dumouriez arrested him and handed him over to the Austrians. The republican citizen army, however, would not follow Dumouriez to Paris, so he, the Duc de Chartres (the future King Louis-Philippe) and the Duc de Montpensier went over to the Austrians on 5 April, only to be imprisoned for a long while. After that, he worked for the royalists in the German states and Russia and settled in England in 1804, secretly advising the British against Napoleon. He remained closely associated with the Duc d'**Orléans**'s family (Chartres inherited the title at his father's execution), and wrote the inscription for the Duc de Montpensier's tomb in Westminster Abbey. He therefore received no recognition from Louis XVIII at the **Restoration**, and died in England.

Duplay, Maurice (1736–1820), and his Jacobin Family

Maurice Duplay was an **active citizen** in the Pikes Section of Paris and a member of the **Jacobin Club**.[36]

Robespierre lodged in Duplay's rented house, 366, rue Saint-Honoré, from 1791 until his death in the **Thermidor coup**, and was treated as an honoured member of his family. Duplay had a prosperous furniture business and was comfortably off from the profits of his business and the rents from the property he owned, though he called himself a cabinet-maker (*menuisier*) as was typical of those who lowered their own social standing to be considered **sansculottes**. (Antoine **Santerre**, the brewer who employed large numbers, was another.) In 1795, he was able to buy his house for over 30,000 francs. It had been part of a former convent, previously sold to someone else as **national property**. Duplay was appointed a juror in the Parisian revolutionary tribunal.

The day after Robespierre went to the scaffold, the whole Duplay family was arrested. Madame Duplay died in prison – perhaps a suicide. Maurice was put on trial along with **Fouquier-Tinville**, but was set free on 17 floréal, year III (6 April 1795). Through association in prison with **Buonarotti**, Duplay was accused as a member of **Babeuf**'s Conspiracy of Equals, but he and his son were acquitted at their trial held at Vendôme in May 1796.

Duplay's strong-minded eldest daughter, Eléonore, was Robespierre's close friend. She was also in prison for a time after Thermidor. She wore mourning for him, and was called 'the widow Robespierre'. Another of Duplay's daughters, Elisabeth, married Robespierre's friend Philippe **Le Bas**, who was a member of the **Committee of General Security** and who also died in the **Thermidor coup**.

The son of the family, Jacques-Maurice, had gone to the armies of the Rhine and Moselle with Le Bas on mission. In the Consulate, he became editor of the newspaper called *L'Indiscret*, and then administered hospices. His cousin, Simon Duplay, had lost a leg at the battle of **Valmy**, after which he worked as a clerk in the *gendarmerie* and then the **Committee of Public Safety**. He was arrested for protesting at the Jacobins about his uncle's arrest. He too went to the Plessis prison, and met associates of Babeuf. On his release he founded a short-lived radical newspaper called *L'éclaireur du peuple*, but soon returned to clerical work at the police office.

Duport, Adrien (1759–98)

Before the Revolution, Duport was an ennobled member of the ***parlement*** of Paris where his legal expertise and opposition to the king's ministers were well known. He was also a **Freemason**, and an enthusiast for the 'animal magnetism' then being popularized by Anton Mesmer. His fellow nobles elected him a Second Estate deputy to the **Estates-General**. He was one of the 46 nobles who joined with the **Third Estate** on their own initiative on 25 June 1789, before the king 'invited' the rest of the **clergy** and the **nobility** to do so.[37]

Duport already had a reputation for a brilliant understanding of the law and was conspicuous in creating the new legal system for the Nation. Together with Antoine **Barnave** and Alexander de **Lameth** (another noble), he formed what became known as the 'triumvirate' that led the patriot group in the **Constituent Assembly**. They were members of the **Jacobin Club**, but also moderates who aimed at bringing the Revolution to a conclusion after what had already been achieved by early 1791. The basis of their participation in the new developments had been respect for the monarchy, in a constitutional rather than an absolute form, and for private property. The king accepted them as his privy counsellors. After his flight to **Varennes**, they took a great number of Jacobins with them to form the **Feuillant Club**. Duport was very much in favour of the fiction that **counter-revolutionaries** had abducted the king when he had set out for the eastern border to make himself independent of the Assembly.

Duport had nothing more to offer after the overthrow of the monarchy and moved to England. He returned to France after **Thermidor** but, when General Augerau had excluded moderates and royalists from the councils in the **Fructidor coup** in September 1797, he left for Switzerland, where he died a year later.

E

Egyptian Expedition

While he was in Italy in 1796, **Bonaparte** thought of a way of disrupting British trade by invading Egypt and making travel to India via the Cape route difficult, menacing it from the Gulf of Suez. This idea was confirmed in his mind when, back in France, he was put in charge of an army at Boulogne to invade England. He saw all the difficulties of transporting sufficient troops across the English Channel. **Talleyrand**, the **Directory's** foreign minister from July 1797, had come to similar conclusions, and the Directory accepted the invasion of Egypt under Bonaparte's command on 5 March. From their point of view it would rid them of Bonaparte's irritatingly challenging presence. His expedition left **Toulon** on 19 May and took Malta on 12 June. On 2 July, Alexandria was taken, and the Mameluke army was defeated at the Battle of the Pyramids on 21 July. Three days later, Bonaparte was in Cairo.

Talleyrand had not expected Great Britain to become hyperactive so soon after the naval mutinies at Spithead and at the Nore in April and June or the financial crisis that had erupted. Pitt's cabinet decided to restore the Royal Navy's presence in the Mediterranean at this same time, thinking that the preparations in Toulon were for a repetition of **Hoche's** expedition to support the Irish. This decision explains Nelson's search along the length of the Mediterranean and his destruction of the French fleet at Aboukir Bay on 1 August.

The Ottoman Empire had been receiving the help of French military experts and, in return, had provided the Republic with war *matériel*.

When Bonaparte took the Ionian Islands, after the partition of Venetian territory at **Campo Formio**, this had changed. After Aboukir Bay the Turks accepted the help of Tsar Paul I of Russia, whose Black Sea fleet reached Constantinople on 4 September.

Bonaparte moved his operations to Palestine on the way to Syria. This achieved little apart from enhancing his personal reputation – for intransigence when he had 3,000 prisoners massacred at Jaffa, and for personal bravery when he went into the plague hospital there. His siege of Acre was frustrated by Captain Sidney Smith's actions off the coast and the advance of a Turkish army from Damascus. His only success was at Mount Tabor. On the way back to Cairo he approved euthanasia for his wounded troops and, once there, had a masquerade triumph. Only Desaix had any military success and that was in Upper Egypt. On 26 May 1799, the Directory had authorized Bonaparte to return, with or without his army, and he embarked with a select few, leaving Kléber (who was assassinated after a year) to explain his departure to the soldiers.

Nevertheless, the presence of the French in Egypt had some positive results. A hospital service was created. Street cleaning was undertaken, cemeteries were provided outside towns, Nile navigation was improved, and a canal system begun. There were windmills and better bakeries. Tribunals were set up for commerce between the various cultures in the country. For France the important result was intellectual. Gaspard **Monge** set up an institute for savants modelled on the Parisian one. A printing works was provided.

The *Description de l'Egypte*, published between 1809 and 1823 by Monge, Berthollet and others, ran to 23 volumes. Archaeology was greatly furthered and Champollion found the Rosetta Stone, which enabled hieroglyphics to be translated later on.[1]

The British sent General Abercrombie to retake Egypt. He landed at Aboukir Bay in March 1801. The remains of the French army, after their surrender, arrived back in France in 1803 after the Peace of Amiens.

Schom, Alan, *Napoleon Bonaparte* (New York: HarperCollins, 1997), chaps 7–11.

Elbée, Maurice-Joseph-Louis Gigot d' (1752–94)

D'Elbée was a French officer in the King of Poland's army like his father, until the family moved back to France and he served in a French cavalry regiment until 1783. Then he retired to live on his Angevin estate at Beaupréau as a *hobereaux* noble.

At the outset of the Revolution, he was with the constitutional monarchists but, when the constitutional Bishop of Angers was elected in spring of 1791, d'Elbée protested against his name being falsely recorded as having voted for him. He left France in November and joined the *émigrés* in the Army of the Princes, but found the high status aristocrats there difficult to get on with, and returned home after less than six months.

Suppressing his doubts about the viability of the insurrection in the **Vendée** and its timing, d'Elbée accepted the request of his neighbours to lead them in it on 14 March 1793. He was wounded at Fontenay, but rejoined the Catholic and Royal Army at Saumur in June, where he supported the choice of **Cathelineau** as commander-in-chief. He besieged Nantes with him until his death. Then, on 19 July, the other officers chose him as overall commander at Chatillon-sur-Sèvre, causing jealousy among higher-ranking nobles. He won in engagements at Coron and Beaulieu. He lost two engagements at Luçon in July and August, but he took Chantonnay and Torfou in September. He suffered serious wounds at the battle of **Cholet** on 17 October 1793. His friends took him to the Isle of Noirmoutier which **Charette** had taken. General Turreau captured him there on 4 January 1794. He was condemned to death by a military tribunal and carried to his execution in a chair two days afterwards.[2]

Emigrés

Between July 1789 and the end of the **Directory**, French men and women emigrated from France in wave after wave, for different reasons and in response to different stimuli. **Artois** (the future Charles X), together with Condé, the Polignac and Rohan clans, the Contis and the Duc de Bourbon, made their 'joyous' emigration on 17 July 1789, three days after the fall of the **Bastille**. After the market women had brought the royal family to Paris from **Versailles** on 7 October, there was the 'timorous' emigration, composed of more nobles, some bishops and many office holders. The pace of departure was speeded up by the 1790 decrees abolishing noble titles, confiscating church lands, and enforcing the **Civil Constitution of the Clergy**.

The Comte de **Provence** (the future Louis XVIII) left France on the evening the king began his flight to **Varennes**. Many noble army officers left France at the end of the **Constituent Assembly** of which they had been members. There was an additional stimulus for them to leave because, after the flight to Varennes, they were required to take a new loyal oath, no longer to the king, but to the Nation, and many refused to do so. They joined the Army of the Princes at Koblenz or at Wörms, intending to return under arms and overcome the Revolution.

The Constituent took some action against the *émigrés* in December 1790, but not until after Varennes was any real attempt made to stop emigration and make it a crime. The **Legislative**, on 9 November 1791, decreed the death penalty for those who did not return by the end of the year. Not many complied. Just before war was declared on Austria in April 1792, there was another wave of emigration. After **Valmy**, the Army of the Princes disintegrated and many nobles returned.[3] Then, on 28 March 1793, the **Convention** declared the *émigrés* to be traitors to the Nation in time of war, confiscated their lands and forbade them to return to France. On 17 September, their relations were declared to be suspects and the municipalities were ordered to record all long absences.

A new wave of departures followed the beginning of the **Terror** in autumn 1793, but this time it was mostly the **bourgeoisie** and **peasantry**[4] who left, fearing reprisals wherever they had taken part in 'federalist' revolts at **Lyon**, Bordeaux, **Marseille** or **Toulon**.

The year 1792 saw the emigration of the **refractory clergy** when the king's veto could no longer protect them. If they did not leave voluntarily, they were to be deported, though many were 'disappeared' on the hulks of **Rochefort** or ships from Bordeaux. Those who went voluntarily found a precarious existence in Spain, in England and the Channel Islands (whence many made their way back secretly into the **Vendée**). George III made them personally welcome and put the Palace at Winchester at their disposal.

After **Thermidor**, the outward flow of *émigrés* slowed down drastically, though the Directory maintained the death threat. Three thousand military nobles who had chosen exile in England were landed on the **Quiberon** peninsula by the Royal Navy in 1795 but were caught and 759 of them massacred by General Hoche. There was, however, a clandestine return under the **Thermidorean Convention**, and a decree of 30 nivôse year IV (20 January 1796) allowed *émigrés* to apply for their names to be removed from the official list. The 'Ultra-royalists' disapproved, but an increasing number did come back.

After **Brumaire**, First Consul Bonaparte encouraged the nobles to return, and the Concordat with Pope Pius VII brought back the surviving clergy. The First Consul issued a general amnesty on 6 floréal, year X (26 April 1802). Only a minority, who had 'learned nothing and forgotten nothing' since 1789, as **Talleyrand** is supposed to have remarked, waited for Louis XVIII's restoration to the throne in 1814. The fortunes of the *émigrés* as a whole were to some extent restored by the *milliard des émigrés* offered to individuals by adjusting payments to *rentiers* down from 5 per cent to 3 per cent organized by Charles X's Prime Minister Villèle in 1825.[5]

Enlightenment

In the middle years of the eighteenth century, the writers and scientists who came collectively to be labelled *lumières* or *philosophes* produced works that cast doubt on many established values. Things that had been taken for granted were called in question, and the tool of all enquiring was to be human reason. Rationality was to be the standard by which all truth was to be established. There was John Locke in England, David Hume in Scotland, and Denis Diderot and Jean d'Alembert in France.

In France, the main manifestation of the Enlightenment was the *Encyclopédie*. D'Alembert wrote the Preliminary Discourse to it (he was co-editor of its many articles by different authors along with Diderot) to assert that René Descartes had freed the human mind for enquiry, but that a realistic appraisal of how things really are came from John Locke and Isaac Newton. **Voltaire** had popularized Newton in France in a book published in 1738. Rules or laws tested by experiment were to be the basis for understanding universal reality and so the Enlightenment gave people liberty to think for themselves. Morality was to be based on civic values. It need not come through the teaching of the Church or be based upon revealed religion. A divine right monarchy could never match with these ideas, and a divine right monarch found it impossible, when all was said and done, to compromise the institution he embodied and had sworn at his coronation to support.

The Encyclopaedists were a diverse collection of essayists, and William Doyle has warned us not to attribute too much 'intellectual symmetry' to their thought. Even so, he points out that they show 'a certain logical self consistency' inasmuch as they all appeared to go against the teaching of established churches (in France, the Catholic Church) and the practices they enforced. The clergy's claim for authority over faith and morality based on revealed religion was being challenged by the *philosophes*, and this was bound to carry matters beyond what was solely a matter of thought. 'The clergy enjoyed temporal power. If Enlightenment were to progress further, sooner or later 'philosophy' would have to turn its attention to practical politics.'[6]

Its practical effect must not be magnified. Deputies in the **Constituent** did not become involved in the 'superfluous issue of abstract metaphysics', as one of them wrote while the **Declaration of the Rights of Man and of the Citizen** was being debated.[7] The reading public was increasing in size, but books by Enlightenment writers had by no means captured a popular market. Donald Sutherland tells us that by far the most frequently purchased book was *The Guiding Angel*, a book of religious devotions. Popular reading, even taking increased literacy into account, remained concerned with marvels, fantasy and the supernatural.[8]

Estates-General

France was faced with a national deficit declared in 1786 to be 112 million livres (£2,464,000 sterling at the contemporary exchange rate), largely caused by the cost of warfare against Great Britain. **Louis XVI** and successive ministers adopted several expedients for regenerating the nation's wealth. When all these had failed, in July 1788, the king agreed to call the Estates-General, a body that had last met in 1614 under the regency for Louis XIII.[9] This consisted of 300 deputies elected from each of the three orders or estates of the nation separately: the **Clergy**, the **Nobility** (called 'aristocrats' pejoratively after the **Terror** began) and the **Third Estate**, which included everybody else from rich merchants to tenant farmers alike. All priests and representative monks voted in each assembly of the *sénéchaussées* and *bailliages*. So did all the nobility. All males in the Third Estate over 21, with their names on a tax register, could vote for a representative in their administrative district assembly. Each estate met separately to vote for their deputies. It was decided, in advance of the meeting called for May 1789 at **Versailles**, that the number of deputies of the Third Estate should be doubled ('doubling the third') so that they would not be out-voted automatically by the clergy and nobility acting together. It was left to be decided after the sessions opened whether the three estates should vote as separate bodies or as one. This issue was not decided for seven weeks, and no business of any importance was done in that time. The only decision made was that the thirds would be calling themselves the Commons (*communes*) from 6 May onwards until further changes. The king and queen were grieving for the dauphin who was ill at nearby Meudon, and died just when decisions became urgent. The thirds maintained their refusal to validate their credentials on their own without the clergy and the nobles.

📖 Tackett, Timothy, *Becoming a Revolutionary* (University Park, PA: Princeton University Press, 2006), Pt 1.

F

Fabre d'Eglantine, Philippe-François-Nazaire (1750–94)
Fabre d'Eglantine is most remembered for his work on the embellishment of the originally stark **Revolutionary Calendar**.

Before the Revolution, Fabre wrote plays and acted and brought his artistic abilities with him when he became a politician. He added '*Eglantine*' (dog rose) to his surname after winning a silver award shaped as such at a festival in Toulouse. He came to act in Paris after touring in the provinces in 1787. His mediocre plays had a revolutionary appeal with evil nobles and patriotic heroes.

When the time came, he joined both the **Jacobins** and the **Cordeliers**, acting as private secretary to **Danton**. He was elected to the **National Convention**, and voted for the king's death, for the **Maximum** and for the exclusion of the **Girondins**. When Gilbert **Romme**'s Committee had finished the Revolutionary Calendar and presented it to the Convention, Fabre gave the months names based on the seasons – they had been known only by ordinal numbers at first.

In November 1793, **Chabot** denounced Fabre to **Robespierre** for peculation in the **Company of the Indies** stock. The plot involved foreigners, which made it worse in Jacobin eyes. There was the Belgian Proli, who had been associated with **Hérault de Séchelles**, a Portuguese Jew called Pereira, a Spaniard called Guizman, and perhaps a few Englishmen, not to mention the Prussian baron 'Anarcharsis' **Clootz**. The suspicion festered until Fabre was arrested and condemned to death along with the Dantonists on 5 April 1794,[1] complaining to **Danton** in the tumbrel that he had been ill-treated.

Faubourg de Saint-Antoine

This eastern suburb of Paris was the centre for a great deal of **sansculotte** agitation for the first half of the revolutionary decade. Many craftsmen in the luxury trades, such as cabinet-makers, worked there. It was also the home of enterprises such as **Réveillon**'s wallpaper factory, and the brewery owned by Antoine-Joseph **Santerre**, who took the part of his workers and became a sansculotte **National Guard** general.

Above it until 1789 were the towers of the **Bastille**, the symbol of the tyrannical aspects of **absolute monarchy**, dismantled by another sansculotte entrepreneur, **Palloy**. Charles Dickens gave the suburb a revolutionary personality of its own, centred on the poor people's wine-shop run by M. and Mme Lafarge. *A Tale of Two Cities* contains a very shrewd understanding of social tension there.

Favras, Thomas de Mahy, Marquis de (1744–90)

As soon as **Louis XVI** was lodged in the **Tuileries** in **October 1789**, several plans to spirit him away to restore his independence were floated and his replies to the question of whether he would co-operate in them were ambiguous. The Comte de **Provence** was living in the **Luxembourg Palace** across the Seine, and one of these schemes is associated with him. He proposed that the king should be abducted by an armed force but was careful not to be personally involved. He made tortuous plans to finance the ambitious adventure. He gave orders to an officer in his entourage, Thomas de Mahy de Favras, a knight of the military order of Saint-Louis, who called himself a marquis so as to be more impressive in the eyes of the German princess to whom he was married. Favras was to arrange a loan of 2 million livres from a bank on the pretext of settling Provence's outstanding debts. The king would be abducted from Paris by armed troops and kept at Peronne, east of Amiens. If the plan succeeded, then Provence could be the regent of France or, if the king were dethroned, he could be king in his place, by-passing the Dauphin Louis-Charles.

Favras talked indiscreetly, and was denounced to **Lafayette** who had him followed and arrested, with his wife, on Christmas Eve 1789. A mysterious figure called 'Barrauz' said that Favras had a letter which revealed a plan to assassinate **Necker**, Lafayette and Mayor **Bailly** and starve the city of supplies (a familiar fear by now). This assertion was circulated in a printed pamphlet at Lafayette's expense so as to alarm Provence and give a warning to anyone else who might be contemplating the abduction of the king. Provence was, indeed, alarmed and decided to go the Hôtel de Ville to confirm that he had told Favras to raise the loan, but to deny any knowledge of assassination plots. **Mirabeau** said that he had added an assertion of his faith in Louis XVI as leader of the Revolution for public consumption.

Favras was put on trial in public. He confessed to the abduction design (but not to the alleged assassination plans), and was hanged (no guillotine yet) on the evening of 18 February 1790 in the place de Grève outside the Hôtel de Ville in the first lawful execution of the Revolution, as opposed to the previous lynchings. A hostile crowd was present. Favras did not implicate Provence. The king and queen were appalled, and Louis XVI had 30,000 livres paid in compensation to Madame Favras through his civil list treasurer. After 1815, Provence (by then Louis XVIII) told his minister de Blacas that he should neither have listened to Favras's plans, nor disavowed him. This might suggest that Favras had planned the abduction himself, and Provence had hoped to benefit from it, rather than having taken the initiative himself.[2]

Mansel, Philip, *Louis XVIII* (London: John Murray, 2005), pp. 48–51.

Federalism/Federalist(s)

When the Revolution began, regionalism was set deep in the French experience, since the monarchy had acquired territory piece by piece over centuries – Provence in 1486, Brittany in 1532, Lorraine in 1766 – but the pope's enclave in Comtat-Venaissin was not incorporated until after the Revolution had begun. Languages – Breton, Provençal and German – were still distinct and opposed by such revolutionaries as Henri **Grégoire**.

The **Mountain** and the **Insurrectionary Commune** gained control of the **National Convention** by expelling the **Girondins** – who were opposed to their centralizing policy – and pursuing them to their deaths. Several provincial centres had thrown over the 'one and indivisible' version of the republic for a federalist one even before that. The **Vendée** was already in revolt, and then Bordeaux, **Lyon**, **Marseille** and **Toulon** declared for independence from Parisian control, imprisoning their local Jacobins and setting up their own administrations. In Toulon, they admitted Lord Hood's Anglo-Spanish fleet and declared for **Louis XVII**. Federalist centres even raised armies with the intention of marching on Paris. A little force from Bordeaux set off in the wrong direction and disintegrated at Langon. A larger force of 3,500 was raised in Marseille, took **Avignon**, and marched up the Rhône to join a supposed force from Lyon, but General Carteaux moved from **Grenoble** to disperse them before taking Marseille itself.

Representatives on mission were sent from the Convention to suppress these uprisings, usually with a measure of brutality: **Couthon**, then **Fouché** and **Collot d'Herbois** in Lyon, **Barras** and **Fréron** in **Marseille** and **Toulon**, **Tallien** in Bordeaux. **Bernard de Saintes** took pre-emptive measures against possible federalists in Vesoul, Besançon and Dijon. At the end of the **Thermidorean Convention**, many of these excesses were covered by an amnesty. By the time the **Directory** was in being, federalism was no longer an issue, and was replaced by outbreaks of 'White Terror'.

Fédérés

These *fédérés* are not to be confused with **Federalists** who objected to the increased power of Paris politicians. *Fédérés* were the volunteers who came to Paris in August 1792 to join forces against the invading force of Austrians, Prussians and French *émigrés*. **Louis XVI** wanted to use his suspensive veto to prevent them camping just outside Paris. The group from **Marseille** arrived singing Captain Rouget de Lisle's new **song** for the Army of the Rhine, renamed as *La Marseillaise*.

Verdun and Longwy had fallen to the invaders, and their commander, the Duke of **Brunswick**, had issued his declaration that Paris would suffer devastation if the king and queen of France were harmed in any way. This had the opposite effect from Brunswick's intention upon the *fédérés*. The soldiers were more afraid of the opponents of the Revolution, who had been arrested and were in all the Paris prisons and the religious buildings now being used as such. It was rumoured, even by authority, in the radical press such as **Marat**'s *Ami du people*, that, as soon as the troops left Paris, the nobles and the clergy would be sprung from prison and would massacre the patriots' families. Volunteer assassins acted pre-emptively, killing around 1,400 prisoners in the **September Massacres**.

The soldiers left and won the battle of **Valmy**.

Fersen, Hans Axel von (1755–1819)

This Swedish Count and General is best remembered for the part he played in the king and queen's flight to **Varennes** in June 1791. The queen's biographers have sometimes asserted that he was her lover.[3] He was certainly her devoted servant.

He joined the French army and was interpreter between General Rochambeau and Washington in the American War of Independence, being present at the British defeat at Yorktown in 1781. He was promoted Colonel of the Royal Swedish Regiment in 1785 and was well liked at **Versailles**. Brief service with Gustav III of Sweden in Finland led to his appointment as Swedish agent in Paris in 1790. He helped plan the king's flight with his family for the evening of 20 June 1791.[4] He had the large black and yellow berline made for the royal family's intended journey to Montmédy and kept it publicly at his own lodgings. He drove the carriage that took them to the Porte Saint-Martin where the berline was waiting for them, travelled with them to Bondy, and then returned to Sweden. His own sovereign, Gustavus III, approved of his participation in the escape, and even moved to Aachen in hopes of greeting Louis XVI.[5]

The Swedish government sent Fersen to Vienna and to Prague for the Emperor Leopold's coronation, and then to Brussels. He returned secretly to the **Tuileries** in early 1792, but realized there was nothing further he could do personally to help **Louis XVI** and **Marie-Antoinette**. He remained a Swedish diplomat until he was accused as an accessory to the crown prince's possible murder in 1810. As he waited to accompany the prince's funeral cortège into Stockholm, the crowd attacked and tore him to pieces.[6]

Festival of the Federation (1790)

When the first anniversary of the taking of the **Bastille** came round, elaborate preparations were made to celebrate the event. Hundreds of citizens turned out to change the landscape at the Champ de Mars (where the Eiffel tower has been since 1889). An 'altar of the *patrie*' was raised up on a pyramid structure. Contingents of the **National Guard** came from all over France to be present.

Talleyrand, who was still bishop of Autun, celebrated mass in the presence of the assembled National Guard under the command of **Lafayette**. It is said that the bishop leaned across the altar to whisper to Lafayette, 'Don't make me laugh.'[7] **Louis XVI** and **Marie-Antoinette** were presiding over the festival which was of national importance. All the major personalities present – the king included – made an oath to uphold the constitution.

In the cantons, similar festivals were held. The National Guard paraded, usually armed with pikes in the absence of other weapons, and speeches were made by mayors and National Guard colonels. Typical of these parades is the one held in Port d'Envaux, along by the River Charente in south-western France. The *curé* (who was to be compelled to leave as a **refractory** soon after) celebrated mass there, after which the National Guard Colonel, whose name was Gallocheau, made a speech containing these words:

> The French have broken their chains. Free from now on, and subject to the law alone, we will not see the balance of justice weighted in favour of the powerful any more, so much so that its sword is powerful for the weak ... Let us open our hearts in recognition towards the enlightened legislators ... Let us swear to maintain a constitution which ought to give happiness to all, and which offers us *for the first time* the inestimable enjoyment of liberty.[8]

Feuillant Club

The Feuillants were a group dedicated to trying to make constitutional monarchy work despite the king's flight to **Varennes** in June 1791, and they took a leading part in drawing up the 1791 Constitution. They had more supporters in the **Legislative Assembly** than the radical **Jacobins** who no longer trusted the king. They met in the empty Feuillants (Cistercian) convent near the **Tuileries Palace**, whose chapel had replaced the one at **Versailles** after the court was brought to Paris in October 1789.

For them, the Revolution was complete with the achievement of constitutional monarchy and they saw the main task of the **Legislative Assembly** as the return to stability. As moderates, they opposed war, thinking that the form of monarchy they supported was too fragile to survive it. Their leaders were the so-called 'triumvirs' – Antoine **Barnave**, Alexander **Lameth** and Adrien **Duport**. Barnave was a barrister, and the other two were former nobles.

Barnave had been in the coach with the royal family all the way back from Varennes. When the king and queen were in the Tuileries Palace once more, he supported the fiction that the king had been abducted in the hope that the monarchy would remain. He wrote the king's speech for the opening of the Legislative Assembly on 5 October 1791. However, in her private correspondence with Axel **Fersen**, the queen said that she and the king were making use of 'wild men' like him to preserve as much as possible of royal authority.[9] The Feuillants' experiment had an air of desperation about it. **Robespierre**'s personal ascendancy, based on his known integrity (dangerous word), brought many Feuillants back to the provincial Jacobin Clubs. The Feuillants 'simply ebbed away'.[10] Barnave did not survive the **Terror**; nor did the Feuillant Club.

Fleurus, Battle of (26 June 1794)

The **Committee of Public Safety** wanted the main impact of the campaign of 1794 to be in **Belgium**, which was again occupied by the Austrians after **Dumouriez** had been defeated at the battle of Neerwinden. **Pichegru** was ordered to take Ypres and move west, **Jourdan** was to go into Belgium from the south, and a mixed force was to advance along the Sambre River.[11] **Saint-Just** went on mission to these forces on 29 April to be a unifying presence, while **Carnot** was overall director from Paris.

The allied command was divided. The Prince of Coburg and the Duke of York did not trust each other. The Emperor Francis II left the Netherlands on 13 June, suggesting that keeping a military presence there was not vital to him. Saint-Just and **Le Bas** were on the Sambre, with the army retreating and counter-attacking across it. While others were at the Festival of the **Supreme Being** on 8 June, Carnot gave instructions – perhaps advised by Saint-Just – for the amalgamation of forces into the Army of the Sambre and Meuse under Pichegru's overall command, with **Jourdan** leading the force in the centre.

Jourdan resumed the siege of Charleroi while Pichegru took Ypres on 18 June. Charleroi surrendered to Saint-Just, just before Coburg arrived with a substantial imperial mixed-nationality force, which he divided so as to watch Pichegru's movements. Action began in the village of Fleurus early on 26 June and lasted all day. Jourdan was left in occupation of the battlefield. Saint-Just rushed to Paris to announce victory. He had just a month left before **Thermidor**. Coburg was left free to withdraw from Belgium undisturbed, and Pichegru and Jourdan both took their armies to Brussels and then advanced eastwards to enter Liège and Antwerp at the same time as **Robespierre**'s fall (9 thermidor, year II, 27 July 1794). The French consolidated the Belgian gains, and Jourdan resumed his march to the Rhine. The British withdrew into Hanover, and the Prussians were blocked when the Armies of Rhine and Moselle laid siege to Mainz. Pichegru waited until the rivers froze in the terrible winter of 1794–5, and then crossed into Holland 'without a struggle' in December and January.[12]

Prieur de la Côte d'Or had been developing military air balloons and one was in use to watch Cobourg's movements, being towed about for nine hours by ropes down which messages were sent.

Floréal Coup (22 floréal, year VI, 11 May 1798)

Six months after the **Fructidor coup**, its results were still in question when the partial elections came round again. The turnout was low, as had become usual, but it was the **Jacobins** who benefited this time. The deputies in the Legislative Councils realized that this time the royalists would not be voting. **La Révellière-Lépeaux** feared he would be assassinated, **Merlin de Douai** (**Carnot**'s replacement) feared a return to **Terror**. Benjamin Constant warned the propertied classes against 'anarchists' as the Jacobins were now being called, though the Jacobins could no longer motivate the **sansculottes** as in 1793–4.

The Directors established by the Constitution of year III found themselves in conflict with the Councils of Elders and of 500, and rigged elections for new ones. They dismissed more than 60 judges and provincial administrators and sent out commissioners with funds to arrange elections. The new councils were due to meet on 1 prairial (20 May 1798), and lists of leftist candidates to be excluded from the councils were prepared. A law was passed on 11 May deliberately to keep seats in eight departments vacant. One hundred and twenty-seven new deputies had their election suppressed, of whom 83 were known to be Jacobins.[13] In other departments, unwelcome candidates were simply excluded. This meant that the legislative councils were completely in the power and patronage of the Directors. On 15 May, François de Neufchâteau was replaced by Jean-Baptiste Treilhard. It was bloodless; but it was a coup. It effectively 'inaugurated a policy of eliminating all opposition'.[14]

Foreign Policy of the Constitutional Monarchy

At the outset of the Revolution, the **Constituent Assembly** undertook never to start a war of aggression. Retrenchment was the only solution to a financial crisis. In 1789, the great powers of Europe had their attention concentrated elsewhere. The Belgian revolution was of more interest to Austria and to Prussia who settled their differences over it in order to concentrate on the partition of Poland, and relations with Russia and with the Ottoman Empire. In Great Britain, Pitt's cabinet had entered a period of careful neutrality.

But this could not last. It was not only French domestic tensions that led to the **declaration of war** with Austria on 20 April 1792.

Nevertheless, things were being said early on by revolutionaries such as **Merlin de Douai** that led the former Austrian ambassador to France, **Mercy d'Argentau**, to observe that the National Assembly had declared war on all other governments. The particular question at issue was Alsace, which had become part of France by the Treaty of Westphalia in 1648, but allowance had been made for the feudal rights of the German princes who were subsumed into the French regency's orbit. Now it was said that it was the will of the Alsatian people that united them with France. The same argument was used about the papal territory of **Avignon** and the Comtat-Venaissin. Besides, too much was being done in public now, while the chancelleries of Europe saw things differently and negotiated behind closed doors.[15] Foreign policy had certainly changed its focus.

Lafayette, on the basis of his own ambition, did not want **Louis XVI** to lose his place at the head of a great European nation. The **Feuillants** clung on to a peace policy, but they were overtaken by the stance taken by **Brissot** and his associates. Brissot and **Isnard** argued that there was an international conspiracy of kings and *émigrés* aimed at restoring the old regime. This was certainly true of the *émigrés* who were trying hard to persuade the kings. They invoked the Gallic diplomatic tradition of honour and glory which was in danger. The **Jacobin Club** went along with this, with the exception of **Robespierre** who said that winning a war would lead to dictatorship by Lafayette, and losing it would mean the end of the Revolution.

The aggressive stance was not one-sided. On 17 January 1792, Austria's attitude was formulated in terms of disbanding French armies being assembled, restoring the rights of German princes in Alsace and Lorraine, returning **Avignon** and the Comtat-Venaissin to the pope, and assuring the safety of Louis XVI and **Marie-Antoinette**. The Prussians agreed and signed a pact with Austria on 7 February. Leopold II died on 1 March, leaving Francis II under pressure for war from his diplomats. The French declaration of war was the result of the usual conflict of the ambitions of great powers, among whom France still had a viable place.

Blanning, T.C.W., *The Origin of the French Revolutionary Wars* (London: Longman, 1986), pp. 73–123.

Foreign Policy of the National Convention

On 19 November 1792, the **National Convention** issued a decree that the French nation would offer assistance to 'enslaved' people who were liberating themselves. This would lead inevitably to French annexation of territories in the desire for natural frontiers on the Rhine, in the Alps and in the Pyrenees in the tradition of Louis XIV's expansionism of a century before. Elections were to be held in these territories, but results were to be manipulated in the interests of French nationalist *raison d'état*. **Carnot** used this justification for annexing Savoy, Nice, **Belgium** and several Rhineland communities. War against the United Provinces (Holland) was in the tradition of outfacing British foreign policy. The Convention showed its Anglophobia. **Dumouriez**, while he was foreign minister, supported the taking of the Dutch fleet to make attacks on British trade. **Danton** talked about 'laying the foundations of French greatness'.

The idea of exporting the Revolution gave way to asserting national interest in reaction to the designs of other great powers. The Austrian minister Thugut was co-ordinating policy with Prussia and Britain in August 1793. The Convention's export of the Revolution to the Low Countries, rather than the execution of **Louis XVI** or the **September Massacres**, was the stimulus for Pitt's government to change from neutrality to armed conflict in its own national interest.

Once **Jacobin** power was consolidated in terms of official **Terror**, any negotiated peace was out of the question. Carnot, the 'organizer of victory', clearly affirmed that the Nation's enemies had to be hated. For the Jacobins of the **Committee of Public Safety**, the only alternative to Revolution was extinction. The war opposed by **Robespierre** in 1792 had, by 1794, become entirely necessary to allow the Jacobins to maintain the impetus of the Terror. The victory at **Fleurus** was the culmination point.

Stone, Bailey, *Reinterpreting the French Revolution: A Global-Historical Perspective* (Cambridge: Cambridge University Press, 2002).

Fouché, Joseph (1759–1820)

Fouché became conspicuous during the **Terror** at **Lyon**, where he was a **representative on mission**, but opposed **Robespierre** in the **Thermidor coup**. He survived as an unscrupulous intriguer to become Napoleon's chief of police and even, despite being a regicide, briefly to serve the **Restoration Monarchy**.

As an Oratorian schoolmaster in Arras Fouché associated with Robespierre before and after the Revolution started. The Oratorians transferred him to Nantes in 1790 to prevent his involvement in the Revolution, but he joined the Nantes **Jacobin Club**. When the religious orders were dissolved in May 1792, he became completely anti-clerical.

Elected a deputy for the Loire-Inférieure in the **National Convention**, Fouché supported the adoption of the Republic. He was sent as a representative on mission against the **Vendéan** and **Chouan** rebels in spring 1793 and then to the Nièvre in central France, where he initiated the de-Christianizing process, closing churches, sending bells to be melted down for cannon, chasing out the **refractory clergy**, and sending church ornaments to the mint, as was being done all over France. He took over a church in Nevers and created his own version of civic religion: a 'festival of Brutus'. He stated that his intention was to substitute the Republic and natural morality for superstition and hypocritical worship.[16] This became the general theme of the representatives on mission, but it was Fouché who originated it. He even gave his daughter a 'republican baptism' at Nevers in August 1793, calling her Nièvre, with appropriate speeches and the **National Guard** band.[17]

In November, he went on to Lyon, along with **Collot d'Herbois**, to carry out reprisals after General **Kellermann** had put down the federalist rebellion there. They called in a large contingent of the Parisian **Revolutionary Army** to terrorize the population. On 4 December, they ordered the *mitraillades* at the cemetery of Les Brotteaux. Sixty men on one day, and two hundred and eleven on the next were brought there in chains, fired at with grapeshot and then finished off by the revolutionary army with hand weapons. Fouché worked hard on a justification for all this carnage: 'Indulgence,' he said, 'is a dangerous weakness liable to rekindle criminal hopes ... Devouring flames alone can express the total power of the people'.[18] One thousand, eight hundred more people were executed there by firing squad or the guillotine before he went back to Paris in April 1794. By that time, the protagonist of de-Christianization, **Hébert**, had gone to the scaffold. It was Fouché who had 'Death is but an eternal sleep' carved above the entrances to churchyards.

Robespierre opposed Fouché's atheism by organizing the Festival of the **Supreme Being** in June 1794. After Robespierre had tried to expel him from the Jacobins, Fouché joined with other former terrorists such as **Tallien** to bring about his fall in the **Thermidor coup**. During the in-fighting of the **Thermidorean Convention**, Fouché was denounced and imprisoned in August. He was amnestied 'for deeds relative to the Revolution' on 26 October 1795.

Fouché gradually came back to power, offering his services to **Barras** who sent him as ambassador to the new **Cisalpine Republic** but moved him to The Hague very soon after. The Directory appointed him Minister of Police in Paris in July 1799 to take action against royalists and Neo-Jacobins alike. He plotted with **Sieyès** in favour of Bonaparte's **Brumaire coup** and was confirmed as police minister.

Despite his great prominence in the Empire – Napoleon made him Duc d'Otranto – he intrigued with **Artois** to help bring about the restoration of the Bourbons. After Waterloo, **Talleyrand** and Fouché were reinstated as ministers and went to meet the returning Louis XVIII at Arnouville. **Chateaubriand** was there too and reminisced:

> All at once a door opens. Vice comes in silently, leaning on the arm of crime, M. de Talleyrand walking with the support of M. Fouché; the infernal vision passes slowly in front of me, goes into the king's office and disappears. Fouché was coming to swear fealty and homage to his lord; the faithful regicide, on his knees, puts the hands which made Louis XVI's head fall between the hands of the martyred king's brother; the apostate bishop stands surety for his oath.[19]

Despite being a regicide, he was at first kept in office and then sent as ambassador to Saxony. But he was exiled in 1816 and died in Trieste four years later.

Freemasonry

Freemasonry was important in the Revolution because members of lodges all over the country were used to hearing the claim that free men were equal, despite the fact that they had to be well up the ladder of affluence in order to be initiated. 'Some 20%' of the deputies elected to the **Estates-General** were Freemasons[20] and brought the experience of the working of their lodges into the Assembly. William Doyle has pointed out that recent studies [in 1984 and 1991] had suggested that 'the elective and egalitarian practices of masonry constituted a potent education in democratic activity which would bear fruit in 1789'.[21]

The king's cousin, Philippe, Duc d'**Orléans**, was Grand Master of the Grand Orient Lodge. Many nobles were lodge members. Naval and military officers had affiliations to lodges and, despite papal edicts against being so, Catholic clergy were members of lodges too. Most freemasons, however, were middle-class men, often lawyers.

Masonic ways of thinking permeated the Revolution because they were close to the ideas of the **Enlightenment**. Masonic symbols, like the all-seeing eye, found their place in the iconography of the Revolution as many of the exhibits in the Musée Carnavalet in Paris demonstrate. The Paris **Jacobin Club** was well provided with freemasons, and the ceremonial of lodges was not far from what went on in its meetings.

@ See online at: http://www.freemasonry.bcy.ca/texts/revolution.html.

Fréron, Louis-Marie Stanislas (1754–1802)

Stanislas Fréron was an ambitious opportunist in the revolutionary decade. As a close friend of **Desmoulins** and an admirer of **Marat**, he began his part in the changes as a journalist. After the **federalist** risings in the south, he wanted to create events rather than report them, as a **representative on mission**. The fury of his reprisals in **Toulon** aroused hostility in Paris and nothing he could do after that could reinstate him. [22]

Fréron's father was a literary critic with connections with Louis XV's father-in-law, the former King Stanislas of Poland, who was godfather to our Fréron. He was a school friend of Camille Desmoulins at the Lycée Louis-Le-Grand, and also acquainted with **Robespierre** there. He inherited his father's literary review but lost control of it to his stepmother's relations and drifted into the **Palais-Royal** circle in Desmoulins's company, to be introduced to **Danton** and Marat, whom he came to admire.

Fréron was elected to represent the Bonne-Nouvelle district in the Paris Commune in 1789, but preferred journalism and took advantage of new press freedom, seeing the success of the newspapers of Desmoulins and of Marat. He wrote and published the radical *Orateur du peuple* (eight pages every two days) to attack opponents such as **Lafayette**, **Bailly** and **Marie-Antoinette**, and spread rumours about a supposed '**Austrian Committee**'. When old-regime authorities still existing in 1790 acted against him, Marat published his reply in his *Ami du Peuple* and Fréron evaded arrest.

As a member of the **Cordeliers** he supported the overthrow of the monarchy and, as a deputy for the Seine in the **National Convention**, voted for the king's death. Appointed with **Barras** as representative on mission to the Hautes and Basses Alpes in 1793, he was active in **Marseille** after General Carteaux had put down the federalist rising there. Barras and Fréron were opposed by the local Jacobins, but used the city as a base for the recovery of Toulon and forced Admiral Hood's departure in December 1793. Fréron showed personal bravery in the attacks on the Toulon forts, but claimed responsibility for shooting 800 army and navy officers and civilians afterwards in reprisal for their rebellion against the Republic. Returning to Marseille, he wanted to punish its people as **Fouché** had punished **Lyon**. Many wealthy merchants were guillotined as federalists, but there was opposition from the **Mountain** to the destruction of the mercantile economy of Marseille.

Fréron returned to Paris, supported the downfall of the Hébertists, connived at the execution of his friends Danton and Desmoulins, but then turned against Robespierre, renouncing the Jacobinism he had upheld with such severity in the Midi only six months before. He made use of the 'Golden Youth' as a vigilante force for the **Thermidorean Convention** against the 'tail of Robespierre'.

Fréron was sent on mission again by the Thermidorean Convention to resist the '**White Terror**' that had broken out in Marseille in reaction against the Republic's suppression of the federalist movement. This time he avoided excesses but on his return to Paris his ambition to be a deputy in the Council of 500 was thwarted, and he narrowly escaped prosecution for his earlier terrorism in the Midi when letters to a supposed friend became public. Moreover, his hopes of marrying **Bonaparte**'s sister Pauline were unfulfilled and he had to accept a minor post in **Saint-Domingue**, where the governor, General Le Clerc, was her husband. Fréron died of yellow fever there in 1802 (as did Le Clerc).

Fructidor Coup (18 fructidor, year V, 4 September 1797)

The *coup d'état* of 18 Fructidor demonstrated how weak the supremacy of the **Directory** was, and that it had to be dependent upon an effective military figure who turned out to be General **Bonaparte**.

Louis XVII had died in the Temple in June and **Provence** had proclaimed himself Louis XVIII. The elections that should have been held in October 1796 to replace a third of the legislative councils under the constitution of year III were delayed until spring 1797 to allow the new system to establish itself.[23] Even so, these elections produced 198 monarchists in favour of ending the war. They were known as Clichyens from the **Clichy Club** of which many of them were members. They had no agreed programme because some were constitutional monarchists and some wanted to return to the old regime. Nevertheless, they gained the repeal of harsh laws against *émigrés* and the **refractory clergy**. They also counted on the support of General **Pichegru**, the commander of the Rhine and Moselle Army, but eventually he would not help them. General Moreau had sent the directors letters found on the Austrian General Klinglin that proved that Pichegru had sold himself to the enemy.[24]

The revelations about Pichegru's perfidy brought **Barras** to ally with **Reubell** and **La Révellière-Lépeaux** in the Directory, and they prepared a coup to forestall the royalist recovery against the other Directors, **Carnot**, now known to be evolving in a royalist direction, and Letourneur, a former marquis.[25] Barras made **Talleyrand** foreign minister, and sounded out Bonaparte who was being so successful in Italy and had only just sent the directors some letters seized from an *émigré*, d'Antraigues, which proved that royalist deputies had decided to overturn the Directory with the help of English money.[26] He was willing to comply by means of his second-in-command, General Augereau, who was on leave in Paris. The Directory's alternative would have been General **Hoche** and they arranged for him to leave the Sambre and Meuse Army to prepare an invasion of Great Britain, which meant he had to pass through Paris with his troops. They appointed him war minister in July 1797, but Bonaparte's compliance effectively prevented these moves (in any case, Hoche was under age to be a minister and died of natural causes on 19 September). The Directory was going to use the army, whereas the Jacobin Republic had used the **sansculottes** to maintain itself in power.

In August, Talleyrand's house became the centre of pro-Bonaparte activity. At 3 a.m. on 4 September (18 fructidor, year V – hence the name for the coup), Augereau's 2,000 troops forced their way into the council chambers in the **Tuileries** and arrested all the royalist deputies. The soldiers went across the Seine to the **Luxembourg Palace** to arrest the two moderate directors. Someone had warned Carnot and he escaped. The newly appointed François Barthélémy was captured in his bed and deported.

In the morning, posters announced the discovery of a royalist plot and the government's foiling of it. Fifty-three royalists were deported to Guiana, known as the 'dry guillotine', and the results of the last elections were annulled. Forty-two newspapers in Paris and the provinces lost their licences. Laws concerning *émigrés* that had been relaxed were severely reinstated in the so-called Directorial Terror. If any returned, they would be shot. Refractory priests were sent to prison hulks off the isles of Ré and Oléron. Known republicans, **Merlin de Douai** and François de Neufchâteau, were the replacements as directors. Bonaparte now supervised foreign policy and dictated the terms of the Treaty of **Campo Formio**.

Furet, François (1927–97)

The sternest and most unrelenting critic of Marxist orthodoxy in the study of the Revolution was François Furet, who has been called 'a revolutionary of the Revolution'. Having been a Communist himself, he re-designated the French **Marxist historians** as 'Neo-Jacobins'. He saw their ideological stance as a straightjacket, preventing any objective reflection on personalities and events of the decade after 1789. Marxist history may have been admirably 'from below', and it may have had an appreciation of the length of time needed for trends to be appreciated (*longue durée*), but the 'classical catechism', as he called it, would not allow any appreciation outside its own parameters.

Furet's influential (and demanding) *Interpreting the French Revolution* was published in Paris in 1978. He claimed in it that the Revolution was over.[27] He did not want to analyse what lay upstream or downstream of it. It had served its purpose as a new beginning for France. He agreed with de **Tocqueville** about how the Revolution, seen as a whole, had developed from tendencies already present in the old regime. If we do not begin with an ideological stance, but let research direct us, we enter areas other – and perhaps more rewarding – than social and economic concerns: culture, for example.[28]

Furet gave clearer guidance about the political completion of the Revolution by claiming that the Third Republic was the true inheritor of the Revolution when President Jules Grévy, along with the Senate and the Chamber of Deputies, took the road from **Versailles** to Paris as King **Louis XVI** and the deputies of the previous century had done, when *La Marseillaise* was finally accepted as the national anthem, and when 14 July became the national holiday. That was in 1879.[29]

To see what can be done when there are no ideological restraints, we only have to look at what he wrote and edited with Mona Ozouf in *A Critical Dictionary of the French Revolution*, published for the bicentenary.[30]

G

Germinal Rising (1–2 April)**; Prairial Rising** (20 May 1795)

During the **Terror**, a new constitution was put before the **National Convention** based on the **Declaration of the Rights of Man and of the Citizen**, on 24 June 1793. It was not implemented as a result of a decree in October which said it was not suitable in the straightened conditions of wartime.

Yet the terrible winter of 1794–5 was the background to the price rises that followed the abolition of the General **Maximum** on prices and wages on 24 December 1794 as part of the Thermidorean reaction, when **Jacobin** ascendancy had been finished with. So now, 'after having blamed constraint for these ills, the people began to blame liberty.'[1] The labourers of Paris challenged the **Thermidorean Convention** with a campaign of posters, demonstrations, petitions and riots culminating with a **sansculotte** demonstration to call for bread, the implementation of the 1793 Constitution, and the liberation of imprisoned patriots on 1 April 1795 (12 germinal, Year III).

Paris was divided in support of it. In the west and near the Treasury (*Bourse*), the sections clamoured for the punishment of four terrorists, **Barère**, **Billaud-Varenne**, **Collot d'Herbois** and **Vadier**, and a rowdy hearing in the tribunal began. The insurrection on the Ile de la Cité was made by women gathering in a crowd in front of Nôtre Dame to march on the Convention. They took more than an hour to break into the **Tuileries** where the Convention sat and stayed four hours reading out their petitions and chanting 'Bread! Bread!' They were eventually persuaded to leave, but the demonstration continued outside. They were dispersed by soldiers, but no one was killed.

This was all repeated in the Prairial rising on 20 May, but this time with more organization. Now the demands were for the 1793 Constitution, the arrest of counter-revolutionaries, and new elections. The demonstration gathered in the eastern suburbs and the centre, especially in very poor sections like Gravilliers, where Jacques **Roux** had operated. Women began it once more. This time there were pikes and cannon available. Their leaders were declared outlaws by the Convention and an appeal was made to 'good citizens' to suppress the demonstration. Line troops and the National Guard were mobilized but how they would respond was uncertain. From 3.30 p.m. until 7 p.m., the convention hall was invaded. One of the deputies, Jean Féraud, was killed. Battalions garrisoned in the west of Paris arrived and the rioters fled, but it took three days for general Menou to 'cleanse' the **Faubourg Saint-Antoine**. The poor sections were disarmed of their pikes, a good number were imprisoned and others deprived of civil rights.[2] The purges in the Terror had deprived the popular movement of its leadership, but the few Montagnards in the Convention who sympathized with the demonstrators were condemned to death.

The immediate result of this action was that opponents of repressed Jacobins and sansculottes implemented the **'White Terror'** in the south and east as vengeance.[3]

Girondins

These were a loosely associated group belonging first to the **Legislative Assembly** and then to the **National Convention**, who took their name from one of the deputies from the Gironde, **Vergniaud**, their principal orator in the Legislative Assembly. There were about 60 of them, and they gave a platform to the Parisian journalist, Jacques-Pierre **Brissot** (hence their contemporary name, *Brissotins*). They associated in Paris salons, such as that of Madame de **Staël**, with the bourgeoisie of banking and sea-borne commerce who favoured a land war from which they could profit. **Clavière**, the Girondin finance minister, was a Genevan banker like **Necker** before him. The Girondins were largely responsible for the **declaration of war** on the kings of Europe.

In the Republic, they opposed the increasing domination of national government by the **Insurrectionary Commune** and the **Jacobin Club**. Girondin political emphasis in revolutionary government was based on the deputies from all the 84 new departments, whereas the Jacobins projected authority emanating from Paris as the indisputable seat of government. The Girondins supplied ministers for the constitutional monarchy from outside the Legislative Assembly. **Roland** was interior minister, Claviére and Servan had the finance and war portfolios, and they opposed the king when he used his veto to protect the **refractory clergy** and in the hope of preventing *fédérés* staying in Paris before leaving for the eastern war front. The king dismissed the Girondin ministers for this on 13 June. They were reinstated after the king was brought back from **Varennes**, as they were again after the overthrow of the monarchy, when they were joined by **Danton** as minister of justice and Gaspard **Monge** as navy minister, until the Legislative was superseded by the Convention on 20 September 1792.

When **Louis XVI** had been declared guilty of treason against the nation in January 1793, the Girondins tried to have his sentence decided by a national referendum, which the Jacobins prevented. Tension grew between these polarized groups in the Convention, leading up to a crisis lasting for three days and ending on 2 June 1793. The Jacobins, aided by Parisian **sansculottes** commanded by François **Hanriot** who surrounded the building with 150 cannon, expelled the Girondins from the Convention and, subsequently, had most of them guillotined as outlaws in the name of the One and Indivisible Republic. The Girondin point of view of the Revolution's aims had come to be known as **federalism**. Rebellions against the Paris government were breaking out in places like **Caen**, **Toulon**, Bordeaux and **Lyon** and were to be brutally repressed by military means and then by Jacobin **representatives on mission**.

William Doyle, in an essay published in 1995,[4] suggested that the Girondins were the real upholders of the principles of 1789, the true revolutionaries, and to call them moderates is inappropriate. It was the Jacobins who were the compromisers, the practical realists under pressure from the sansculottes.

Gobel, Jean-Baptiste-Joseph (1726–94)

The constitutional archbishop of Paris became famous for renouncing his belief under pressure from the de-Christianizers, and went to the scaffold, condemned with the Hébertists.

Gobel was born to humble parents in Alsace, and studied at Porrentruy. Porrentruy was ruled by the Bishop of Basel who encouraged, educated and ordained the young man. He later made him his suffragan as Bishop of Lydda *in partibus*. The clergy of Huningue elected him their deputy to the **Estates-General**. He took the Oath to the **Civil Constitution of the Clergy**. Then he was elected constitutional bishop in several dioceses, from which he chose the Archdiocese of Paris, and was consecrated in March 1791 by the seven French bishops who had taken the oath, including **Talleyrand**. He was intruded into the place of Antoine-Eleonor-Léon de Juigné who had refused the oath and was understood in law to have resigned.

Eighteen months later, Gobel became administrator of Paris and actively anti-clerical, even taking up the revolutionary demand that constitutional priests should marry. A year afterwards, he came to the bar of the Convention and formally renounced his archbishopric and his religion, persuaded to do so by **Hébert**, **Clootz** and **Chaumette** from the **Cordeliers**, and given a large sum of money by the **Jacobins**. The de-Christianizers saw him as a prize in their campaign, and **Robespierre** regarded Gobel as an atheist, though he never said he was. In fact, he went back on his renunciation afterwards, and took steps to become a Catholic again. But he was too late to avoid Robespierre's attack and was executed with Hébert on 24 March 1794.[5]

Golden Youth (*Jeunesse Dorée*)

After the fall of **Robespierre** in July 1789, gangs of self-consciously dressed middle-class young men, accompanied by young women known as *Merveilleuses,* equally extravagantly dressed, met in cafés and developed an organization in Paris to launch attacks with their canes and clubs on any recognizable **Jacobins** and **sansculottes** they encountered in the streets. These were the *Jeunesse dorée* who represented the Thermidorean reaction to **Terror**, the remaining Jacobins – known as the 'tail of Robespierre'

– and the whole sansculotte ethos. These gangs included conservative republicans, constitutional monarchists and outright reactionaries. Some of them, indeed, were avoiding conscription or had deserted from the Republican **Army**, but many others had just been released from prison awaiting the **revolutionary tribunal** and the **guillotine**.

They were important mainly because of their nuisance value. They forced the removal of **Marat**'s remains from the Pantheon on 8 February 1795.[6] They would later be called 'Fréron's Young Men', or 'Fréron's Army'. Stanislas Fréron, on his return from the subjugation of federalist rebels in **Marseille** and **Toulon**, renounced his Jacobin beliefs for those of the Thermidoreans, and made use of the Golden Youth to achieve his new aims. 'From being a private militia (*milice*) at the outset, they later became one of the main essentials of the reactionary dynamic and one of the central explanations of the Thermidorian phenomenon.' (My translation).[7] They did not take kindly to being disowned by him. The **Jacobin Club** was rumoured to be plotting to assassinate leaders of the **Thermidorean Convention**, so they closed it down with the support of the *jeunesse* on 19 November 1794. Thérèse Tallien turned the key in the lock.[8]

Gossec, François-Joseph (1734–1829)

Gossec (born Gossé) had been in Paris for a long time, originally as Rameau's pupil. By 1789, he was in charge of the Royal Song School, but soon associated himself with the Revolution. His prolific musical output for it was the composition of set pieces, such as a *Requiem*, performed in the district of Saint-Martin-des-Champs 'for citizens who had died in the common cause' in 1789,[9] a *Te Deum* for the **Festival of the Federation**, and music for several state funerals, from the *Marche lugubre* for **Mirabeau**'s funeral, to the *Cantate funèbre* for the French plenipotentiaries murdered at the **Rastadt Conference** in 1799. He wrote music for the transfer of **Voltaire**'s remains to the Pantheon in 1791, and the tune for Desorgues's hymn to the **Supreme Being** for **Robespierre**'s festival in June 1794. He was responsible for the definitive orchestration of *La Marseillaise* for a performance in the Paris Opera in 1792.[10]

Gouges, Olympe de (1748–93)

Olympe de Gouges was a different kind of feminist from **Théroigne de Méricourt**. She did what she could for her cause as a writer – originally of plays with short runs in Paris theatres. The work for which she is mainly remembered is the *Declaration of the Rights of Woman and the Female Citizen*[11] ('Citizeness' is an ugly translation of *citoyenne*) published in 1791. This sailed full in the face of **Jacobin** misogyny which meant the *citoyenne* had the right only to bear children and bring them up as good republicans.

She was a butcher's daughter, born as Marie Gouze in Montauban (Tarn-et-Garonne), who believed she was the illegitimate child of a marquis who did not acknowledge her. She was married to someone for whom she felt revulsion. He only lived long enough to beget her son with whom she moved to Paris in 1770.

De Gouges voiced her opposition to the king's execution. A crowd surrounded her lodging and she protected herself by going to confront them and making them laugh. When the **Girondins** were excluded from the **National Convention** and hounded to their deaths, she was known to be their supporter. She produced a placard offering three possibilities from which the French Nation could make its choice: the One and Indivisible Republic, the Girondin proposal of some local autonomy, or constitutional monarchy. She challenged **Robespierre**, and that had the inevitable result of her execution. She was arrested and went to the scaffold after three months in prison in November 1793.[12] She was as much a target for the Jacobin brand of virtue as any of the **refractory clergy**.

@ The text of the Declaration of the Rights of Woman and the Female Citizen can be found online at: http://www.pinn.net/~sunshine/book-sum/gouges.html.

Great Fear (July to August 1789)

Soon after the **Estates-General** met in May 1789, rumours circulated – and were believed – that certain court nobles were conspiring against the growing influence of the **Third Estate**. This coincided with the intensifying food crisis. Regiments made up of foreign soldiers were ordered to surround Paris, while the Parisian bourgeoisie armed the first contingents of the **National Guard** to protect their property. After the fall of the **Bastille**, beggars were expelled from the capital to prevent any more violence there. Rumours circulated in most of France that the Revolution was being threatened by large bands of these beggars turned 'brigands' moving around the country in the pay of counter-revolutionary courtiers.

Most towns formed National Guard contingents on the Parisian model to withstand the threat they seemed to offer. In rural areas, it was feared that the brigands were intent on destroying the harvest before it was ripe to starve the Third Estate into submission. There were 'sightings' of thousands of strangers moving along valleys and across plateaux, causing village populations to arm themselves and take to the woods for safety. This often led to real attacks on noblemen's *châteaux* and *manoirs* by tenant farmers who destroyed their title deeds, hoping thereby to avoid paying **seigneurial dues** in future. They also hoped to have the hunting guns which some seigneurs had confiscated before the Revolution restored to them. Many nobles, after being threatened in this way, and sometimes having their houses actually destroyed, left France and became *émigrés*. This wave of violence, motivated by fear, led to the seigneurial system being dismantled. The great nobles and the higher clergy themselves abolished feudal dues – in principle but not in fact – on the **Night of 4 August 1789**.

Later on, some villagers accused their former seigneurs before the new **justices of the peace** of having used false measures at harvest time when dues were paid in kind.

Lefebvre, Georges, *The Great Fear of 1789: Rural Panic in Revolutionary France*, trans. Joan White (New York: Schocken Books, 1973).

Grégoire, Abbé Henri (1750–1831)

Baptiste-Henri Grégoire was a First Estate deputy from Lorraine in the **Estates-General** and was among the first of the **clergy** to join the **Third Estate** deputies who had made their **'Tennis Court Oath'** not to disperse until they had been recognized by the king as the National Assembly.

Grégoire was a leading opponent of slavery and had won a prize in the Academy of Metz for an essay on making the **Jews** happier and more useful to France. He joined the Breton Club in **Versailles**, and then the **Jacobins** after the Assembly moved to Paris in October, and found himself among the progressives. In fact, he anticipated being arrested for his advanced views when it seemed as if the king and the court were attempting to destroy the Assembly in the egg during the July crisis of 1789, which led to the taking of the **Bastille**. He even deposited some of the Assembly's files for safekeeping with Madame Emmery, the wife of a Third Estate deputy from Lorraine.[13] He certainly expressed his radicalism in relation to the **Night of 4 August 1789**.[14]

Grégoire was one of the 30 or 40 **Jansenists** out of nearly 300 clerical deputies, and was on the ecclesiastical committee that devised the **Civil Constitution of the Clergy**. Moreover, he was one of the eight Jacobin deputies making most speeches in the Assembly between May 1789 and July 1790, when the clergy constitution decree was passed.[15] When this was adopted and the power of the old-regime bishops was broken, a 'constitutional' bishop was to be elected for each one of the 83 new departments. To be eligible for the new bishoprics, priests were to have been in office as parish priests for not less than 15 years. Grégoire himself was elected constitutional bishop of the Loir et Cher department, with his cathedral at Blois. In the **National Convention** he defiantly continued to wear his purple cassock in public even during de-Christianization and the **Terror**.

Grégoire was elected as a member of the Council of 500 under the **Directory**. He refused, however, to accept **Bonaparte's** *Concordat* in 1801.

📖 Sepinwall, Alyssa Goldstein, *The Abbé Grégoire and the French Revolution: The Making of Modern Universalism* (Berkeley: University of California Press, 2005).

Grenoble, Day of the Tiles (7 June 1788)

The day of popular protest in support of the ***parlement*** of Dauphiné province, in which four people died and about forty suffered injuries, has been taken as an opening salvo of the Revolution against royal government. There had been outbreaks of violence before that, in Rennes to support the Breton *parlement*, and in Pau for the sake of that of Béarn. These events are sometimes referred to as the 'noble revolt'.[16]

The **Assembly of Notables** had met between February and May 1787, and had not co-operated, either with **Calonne** or with **Loménie de Brienne**, in attempts to regenerate the nation's finances and morale. The ennobled magistrates in the *parlements* objected to the attempt to by-pass their authority which Calonne had made by summoning the Assembly of Notables, and began their call for the **Estates-General** as the only competent body to raise new taxation. The king and Brienne tried to abolish the *parlements* altogether, instead of sending them 'on vacation' to another town nearby, as had often happened in the past (e.g. Paris to Troyes, Bordeaux to Libourne). By the 'May Edicts' of 1788, they were to be replaced by an entirely new plenary court of law.

The magistrates (*parlementaires*) of Grenoble – though they were not alone among the *parlements*: Pau and Rennes and Bordeaux reacted similarly – responded on 7 June by meeting in their president's house in the town to set up the provincial estates. Brienne issued orders to the military commandant of Dauphiné, Clermont-Tonnerre, to arrest them, and issued the *lettres de cachet* for the purpose. A popular rising then burst out. All the market stalls and shops closed, people took to the roof of the former Jesuit College and hurled tiles down upon the soldiers, some of whom reacted with shot and bayonets. The rioters then ransacked the governor's house. The magistrates negotiated with Clermont-Tonnerre, and order returned. A young Protestant lawyer called Antoine **Barnave** had written a memorandum defending the *parlements* as a last rampart against despotism, and he was backed up by an equally young judge, Jean-Joseph **Mounier**. On their initiative, it was agreed on 14 June that there would be a token meeting of the three orders in the provincial estates.[17] This was held on 21 July in the Château de Vizille outside the town, the property of a rich industrialist called Claude Périer. Clermont-Tonnerre's successor Marshal de Vaux permitted it. The magistrates walked there in their red and ermine robes, joined by 50 from the clergy, 165 nobles and 276 from the **Third Estate**. (Even so, none of the large towns in the

Dauphiné were represented, and of the province's 1,212 parishes, only 194 sent representatives.) The assembly decreed the re-establishment of the Dauphiné Estates abolished in 1628, with double representation for the Third Estate, the end of clerical and noble tax privileges, and admission of *roturiers* (commoners) to all offices. They also asked the king for the Estates-General to be summoned. There was considerable reaction to this all over France and the Vizille assembly became something of a model for what happened nationally.[18]

On 8 August 1788, Brienne abolished the plenary court and set 1 May 1789 as the date for the convening of the Estates-General for which elections would have to be arranged at provincial level. [19]

Grétry, André-Ernest Modeste (1741–1813)

Grétry grew up in Liège in the Austrian Netherlands and part of his musical training had been in Rome. He had been in the musical establishment in Paris for 20 years before the Revolution began. He was a prolific composer of comic opera, and supported the French rather than the Italian party in the great contemporary musicians' dispute known as the *querelle des bouffons*.[20] He was acquainted with **Voltaire**. He accommodated himself to the Revolution and became an inspector of the *Conservatoire,* and a member of the *Institut de France*. He wrote memoirs, which contain his reflections on the relation between a musician's art and his political environment.

Unenthusiastically, he wrote acceptable works such as the one-act opera *La fête de la raison,* the lyrics of which were written by the atheist Sylvain Maréchal, performed after **Thermidor** as *La rosière républicaine*, at the Paris Opera on 2 September 1794. He also wrote an opera about the boy-martyr for the Republic, Joseph **Bara**. In the last year of the **Directory** (though no one knew it was), in March 1799, he wrote *Music for the Planting of a Tree of Liberty* as a sextet for wind instruments.[21]

During the Empire, he received the cross of the Legion of Honour and was given a pension.

📖 Charlton, David, *Grétry and the Growth of Opéra-comique* (Cambridge: Cambridge University Press, 1986).

Gros, Antoine-Jean, Baron (1771–1835)

Gros became associated with **Bonaparte** in Italy in 1796, and benefited from his patronage as a painter of themes and portraits. Such paintings as *Bonaparte Visiting the Plague Victims of Jaffa* and *The Battle of Eylau* were to be significant in creating the Napoleonic legend during the Empire but, before that, Bonaparte's patronage as a mere general was fruitful.

Gros's parents were artists and they passed on their skills to their son at an early age. He joined **David**'s studio in 1785, while he was still at the Collège Mazarin. After he had tried and failed to win the Rome Prize, he painted portraits with deputies in the **National Convention** as his sitters. Unlike David, Gros was not committed to supporting the official **Terror** in 1793, and left for Genoa, living on his portrait commissions. He encountered Joséphine Bonaparte and followed her to Milan, where she presented him to the victorious Bonaparte.[22]

Gros was given a post with the **army** after the battle of Arcola. In 1797, on Joséphine's recommendation, Bonaparte appointed him as head of the commission to choose the paintings and *objets d'art* to be taken to the Louvre as prizes of war. He was fulfilling commissions all the time. Gros escaped from besieged Genoa in 1799, and made his way to Paris, where he set up his studio in the Capucins, winning the prize offered by the consuls with his painting of *The Battle of Nazareth* in 1802. Other battle paintings followed.

He was painter to the Empire and, after Napoleon's defeat, worked under the restored Bourbons. His decoration of the ceiling of the church of Sainte-Geneviève (the Pantheon in the revolutionary years), begun in 1811 and completed in 1824, gained him a barony from King Louis-Philippe.[23] He continued to benefit from David's advice when he visited him in exile in Brussels. But his neo-classical style was being replaced by that of the romantic painters, and he lost pupils from his studio. He committed suicide in 1835 and his body was found in the Seine on 25 June.

Guillotin, Joseph-Ignace (1738–1814)

There is an 'apt fable'[24] that Joseph-Ignace Guillotin's premature birth was provoked by the screams his mother heard from a man being broken on the wheel as she walked along the bank of the Charente at Saintes. Be that as it may, 51 years later, he proposed to the **Constituent Assembly**'s committee on capital punishment that all criminals condemned to death, whatever their social status, should be decapitated by 'a simple mechanism'. Deputies laughed at the thought of heads rolling away, but they accepted the proposal.

By then Guillotin was a medical doctor in Paris, having graduated with a good degree from the Academy of Medicine. In 1784, he had served on a royal commission to examine the claims of Anton Mesmer about 'animal magnetism'. He also wrote a pamphlet containing suggestions about how the **Estates-General** should be organized, and was elected as one of the 10 deputies for Paris as a result.

Once at **Versailles**, it was found that the **Third Estate** deputies could not hear the speakers, so he proposed that the seats should be arranged in a semi-circle with the tribune placed centrally, as all national assemblies have been arranged ever since. When the Third Estate seemed to have been locked out of their usual meeting hall, it was Guillotin who suggested they should go to a nearby real tennis court.[25]

This compassionate man spoke in the Assembly's debate on 1 December 1789 in favour of the death penalty being phased out altogether. As a first step towards this end, he proposed on 20 January that the death penalty should be the same for all without distinction. His motion was adjourned, but raised again on 3 June by **Peletier de Saint-Fargeau** and it formed the basis of a decree adopted on 25 September. He was appalled when the name *Guillotine* was given to the machine that was put into use, especially when its use became so frequent in the **Terror** and a public spectacle.

Politically, Guillotin was a **Feuillant**, and he resumed his medical career as chief surgeon of the military hospital in Arras. He returned to Paris in 1795 and was imprisoned for four weeks after making inflammatory comments as secretary of the primary assembly of the Halle-au-blé section at the time of the **Vendémiaire** rising. After examination by the **Committee of General Security** – a more balanced procedure under the Thermidorean Convention than previously – he was set free, and left active politics to take up his medical practice again.[26]

Guillotine

There were precedents for the guillotine in other countries, such as the Halifax Gibbet, the Scottish Maiden, and Swiss and Italian ones, dating from the Middle Ages. In France in earlier times, only nobles were beheaded, but sometimes the process was excruciatingly inefficient. Commoners were hanged with no deep-drop device, so that could take a long time too. Breaking on the wheel, by which the executioner tied the condemned man to a cartwheel and broke his limbs with an iron bar, was banned early in the Revolution.

Then a committee was set up in 1789 to make recommendations for a means of execution to be applied all over France in the newly prevalent spirit of national uniformity. The committee's president was Dr Antoine Louis. Dr **Guillotin** was one of its members. Guillotin's proposal for decapitation by a 'simple mechanism' was intended to be as humane as possible. Six months after Dr Guillotin's proposal, Justice Minister Roederer ordered a design for such a mechanism from Dr Louis, since he was the Permanent Secretary of the Academy of Surgery (so it was nearly called the 'Louisette'). The prototype was made by a piano manufacturer, Tobias Schmidt,[27] who took out a patent on it. The highwayman Nicolas Pelletier was the first to undergo this legal death penalty on 25 April 1792.[28] The military kept the firing squad as an alternative, as did **Fouché** at **Lyon** and **Hoche** after the **Quiberon** invasion. **Fréron** regretted not having a guillotine at **Toulon**.

The humanitarian principle behind the invention was soon made redundant when the official **Terror** gathered momentum after June 1793 and the 'National Razor' was in great demand in Paris and ordered by **representatives on mission**. Collenot d'Angremont, a royalist who led a conspiracy just before the **'Day' of 10 August 1792**, was the first political victim of the guillotine, condemned by the special tribunal on 17 August and decapitated on 21 August.[29] After that, anything between 16 and 40 thousand were executed by it on a national scale during the Revolution.

In Paris, execution by the guillotine became a public spectacle on the scaffold in the Place Louis XV, renamed as Place de la Révolution (and later Place de la Concorde). Personalities such as **Danton** made execution their final performance. The king's attempt to speak to the crowd was drowned by drum rolls. Most died with dignity, exceptions being Camille **Desmoulins** and Madame du Barry, Louis XV's last official mistress.

Its use was abolished in 1981 while Robert Badinter, co-biographer of **Condorcet** with his wife Elisabeth, was Minister of Justice.

Arasse, Daniel, *The Guillotine and the Terror*, trans. Christopher Miller (London: Penguin Books, 1991).

H

Hanriot, François (1761–94)

François Hanriot's part in the Revolution was as **National Guard** commander of the Parisian battalions, principally when the **Girondins** were expelled from the Convention and in his attempt to rescue **Robespierre** during the **Thermidor coup**.

His parents were peasants who had become servants in a bourgeois household in Nanterre. He was clerk in a notary's office as a young man and was working for the Farmers-Generals' tax office when the Revolution started. The building where he worked was set on fire, and he joined in the riot on 12 July to the extent of burning the files he had been working on, for which he was sent to the Bicêtre prison. **Marat**'s press campaign gained the rioters their freedom.[1]

Hanriot lived in the Jardin des Plantes section of the over-populated Saint-Marcel suburb and, as the section secretary, became the mouthpiece of the **sansculottes** there. He was in armed combat during the attack on the **Tuileries** on the **'Day' of 10 August 1792** against the king's Swiss Guards, and was elected commander of his section's National Guard Battalion on 2 September, the first day of the **September Massacres**.

He was promoted to command the Paris National Guard on the evening of 30 May 1793, in time to direct 80,000 sansculottes in their action against the **Girondins** in the **National Convention** during the following three days. Marat called him the 'saviour of the country' for what he did. Nine days afterwards he offered his resignation, but the Paris Commune would not let him go until they had found a replacement. He was re-elected by

9,087 votes out of 15,152 on 1 July[2] and given the rank of brigadier on 3 July. On 19 September he became a general.

Hanriot differed greatly from his two predecessors, **Lafayette** and **Santerre**, but he was the 'incarnation of the new political choice.'[3] He was entrusted with maintaining order in the capital in the winter of 1793–4, and it was said of him that he was more like the father of a family than a commanding officer, bringing out a sense of republican morality and sanculotte values in his troops. His order of the day of 6 brumaire year II said: 'In a free country, the police ought not to take action with pikes or bayonets, but with reason and philosophy ...'[4] Here, of course, he was talking about maintaining order, rather than intimidating the uncommitted deputies in the Convention (who were known as the Plain or Marsh) to exclude the Girondins, as he had called the sanculottes to do five months earlier.

As a member of the **Cordeliers**, he was associated with the Hébertists, but **Robespierre** protected him when **Hébert** was executed. He stood up against **Carnot** who wanted to take cannon away from Paris. He was dismissed by the Convention as the Thermidor coup gathered momentum. He tried to rescue Robespierre, **Couthon**, **Saint-Just** and **Le Bas** from the Hôtel de Ville in the confusion of the night of 9–10 thermidor, but he was outlawed himself on the Convention's orders. He tried to hide, but was found, wounded in the head, in a yard alongside the Hôtel de Ville. He was guillotined on the evening of 28 July with the other Robespierrists.[5]

Hébert, Jacques-René (1757–94)

Hébert was one of the Revolution's radicals, with ideas, but not a lifestyle, in conformity with the **sanculottes**. His major contribution to events was as a journalist and newspaper publisher. *Le Père Duchesne* consisted of a running commentary on events and personalities. Père Duchesne himself was a pipe-smoking stove maker with a good line in the language of the street.

His father had been a goldsmith and a member of the chamber of commerce in Alençon, but he died young, and Hébert had a struggle for existence. He went to Paris, where he worked in street theatre and tried to write plays. He lived from hand to mouth among the workmen and masons of the Place Maubert, where he became very conversant with the popular language of which he made such effective use. When the

Revolution started, he wrote pamphlets, and had found a place in the **Cordeliers Club** by 1791. *Le Père Duchesne* first appeared in 1790 and lived as long as its creator, commercially successful as well as promoting the radical cause.[6]

Hébert was a constitutional monarchist at first, with friendly mentions of 'that good old bloke (*vieux bougre*) the king'. The king's flight to **Varennes** changed that, and the paper was increasingly radical. He took up the causes of popular sovereignty and the right to work. The Paris Commune and successive war ministers bought up copies of *Le Père Duchesne* to distribute free to poor people and soldiers. His jibes at the king and queen became increasingly insulting. He was present when the **National Guard** fired into the crowd on 17 July 1791 at the Champ de Mars. The verbal abuse against public figures became sharper as a result. He was a delegate from the Bonne-Nouvelle Section in the **Insurrectionary Commune** of 10 August 1792. By that time he had his own printing press for his two journals, the other being the *Journal du soir sans réflexions,* a daily account of the **Legislative Assembly**. He wrote approvingly of the **September Massacres**. In December 1792, he was elected to a legal post in the Paris Commune. He joined the **Jacobin Club** in January 1793 and was **Marat's** ally when the **sansculottes** helped with the expulsion of the **Girondins** from the Convention, and supported the rounding-up of **Brissot** and the others for execution afterwards.

He was instrumental in the *journée* of 5 September 1793 along with **Chaumette**. He opposed the **Maximum** on Prices and Wages introduced in September 1793 because it favoured hoarding, and was imprisoned for three days following his outburst against it. When the **Revolutionary Calendar** was adopted in October, Hébert was among the leaders of de-Christianization. **Robespierre** and **Saint-Just** disliked his atheism, favouring belief in the **Supreme Being**. In the Republic of Virtue, any other viewpoint was counter-revolutionary.

The **Committee of Public Safety** ordered **Fouquier-Tinville**, prosecutor in the Revolutionary Tribunal, to draw up charges against Hébert, **Vincent**, **Ronsin** and the printer **Momoro**. Saint-Just told him to 'amalgamate' the evidence against them in the absence of hard fact.[7] Others were charged at the same time, so as to add evidence of a foreign plot against the Convention. Witnesses were suborned, and there was no written evidence against the Hébertistes. No defence witnesses were permitted. The trial filled the three days needed for the jury to accept that all of them were guilty. On 24 March, the verdict was given in the morning and the executions were carried out in the afternoon.

@ Extracts from *Le Père Duchesne* are given online at:
http://www.marxists.org/history/france/revolution/hebert/index.htm

Helvetic Republic

Switzerland had always maintained its independence though its ties with France were significant. In 1790, a Helvetian Club was set up in Paris to diffuse the ideas of the French Revolution to the Swiss cantons. This provoked popular risings in many places and the French annexed Porrentuy province in 1791 with **Bernard de Saintes** as **representative on mission** at the time.

Switzerland took no part in the **War of the First Coalition**. There was an anti-French backlash after the **'Day' of 10 August 1792**, when so many Swiss mercenary breadwinners were cut down by the **sansculottes** of the **Insurrectionary Commune**.[8] However, there were plenty of radicals there who were willing, after the Peace of **Campo Formio** in 1797, to welcome French expansion. Peter Ochs, tired of the decaying federation with which he had been associated since 1776, negotiated with **Reubell** and **Bonaparte** in December to plan a French takeover. A rising in the Vaud in February 1798 led to General Brune invading the country with little opposition. Mulhouse and Geneva were annexed by France, but the new Helvetic Republic was formed out of the other 23 cantons with its capital at Lucerne. It was to be governed by a French-style directory. A treaty with France assured French control of the Alpine passes.

The final year of the French republic saw attempts by Austrians and Russians in the Second Coalition to wrest the country away from France in support of popular risings. The advent of Bonaparte as First Consul with his Act of Mediation in 1802 stabilized the situation, and the republic changed its name to the Helvetic Confederation.[9]

Hérault de Séchelles, Marie-Jean (1759–94)

Hérault de Séchelles stands out as one who, born into noble circumstances, profited from patronage, but rejected his old-regime life for an extreme position in the Revolution, only to become a victim of the **Terror** himself.

He was educated by the Oratorians at the prestigious college of Juilly and qualified as a lawyer at the Châtelet in Paris at the age of 20, to become advocate-general in the Paris *parlement*. He had met and talked to **Rousseau**, and cultivated literary interests. André **Chénier** compared him to Cato and to Catullus alike. He was related to, and under the patronage of, the **Polignac** family, who helped him into his position of responsibility in the Paris *parlement* and presented him to the queen. He lost credit at **Versailles**, however, by having some implication in the **Diamond Necklace Affair**. The **nobility** of Mantes distanced themselves from him at election time in 1789, so he was not a Second Estate deputy in the **Estates-General**. Hérault was present in person at the storming of the **Bastille**, although perhaps no more than as an observer.

He travelled in Switzerland for a while and, on his return in December 1789, was elected as a judge in Paris and then to the civil tribunal of the Paris Department. He joined the **Jacobins**, left with the **Feuillants** after the king's return from **Varennes**, and then was elected as a Paris deputy (14 out of 24) in the **Legislative Assembly**. He spoke in support of the war party after the declaration of **Pillnitz**. As a member of the diplomatic committee, it was he who had to propose the decree on the *patrie* in danger on 11 July 1792 which raised the level of enthusiasm for the war. When the monarchy had been overthrown in August 1792, he criticized the **Insurrectionary Commune**, and was not elected by the capital to the Convention. He was in the **National Convention** as a deputy for the Seine et Oise.[10]

Hérault was considered to be among the substantial number of deputies in the National Convention who were loyal neither to the Jacobins nor the **Girondins**, and was sent on mission to the new department of Mont Blanc in November 1792. He delayed his return until April 1793 (so as to stay with Adèle de Bellegarde), and was away for the king's trial and execution. He returned to be president of the Convention on 31 May when the Girondins were being excluded. Then he was elected to the **Committee of**

Public Safety and was in charge of foreign relations. His moment of glory was on 10 August 1793 at a fête for the first anniversary of the overthrow of the monarchy, making speeches at six halts of a procession from the Champ de Mars to the Place de la Bastille.

During his subsequent tours as a **representative on mission**, he was under suspicion and reports came back to Paris about his meetings with foreigners. He allied with the Hébertists over the Cult of **Reason**. **Robespierre** did not trust him because he was a former noble and an atheist. He was denounced as being a friend of Proly, the natural son of the Austrian minister Kaunitz, of a Portuguese called Pereira, and of **Clootz**. He offered to resign from the Convention but he was made to stay and 'justify his conduct', as was said. He left the Committee of Public Safety in February 1794 and was denounced for retaining contacts with aristocrats and for his liaison with Adèle who was the wife of an Austrian general.

Fabre d'Eglantine charged Hérault with harbouring an *émigré* and caused his arrest on 15 March. He was included in the accusations brought against the Dantonists by **Saint-Just** a fortnight later. On the way to the scaffold on 5 April, he tried to lend some courage to the desperate Camille **Desmoulins**.[11]

Hoche, Louis Lazare (1768–97)

Hoche had a distinguished career, one of the Revolution's success stories. He joined the army in the ranks as a boy soldier in 1784 and used his spare time to educate himself. His original regiment was disbanded in 1789 and he served in several others before being commissioned in 1792. A year later he was a general.

He was at Neerwinden as an aide-de-camp in the Austrian Netherlands when the Prince of Coburg defeated **Dumouriez** on 18 March 1793, and was a suspect under arrest after Dumouriez defected to the Austrians. Upon release he served in the defence of Dunkirk and Thionville. He was the general commanding the Army of the Moselle in October 1793, but lost his first battle at Kaiserslautern at the end of November against the Prussians. He was not deprived of his command, however, having impressed the **Committee of Public Safety** with his energy. On 22 December, he attacked Wurmser's Austrian force at Fröschweiler and was put in command of the Army of the Rhine by the **representatives on mission**. At the battle of Wissembourg which followed on 26–27 December 1793 against a combined Austro-Prussian force, Hoche forced the enemy back across the Rhine and regained Alsace for the Republic.

His predecessor in the Army of the Rhine was Charles **Pichegru**, who had him charged with treason in March 1794 (just after his marriage). He remained in prison until the fall of **Robespierre** at the end of July, and then was given command against the **Vendée rebellion** in August. He made the truce at La Jaunaye with **Charette** on 15 February 1795, but it did not hold. The British Navy landed a force of *émigrés* on the **Quiberon** peninsula on 16 July and he and **Tallien** had 750 of them executed after their defeat. A year later, it was considered that he had pacified the west after more than three years of bitter struggle.

In February 1796, Wolfe Tone, the leader of the United Irishmen, presented a plan to the Directory for Franco-Irish collaboration against the British, asking for a general and 30,000 men. Hoche's services were offered because he had been successful in the west. He met Tone in Paris, and accepted the command, with 15,000 of his troops. The expedition was ill-prepared and called off by the **Directory** but, learning that Ireland was in full rebellion, he set out on 17 December. A tempest prevented any landing, and Hoche was back within a month. The Army of Ireland was dissolved in February.[12] Hoche went to lead the Sambre and Meuse Army. He returned to the Rhine and won an important engagement with Werneck's Austrians at Neuwied on April 18 1797. His success there contributed to the Peace of Leoben.

He entered political life to become war minister under the Directory, who saw him as an alternative to **Bonaparte** in defending them, but he soon resigned to return to the Rhine. He died of consumption in September 1797, depriving Bonaparte of his only serious rival.

Houchard, Jean-Nicolas (1739–93)

Houchard was a career soldier in the old régime, never promoted above the rank of captain. His main contribution as a revolutionary general was his unappreciated victory at Hondschoote against the Duke of York. After that, this first non-noble general became the victim of mixed messages in the **Committee of Public Safety** at the time when the **Law of Suspects** was being planned.[13]

The Revolution had shown Houchard to be a man of **sansculotte** convictions, even to the point of wearing a **Phrygian bonnet** on parade on one occasion. Nevertheless, he had been denounced by the Jacobins in his home in Strasbourg as soon as he was put in command of the Army of the North.

While the '**Day**' of **5 September 1793** was in full spate, **Carnot** received a complaint from General Houchard on the eve of his battle that he was insufficiently supplied with men and war *matériel* and had to rely on weak subordinate officers. Nevertheless, he engaged the British and Hanoverian forces in a three-day action, dispersed his adversaries and occupied Dunkirk. Despite this being the first victory of the Republic after six months of reversal,[14] it was not in accordance with the Committee of Public Safety's orders. They had wanted a knock-out blow sufficient to raise a revolution in England. Houchard did not pursue the Duke of York's army. It was left intact, and he had dissipated his own forces contrary to Carnot's explicit orders. Carnot and **Bouchotte** found him at fault. He was charged with treason as well as disobedience: letters found in his headquarters showed him to be in contact with enemy aristocrats.

Houchard was imprisoned and sent before the **Revolutionary Tribunal**. Despite showing his gallantly acquired wounds, he was guillotined on 17 November (26 brumaire, year II). He had commanded the Army of the North for only six weeks. He was succeeded by **Jourdan**.

Hulks (*pontons*) of Rochefort

Navy Minister Dalbarade had devised a scheme for dealing with **refractory clergy** who had not voluntarily left France, and the **National Convention** accepted it. The plan to deport them all to Guiana in 1793 and turn them into cattle farmers was unworkable, but they were brought from all over France on horrifying journeys to Bordeaux and to Rochefort with the intention that these subversive 'fanatics' should disappear from French life.

In Rochefort, 1,100 of these clergy were put on old slave ships (hulks) and left for 11 months in deliberately squalid conditions offshore in the Roads of Aix. After several months, an epidemic of typhus caused Chevillard, the naval commander in Rochefort, to move them to a tented encampment on a very small island that had become a national property – the Ile Madame (renamed Citoyenne). Two hundred and forty-one of them died there. The survivors were put back upon the hulks. After **Thermidor**, they were a little better treated, but were not released, except in special cases.

They were joined in the Roads of Aix by three other ships loaded with refractory clergy that had set out from Bordeaux for Guiana but were prevented by the British Navy from leaving the shelter of the coast. The original ships moved into the port of Rochefort in January 1795. The priests were taken to Saintes where they were kept in semi-liberty in the empty Abbaye aux Dames and then dispersed to their home departments. The priests from the Bordeaux ships were taken to the derelict fortress of Brouage near Rochefort and left under guard in the bitter cold. Eventually they too were released. The decision to release both groups rested in the hands of the **Committee of General Security**, but it was casually done on the basis of a hastily drawn-up list which left many at Brouage for much longer than they need have been.

In 1798, the so-called 'Directorial Terror' sent many of them back to the islands near Rochefort, where they were detained again on hulks and in the fortresses of Ré and Oléron almost until the signing of the *Concordat* in 1801 by First Consul **Bonaparte** and Pope Pius VII, when they were reincorporated into life in France.[15]

I

'Infernal Columns' (January 1794)

On 23 December 1793, the Catholic and Royal Army of the **Vendée** had been defeated at Savenay. The only rebel force still in the field was **Charette's**. General Louis-Marie Turreau was appointed commander of the Army of the West and presented his plan for a scorched earth policy of aggression. Twelve infantry columns would advance in parallel from east to west over territory held by the rebels holding out beyond **Cholet** towards General Haxo's troops on the coast. The **Committee of Public Safety** accepted his plan. It was nothing new in fact. The 'extermination' of the Vendée had been ordered by the Convention at the beginning of August, and was already being carried out. **Carnot** decided that France had not enough resources to fight on two fronts beyond 1795, and that the Vendée war must be ended in spring 1794. To meet this requirement, Turreau's strategy of severe repression seemed ideal in the climate of official **Terror**. Turreau tried to evade responsibility by having the Convention issue a clear warning of the possible massacre of women, children and old people. The Committee of Public Safety would not give it, but repeated the extermination order of 1 August. They gave a blank cheque to Turreau and to the **representative on mission**, one of the committee, **Prieur de la Marne,** to take all measures necessary for public safety.[1]

The **sansculottes** now in charge in La Rochelle agreed that the town should provide horses and carts in exchange for all the grain and livestock likely to be acquired by them in this action. Turreau's 'columns from hell' advanced from Parthenay, Bressuire, Doué and Angers on 22 pluviôse (10 February 1794) with a force of 70,000 gathered from all over France. They obeyed their orders to slaughter men, women and children indiscriminately. This was deliberate policy in the villages of the Vendée, even to the extent of using bayonets to economize on shot.

Disgusted as much as frightened, many republican soldiers deserted. The wounded in hospital in La Rochelle prolonged their stay there as much as possible, and were registered as suffering from the 'sickness of the Vendée'. Young soldiers were terrified by stories of atrocities perpetrated on captured republicans by the rebels' families. It was a mutual horror.

Protests were immediately made. **Robespierre's** own confidant, Marc-Antoine **Jullien**, complained from La Rochelle that inhabitants of communes in the Vendée where the houses had been set on fire by the 'Blues' were themselves arresting other rebels in order to hand them over to the republicans in self-protection. He went on:

'Can you believe that, on the pretext of following your orders, they [republican soldiers] cut the throats of children, women and municipal officers in their sashes ... or that your generals set the example of pillaging to make the sublime task of a defender of the *patrie* degenerate into the vile occupation of a *voleur*?' [2]

Turreau's subordinate generals also made protests. The Vendéans were now more determined to resist, and a spirit of revenge brought more recruits into the ranks of the counter-revolutionary army led by Charette and **Stofflet**.

Turreau's disgrace lasted only until 1797, and he served subsequently in the Army of Italy.

Insurrectionary Commune

The Insurrectionary Commune was the body responsible for instigating the attack on the **Tuileries Palace** on the **'Day' of 10 August** that ended with the suspension of the monarchy, the loss of 400 **sansculotte** lives and the massacre of the king's Swiss Guards.

Developments towards it began on 27 July when the Paris Commune council set up an office to enable the 48 sections of the capital to correspond with each other. On 30 July, the section assemblies began to admit 'passive' citizens to their meetings. The next day, the Mauconseil section (which included part of the **Faubourg Saint-Antoine**) declared its non-recognition of **Louis XVI** as King of the French. On 3 August, delegates from 47 sections (the exception was the Temple), went to the bar of the **Legislative Assembly** to demand the removal of the king. The assembly made no decision, so the section Quinze-Vingts (off the rue Saint-Denis) gave it an ultimatum and invited other sections to pressurize the deputies. Common action was resolved upon and, in the evening of 9 August, an assembly of section representatives, led by the Quinze-Vingts, invited the sections to send three representatives each to the Commune 'to advise on saving public affairs'. The representatives sat in a room next to the one used by the Commune's general council in the Hôtel de Ville, and declared themselves the true general council at first light on 10 August. They dismissed the former *chevalier*, Antoine Mandat, **Lafayette**'s recent successor, from command of the Paris **National Guard** (he was to be assassinated by the end of the day) to be replaced with Antoine **Santerre**, the brewer who identified with the sansculottes.[3]

They kept **Pétion** as mayor, who was caught between his need to maintain order and his fear that the attack on the palace would fail. Santerre mobilized the National Guard through the sections, although previously it had had no links with them, and the officers – some of whom were royalists – were hesitant to obey. This made the presence of the *fédérés* in the capital so important to the radical insurrectionists, who made a great effort to recruit them for the attack on the **Tuileries Palace** on the morning of 10 August and to make an alliance between them and the city's sansculottes.[4] An army of 20,000 men was formed virtually overnight.

There was no certainty about the outcome. The palace was defended by some 4,000 men, including the Swiss regiment and aristocratic bodyguards who would not be hesitant in resistance.[5] They had affirmed their loyalty to the king the day before. It was to these that the queen drew attention in the morning when the king decided to seek refuge in the Assembly.[6]

When the violence was over, the Legislative Assembly recognized the Insurrectionary Commune, which remained in being until 2 December, and promised to call a **National Convention** to draw up a new constitution. The Commune changed its membership from 3 members per section to 6, making a body of 288, including the inevitable lawyers, some writers, civil servants, medical men and skilled artisans. There were only two working men. At the outset there were no big names. **Robespierre**, **Billaud-Varenne**, **Collot d'Herbois**, **Marat**, **Tallien**, **Carra**, **Santerre** and **Danton** were added on 11 August, although, as minister of justice, Danton had a hand in organizing what happened at the palace, and the future mayor, **Pache**, was brought in on the day after.[7]

The Insurrectionary Commune sat every day without being summoned, and set about a raft of radical decrees for the city. It abolished the distinction between **active** and passive citizens. The statues of Louis XIV and Henry IV were taken away, the busts of **Necker**, Lafayette and **Bailly** were broken, delegates were sent to the departments and armies, a surveillance committee was set up, **Chaumette** was given full power to arrest and set free. **Refractory priests** and royalist journalists were rounded up by the victors of 10 August, some of whom wore pieces of dead **Swiss Guards** uniforms and had royalists' ears sewn on their hats. There was hostility from the **Girondins** in the Legislative. They wanted the Department of the Seine to control the new commune.[8]

Isnard, Maximin (1755–1825)

Maximin Isnard's revolution involved a certain amount of inconsistency, some luck as a **Girondin** and the utterance of an elegant and memorable saying.

In 1791, he was a businessman at Draguignan in the Var and was elected as a deputy for the Var department in the **Legislative Assembly**. He allied himself with the emerging Girondins. As opposed to the nominees of **Brissot**, who became ministers in the constitutional monarchy, he attacked the court in the **Tuileries** and pressed the idea that there was an '**Austrian Committee**' working against French interests. Nevertheless, during the '**Day' of 20 June 1792**, when the **sansculottes** burst into the palace and threatened the king, Isnard and some other deputies stood near him to offer protection. Even so, he was chosen to go to the Army of the North to explain what had happened on the '**Day' of 10 August**.

In the **National Convention** he voted for the king's death. He was an original member of the **Committee of General Security** in January 1793. On 25 May, when the Paris Commune petitioned for **Hébert's** release from detention, Isnard was president and made the observation: 'If, through these continually renewed rebellions, the principle of national representation suffers, I tell you in the name of France that people will soon be searching the banks of the Seine to see if Paris ever existed.'[9]

Despite this, Isnard was allowed to resign as a deputy on 2 June 1793 in time to avoid involvement in the fate of the 29 Girondins who were arrested. When arraigned with others like him on 3 October, he escaped and went into hiding. In March 1795, he came back to the Convention in support of the **Thermidorean** reaction. He was on mission in the Midi and did nothing to prevent the massacre of the revolutionaries detained in Fort Saint-Jean in Marseille during the **'White Terror'** of May 1795. On his return, he was charged with favouring the royalists, but defended himself successfully. The outcome was his election to the Council of 500.[10]

He was not returned in the partial election of 1797 and went home to Draguignan to write in favour of Catholicism and, later, the Empire. He was made a baron of the Empire and supported **Napoleon** in the 100 Days. Nevertheless, the **Restoration Monarchy** left him in peace for his last ten years.

Italian Campaign (1796–7)

General **Bonaparte** was appointed by the Directors to command the Army of Italy on 2 March 1796 and joined it on 27 March. The **Directory's** strategy was that he should provide the southern jaw of a huge pincer movement, of which the upper jaw should be an attack on the Rhine by Moreau and **Jourdan**. Whatever conquests Bonaparte might make in Italy would be used as bargaining counters at a peace conference after a putative victory.

Bonaparte made his headquarters at Savona on 9 April and advanced towards Turin to impose peace terms on Piedmont on 28 April. On 10 May, he defeated Beaulieu's Austrians at Lodi and sent Masséna to occupy Milan after three days. Bonaparte went to Milan and authorized the removal of art treasures to Paris and also war indemnities so that the campaign should not increase the strain on the French treasury.

Bonaparte soon chased the Austrians out of the whole of Lombardy. His siege of Mantua had to be abandoned on 31 July, although the Austrians under Würmser were repulsed at Castiglione on 5 August. Bonaparte moved to Trent in the Tyrol, which he took on 5 September. Würmser evaded Bonaparte and returned to Mantua, only to be forestalled by **Masséna**'s arrival there. Bonaparte founded the **Cisalpine** and **Cispadine** republics to allow control sympathetic to France. The Austrians Avanti and Davidovich went on the offensive in early November and forced Bonaparte back to Verona. Despite being outnumbered, he was victorious at Arcola on 17 November after three days' fighting. Avanti was halted at Rivoli on 15 January 1797. Mantua fell on 2 February. Bonaparte drove Archduke Charles back and then imposed a provisional peace on 17 April at Leoben. In October, its terms were made formal in the Treaty of **Campo Formio**.

The Directors found that policy was being dictated by the general, and they had no choice but to go along with it.[11]

J

Jacobin Club

After the **Constituent Assembly** moved to Paris in October 1789, a rented room not far from the *Manège* in the Dominican Convent of Saint-Jacques became the venue for a group calling themselves 'the committee of the Revolution'. This name was soon changed to the less provocative 'Society of the Friends of the Constitution'. By January 1790, they were calling themselves the Jacobins, after their meeting place. Many of them had been in the Breton Club at Versailles, which had been essentially for deputies from Brittany, though it had other adherents, such as **Robespierre** from Artois. Others came from the **Palais-Royal** coalition, such as **Mirabeau**, **Le Chapelier**, **Duport**, **Barnave** and the **Lameth** brothers. The Jacobin Club was a new organization. Its purpose was to review the working of the assembly and to plan strategies for legislation as the issues arose, subject to their own guiding principles.

The formation of the Club for 'patriots' (the contemporary meaning of which was lovers of liberty[1]) was a reaction to the power being asserted in the **Constituent Assembly** by the nobles and the clergy. **La Révellière-Lépeaux** (later one of the executive directors) recorded in his memoirs that the aristocratic party used to hold meetings in which they arranged for the election of the assembly's officials. The left decided to take similar action. Timothy Tackett has argued (against François **Furet**) that, at least until 1790, the Jacobins were in a minority in the Constituent Assembly, while the king and the rightist coalition held genuine power. These first months of the assembly's existence were a period of intense struggle between the right and left for the support of a non-aligned centre group. What Tackett calls 'the dialectic of interaction'[2] was to intensify into the spring of 1790.

With increasing numbers, the Club moved into the Jacobins Library, a long room like the *Manège*, with benches facing each other and the president's rostrum in the centre of one side. They formed committees as in the assembly itself, with a steering committee to guide business, the initial members of which were Mirabeau, Barnave, Duport, Alexandre Lameth and Robespierre. The leadership was certainly radical from the outset. Barnave drew up regulations which were accepted as official in February. There were three principles: upholding the constitution, regarding all men as equal (despite the lack of success until the foundation of the Republic in removing the distinction between 'active' and 'passive' citizens), and unmasking and combating counter-revolutionary conspiracies.[3] From then on, a new intense idealism appeared in the members' attitudes. Constitutional clubs all over France soon began to exist under its umbrella. On the basis of these, the Jacobins would claim to represent the will of the nation.[4]

The idealism became even more intense when they became the **Mountain** in the **Legislative Assembly**, and then in the **National Convention**, when the Jacobins dominated the **Committees of Public Safety** and **General Security**, sending out **representatives on mission** such as **Barras**, **Carrier**, **Tallien**, **Collot-d'Herbois**, **Fouché**, **Fréron**, **Lequinio** and **Bernard de Saintes** to overcome any tendencies towards **federalism**. Their authority lasted until the **Thermidor coup** of July 1794.

Then, with Robespierre and his faction gone, the **Thermidorean Convention** dismantled much of the Mountain's programme and on 19 November (29 brumaire, year III) the Club's premises were locked up by Teresia Tallien, surrounded by a crowd of **'golden youth'**.

Jansenists

Many parish clergy and some of the lawyers in the *parlement* of Paris had adopted the teaching of the seventeenth-century Bishop of Ypres, Cornelius Otto Jansenius, with its distinctive spirituality and ideas on church organization. Ten per cent of the **clergy** elected to the **Estates-**

General were Jansenists. They energetically represented a large, deliberately inconspicuous, but influential sub-culture in the French Catholic Church. The bishops, on royal authority, had tried unsuccessfully to suppress Jansenism as a heresy all through the eighteenth century.

The Jansenist deputies obtained the **Constituent Assembly**'s adoption of the **Civil Constitution of the Clergy** in July 1790, based upon their principles.[5] The parish clergy were to become paid functionaries of the French nation, regardless of papal authority, and elected by active citizens. In November, another decree required all bishops and priests to take an oath to maintain the Civil Constitution in return for their not inconsiderable salaries, or be regarded as having resigned. Many of the clergy who took the oath in order to become elected constitutional curés were Jansenists. Among them was the Abbé Henri **Grégoire** who became constitutional bishop of the Loir et Cher department, based at Blois, and remained in the **National Convention**, wearing his purple cassock throughout the **Terror**, despite Archbishop **Gobel**'s having given in to de-Christianization.

The importance of the Jansenists for the Revolution was in their popularizing of the idea that obedience to an impersonal law was preferable to any arbitrary authority,[6] but the decisions made in 1790 'blew Jansenism apart'.[7]

 Doyle, William, *Jansenism* (Basingstoke: Macmillan, 2000), chap. 8.

Jemappes, Battle of (6 November 1792)

Following on from the victory at **Valmy** on 20 September 1792, **Dumouriez** moved north to invade the Austrian Netherlands and scored a second success at Jemappes with his superior numbers (32,000 infantry and 3,800 cavalry with 100 cannon) against the Austrians under Saxe-Teschen (with 11,600 infantry, 2,100 cavalry and 56 cannon dug in on a ridge near Mons), and by repeated charges. The name of the battle comes from a village at the north end of the ridge. The Duc d'**Orléans**'s son, the Duc de Chartres (future King Louis-Philippe), had command of the centre of the line and effectively dislodged the Austrians.[8]

This left the way to Brussels open and allowed the Revolution to be exported for a few months. The Austrian Netherlands were in French hands by 14 November, only to be lost again at the battle of Neerwinden five months later.

Jews in France during the Revolution

The Jewish minority population had been legally excluded from France since 1394, but the Revolution made Jews active citizens in the new nation. The emancipation decree was passed by the **Constituent**, but not until after anti-Semitism had surfaced in the national debate.[9]

In the years before the Revolution, Jews numbered around 39,000 out of a total population of the hexagon of 28 million. They were tolerated under strict conditions in Alsace and Lorraine. They also lived in **Avignon** and the Comtat-Venaissin, still Papal territory, and in Nice, ruled by the House of Savoy. In these areas, they were usually money-lenders or peddlers. Supplying horses and grain for the **army** gave them privileges in Strasbourg and Nancy. In Paris, 500 Jews were accepted as temporary residents, the law having turned a blind eye, as élite traders.

Portuguese Jews were allowed to live in Bordeaux and around Bayonne (though only after going through the motions of Christian baptism until 1776). Some were involved in lucrative colonial trading. Some small concessions were made in the 1780s and **Louis XVI** ordered Malherbes to examine the condition of French Jews as well as that of Protestants who received an edict of civil toleration in 1787.

The **Declaration of the Rights of Man and of the Citizen** proclaimed the equality of all born and living in France, and asserted that 'no one should be disturbed on account of his opinions, even religious'. Nevertheless, real changes were slow in coming, and met with opposition. The votes in the **Constituent Assembly** for Sephardic Jews to live in Bordeaux and Avignon were 374 to 280. Decisions about the admission of Ashkenazi Jews on the eastern borders and the abolition of all discrimination were delayed until 27 September 1791. It was, however, taken for granted by the legislators that the Jews in France were to be Frenchmen. Dual nationality was not acceptable. As a result, prominent Jews were subject to the same pressures as everyone else in the **Terror**. Hébertist atheism had the same effect on the Synagogue as on the Church in 1793–4. Prominent Jews and their rabbis went to the scaffold. Synagogues were closed and observance of the Sabbath forbidden. On the other hand, there were Jews who became enthusiastic **Jacobins** in Paris, and in Bordeaux. At Saint-Esprit-lès-Bayonne in the Landes, the Jacobin Club was almost exclusively Jewish.[10] When the French took Rome, the walls of the ghetto there were razed, and Jews were enthusiastic in planting trees of liberty in Frankfurt and elsewhere. Some Jews in the south-east were victims of the 'White Terror'.

Hyman, Paula, *The Jews of Modern France* (London and Berkeley, CA: University of California Press, 1998), chap. 2.

Jourdan, Jean-Baptiste (1762–1833)

Jourdan, like **Hoche**, represents a career open to the talents which the Revolution fostered. He had been a silk merchant's apprentice, then a boy soldier in the American War of Independence during which he was wounded and invalided out. He volunteered for the **army** again when the constitutional monarchy declared war on Austria in 1792. He was a general officer by 1793, a rise more rapid than Hoche's, and **Carnot** chose him to replace **Houchard** in command of the Army of the North in time to win the battle of Wattignies on 15–16 October 1793. He and Carnot secured the plateau and forced Coburg to lift the siege of Maubeuge and retreat.

He became a suspect in Jacobin eyes immediately afterwards, but Carnot and **Barère**, as members of the **Committee of Public Safety**, protected him and he went home to Limoges. The year 1794 saw him in command of the Army of the Sambre and Meuse, where he won the battle of **Fleurus** on 26 June, which brought the French frontier to the Rhine. In 1796, his army was the left wing of a broad advance on Vienna, with Moreau in the centre on the Danube and **Bonaparte** on the right in Italy.

Jourdan and Moreau were repulsed by Archduke Charles, and this led to Jourdan having no further command for two years. In the **Directory** he became a deputy in the Council of 500 and the Jourdan Law on conscription of 5 September 1798 was named after him. Its preamble stated: 'Any Frenchman is a soldier and owes himself to the defence of the nation.'

In the war against the Second Coalition which began in 1799, he was defeated by Archduke Charles in March, and stood down in favour of General **Masséna**. In spite of his opposition to Bonaparte's **Brumaire coup**, he accepted appointments from the First Consul and became a Marshal of France at the beginning of the Empire, serving in Italy and Spain, and suffering defeat at the hands of Wellington at Vitoria in Spain.

Despite supporting Napoleon in the 100 days, he accepted office under the Bourbons after Waterloo. In 1819, he was made a Peer of France. He ended his days as governor of Les Invalides.[11]

Jullien, Marc-Antoine (1775–1848)

Marc-Antoine Jullien's father was a deputy for the Drôme in the **National Convention**. At the age of 15, Marc-Antoine was working on a Paris newspaper. He joined the **Jacobin Club** only a year later, and is known to have opposed the **Declaration of War**. He was noticed by the new powers in the land and sent to London by **Condorcet** as a mediator between the **Girondins** and the British Whigs. January 1793 saw this 18-year-old briefly a government inspector of the Army of the Pyrenees.

He was then employed by **Robespierre** as his ears and eyes on various missions for the **Committee of Public Safety**. Jullien denounced General Turreau for the excesses of his **'infernal columns'**, **Carrier** in Nantes for his barbarous reprisals and, yet, **Tallien** and Thérèse **Cabarrus** in Bordeaux for their clemency. He was recalled to Paris on 24 April 1794 and placed on a committee to deal with public education. Then, back in Bordeaux, he carried out a purge to make sure there were no Girondins left there. After Robespierre fell, Jullien was arrested and stayed in prison until his father gained his release on 14 October 1795. By then, he had written a denial of his loyalty to Robespierre.

Jullien was a founder member of the **Pantheon Club**, and returned to journalism. He was employed by the police ministry in March 1796 to keep registers of *émigrés*. He went into hiding from May until October 1796, accused of complicity with **Babeuf**'s 'Conspiracy of Equals'.

He edited a newspaper during Bonaparte's Italian campaign and then accompanied the general to Egypt. He returned to administer the Parthenopean Republic (Naples). He welcomed the **Brumaire coup** and became more prominent in the Consulate and Empire, although he was interned for his contacts with Germaine de **Staël** in 1813. Subsequently he worked in the field of education during the **Restoration Monarchy**.[12]

Justices of the Peace (*Juges de Paix*)

The stabilization of the law and its availability to every citizen was a priority of the early phases of the Revolution. The control of law on a local scale by the seigneurs and the lawyers they employed in their courts had been overthrown on the **Night of 4 August 1789** by the National **Constituent Assembly** at **Versailles**. Under the old order, the course of justice was slow, arbitrary and often prolonged because the longer cases lasted, the more fees the lawyers could command in civil disputes. When it came to criminal cases, serious crimes were frequently not brought to court because it cost the seigneurs too much to prosecute someone against whom an accusation had been made. Rural law enforcement in the seigneurial courts was too weak to make criminal justice possible in any reliable sense.[13]

Yet it has been pointed out that the real problem with seigneurial justice was that it was anomalous.[14] A more public justice was being sought in the countryside, and this was close to being offered before the changes were made. Justice had to be seen to be done. A private court in which the lawyers drew larger fees for taking a long time over a decision was no longer appropriate from anyone's point of view. Improving the system was expected in the **statements of complaint**. Seigneurs hoped that former vassals would pay the redemption prices for their feudal dues on land authorized by the decree of 15 March 1790, but they could not prosecute them for the money because seigneurial courts were abolished by another decree of the Constituent in August.[15]

A revolutionary form of justice was implemented by laws passed in the Constituent Assembly on 16–24 August 1789, and on 19–22 July 1791. These laws set up the post of justice of the peace in every canton so that law could be readily available at a local level in small disputes, and virtually free to plaintiffs. The law also provided for the justice of the peace to be supported by two non-specialist assessors. The **active citizens** were to elect the *juge de paix* on the basis of his local reputation for probity and integrity, and his task was seen as a mediating one in civil disputes involving sums of money of less than 50 livres. No professional counsel need be involved in his cantonal court: their role was confined to district and higher courts and, even in those, a defendant could name his own defence counsel, who need not be a qualified lawyer. Small legal actions could now be resolved in a period of weeks, sometimes a few days, as opposed to the years that some cases had taken before the Revolution to the financial ruin of many involved, both innocent and guilty, with fines to be paid and costs to be settled amounting to several years' income.

Crubaugh, Anthony, *Balancing the Scales of Justice: Local Courts and Rural Society in Southwest France, 1750–1800* (University Park, PA: Pennsylvania State University Press, 2001).

L

Lacombe, Claire (1765–?)

Before the revolutionary years Lacombe had been a mediocre actress in **Marseille** and **Lyon**. Having arrived in Paris, she went to the **Cordeliers Club** to listen to the discussions. On 25 July 1792, she read a speech at the bar of the **Legislative**, dressed as an Amazon, to offer to fight against tyrants while demanding the arrest of General **Dumouriez**. She was awarded a civic crown for her belligerent presence in the **Tuileries** on the '**Day**' **of 10 August** with a battalion of *fédérés*.

In the winter of 1792, she had associated with the *enragés*, and lived with one of the group's leading men, Théophile **Leclerc** (though he later married Pauline **Léon**). Lacombe and Léon shared the *enragés*' rancour against high prices, low wages, unemployment and hoarding. They asked for the right of single women and widows to fight for the Republic in the **Vendée**. In April 1793, Lacombe proposed to the Jacobins that hostages should be taken from aristocratic families.

Claire Lacombe's most conspicuous part in the Revolution was as co-founder with Pauline Léon of the Society of Revolutionary Republican Women in February 1793. This society met at first in a room at the **Jacobins** – next to where the Club had its meetings while the women were still supporting the programme of the **Mountain**. After the king's execution in January 1793, it moved to the crypt of the former church of Saint-Eustache, right by the market halls, to state the society's independence. This aroused the hostility of the market women, who objected to the society's members patrolling the streets dressed as male **sansculottes** looking for women who were not wearing **revolutionary cockades** and subjecting them to aggravation.[1]

Lacombe took part in the events which led to the downfall of the **Girondins** between 31 May and 2 June 1793. She drew up petitions: one in August to demand that all the remaining nobles in the army should be dismissed and, during the **'Day' of 5 September**, that the government should be purged. She arrived at the bar of the **National Convention** on 7 October to denounce the oppression women found themselves having to bear. The **Mountain** found something they could use as a pretext for acting against her. The market women accused the Society of Revolutionary Republican Women of having forced them to wear **Phrygian bonnets**, which were only for men. They threatened to give her a whipping as they had done to **Théroigne de Méricourt**. This disorder in a public place served as the pretext for the government to ban all women's associations. She was arrested on 16 September and her lodgings were ransacked. She was set free the next day because it was reported that 'nothing but what breathed pure patriotism' had been discovered in her letters.[2]

During the Jacobins' attack on the *enragés* and the Hébertists she hid for a while, but was arrested on 2 April 1794 with Pauline and Théophile Leclerc. She remained in prison until 18 August 1795. She then went back to acting, and moved to Nantes where she wrote a few letters to her friends but, after that, left no trace.

Moore, Lucy, *Liberty: The Lives and Times of Six Women in Revolutionary France* (London: Harper Press, 2006).

Lafayette, Marie-Joseph Paul Yves Roch Gilbert du Motier, Marquis de (1757–1834)

Lafayette's ambition was to be the indispensable leader of the moderates in the Revolution. He had fought in two campaigns of the American War of Independence, been wounded at the battle of Brandywine, effected an alliance between the states and the five Indian nations and returned as the 'hero of two worlds'.[3] **Louis XVI** had made him a brigadier. He was a **Freemason** and a member of the *Société des **Amis des Noirs***. He bought land in Guiana so as to develop philanthropic projects. In Paris, he became prominent in the pre-revolutionary salons and a member of the liberal **Committee of Thirty**.[4]

As one of the wealthiest nobles in France, Lafayette had been called to the 1788 **Assembly of Notables**. In the **Estates-General** he was a Second Estate deputy for Riom, one of the 46 nobles who joined with the **Third Estate** after the **Tennis Court Oath**. He proposed a **Declaration of Rights** based on the one Jefferson drew up for Virginia. He was also elected commander-in-chief of the Paris National Guard on the day after the taking of the **Bastille** in the interests of restoring order. When he failed to prevent **Bertier** and Foulon being lynched, he tried unsuccessfully to resign.

Opposition from what became the **Jacobin Club** hardened against him over the next few months. He would be accused of 'Caesarism'. When the market women of Paris marched out to **Versailles** on 5 October, Lafayette followed them at a distance with his National Guardsmen. He did not prevent the violence of the following night, but persuaded Louis XVI and **Marie-Antoinette** to appear on the balcony for acclamation by the crowd and to agree to go to Paris in the morning. The court nobles hated him as a result.[5]

Making Paris his power base, he formed the Society of 1789 with Mayor **Bailly** and Emmanuel **Sieyès**, having distanced himself from the Jacobins and **Mirabeau**. He was on parade in the Champ de Mars on 14 July 1790 to make the civic oath. Patrice Gueniffey suggests that 'on that day the idol began to crumble'.[6] He could not hold the middle ground between the king and the **Constituent Assembly**, and the press began to treat him with derision.

He was caught between two fires. He acted against the left when there was a serious mutiny in the politicized garrison at **Nancy** in August 1790 and supported the stern reaction of General **Bouillé** and war minister **de La Tour du Pin**. Courts-martial punished the soldiers severely, enraging the Jacobins.[7] Then again, on 28 February 1791, workers from the **Faubourg de Saint-Antoine** marched to the Château de Vincennes to the east of Paris, fearing it was to become a new Bastille. Lafayette took his **National Guard** to disperse them. But, on his return, he disarmed 400 royalists at the **Tuileries Palace** who were attempting to protect the unguarded king on the 'Day of the Daggers'. Lafayette was later to maintain that the march from the Faubourg de Saint-Antoine to Vincennes had been planned in order to make the National Guard leave Paris for long enough for the king's partisans to seize the Tuileries.[8] This deepened the rift between himself and the courtiers while the Jacobins accused him of arranging the event.

On 17 April, the Paris crowd stopped the king from leaving for Saint-Cloud to receive his Easter communion from a **refractory priest** and Lafayette stayed inactive. The royalists saw this as interference, and the Jacobins asserted that he had encouraged the king to try to leave to prove that he was not at liberty.[9] In June, when the king had escaped from the Tuileries and been brought back from **Varennes**, **Danton** charged Lafayette with complicity in the flight, although he had been by-passed by the king and queen and **Fersen** as plans were made. He was offered an alliance by the **Feuillants** and supported the claim that the king had been abducted by counter-revolutionaries, which the Assembly accepted. As a result, Lafayette was seen as increasing surveillance over the king so as to humiliate him excessively and defend himself from further accusations of complicity.[10]

Danton and the **Cordeliers** arranged for a petition for a republic to be signed on 17 July at the altar remaining in place from the previous year's taking of the civic oath. Lafayette and Bailly were held responsible for the deaths of upwards of 50 demonstrators (massacre of the Champ de Mars). It is an open question whether Lafayette gave the order to fire, but **Desmoulins** asserted that he had done so, 'like another Charles IX' (who, by an unconsidered remark – 'Then kill them all! Kill them all!' – was said to have brought about the Massacre of Saint-Bartholomew's Day in 1572[11]). The Jacobins agreed.[12] Yet Donald Sutherland's 2003 study of the Revolution asserts categorically that neither Lafayette nor Bailly displayed the red flag to declare martial law, nor did they tell the crowd to disperse. 'Instead, someone in the crowd fired a shot, the National Guard panicked, let loose a fusillade and charged the petitioners.'[13] Whatever actually happened, Lafayette's unpopularity in Paris was added to that on the part of the court and the Jacobins. **Pétion** was elected mayor with a majority over Lafayette of 8,000 votes out of 11,000[14] and, when the Constituent

Assembly gave way to the **Legislative**, he had to relinquish his command
of the National Guard. In December, he was given command of the Army
of the Centre. When war with Austria began, his enemies accused him of
trying to provoke civil war and seeking to be another Cromwell – 'Cromwell
had character, but Lafayette has none,' was **Brissot**'s comment.[15]

Ten days after the monarchy was overthrown, Lafayette was relieved of
his command and declared a traitor. He fled across the frontier, and the
Austrians imprisoned him for five years at Olmütz in Bohemia until he
was released in September 1797 under the terms of **Campo Formio**.[16]

Lafayette returned to France after **Brumaire** as an amnestied *émigré*,
but lived quietly until he became a deputy in the 100 days and demanded
Napoleon's abdication after Waterloo.[17] He was in opposition under Louis
XVIII and Charles X, and then, in July 1830, was elected commander of
the Paris National Guard once more at the centre of another revolution in
Paris, and was able to give support to a constitutional monarchy such as
he had supported 41 years before.

Gueniffey, Patrice, 'Lafayette', in François Furet and Mona Ozouf (eds), *A Critical
Dictionary of the French Revolution*, trans. Arthur Goldhammer (London: The
Belknap Press of Harvard University Press, 1989). References above are from
the French edition.

Lally-Tollendal, Trophime-Gérard, Marquis de (1751–1830)

Lally-Tollendal had a typical noble's military career and was then elected
to the **Estates-General** by the Parisian Second Estate. He was at first
hostile to the changes being made, but then he supported the union of
the three estates on 27 June. He thought that the only means of slowing
the Revolution down was to 'take part in it' (*s'y prêter*). On 13 July, he
supported the return of **Necker** to office, and then made two reconciliatory
speeches at the Paris Hôtel de Ville. By the **Night of 4 August** he was
secretary to the Assembly and tried to have the session suspended before
things went too far. It was he, however, who was responsible for giving
Louis XVI the title 'restorer of French liberty'. He sat on the constitutional
committee and argued, together with other *monarchiens* such as **Mounier**,
for a two-chamber legislative along British lines and for an absolute veto

for the king. When those demands were rejected, he left the committee. After the **October Days**, he resigned and went to Switzerland. He returned to France in 1792 and was supposed to have become a member of the **'Austrian Committee'**. When the monarchy had been overthrown, he was arrested on 17 August and put in the Abbey prison, but released on 31 August.[18] Then he went with the Princesse de Henin to England and lived for a few months in Juniper Hall in Surrey with the colony of *émigrés* already there.[19] He offered to help with the king's defence in December.

Lally-Tollendal did not return to France until after **Bonaparte**'s **Brumaire coup**. He lived quietly during the Consulate and the Empire, but received honours from Louis XVIII during the **Restoration Monarchy**.

Lamballe, Marie-Thérèse-Louise de Savoie-Carignan, Princesse de (1749–92)

Perhaps Queen **Marie-Antoinette**'s closest friend at **Versailles** and the **Tuileries Palace**, the Princesse de Lamballe was murdered in La Force Prison on the second day of the **September Massacres**.

She was from Savoy and, in 1767, had married the Prince of Lamballe, whose father was a legitimized son of Louis XIV. He died within the year. Marie-Thérèse lived at Versailles from the time of Louis-Auguste's marriage to Marie-Antoinette in 1770, and was put in charge of the queen's household in 1775. When the royal family was brought to the Tuileries in October 1789, her Paris salon was a focus for royalists who were also members of the **Constituent Assembly**. She went to England for a short time but returned to Paris and was supposed to be representing the queen on an **'Austrian Committee'** contacting the foreign enemies of the Nation.

When the king and queen, the princess royal and the dauphin were put in the Temple Prison on 10 August 1792, the Princesse de Lamballe went with them. After nine days, she was taken to La Force Prison, where she refused to take an oath against the monarchy. She was a prime target for the *Septembriseurs*. News of her death spread quickly all over France, through the usual process of letters from deputies to the local clubs. They wanted to make Marie-Antoinette see her head at the end of a pike, presenting it to her under her windows in the Temple, but she did not appear.

More monstrous things than the cutting-off of her head were reported as time went on, but recent scholarship has refuted them.[20] Even so, her death represents horror on a national scale, and it was made an issue by the **Girondins** who blamed **Danton** and **Marat** for the deaths of at least 1,400 people – by no means all of them nobles or **refractory clergy**.

Lameth, Alexandre, Comte de (1760–1829)

Lameth was from the military **nobility** who had served in the American War of Independence and had been a cavalry colonel in the old regime since 1784. His prominence in the Revolution was as an advocate of constitutional monarchy, a founder member of the **Feuillants Club**.

He was a noble deputy in the **Estates-General**, who joined with the **Third Estate** in the **Constituent Assembly**. Associating himself with Antoine **Barnave** and Adrien **Duport**, he was instrumental in abolishing seigneurialism and the centrality of the royal court in government, although he did not favour a second chamber for peers on the English model.

Lameth offered himself as an adviser to **Louis XVI** even after his flight to **Varennes** in June 1791. Lameth, Barnave and Duport drew members of the **Jacobin Club** into the Feuillants Club which met in a closed convent chapel close to the **Tuileries** and remained in being until the **declaration of war** in April 1792.

Lameth served with the Army of the North and emigrated with **Lafayette** after the republic was proclaimed. The Austrians imprisoned him and, on his release in 1796, he went to Hamburg. First Consul **Bonaparte** made him a prefect. During the **Restoration Monarchy** he was in the Chamber of Deputies in opposition to the successive ministries that served Louis XVI's brothers.[21]

La Révellière-Lépeaux, Louis-Marie (1753–1824)

During the Revolution, La Révellière-Lépeaux went through all the stages of national elected office that he could, and was one of the National Directors.[22] He is also remembered for his sponsorship of the cult of **Theophilanthropy**, which he tried to have adopted as a replacement state religion after the de-Christianization of the Catholic state and the discrediting of **Robespierre**'s **'Supreme Being'**.

He was a deputy for Angers in the **Estates-General** and a member of its constitutional committee. He voted for the exclusion of members of the **Constituent Assembly** from the **Legislative**. He worked in the Maine et Loire department until they elected him to the **National Convention**. He was a **regicide** and voted against the motion to choose ministers from among the deputies. He voted for the prosecution of **Marat**. When he defended the **Girondins**, he was prosecuted by the **Mountain**, hid in the hermitage of Saint-Radegonde in the Montmorency forest for a year and returned to his place in the Convention after Robespierre's fall. He voted for treating the **refractory clergy** who had not left French territory as if they were *émigrés*. The Thermidoreans put him on the **Committee of Public Safety**.

The next step for La Révellière-Lépeaux was to be elected to the new Council of Elders in 1795 by 31 departments, out of which he remained faithful to the Maine et Loire. He was chosen as a Director. He congratulated **Bonaparte** in letters on his victories in Italy. When partial elections in year V produced a royalist majority, La Révellière-Lépeaux was one of the initiators of the **Fructidor** *coup d'état*.

In May 1799, the **Prairial coup** excluded him from the **Directory**. In the Empire he would not take the required oaths and lost his place in the Institute and left Paris. He refused a pension that **Fouché** arranged for him and lived privately for the rest of his life, even avoiding being exiled as a regicide in 1816 as many others from the Convention did not.

La Rochejaquelein, Henri du Vergier, count of (1772–94)

At the age of 20, La Rochejaquelein held a commission in **Louis XVI**'s Constitutional Guard. This guard was dissolved on 29 May 1792, but, on 9 August, La Rochejaquelein went to the **Tuileries** to make himself available and fought against the assailants on the **'Day' of 10 August**.[23] He escaped the retribution that many had to suffer, and went home to Bas-Poitou (the **Vendée**) where he refused to respond to the **Convention**'s demand for 300,000 troops from all over France to fight the kings of Europe in February 1793. Instead he became a leader of the rebellion in April, joining forces with a cousin of his, under the command of Louis d'**Elbée**. He was present at the taking of Bressuire, of Fontenay-le-Comte and of Saumur in

May and June. He was in command at the Vendéan victory of Chantonnay in September, but was one of the vanquished at **Cholet** in October.

La Rochejaquelein was elected commander-in-chief when still only 21 to replace d'Elbée who had been wounded. A spy was sent to offer British help to the Vendéan commanders, who agreed to make a move to Brittany since supporting troops could land at Saint-Malo. La Rochejacquelein crossed the Loire in force, but still had not decided which port to make for. After two more *émigrés* arrived with letters signed by Pitt and Dundas, La Rochejacquelein chose Granville to take the port for a British landing. The **Committee of Public Safety** made a priority of having an army on the Breton coast before the rebels did, but no republican force prevented the Vendéans from reaching Granville. The British ministers had not made any concrete offer to the Vendéan leaders because of confused intelligence about their whereabouts and the republicans' plans.

The Vendéans besieged Granville for 26 hours on 13–14 November. No help arrived and he went south again. Lord Moira's fleet arrived off Cherbourg and then returned to Cowes with its *émigré* passengers smitten with disease. The Vendéans were defeated by Kléber and **Westermann** at Le Mans on 12 December and at Savenay on 23 December.

La Rochejaquelein took his survivors back across the Loire. He and **Stofflet** offered to work together along with **Charette**, but he did not accept the offer.

'Monsieur Henri' tried to set up another army in the Angevin *bocage* countryside (small, hedged fields, undulating terrain, sunken lanes, good for irregular fighting), but was hunted down and shot by a republican grenadier at Nuaillé, near Cholet.[24]

La Tour du Pin Gouvernet, Jean-Frédéric, Comte de (1727–94)

De La Tour du Pin had old-regime values which he tried to accommodate to the changed political scene of the Revolution. He made a sincere attempt to work in the new conditions, but found that compromise was impossible for him, so he was a victim of the **Terror**.

He had been a professional soldier who had received his commission as a youth and had served with distinction in the Seven Years' War. His marriage made the province of Saintonge his personal centre of operations and **Louis XVI** appointed him military commandant there. The **nobility** of Saintes elected de La Tour du Pin as one of their two deputies in the **Estates-General**, and he declared himself in favour of necessary change. He was one of the first out of the small number of nobles who allied with the **Third Estate**. He kept a good table at Versailles, welcoming fellow deputies of all political colours at twice-weekly dinners. Choderlos de Laclos (the author of *Les Liaisons dangereuses*) and Maximilien **Robespierre** were on his guest list.

As war minister he did what he could to re-establish the **army** after its loss of nerve in 1789, adopting the *tricolore* as the military banner. He had worked towards the re-establishment of discipline, but this backfired on him after troops mutinied at **Nancy** in August 1790 and punishments handed to them were as harsh as they had ever been before the Revolution. This led to his resignation after he was denounced along with other ministers by **sansculottes** in the streets of Paris and by Georges **Danton** in the **Constituent Assembly**.

De la Tour du Pin was in England when Louis XVI was put on trial, but returned to Paris to do as much as he could to preserve the idea of constitutional monarchy. When it became plain that there was nothing he could do, he retired to Auteuil, where he was arrested on 31 August 1793. He was brought from prison to be a witness at the queen's trial. He defended her courageously, continuing to give her the respect he saw due to her by using her royal titles and refusing to call her 'the widow Capet' as the prosecutor, Antoine-Quentin **Fouquier-Tinville**, wanted him to do.

His renewed imprisonment lasted nearly seven months and then, on 28 April 1794, he was condemned and executed on the same day – as was usual during the Terror.

La Tour du Pin, Lucie de (1770–1853)

Lucie Dillon married Frédéric-Seraphim, who became the Comte de La Tour du Pin when his father, the war minister, was guillotined. She is important as a chronicler of the Revolution, who managed to spend the worst months of the **Terror** living by the Hudson River in the United States, having arranged her escape from Bordeaux with her husband through the influence of Thérèse **Cabarrus** on **Tallien** when he was **representative on mission** there in 1793.

📖 Moorhead, Caroline, *Dancing to the Precipice: Lucie de La Tour du Pin and the French Revolution* (London: Chatto & Windus, 2009).

Lavoisier, Antoine-Laurent de (1743–94)

Lavoisier had a scientific reputation in Europe continuing into the years of the Revolution, but his involvement in money-raising caused his downfall in the new climate of the **Terror**. Although qualified as a lawyer, he began scientific research, travelling a good deal around France making observations. He interested himself in such matters as street lights. He was elected to the Academy of Sciences in 1768, presenting results of work carried out in his laboratory in the Paris Arsenal. The king's minister Turgot had placed him in charge of gunpowder supplies. He replaced the elderly member of the Farmers-General, whose assistant he had been, in 1779, and used what he gained from the revenues to finance his scientific work.[25]

The Farmers-General dated from Colbert's time in the seventeenth century and were responsible for raising half the revenue of the nation. The authority to collect taxes was leased to this company of private individuals designated as tax farmers. They collected the revenue, paid what was expected to the treasury and kept (farmed) the surplus. This associated them closely with the king, and they even had the right to have a company of armed collectors. They had recently built the Wall of the Farmers-General around Paris so that charges on produce brought into the capital's markets could be collected more systematically. Only a few admired the neo-classical elegance of the gates designed by Claude-Nicolas Ledoux, finished and ceremoniously inaugurated in June 1790 – a year after the attacks upon them in 1789. Generally, the gates – and the Farmers – were objects of loathing. A French pun was made: '*le mur murant Paris qui rend Paris murmurant*' (The wall surrounding Paris that makes Paris murmur).[26]

As a landowner, Lavoisier was elected to the provincial assembly of Orléans for the **Third Estate**, although he was a noble, and worked on fiscal reform, creating a regional discount and savings bank, and a life insurance company. When the Revolution came, he was a member of the Society of 1789 and presented a paper about the *assignat*. He also worked on national statistics, and was a member of the body that issued research grants. Meanwhile, he was being criticized as a Farmer-General by **Brissot** and the popular societies, and lost his lodging and laboratory at the Arsenal.

The Convention transferred the funds of the Farmers-General to the Treasury and put seals on the individual farmers' offices in June 1793, ordering their arrest. Eleven of them were executed over several months.[27] Influential people tried to save Lavoisier, but he was sent to the scaffold on 8 May 1794.

Law of 14 frimaire (4 December 1793)

The **National Convention** retained hold of the reins of government, but delegated its authority to the **Committee of Public Safety** by this law. There were still ministers until April 1794, but they were solely administrative. The Committee could exercise control over the hitherto independent actions of **representatives on mission**. Its effect was not immediate. Representatives still behaved like proconsuls, and the **revolutionary armies** were still manically pursuing hoarders. But gradually this law became the means of asserting the power of the One and Indivisible Republic, so that it did not need to rely on the **sansculottes** to enforce its policy. It has been called 'the constitution of the reign of **terror**'.[28]

Law of 22 prairial (10 June 1794)

Robespierre and **Saint-Just** pushed the Law of 22 prairial, year II through the **National Convention** on the basis of their positions on the **Committee of Public Safety**. The nation was still in danger, in spite of recent military victories, and the 'revolutionary razor' was made to work longer hours. This law ushered in what was known as the 'Great Terror', because it did away with defence counsel in the **Revolutionary Tribunal** and refused the testimony of defence witnesses, which ensured speedy judgements on the basis of the jury's 'moral certainty' after three days.

The only sentence possible for those found guilty in the Tribunal after June 1794 was death, and more personnel were taken on to cope with the increased pressure of business. The number of death sentences accelerated. In March 1794, there had been 100. April saw 244, then, in May, there were 339. In June, when the law was passed, the figure reached 659, and peaked at over 900 in July.[29] After **Thermidor**, the Tribunal was wound down.

Law of Suspects

From the spring of 1793 onwards, more and more people had been arrested, despite there being as yet no real definition of who was a suspect and who was not. Then the **Jacobins** forced the Law of Suspects though the **National Convention** on 17 September 1793 so as to make the selection and imprisonment of 'enemies of the people' easier. The suspects were to include not only counter-revolutionaries, but also those with no positive enthusiasm for the changes made so far. In addition, the uncompromising **Law of 22 prairial** (10 June 1794) gave unrestricted authority to **surveillance committees** all over the country to act severely against suspects, often leading to automatic death sentences. These laws stayed in use until after the **Thermidor coup**.

The Law of Suspects was so imprecise that anybody could be sent to the **Revolutionary Tribunal**. Since the former nobles were assumed to be willing to co-operate with the Austrians and Prussians to erode the Revolution, they had to be made harmless. Anyone known to have contact with *émigrés* would certainly be in danger of arrest. This was a process that had been gathering momentum since the **September Massacres** a year before, and plenty of people were in the prisons not knowing what would befall them.

Bachelors between 18 and 25 who had not presented themselves for the army were suspect, even if they were fervid republicans. After 2 June 1793, being a known supporter of the **Girondins**, who had now been crushed, was sufficient qualification for becoming a suspect. The only way not to be suspect was to apply for, and be granted, a **certificate of civism** from the municipality where one lived. Even with such a certificate, one had to be in good standing with the local surveillance committee.[30]

Law of Two-Thirds

When the **Thermidorean Convention** was coming to an end, on 22 and 30 August 1795, the Law of Two-Thirds was decreed. This meant that two-thirds of the deputies from the Convention were to pass into the Councils of Elders and the Council of the Five Hundred in the new Constitution of Year III – the **Directory**. The universal male suffrage which elected the **National Convention** two years before was a thing of the past now. The Directory would keep itself in place by a series of coups, until a coup they had not organized – **Brumaire** – replaced it with the Consulate.

Le Bas, Philippe-François-Joseph (1762–94)

Le Bas was elected to the National Convention as a deputy for the Pas-de-Calais, and took his seat with the **Mountain**. He voted for the king's death and was on mission with the Army of the North in August 1793, arresting suspects. He was elected a member of the **Committee of General Security**, but remained close to **Robespierre**, **Couthon** and **Saint-Just** on the other Committee. Again on mission to the Army of the North, he and Saint-Just set up the organization that made **Jourdan**'s victory at **Fleurus** possible.

Le Bas's marriage to Elisabeth Duplay, daughter of Maurice **Duplay**, Robespierre's landlord, meant a close association with Robespierre as well as Saint-Just. When Robespierre and the others were arrested, on 8 thermidor, Augustin Robespierre stood by his brother, and Le Bas by Saint-Just. As troops sent by the Convention came to arrest the group as outlaws in the Hôtel de Ville, Le Bas shot himself and was already dead when he was guillotined on 10 July 1794. His wife, his father and his son were imprisoned for several months.[31]

Le Chapelier, Isaac-René-Guy (1754–94)

Le Chapelier's surprising contribution to the early days of the Revolution was the Law of 14 June 1791 that bears his name. It declared all workers' or employers' associations illegal, which had much more effect on workers than it could on employers. It governed workers' relations with employers until Napoleon III changed trade union legislation in 1864.[32]

One of the many lawyers in the Revolution, Le Chapelier had been elected to the **Estates-General** as a **Third Estate** deputy for Rennes, where he had previously held aloof from aristocratic attacks on law students since he had just inherited his father's title.[33] While the **Constituent Assembly** was still at **Versailles**, he was the informal leader of the Breton Club[34] which became the **Jacobin Club** after the move to Paris in October 1789. He was president of the Constituent on the **night of 4 August 1789.**

After the king's flight to **Varennes**, he left the Jacobins to join the constitutional monarchists of the **Feuillant Club**. He ceased to be prominent as a revolutionary, and spent some time in England. After his return during the **Terror** he was arrested and executed on 22 April 1794.

Leclerc, Théophile (1771– after 1804)

Théophile Leclerc was a member of the **Cordeliers Club**, closely linked to the Society of Revolutionary Republican Women, and associated with Jacques **Roux** and Jean-François **Varlet**, the *enragés*.

He was the fifth child of an engineer with the Bridges and Roads (*ponts et chaussées*) and joined the **National Guard** at Clermont-Ferrand in 1789. In March 1790, he sailed from Bordeaux to Martinique to join his two brothers. The inhabitants of the island had risen against their governor. Théophile joined the revolutionaries and was arrested.

He was sent back to France and landed at Lorient without any resources. The **Jacobin Club** of the Morbihan helped him. He joined the 1st Morbihan Battalion, in which he served until February 1792. He volunteered to conduct 17 other revolutionaries from Martinique to Paris and guard them. With the Jacobin Club's money he presented himself in Paris in March 1792 to plead their cause in the **Constituent Assembly**. He gained their acquittal and was fêted at the Jacobins.

He joined the Army of the Rhine to work in mobile hospitals and was present at the battle of **Jemappes**. In February 1793, he was transferred to the Army of the Alps in **Lyon**, where he associated with the Jacobin leader, Marie, Joseph **Chalier**, whom he had met before. Chalier sent him to the Parisian Jacobins on 4 May, hoping to speed up the formation of the promised **revolutionary army** since the situation in federalist Lyon was becoming dangerous for patriots. His time as an *enragé* was the result.[35]

He was a member of the insurrectionary committee who organized the fall of the **Girondins** in the *journée* of 2 June 1793, and intervened in the debates of the **National Convention** to demand the severest penalty for them. On 30 June, he supported Jacques Roux and the address he gave at the bar of the Convention on 25 June. Like Roux, he saw himself as a successor to **Marat**, assassinated by Charlotte **Corday** on 13 July 1793. He published *L'Ami du peuple par Leclerc*, in which he argued for a price maximum, the creation of a revolutionary army made up entirely of enthusiasts for the Terror, and the execution of all suspects. The government held back from taking these measures, but he continued with his newspaper and increased the intensity of his attacks on the Convention.

The Jacobins intimidated him and he abandoned his newspaper on 15 September. He married Pauline **Léon** on 18 November. The **Committee of General Security** ordered his arrest on 3 April 1794, along with his wife and his former mistress, Claire **Lacombe**, the two founders of the Society of Revolutionary Republican Women. They were in the Luxembourg prison from 6 April until 22 August.

Théophile and Pauline disappeared from sight after their release from prison until 1804, the date of an extant letter from Pauline Léon which said that she was a primary school teacher in Paris and that her husband was still alive. Pauline is known to have died at La Roche-sur-Yon in 1838.

Lefebvre, Georges (1874–1959)

Lefebvre was perhaps the most influential French writer on his country's Revolution in the middle years of the twentieth century. He held a **Marxist** view of history, seeing the rise to political power of a capitalist bourgeoisie as the Revolution's main cause. Any reader is impressed by the subtlety of the use of this idea in Lefebvre's work. He developed the emphasis on history 'from below',[36] from an idea of the socialist politician Jean Jaurès who influenced Lefebvre significantly as a young man.

The kind of social mobility that allowed Lefebvre eventually to become a professional scholar was rare when he graduated from Lille University in 1898. He became a university teacher at the age of 50 after many years in schools. Given that the Marxist interpretation was in the ascendant when Lefebvre was young, his study, long in preparation, entitled *The*

Peasants of the North during the French Revolution (1924), had to be a socio-economic appraisal. It used the evidence of tax-rolls, documents from notaries' offices and the minutes of local municipalities to observe, among much else, the effect of the purchase of **national property** by outsiders. This thesis gained him professorships at Clermont-Ferrand and Strasbourg. Then he was appointed to the Sorbonne in 1937, from where he published his short study of the Revolution, called simply *1789*, for the 150th anniversary in 1939, which the Vichy government ordered to be burnt a year later. He was a socialist until 1940 and then, from the 1944 Liberation of France onwards, he was a fellow-traveller of the Communist Party.[37]

Furet refers to Richard Cobb's characterization of Lefebvre as 'an old solitary, a little eccentric, remaining the statue of republican virtue … dry, not very friendly, and suspicious of enjoyment and life's graces.'[38] Like **Mathiez**, he detested what went before the Revolution and came after it: the aristocratic world and Thermidorean society. Both historians ignored the parts of the Revolution that did not turn out as they wanted them to. Lefebvre summarily dismissed Albert Cobban's criticism of his social interpretation of the Revolution. Yet, unlike Mathiez, he had no time for partisanship over the Revolution's personalities, as in the Mathiez/**Robespierre** dispute with **Aulard/Danton**. Lefebvre is more objective, letting Robespierre rediscover a position as a centrist politician, the temporary arbitrator in a fragile alliance, and becoming a character less worthy of reverence.[39]

Doyle, William, *The Origins of the French Revolution*, 3rd edn (Oxford: Oxford University Press, 1999), Pt I.

Furet, François, *Academic History of the Revolution*, in François Furet and Mona Ozouf (eds), *A Critical Dictionary of the French Revolution*, trans. Arthur Goldhammer (London: The Belknap Press of Harvard University Press, 1989), pp. 881ff. References here are to the French Edition.

Selected works by Georges Lefebvre in English translation:

1789, trans. R.R. Palmer as *The Coming of the French Revolution* (University Park, PA: Princeton University Press, Bicentennial Edition, 1989).

The French Revolution, vol. 1: *From its Origins to 1793*, trans. Elizabeth Moss

Evanston (New York: Columbia University Press, 1962).

The French Revolution, vol. 2: *From 1793 to 1799*, trans. John Hall Stewart and James Friguglietti (New York: Columbia University Press, 1964).

Legislative Assembly (October 1791–August 1792)

All who had been members of the **Estates-General** and the **Constituent Assembly** were excluded from the newly elected Legislative Assembly, which met in the former riding school by the **Tuileries Palace** in October 1791 and which was predominantly bourgeois. There were no separate noble or clerical elections as there had been for the Estates-General. Only 8 per cent of the noble heads of families had become *émigrés*, but those who remained adopted a low political profile for the most part. The **refractory clergy** were beginning their exile in Britain, Spain or a German state. The constitutional clergy voted with everyone else in the elections, and a few of them became deputies. The power base of the new assembly was narrow because less than a quarter of qualified voters actually exercised their right. In Paris, the turnout was no more than 10 per cent of active citizens.[40]

The Legislative (it is usual to leave out the word 'Assembly' after using it once), elected by **active citizens**, was dominated by members of the liberal professions with a preponderance of lawyers. Its purpose was to be the legislative for the constitutional monarchy which was still in existence despite the king's flight to **Varennes** and his humiliating return. The fiction that **Louis XVI** had been abducted in June 1791 was accepted as soon as he had returned under duress, and he remained executive head of state for another 13 months.

Several crises had to be weathered during that time. Counter-revolutionary outbreaks occurred in the **Vendée** as soon as the deputies took their seats. The *émigré* nobles were joining the Army of the Princes across the Rhine and had their property in France confiscated by the new assembly's subsequent decree. Many of them had been deputies in the Constituent and, if they were military officers too, refused to take the new oath to the Nation instead of to the king. Further measures were taken against refractory Catholic priests who had not yet left France or who had returned to ferment opposition.

The Legislative had demanded Austrian renunciation of treaties which threatened French sovereignty in January 1792. By 20 April, this had not been done and Leopold had died. Louis XVI, now a constitutional monarch, came to the assembly to declare war on Leopold's son, King Francis of Bohemia and Hungary (not yet elected Emperor), on 20 April 1792. Prussia and other German states allied with Austria against France.

The monarchy was suspended on 10 August, and the Legislative assumed emergency powers in the face of the Duke of **Brunswick**'s invasion and occupation of Longwy and Verdun by 1 September. It found sufficient organizing strength to gather a Republican army to defeat the Austro-Prussian invaders in the artillery battle at **Valmy** on 20 September, the day of its final meeting. Once the monarchy had gone, however, the Legislative had lost its reason for existence. In its last month, it shared power with a Provisional Executive Council and the **Insurrectionary Commune**[41] in making arrangements for the election of the **National Convention**, which would be both executive and legislative for the new Republic.

Léon, Pauline (1758–1838)

Pauline Léon made chocolates and feminist protests during the first half of the Revolutionary decade. With Claire **Lacombe**, she founded the Society of Revolutionary Republican Women and was associated with the *enragés*, becoming the wife of Théophile **Leclerc**.

Her mother was widowed and she helped her make the chocolates and look after the other children where they lived in one of the poorer streets of the Faubourg Saint-Germain.[42] It is said that she was fired up to take a radical stance by hearing of the execution of some participants in a bread riot. Like Lacombe, she frequently attended the meetings of the **Cordeliers Club**.[43] She made a speech to the **Constituent Assembly** on 6 March 1791, proposing that a women's militia should be raised to protect homes and businesses from counter-revolutionaries. She signed the petition for the establishment of a republic, which provoked the massacre at the Champ de Mars in July 1791.

When the Society of Revolutionary-Republican Women was in existence, she was elected as its president. She was at the head of the women **sansculottes** during their patrols to make other women wear the revolutionary cockade and even the **Phrygian bonnet** usually reserved for men. Léon and Lacombe both focused their hatred on **Lafayette** because of his personal ambition during the period of the constitutional monarchy.

Léon was put in the Luxembourg prison with her husband and Claire Lacombe on 4 April 1794, but released after **Thermidor**. All that is known of the Leclercs after that is from Pauline's letter dated 1804, which says she was a primary school teacher in Paris and that Théophile was still alive. She died at La Roche-sur-Yon in 1838.

📖 Moore, Lucy, *Liberty: The Lives and Times of Six Women in Revolutionary France* (London: HarperCollins, 2006).

Le Peletier, Louis-Michel, Marquis de Saint-Fargeau (1760–93)

Le Peletier ranks with **Marat** and **Chalier** as a Jacobin martyr. He voted for the king's death, focusing the hatred of royalists upon himself. On the night before **Louis XVI**'s execution, a member of the royal bodyguard, Philippe de Pâris, found him in a restaurant in the **Palais-Royal**, killed him with his sabre without the rest of the diners noticing, and escaped from the room.[44] The threat of **counter-revolution** was never far away.

Le Peletier came from a noble and wealthy family; his great-grandfather had been Controller-General of the Finances, he was president of the court of the Paris *parlement*, then its advocate general. He was elected to the **Estates-General** for the **nobility** of Paris-ville, but took his time over joining the thirds in the National Assembly. He became progressive in his views, proposing the abolition of the death penalty and the galleys in the **Constituent Assembly**. 'Distanced by character and principle from extreme ideas, my system was that of conciliation which I did not believe was impossible,' he commented.[45] He took his turn as president of the assembly. Some called him the 'Alcibiades' of the Revolution.

Barred from the **Legislative Assembly**, Le Peletier was President of the Departmental Directory in the Yonne, and was a deputy for the same department in the **National Convention**. His interests included providing the new Republic with a uniform system of education in state schools for boys and girls alike, who would then imbibe the Revolution's ideals.

Le Peletier was given a state funeral in the Pantheon after what amounted to a lying-in-state in the Place Vendôme on the pedestal where Louis XIV's statue had been. Jacques-Louis **David** produced a portrait of him comparable with the one of **Marat** he was later to paint, but it was destroyed by his royalist daughter.

Lequinio, Marie-Joseph (1755–1814)

Lequinio was a zealous, energetic and uncompromising extremist during his time as a **representative on mission**, principally in the Charente-Inférieure (now Charente-Maritime) in the latter part of 1793. With his colleague Laignelot he reorganized La Rochelle as a base against the **Vendée** rebellion across the Sèvre river, purging the administration of non-Jacobins, motivating **sansculottes** in the town, acting against the remaining nobility and clergy, arresting suspects, requisitioning food, grubbing up vines to turn the land back to grain production, and organizing municipal cleansing and burial grounds.

Lequinio turned to the naval port of Rochefort in October 1793, where he claimed to have evidence that the British would try and take over as they had briefly in **Toulon** since August. Two Rochefort 80-gun warships, *Apollon* and *Généreux*, had been in Toulon. Admiral Hood had disarmed them and sent them back to their home port under flags of truce. When they arrived, Lequinio put the officers and some of the crews on trial before a **revolutionary tribunal**. They were executed, and he reported popular approval to the **Committee of Public Safety** straight afterwards. Then he extended his activities to de-Christianization all over the department, closing churches, re-educating constitutional clergy, agreeing with the 'disappearing' of **refractory clergy** on two old slave ships in the Roads of Aix off Rochefort, and enforcing the **new calendar** with its ten-day weeks and tenth-day festivals in the Temples of Truth, as the churches were now called. Apart from his twice-born atheism which **Robespierre** did not support, this was thoroughgoing Jacobin policy.[46]

Lequinio also hounded a fellow deputy in the Convention, Gustave Dechézeux from the Ile de Ré, who had voted for the king's guilt but against his execution, and had been in modern terms de-selected by his radical constituents. Lequinio had him arrested and put on trial in Rochefort.

He was executed in January 1794, to be reinstated posthumously by the **Directory**.

The townspeople of Rochefort denounced Lequinio after **Thermidor**. He went into hiding until the amnesty in October 1794 for 'deeds committed as a result of the Revolution', but his election to the Council of 500 was quashed. He worked as a paid inspector of forests in the Nord department until he was sent as trade commissioner to Newport, Rhode Island, and then Savannah, Georgia, by First Consul **Bonaparte**.

There followed his astonishing marriage to a former nun from a noble family, who had lost a brother to the guillotine. 'The torments of the revolution were finished a long time ago,' he wrote to her in 1798.[47]

Lesueur, Jean-Baptiste (1749–1826)

There is a series of colourful, simplistic cut-out gouaches mounted on blue paper portraying petty-bourgeois characters often looking happy. One of them, of four cheerful **sansculottes** carrying a model of the **Bastille** carved out of one of its stones, is on the jacket of Simon Schama's *Citizens*. It used to be thought that these images were the work of two brothers called Pierre-Etienne and Jacques-Philippe Le Sueur. Philippe de Carbonnières of the Musée Carnavalet[48] has pointed out that the brothers were, indeed, officially appointed artists in the revolutionary epoch, but Pierre painted landscapes, and Jacques was a sculptor. So their works have no strong connection with these gouaches.

They are in fact by Jean-Baptiste Lesueur, whose house on the Boulevard Saint-Denis (since 1830, rue Neuve d'Orléans) is the Paris address of the Bidault de L'Isle family, owners of the collection. Lesueur worked for a long time at the same address, as is shown by contemporary commercial almanacs. It is not known how many of these gouaches he made. Important scenes like the storming of the Bastille are absent, though its demolition is represented.

There was probably a lapse of time between the events and their portrayal. After **Thermidor**, image-making was less restricted. M. de Carbonnières suggests that the pictures were used in a model theatre at home or for the neighbourhood to see. That is why they were cut out and pasted on card, especially since there are signs that they were glued to a piece of wood to make them stand up so that they could be pushed on to the stage from either side. This would also account for some being missing and some being rather battered.

Lesueur did pay attention to violence in the provinces, such as the massacre of the ice-pit (*glacière*) at **Avignon** or scenes from the **Vendée**, but he seemed more interested in everyday Parisian life. There is a wonderful image of a man and his wife and their two children happily going to the *guingette* (a little restaurant where there was singing and dancing) and several pictures reprove the Revolution's repressive character. He seems to have been moderate in his support for the Revolution. Although his name is on a list compiled in 1801 of those involved in the **Terror**, he tried to resign from the section committee of which he was a member in 1794.

Lesueur gives us what nowadays we would see in comic books (the *bandes dessinées* enjoyed by many French adults). They are close to events: the popular mobilization of July 1789, the planting of a Liberty Tree, the market women bringing the king to Paris, **Marat** carried shoulder-high after his release on 27 April 1793, the arrest of **Louis XVI** at **Varennes**, soldiers' response to the Nation in danger, or giving their allegiance to **Bonaparte**. Clothes and uniforms may be from the **Directory** years rather than the constitutional monarchy or the **Jacobin** republic, but they resemble what we see on commemorative plates in the Carnavalet and many a provincial museum. If we ask 'What was it like for ordinary people?', Lesueur gives us an informed reply.

Ligurian Republic

The Republic of Genoa, like that of Venice, had tried to remain neutral in the face of French expansionism. Nevertheless, a Jacobin movement grew there and made itself a significant force in May 1797 with street demonstrations against dominance by the rich bourgeoisie. These Jacobins issued an invitation to General **Bonaparte** to support them in their struggle with the conservative rural backlash in the hinterland. He responded, and the Ligurian Republic came into being on 6 June 1797 with a moderate regime. The archbishop announced his support for the new arrangements a month later, since Bonaparte supported the Church and Genoese commerce. At first, there was still a doge and senators, but a new constitution based on the French Directory was soon adopted, and a declaration not only of rights but also of duties was promulgated. A plebiscite of qualified voters accepted this on 2 December 1797. A *coup d'état* on 31 August 1798 allowed greater French control.

The Ligurian Republic had a measure of independence shown by the war conducted against Piedmont in June 1798, influenced more by Piedmontese exiles than by the French. The King of Piedmont had invaded the Ligurian Republic and war was the result. The French intervened in July, and ended by annexing Piedmont, with Carlo Emmanuele IV exiled to his other territory of Sardinia.[49]

Lindet, Jean-Baptiste Robert (1746–1825)

Lindet was a member of the **Committee of Public Safety**, whose gifts in the administrative sphere were shown in his presidency of the National Food Commission during the **Terror**, when he adopted a less doctrinaire line than his colleagues.

Like so many of the revolutionaries, he was trained as a lawyer and was then elected to the **Legislative Assembly** in 1791 and the **National Convention** in 1792. At first he sided with the **Girondins**, and was entrusted with drawing up an indictment of the king's alleged crimes in December 1792. While he worked on it, he became a thoroughgoing **Jacobin**. He voted for the king's death without appeal. Now against the Girondins, he supported their expulsion from the Convention, and took part in the setting-up of the **Revolutionary Tribunal**. He was elected to the Committee of Public Safety in April 1793 to organize food supplies for the nation by enforcing the General **Maximum**.

He went as **representative on mission** successively to the Rhône, the Eure, Calvados and Finisterre without resorting to excesses in resisting rebellion as did **Carrier** in Nantes, **Fouché** in **Lyon** and **Fréron** in **Toulon**. He refused to sign **Danton**'s death warrant, famously and courageously telling **Saint-Just** that he was there to feed the people, not to kill patriots.[50] He took a neutral position towards **Robespierre** and did not associate himself with the **Thermidorean** reaction. He continued to justify the exclusion of the Girondins and the subsequent arrest of their supporters, the necessity of the Maximum, and the actions of the Jacobin Committees.

Moreover, when **Barère, Billaud-Varenne** and **Collot d'Herbois** were indicted for their part in the **Terror** in March 1795, he defended them. In May 1795, he was denounced, but was, in turn, defended by his brother, the constitutional bishop of Evreux, and benefited from the amnesty passed on 26 October (4 brumaire, year IV). He was arraigned with other remaining Jacobins, imprisoned and excluded from the Convention in July 1795.

He had not renounced his extreme views, however, and was associated with **Babeuf's** Conspiracy of Equals in 1796. He was tried at Vendôme and acquitted. Nevertheless, when he was elected by the Nord department to the Council of 500 in September, the election was quashed, and he was prevented from taking his seat in the Council as a result.

He was elected again in April 1798 and became minister of finances in July 1799, after supporting the **prairial coup**. He raised a forced loan, but it was rendered obsolete by Bonaparte's **Brumaire coup** in November. He did not co-operate with the Consulate, and neither supported the Empire nor Napoleon's '100 Days' in 1814–15.[51]

Loménie de Brienne, Louis-Etienne-Charles de (1727–94)

Louis XVI appointed Loménie de Brienne, the queen's protégé, to replace **Calonne** as head of the finance council in May 1787. Brienne tried to implement a modified version of Calonne's proposals to the **Assembly of Notables**, in which he had been a prominent opposition member.[52] Three and a half weeks later, the Assembly of Notables was dismissed, leaving Brienne to deal with the Paris *parlement* which the Assembly had been intended to by-pass.

Some major edicts were implemented in his time. The *corvée* (work service to repair roads and bridges) was changed to a money payment, there was to be unrestricted internal trade in grain, provincial assemblies were to be established, there was a decree of toleration for Protestants and economies were made in the face of the national deficit. Nevertheless, when the *parlement* refused to register the modified land tax, the king insisted upon it. The *parlementaires* were exiled to Troyes, amid popular protest.

In August, Brienne was designated as *ministre principal*, the closest anyone came to being prime minister in the old regime. After some negotiation over the finances, the *parlement* returned to Paris. In November, there was agreement on the summoning of the **Estates-General** before 1792 at a royal session during which the Duc d'**Orléans** protested. The *parlement's* opposition continued, so Lamoignan, the Keeper of the Seals, issued the 'May Edicts' in 1788, in which he set up a new Plenary Court made up of princes of the blood and royal officials, effectively to replace all the *parlements* for the registration of royal financial edicts. (The court met only once.) The nobility opposed this – spoken of as the 'aristocratic revolt' – and instigated riots against the edicts in several towns where there were *parlements*, the most serious riot being in **Grenoble**, where the 'Day of the Tiles' took place. Brienne accepted the summoning of the Estates-General for 1 May 1789 (not 1792 as he originally agreed), and suspended payments on some state loans which led to **Artois** contriving his resignation in August 1788. Government credit had gone, the urban building boom collapsed. The king's reluctant recall of **Necker** is regarded by historians as the collapse of **absolute monarchy**.[53]

Brienne had been Archbishop of Toulouse from 1763 until he had himself translated to Sens while he was finance minister. The king would not appoint him Archbishop of Paris because, he said, he thought the occupant of that office ought to believe in God, but **Pope Pius VI** agreed to his becoming a cardinal. He spent two years in Rome and then returned to France. He was one of only 7 bishops out of the total of 136 who took the Oath to the **Civil Constitution of the Clergy**. He retired to a secularized abbey in Sens which he bought as a **national property**, and repudiated his Catholic faith (which, despite his high office, had always sat lightly on him). He was arrested as a **suspect** during the **Terror** in November 1793, and died, perhaps from swallowing the medicaments he used for his eczema, three months later.

Louis XVI (1754–93)

Louis-Auguste, Duke of Berry, did not expect to be the King of France until he was ten, but his father, the Dauphin Louis-Ferdinand, and his elder brother, Louis Duc de Burgundy, died before Louis XV. He went hunting with Louis XV, gaining a lasting enthusiasm for it: on 14 July 1789 he was to write in his diary, '*Rien*', but it was only a hunting diary. He liked tinkering with locks and clocks and was often met chasing cats through the apartments in the attics where courtiers lived. He was by no means unintelligent, as his incisive appreciation of complicated policy in marginal notes on state papers later showed.

Louis-Auguste had two younger brothers, both of whom were to be king in turn, Louis-Stanislas, Comte de **Provence** and Charles-Philippe, Comte d'**Artois**. There were other princes of the blood royal, but only Philippe Duc d'**Orléans**, his cousin, sided with the Revolution, calling himself 'Philippe Egalité'. The others formed the Army of the Princes as *émigrés*.

There had been a 'diplomatic revolution' in which France allied herself with Austria by the Treaty of Versailles in 1756. Louis XV's minister Choiseul organized the marriage of Louis-Auguste and **Marie-Antoinette** as a significant part of it in 1770. The hesitant young man of 16 found himself the husband of a lively 14-year-old girl. Courtiers who watched the Dauphin eating with the rest of the royal family in public remarked upon how much he still enjoyed his food …

At the outset of Louis XVI's reign, when the nation expected an obvious symbol of potency (William Doyle's phrase about Louis XV), Marie-Antoinette had not borne him any children in spite of their being married four years. Louis XVI never had an official mistress as his predecessors did. The king and queen had been too innocent to understand the processes of generation until advised by the queen's brother, Joseph II of Austria, in 1777, after which all was well. Yet out of four children, only one survived into mature life, Marie-Thérèse, who was to be married to Artois's son and become Duchesse de Angoulême. (She returned to Paris in 1814 during the first **Restoration** to find and rebury her parents' remains.) The first dauphin died on 4 June 1789 just as the **Estates-General** was opening. The second dauphin, Louis-Charles, became **Louis XVII** to royalists as the captive of the Temple Prison, where he died in June 1795. Another daughter had lived under a year.

***

Despite the famine conditions of the 'Flour War' when stern repression was used against poor people, an impressive coronation was held at Reims. Apart from the journey there, a visit to Cherbourg to open new naval facilities, and what was to become known as the 'Flight to **Varennes**', Louis XVI's horizons were limited to the parks of the royal palaces. He was lacking in management skills and had not been adequately trained in them. His diffidence showed at all the major crisis points of his reign except the last, when there were no decisions left for him to make. It was publicly said that he had no will of his own at a time when public opinion counted for more than the king's will in any case. He never inspired real confidence, and his decisions were not taken as irrevocable, so he was often regarded as a hypocrite or untrustworthy. He could never control court intrigue, nor the machinations of assemblies he had summoned, nor popular agitation, and he went from humiliation to humiliation.[54]

The foreign policy of **absolute monarchy** continued anti-British as shown by the support given to the American colonies from 1778 to 1782 and to Tipu Sahib in India. Naval action involved huge expense, financed by loans raised on royal credit while the Swiss banker **Necker** was finance minister. Louis aligned himself with **Calonne**'s attempts at reform. He did his best to control and then by-pass the Paris *parlement*, but without success. The hand-picked **Assembly of Notables** refused to regenerate royal finance, and the Bourbon version of absolute monarchy was seen to have failed. A collapse of initiative was noticed in the king himself after that. He reappointed Necker. The king's indecisiveness was embarrassing and disastrous for government. Dislike for it was expressed in many of the **statements of complaint** (*cahiers de doléance*) in 1789 by the assertion that ministries were too short-lived to be effective, and each one undid what the one before had decided. It was said of Louis XVI by a **Third Estate** deputy in 1789, 'The king has spent his life recounting in the evening what he had got wrong in the morning.'[55]

Louis agreed to the election of deputies for the Estates-General, which had not met since 1614. He also called for each *bailliage* and *sénéchaussée* in the kingdom to draw up a statement of complaint about his government for the deputies to bring to **Versailles** for consideration. Economic distress increased with working men's families having to spend all their income on food by May 1789, when the deputies were assembling, yet many a rural statement of complaint still expressed confidence that the king would put things right by decisive action of some kind – that was what kings were supposed to do. There was the **Tennis Court Oath** on 20 June. Then the king accepted the Third Estate's National **Constituent Assembly** and 'invited'[56] the **clergy** and **nobility** to join it on 27 June. Court intrigue led to Necker's dismissal on 11 July.

The king ordered regiments of foreign soldiers to surround the capital. The Parisians feared deliberate creation of famine on the part of the courtiers to destroy all that had been achieved in the Revolution so far. The price of grain peaked on 14 July, the day of the fall of the **Bastille**. When the king asked the Duc de La Rochefoucauld if there was a revolt in Paris, he famously replied that it was a revolution. Generals had told the king that they could not rely on their officers' loyalty. The troops were withdrawn. Necker was reappointed. Louis XVI went to the capital in person on 17 July to put on the national cockade and confirm Sylvain **Bailly** in the new post of mayor. Seigneurialism was ended on the **Night of 4 August** in the Constituent Assembly. In all these developments, the king was increasingly hesitant and incompetent,[57] with surges of activity and periods of apathy, all the marks of a depressive state. He had lost his son, he had to accept a constitutional compromise. There were few he could trust.

Parisians had not seen any improvement in their conditions. The market women marched to Versailles. There was a night of violence on 6–7 October, and the royal family was brought to live under supervision in the **Tuileries Palace**. The king wrote to his Bourbon cousin, Charles IV of Spain, five days later to tell him what had happened, and to make his 'solemn protest' (*protestation solennelle*) against it. 'I owe it to myself, to my children, to my family, and to all my house not to allow the royal dignity that a long succession of centuries has confirmed in my dynasty to be debased in my hands.'[58]

***

Before the king was brought to Paris, the Constituent Assembly had set up the constitutional monarchy with the king as executive and itself as legislative body. The king was allowed a suspensive veto on the assembly's legislation. He used it twice in the summer of 1792 – against the *fédéré*

National Guardsmen camping around Paris and the exile of **refractory clergy** – and it was a factor in the overthrow of the monarchy itself.

At the end of 1789, Church lands were nationalized and the process of selling them off was begun. The *parlements* were suspended and never met again. The following year, the new **administrative framework** of the kingdom was set up, and the **Civil Constitution of the Clergy** became law. All these changes were enacted with the king's reluctant acquiescence. Once Pope Pius VI's opinion on the ecclesiastical changes was declared, the king expressed his own disapproval of them by trying to leave Paris for Saint-Cloud to receive his Easter communion from a refractory priest. He was prevented from doing so by a militant crowd and the **National Guard** commanded by **Lafayette**. This led to his decision to leave the capital for the eastern border of France and declare himself independent of the Assembly, explaining his action in a letter that was meant to be found when he had gone. What is always called 'The Flight to **Varennes**' took place on 20/21 June 1791. Varennes is the place where he was caught. He had set out for Montmédy on the eastern frontier. He did not understand the extent of the changes in the mind-set of the citizens over just three years, still regarding them as his subjects.[59]

On his return to Paris, the Assembly accepted the fiction that he had been 'abducted' by royalists. Not many in the **Jacobin Club** believed it was the truth, but a letter from General **Bouillé** assuming all responsibility for the event allowed the Assembly to let it become the official version of the events. The Paris Commune maintained that the king had left of his own accord and did not trust him.

Nevertheless, the **Feuillants** and the **Constituent Assembly** tried to make constitutional monarchy work. The Constitution of 1791 was adopted in September. The king came to the Assembly to **declare war** in April 1792. But the Parisian mistrust grew, and on the **'Day' of 20 June**, a **sansculotte** crowd burst into the Tuileries, cornered the king on his own, to make him wear a **Phrygian bonnet** and drink the nation's health. When Mayor **Pétion** arrived after two hours to restore order, the king asked him why it had taken him so long. This was a prelude to the **'Day' of 10 August 1792**.

***

The monarchy was suspended on the 'Day' (*Journée* is the French word used for these cataclysmic occasions) of 10 August 1792 amid the violence at the Tuileries. The royal family was confined in the Temple Prison on the orders of the Paris Commune. The Duke of **Brunswick** led the Prussian army into France, threatening severe reprisals if the king and queen were harmed, which stiffened the resistance of the patriots. Royalists were massacred in the Paris prisons in **September**. The newly assembled **National Convention** declared that France was a republic on 20 September, the day before the republican army's victory at **Valmy**. The decision was made to put 'Louis Capet, former king of the French' on trial 'for conspiracy against public liberty and against the general security of the state.' The king's secret strongbox (*armoire de fer*) was found in the vacant Tuileries Palace and still contained compromising correspondence between him and **Mirabeau**, Lafayette and **Dumouriez**.

The trial began on 15 January 1793 and took 37 hours of the Convention's time. The former minister **Malherbes** did his best as defence counsel. When Louis XVI's guilt had been unanimously decided upon, each of the deputies present was required to go in person to the tribune to make his declaration about the sentence to be passed. Intimidating sansculottes looked down from the galleries. A typical Jacobin response was given by a deputy from the Charente-Inférieure (as it was called then), **Bernard de Saintes**: '... as I am deeply convinced that the greatest service that can be rendered to the human race is to rid the earth of the monsters that devour it, I vote for the death of the tyrant with the shortest delay.' In the closest possible vote, 361 out of 721 deputies agreed. The **Girondins** sponsored the idea of a national referendum to confirm the verdict if the Convention found the king guilty, but their proposal was rejected.

***

On 21 January 1793, Louis XVI went to the scaffold. His intended words to the people at the scaffold were drowned out by specifically ordered drum rolls. Afterwards, people collected his blood on their handkerchiefs. He was buried in the common grave.

When all was said and done, Louis XVI was unable to adapt himself to constitutional monarchy. The programme of the *monarchiens* was not what he wanted for himself. He did not entirely go along with the Feuillants. He could not work with the Girondin ministers imposed upon him, and had his own reasons for declaring war on the queen's relations. After Mirabeau had died, he had no real link with the Assembly. He preserved his absolutist temperament. He also kept his place in the collective sub-conscious of the French nation: it is said that even Communist mayors issued invitations for the Requiem Masses held for him in 1993.

Hardman, John, *Louis XVI* (New Haven and London: Yale University Press, 1993).

Lefebvre, Georges, *1789*, trans. R.R. Palmer as *The Coming of the French Revolution* (University Parks, PA: Princeton University Press, Bicentennial Edition, 1989).

Price, Munro, *The Fall of the French Monarchy: Louis XVI, Marie-Antoinette and the Baron de Breteuil* (London: Macmillan, 2002).

Louis XVII (1785–95)

The 'First Dauphin' had died at Meudon in the opening weeks of the **Estates-General** and, when the king was pressed to make decisions, he replied, 'There are no fathers then among the Third Estate.'[60] When the queen was on trial in October 1793, and accused of sexually abusing the 'Second Dauphin', her response was, 'I appeal in this matter to all mothers present in court.'[61]

Louis-Charles was taken from the rooms in the Temple where he lived with his mother, his aunt, Madame Elisabeth, and his sister, Madame Royale, and kept on his own. With remarkable courage, the journalists and editor of the *Courier Universel* reported the changes made to the supervision of the child on 24 November 1794. They were arrested for it immediately.[62] The boy died on 8 June 1795. Royalists in the **Vendée**, in Brittany, in **Toulon** and in exile clung to Louis XVII's name until then. When Admiral Hood took Toulon, he did so in exchange for the Toulonais' accepting Louis XVII as king and forced the British ministers' hands to support a Bourbon restoration to which they had not yet committed themselves. Many of them thought that, while she was still alive, the queen should have been regent for Louis XVII after 21 January 1793, but **Provence** assumed the regency and then the throne in exile.

In the nineteenth century, there were several men who claimed to have been Louis-Charles escaped from prison. His sister, the Duchesse d'Angoulême, did not acknowledge them. DNA testing was carried out on the heart buried in the royal mausoleum in the Abbey of Saint-Denis and the positive results were made public in Paris on 19 April 2000. Louis XVII died as the 'Prisoner of the Temple', as newspapers announced in surprising detail in 1795.

Cadbury, Deborah, *The Lost King of France: The Tragic Story of Marie-Antoinette's Favourite Son* (London and New York: Fourth Estate, 2002).

Luxembourg Palace

Marie de Medici's Luxembourg Palace suffered several changes of use in the revolutionary years. At the outset it was the residence in Paris of 'Monsieur' – **Provence** – which he used as well as his apartments in **Versailles**. Once he had left as an *émigré* at the same time as the king's flight to **Varennes**, it was left empty.

As the need for places to confine political prisoners grew more acute, it lent itself well enough to the detention of several of the personalities of the Revolution. This constituted no more than occasional use, it seems.

The adoption of the Constitution of Year III meant that the five Directors in their bizarre uniforms designed by **David** (*directoires* were the type of underwear worn by women during the middle years of the twentieth century) needed impressive housing. The Luxembourg served very well when converted into five apartments for a succession of Directors, and for **Barras** the whole time until he agreed to go after the **Brumaire coup**.

Lyon: Federalist Rebellion (1793)

Lyon's prosperity was traditionally based on the production and weaving of silk. With the departure of the *émigrés* and the end of the court at **Versailles**, where wearing silk clothes had been compulsory, the demand for the Lyon silk-workers' product almost completely dried up.

Unemployment in Lyon soared and half the workers and their families were in receipt of charity. According to Arthur **Young**, who visited Lyon in December 1789, the trade treaty with Britain of 1786 made by **Calonne** added to the misery, with cheaper British goods available as alternatives to French products. Besides, the misery was being increased by the *octroi*, the high tax to be paid at the town gates to bring in produce for sale.[63]

In September 1790, the Lyonnais **sansculottes** created popular societies in the 32 sections to counteract the bourgeois clubs affiliated to the Paris **Jacobin Club**, whose membership fees were costly. Delegates from the sections' popular societies met in a Central Club. This was controlled at first by people sympathetic to **Roland**, but it was then taken over by the associates of the radical **Chalier** (collectively called Chaliers). A Rolandin called Vitet was elected mayor, and the directors of the Rhône-et-Loire department, who shared the Hôtel de Ville, were constitutional monarchists too. After the overthrow of the monarchy on 10 August 1792, there were copycat **September Massacres** in Lyon – eight officers and four priests died. Vitet was elected to the **Convention** (Roland was a minister again), and another Rolandin, Nivière-Chol, became mayor. Economic stress was worsening. In February 1793, the Central Club demanded a **revolutionary tribunal**. Nivière-Chol opposed it and would have called in troops to resist the popular societies. On 9 March, there was a popular rising. Nivière-Chol resigned but was re-elected. The Chaliers denounced the 'aristocrats' linked to the Rolandins. Workers opposed the Chaliers, however, since they remained loyal to those who might be able to provide work again. Nivière-Chol stood down, and another moderate replaced him, and was replaced in turn by a Chalier, Bertrand.

Thus began the '80 days of the Chaliers', when a whole series of Jacobin local measures were decreed including the **Maximum** and a Lyonnais **Revolutionary Army**, which was authorized to take weapons from the bourgeois **National Guard** on 14 May. First seven sections, then twelve, and then a majority opposed the decree. The Lyonnais **Girondin** deputy at the National Convention had this contravened and four **representatives on mission** were sent to Lyon, including **Dubois-Crancé**. Twenty-six sections meeting at the Arsenal rejected the order of 14 May. The struggle between the moderates and the Chaliers began on 29 May. Two representatives on mission (two had already left) were arrested by the moderates. The Chaliers were arrested too and put on trial as 'anarchists'. On 29 May, Lyon had a 'Day' exactly the reverse of the 'Day' in Paris on 31 May, when the Jacobins began excluding the Girondins from the Convention.

The Convention reacted quickly, realizing this was a 'federalist' rising, linked with others in Normandy, the south-west and the Midi, and the east against the centre. The moderates made contact with Marseille, Nîmes and Bordeaux to demand an alternative convention at Bourges. The Chaliers' plan for an army was implemented by their opponents. The leaders were royalists like the Comte de Précy and the Marquis de Clermont-Tonnerre (whose titles had been abolished). Robert **Lindet** tried to negotiate but to no avail. Decrees of the Convention against the federalists were issued and, in reply, Chalier was executed in Lyon (another Jacobin martyr) along with two of his supporters, and another was lynched in the street. The Lyonnais citizens stood solidly behind their new leaders with a vote of 11,300 to 67.

Kellermann, Dubois-Crancé and the Army of the Alps were held up by a Piedmontese offensive in Savoy, and did not arrive before Lyon until 10 August 1793. The town was bombarded from 29 August onwards. **Couthon** arrived in October. Précy and Clermont-Tonnerre fled to Switzerland. The siege ended after 67 days. On 12 October, the Convention passed its famous decree: 'Lyon shall lose its name. It shall be called 'Freed Town. It shall be destroyed. All that was inhabited by the rich shall be demolished. Only the house of the poor man shall remain …' Couthon was taken to the Place Bellecour in his wheelchair and began the demolition of the elegant bourgeois houses there and along the Rhône quays, but his heart was not in it, and he was soon replaced by **Fouché** and **Collot d'Herbois**.

These two showmen put on a display starting with a de-Christianization ceremony (which, of course, had a political rather than religious purpose). The executed Jacobin Chalier was given a eulogy while his body was exposed for 'public veneration', as Collot reported when he sent his head to Paris like a holy relic. There was a travesty of a religious procession: an ass wearing a bishop's mitre. Objects considered holy by Catholics were smashed on Chalier's (empty) tomb. Collot intended all this to be liberating as well as blasphemous. The mass shootings were theatre too, meant 'to imprint terror without exciting pity' as those responsible for them said. Fouché added that it was to 'express the total power of the people' that on successive days, 60 then 208 federalists were shot – at first with cannon – and their bodies thrown into prepared graves dug in a meadow called Les Brotteaux. There were only two *mitraillades*, so sickening that they were replaced by the usual methods of execution (935 people were shot and 732 guillotined over 130 days).[64] The surviving bourgeois were brutally taxed.

Fouché went back to Paris and provoked the **Thermidor coup**. Vitet returned to Lyon at the end of August, and the Jacobin mayor Bertrand was dismissed. New representatives on mission dismantled the **Terror**. Lyon's name was taken back on 4 October, and the **Thermidorean Convention** received an address from the new municipality on 7 October, with not even Fouché objecting.[65] The economy was ruined and the population had been diminished by 20 per cent. Vengeance in the form of the **'White Terror'** soon took place, with Jacobin terrorists tracked down and killed – in their prison cells and even in their hospital beds.[66]

M

Maistre, Joseph-Marie, Comte de (1753–1821)

Like **Bonald**, Maistre was regarded by his constitutional and republican opponents as a 'prophet of the past'.[1] He was from a French family who lived in Savoy (part of the Kingdom of Sardinia) and had been ennobled there. He was a member of the Savoyard senate from 1787 until 1792 and, during the Empire, was Savoyard ambassador to St Petersburg.

The **'alliance of throne and altar'** was for Maistre the only true form of government. Hereditary monarchs and the pope were God's only accredited representatives in Christian Europe. He unfailingly supported the Jesuit Order, but was also, surprisingly, a **Freemason**. He was in favour of **Louis XVI** calling the **Estates-General**, since he owned land in France and could have been elected as a deputy. His support for reform evaporated with the decisions of the **Night of 4 August 1789**.

When a French army invaded Savoy in 1792, Maistre left home and became an exile in Switzerland, where he visited Germaine de **Staël** in Coppet and joined in the conversations in her salon there. His exile lasted until he went to Russia in 1803 as Piedmontese ambassador, and a good deal of counter-revolutionary writing was the result. His purpose was to deny any legitimacy to institutions derived by human will and without depth in the long term of history. It has been pointed out, however,[2] that his polemic was most fragile when he used it against the institutions that arose from the Revolution.

On this subject, in fact, the thought of Maistre is not without contradictions. On the one hand, he conceives the Revolution as a pure nothing, a satanic work coming from the negative tendency written into the human condition; on the other, he insists precisely and eloquently on the fact that the Revolution was not a simple episode, that it is an epoch open to the past and the future, for which precedents can be found in compiling the genealogy of the spirit of opposition in France, the inheritors of which were still at work after the Restoration [of the monarchy].[3]

The impact of the French Revolution is not something that even a reactionary polemicist can deny.

 de Maistre, Joseph, *Considerations on France,* ed. Richard A. Lebrun with an Introduction by Isaiah Berlin (Cambridge: Cambridge University Press, 1974 and 1994).

Malherbes, Chrétien Guillaume de Lamoignon de (1721–94)

Malherbes had been chief censor of the press in Louis XV's reign while his father was chancellor and had adopted a liberal policy towards Diderot over the publication of his *Encyclopédie*. When he opposed Louis XV's suppression of the Paris *parlement* in 1771, he was ordered to leave **Versailles**.

Louis XVI appointed him minister for the royal household on his accession in 1774, but he resigned after two years to campaign on behalf of legal recognition for Protestants and Jews. He held ministerial office again in 1787, but did not remain. He offered to act as counsel for Louis XVI's defence in December 1792, a task he carried out as best he could in the circumstances. Having declared himself publicly as a royalist, it was not long before he and all his family suffered the same fate as the king.[4]

Mallet du Pan, Jacques (1749–1800)

Mallet du Pan was a royalist. During the early part of the Revolution, he was entrusted by **Louis XVI** in person with a mission to liaise with the princes of the blood royal and some German rulers in Frankfurt in 1791 to try to provide some concerted policy. This failed, mainly due to the intransigence of **Artois**.

Like **Necker**, he was a Protestant from Geneva. He attracted the attention of **Voltaire** and was appointed to a professorship in the academy at Cassel which he soon gave up. He moved to London and involved himself with a newspaper run by Linguet, who returned to France, insulted a marshal of France and spent two years in the **Bastille**. Mallet kept the newspaper going in London, but gave it up when Linguet wanted it back upon his release from the Bastille.

After his secret mission to the princes, he went to Berne, and made commentaries on the Revolution for the Habsburg Emperor and for the King of Prussia and the Court of Portugal. He attacked **Bonaparte** and the **Directory** for dismantling the Venetian Republic in 1797 and handing it over to Austria. The French government pressed for his exile from Switzerland as a result. This took him once more to London, where he brought out another version of his paper, the *Mercure britannique*, and died of consumption in 1800.[5]

Marat, Jean-Paul (1743–93)

Marat's contribution to the Revolution was through his outspoken newspaper, and the manner of his death. *L'Ami du peuple* (The Friend of the People) spoke for the **sansculotte** outlook. In its pages, Marat monitored events for a popular audience from September 1789 until July 1793, when Charlotte **Corday** murdered him in his medicinal bath.

In 1789, at the age of 46, he was older than most of the front-row revolutionaries. He had already experienced a career as a private tutor, scientist, medical doctor and political theorist. The violent language he used as the Revolution's commentator is in contrast to the gentleman's life that he evidently led before 1789.[6]

Marat gave this gentility up as the elections for the **Estates-General** were being held in spring 1789. His *Appeal to the Nation* covered similar ground to **Sieyès**'s work. He made suggestions for an appropriate constitution for France, criticizing those who were strongly supporting the English system. He gave a detailed account of the **October Days** in the newly launched *Ami du Peuple*, using reports of eye-witnesses, creating a culture of suspicion, ever on the look-out for 'enemies of the people' and denouncing them as such. But, on 8 October, he was arrested for insulting the Paris municipality and went into hiding. Even so, in November, he launched a series of pamphlets against **Necker**, 'unfaithful minister, sold to the court'. Despite the protection of **Danton** and the **Cordeliers** he had to seek safety in London for several months.[7]

On his return to Paris in spring 1790, *L'Ami du Peuple* re-emerged to denounce **Mirambeau** ('the infamous Riquetti') and unveil **Lafayette**'s personal ambition. He saw a court-based conspiracy in the repression of the **Nancy** mutineers. His uncanny predictions began with the king's flight to **Varennes**, which he announced in advance. After the Champ de Mars massacre he was silenced again, nearly returning to London, but staying instead to be with Simone Evrard, who shared his life until his murder. He directed his invective next against the **Girondins**, whom he saw as irresponsible rabble-rousers promoting a dangerous war with the kings of Europe.[8]

After the **'Day' of 10 August 1792**, he issued his *Address to the Brave Parisians*, calling for them to consolidate their victory over the suspended monarchy by appointing a triumvirate of **Robespierre**, Danton and himself to govern. He became a member of the Paris **surveillance committee** at the same time as the **September Massacres** began. He had previously called for the physical elimination of counter-revolutionaries. In the event, he tried to limit what was happening, but he did co-sign the circular justifying popular violence.[9]

On 9 September, he was elected a Paris deputy in the **National Convention** and sat with the **Mountain**. He changed the name of *L'Ami du Peuple* to *Le Journal de la République française*. He intended to be less cavalier and to stand for revolutionary discipline. He only now joined the **Jacobin Club**[10] and took sides with Robespierre, seeing conspirators everywhere. His newspaper 'invented the language of the Terror'.[11] He used it to express violent outbursts against the **Girondins**, calling for them to be lynched.[12] He voted for the king's death and vehemently endorsed it in anticipation on 19 October. The Girondins accused him of aspiring to a dictatorship with Robespierre and Danton. Abandoned by the Mountain, he defended himself, appealing again for a dictatorship. Since 96 of the 128 deputies on mission were Jacobins, and 238 more stayed away, the Girondins could mobilize enough of the uncommitted deputies in the Convention (known as the Plain, or the Marsh) in a roll-call vote to have Marat impeached before the **Revolutionary Tribunal** on 14 April 1793, with only 93 voting against.

Marat evaded arrest, then settled in comfort in the **Conciergerie**, visited by members of the Paris Commune. He came before the Revolutionary Tribunal on 24 April, amid applause from the public galleries. He defended himself and was acquitted the same day. The crowd carried him back to the Convention in triumph – one of **Lesueur**'s miniatures depicts this – and he was afterwards fêted in the Jacobins. No wonder that Marat was instrumental in gaining sansculotte support for the Girondins' exclusion from the Convention on 2 June.[13]

Marat's health was deteriorating, so he withdrew from the Convention and the Jacobins, though he kept up his letter writing and journalism. After Charlotte Corday murdered him he became an icon of the revolutionary spirit through **David**'s eulogy of him in paint and ceremony at his funeral. On 25 November, his body was moved to the Pantheon, but his apotheosis did not outlast the **Thermidorean Convention**.

Ozouf, Mona, 'Marat', in François Furet and Mona Ozouf (eds), *A Critical Dictionary of the French Revolution*, trans. Arthur Goldhammer (London: The Belknap Press of Harvard University Press, 1989), pp. 242ff. References here are to the French edition.

Marie-Antoinette (1755–93)

Married at 14 to a prince little older than herself who was short of self-confidence, Marie-Antoinette had to take on all the tensions of the old regime and then submit to the Revolution's **Terror**. Guides at **Versailles** used to say she was *superficielle*, but all that has changed. 'Let them eat cake,' had been said frequently by many others for a very long time before she was accused of insulting the hungry people of Paris from her little theatre, the pillars of which, they said, were made of solid gold. She is the tragic queen who learned how to be regal in the hardest possible way.

She grew up ill educated in Vienna as the fifteenth child of Empress Maria Theresa and the late Francis I. She married the Dauphin of

France in the final stages of the diplomatic revolution of rapprochement between France and Austria, in 1770. At Versailles, she was advised by **Mercy d'Argenteau**, the Austrian Ambassador. He wrote reports to her mother, who replied direct with reproaches. Marie-Antoinette became queen in 1774. It took seven years for **Louis XVI** to beget their first child. Their first male child died at the same time as the **Estates-General** opened.

Marie-Antoinette was the leader of fashion in dress and culture, and went secretly to Paris theatres and casinos with close friends. All that contributed to malicious representations of her in pamphlets as a spendthrift with insatiable sexual desires. The Princesse de **Lamballe** was her household superintendent, and the Duchesse de **Polignac** was put in charge of the royal children. They were both the recipients of large expense accounts. The latter was the king's friend too. The queen was accused of adultery with the king's younger brother, **Artois**, and there are illustrations of her as a mythical harpy, harking back to Mélusine. Further complications arose when it was whispered that the King of Sweden's envoy, Axel **Fersen**, was her lover.[14]

The charge of extravagance against her was increased when the Petit Trianon at Versailles was embellished for her from 1774 onwards, and when she had the Queen's Hamlet built in its grounds. The **Diamond Necklace Affair**, beginning in 1784, together with the king's purchase of the Saint-Cloud Palace as a present for her caused further unpopularity, especially when the extent of the national deficit was made public by **Calonne**. Two nicknames used against her were *Madame Déficit* and 'The Austrian Woman'.

Not until after Calonne had failed to convince the **Assembly of Notables** of the need for financial reform in 1787 did the queen have any real influence over the king's appointments. It was then that she gained the appointment of her protégé Archbishop **Loménie de Brienne**.[15] Nevertheless, she had no say in replacing Vergennes as Foreign Minister with Montmorin at the same time.

From her thirtieth birthday in 1785 onwards, Marie-Antoinette was perceived by those who knew her as increasingly serious about her status as queen and mother of the royal children. Nevertheless, the *libellistes* (writers of scurrilous pamphlets) took advantage of every turn of events. Her principal enemies became **Hébert** and his creation *Le Père Duchesne.*

After the fall of the **Bastille**, although she was associated with **Necker's** dismissal, she stayed at Versailles while Artois and Yolande de Polignac emigrated. On the night of 5–6 October 1789, she became the main target of the march of the market women. Two of her bodyguards were slaughtered and her bedroom was ransacked with murderous intent just after she had fled to the king's side. She stood with him on the balcony in the morning when he agreed to go to Paris. Once in the **Tuileries**, she was active in making plans to escape from France. Her loving friend (*ami amoureux*) Fersen and the Baron de **Breteuil** organized the flight to **Varennes** with her support, which the king accepted after he was not allowed to go to Saint-Cloud for Easter in 1791.

With the acceptance of the fiction that the king was being abducted by royalists and of the 1791 Constitution, the queen's new nickname became *Madame Veto*. In the prelude to war, her contact with her brother, Emperor Leopold II, was regarded as treachery, and this continued when war had been declared on the next emperor, Francis II. On the *journée* of **20 June 1792**, she had to hide from the **sansculottes** in a room in the Tuileries. On the '**Day' of 10 August**, she pointed out that there might be enough loyal soldiers in the Tuileries to defend the king, but she took refuge with him in the **Legislative Assembly** to hear that the monarchy had been suspended.

The Insurrectionary Commune took them as prisoners to the Temple and, after the king's trial and execution, 'the Widow Capet' was left there with Madame Elisabeth (Louis XVI's sister), the eight-year-old **Louis XVII**, and her daughter Marie-Thérèse (who was later released in exchange for four French prisoners of the Austrians and married to her unprepossessing cousin, the Duc d'Angoulême). The queen could have been deported or exchanged, but the intensity of hatred from Hébert and the **Jacobins** caused her to be transferred to the **Conciergerie** – the ante-room of the **guillotine** – for her show trial before Herman and **Fouquier-Tinville** in the **revolutionary tribunal**. The verdict was prearranged, and she went to the scaffold on 16 October 1793. That date is often regarded as the beginning of the official **Terror**.

The main charge against her, expressed in the second day of the hearing before the revolutionary tribunal was that she had exercised an ascendancy over her indecisive husband and so was guilty of the tyranny for which he was executed.

 Fraser, Antonia, *Marie-Antoinette: The Journey* (London: Weidenfeld and Nicolson, 2001).

Thomas, Chantal, *The Wicked Queen: The Origins of the Myth of Marie-Antoinette*, trans. Julie Ross (New York: Zone Books, 1999).

Zweig, Stefan, *Marie-Antoinette: The Portrait of an Average Woman*, trans. Eden and Cedar Paul (New York: The Viking Press, 1933; repr. Grove Press, 2002).

Marseille: Federalist Rebellion (1793)

As early as March 1793, moderate republicans in Marseille were alarmed at hearing of mob violence and extremism in Paris and saw **representatives on mission** as agents of Jacobin dictatorship.

On 19 March, **Fréron** and **Barras** arrived as representatives in a Marseille about to erupt into rebellion.[16] Weapons had been confiscated by their predecessors, and the **Jacobin Club** acted against the moderates in the city's sections. A **revolutionary tribunal** was in being and a **guillotine** set up. There had been a forced loan from the wealthy merchants. Yet the moderates on the section councils had enough political clout to close the Jacobin Club and assume power. Barras and Fréron had to escape to Montelimar on 27 April. The moderates all over the Midi – Aix, **Avignon** and Arles – acted similarly. Two other representatives, Jean-Baptiste Bo and Charles Louis Antiboul, were arrested in Marseille. The moderate movement grew and included royalists. A federalist force began a march up the Rhône Valley to be dispersed by Jean-Baptiste Carteaux's new Army of the Midi, which moved from Grenoble to Avignon in July. Carteaux took Marseille on 25 August. Many moderates fled to **Toulon**, which had just admitted British and Spanish naval squadrons to its harbours, to continue their struggle.

Antoine Christophe **Saliceti** and Thomas-Augustin Gasparin, representatives in the Midi as a whole, entered Marseille with Carteaux. The Jacobin Club reopened. The ship owners held responsible for revolt had to raise a forced contribution of 4 million livres within 24 hours. Churches and convents in the Provençal departments were ransacked for metal for cash and cannon. Marseille was to supply the siege of Toulon with troops, provisions and armaments. The radicals who had been imprisoned were freed and placed in authority in the city council. The revolutionary tribunal reappeared. A **revolutionary army** of **sansculottes** was formed. No fewer than five representatives were in Marseille and they instituted martial law with the **National Convention**'s approval on 16 December. The local Jacobins objected, however, and withdrew their battalions meant for Toulon. The representatives replaced the new council and brought in a regiment from the Drôme. Then they had to subdue Toulon.

On their return from Toulon, Barras and Fréron wanted the entire city punished and called 'Without a Name' and the departmental administration to be moved away to Aix. Admiral Hood's captured correspondence showed that Marseille moderates had been negotiating with the allies of the coalition and had caused the rising in the entire Midi.

Even so, the **Committee of Public Safety** would not agree to the destruction of so important a commercial centre which had earlier supported the Revolution to its utmost. The president and vice-president of the Jacobin Club were sent to Paris, charged with taking bribes to save wealthy people from the revolutionary tribunal (they were acquitted and reinstalled after a month). Barras and Fréron set up a military commission of sansculottes to execute 30 merchants and confiscate their property. The Committee of Public Safety did not approve of their actions and replaced them with the more biddable Etienne Chrisostome Maignet.

Marxist Historians
In the middle years of the twentieth century – spanning the Second World World War – the 'classic' interpretation of the French Revolution was in the hands of Marxist historians in France. The important names are Albert **Mathiez** (1874–1928), Georges **Lefebvre** (1874–1959) and Albert **Soboul** (1914–82). Their interpretation depended on a concept, first introduced by the socialist politician Jean Jaurès before 1914, developed as 'history from below'. A lucid and accurate summary of the Marxist position was provided in 1998 by the American historian Gary Kates in terms like

this: the Revolution was not just a struggle in political terms between faulty **absolute monarchy** and wholesome democratic republicanism, but took place on a deeper level as a change from feudalism to capitalism. The elite **bourgeoisie** with disposable liquid capital made an alliance with artisans and peasants to confront the **nobility** whose wealth was in land. This was initially successful, but strained at the seams by 1791 when class conflict arose between the bourgeois elements and the popular classes. The resulting struggle produced an urban movement led by the **sansculottes** who had a vision which nineteenth-century radicals came to share. The apogee of the sansculotte movement was the **Terror**, when the **Jacobins** established a modern democracy, albeit for a short time. 'Thus the French Revolution was essentially a class struggle in which one class was destroyed (the nobility), one class was awakened (the sansculottes), and one class won control of the state (the bourgeoisie).' [17]

The Marxists' emphasis was on social and economic history, areas of study where other ideas from Camille-Ernest Labrousse (1895–1988) had been influential. A long view of historical progress led to comparisons with events in Russia in the decade following 1917, whereupon the interpretation became Leninist rather than Marxist.

The Marxist approach held the field until challenged by a British historian, Alfred Cobban, and an American, George V. Taylor, who re-emphasized the political aspects of the Revolution, in the 1950s. Not until François **Furet** (1927–97) turned away from Marxism was any change made in France. Albert Soboul called the Marxist interpretation the classic one. Furet preferred to call it a neo-Jacobin one. Furet's subsequent work, both on his own and in collaboration with Jacques and Mona Ozouf (such as the *Critical Dictionary* he and Mona Ozouf edited in 1989), produced a view of the revolutionary decade without Marxist historical presuppositions. The new 'revisionary orthodoxy' appears to see no single, clear-cut guiding principle, since it is concerned with the whole spectrum of human interest from politics to culture. A very important contribution to the debate, accessible in English to non-specialists, is William Doyle's 1985 translation of Guy Chaussinard-Nogand's 1976 study of the French nobility, with its conclusion that there was a 'convergence of interests' which mobilized nobles and bourgeois alike against the way

229

the court and the monarchy had come to typify and monopolize the state.[18] More constructive conclusions can emerge if noble and bourgeois contemporaries are allowed to speak for themselves in their **statements of complaint** (*cahiers de doléance*), without any over-arching ideology imposed upon them by historians long after the actual events.

In France, Claude Mazauric continues to defend the Marxist position. His latest book is from 2009, *L'Histoire de la Révolution française et la pensée marxiste* (Presses Universitaires de France).

Chaussinand-Nogand, Guy, *The French Nobility in the Eighteenth Century*, trans. William Doyle (Cambridge: Cambridge University Press, 1985).

Doyle, William, *The Origins of the French Revolution*, Second Edition (Oxford: Oxford University Press, 1988), Pt I, *The Marxist Orthodoxy and its Critics*. The 3rd edn, 1999, starts its appraisal in 1939.

——, 'Reflections on the Classic Interpretation of the French Revolution', in *Officers, Nobles and Revolutionaries, Essays in Eighteenth-Century France* (London and Rio Grande: The Hambledon Press, 1995).

Furet, François, *Interpreting the French Revolution*, trans. Elborg Forster (Cambridge: Cambridge University Press, 1981).

Furet, François and Mona Ozouf (eds), *A Critical Dictionary of the French Revolution*, trans. Arthur Goldhammer (London: The Belknap Press of Harvard University Press, 1989), particularly the entry on *The Academic History of the Revolution*.

Kates, Gary (ed.), *The French Revolution: Recent Debates and New Controversies* 2nd edn (New York and London: Routledge, 2006).

Lefèbvre, Georges, works cited after his entry, above.

Masséna, Jean-André (1758–1817)

Masséna became a general in the wars of the Revolution with a tremendous reputation as 'the dear child of victory'. He was one of the original 18 marshals appointed by the Emperor Napoleon.

His father, a shopkeeper in Nice, died when he was six, and his mother did not take him with her when she married again. In 1771, he was a cabin boy on a merchant ship which made voyages in the Mediterranean and to the French colony of Guiana. On his return to Nice in 1775, he joined the French (not Sardinian) army and had risen to be a warrant-officer by 1789 when he left the service. He was a smuggler for a while and then rejoined the army in 1791. There were no bars on able soldiers being commissioned by then, and he was soon a colonel. When war was declared in April 1792, he was stationed in the south-east and his battalion was soon incorporated into the Army of Italy. In August 1793, he became a brigadier, and a general in December.

When Bonaparte was given command in Italy in 1796, Masséna was in charge of two of its divisions. He took part in all the actions in **Bonaparte**'s Italian campaign, fording the bridge at Lodi and entering Milan.[19] After Bonaparte left for Egypt, Masséna commanded in Switzerland. The **Directory** was less intransigent about defeats than the **Committee of Public Safety** had been and, although defeated by Archduke Charles at the first battle of Zurich, he won the second battle there against the Russian Korsakov. As a result, Tsar Paul withdrew from the **Second Coalition**.[20]

Masséna was made a Marshal of France and a Duke by Napoleon. He fought in the Peninsula War facing Wellington at the Lines of Torres Vedras. He was in command at Marseille when the Empire fell, and kept his rank at the **restoration of the monarchy**.

Mathiez, Albert (1874–1932)

Albert Mathiez was designated as '**Aulard**'s unfaithful disciple'[21] by François **Furet**. His 1904 doctoral thesis about religious cults in the Revolution, such as **Theophilanthropy**, grounded him in the study of the Revolution.

He was born in the rural Franche-Comté and won a place at the Ecole Normale Supérieure, graduating in 1897. He taught in schools for a while and then became a pupil of the Revolution specialist Alphonse Aulard in Paris. He taught in a Parisian *lycée* in 1906 and then had university posts at Besançon in 1911 and Dijon in 1919. He failed to gain Aulard's professorship at the Sorbonne in 1923 (Philippe Sagnac was appointed), but taught in Paris from 1926, at the Sorbonne, in charge of courses, and simultaneously at the Ecole Pratique des Hautes Etudes. He was of a very irascible temperament, and died from a stroke in 1932.[22]

Mathiez quarrelled famously with Aulard in 1908 at the moment when he joined the society for Robespierrist studies, founded the year before, and contributed to the first issue of *Annales révolutionnaires*, which broke the monopoly in this field of Aulard's own review, *La Révolution française*. Aulard had been a 'pontiff' until then, identifying his subject with his professorial chair and even with himself.[23] Mathiez had been champing with impatience at his *lycée*, and it was surprising that the clash had not come earlier. Aulard was a radical, bourgeois republican and Mathiez a socialist who believed in a future of working-class supremacy. Aulard admired **Danton**, and Mathiez, **Robespierre**.[24]

The type of socialism Mathiez espoused at this time is elusive, being more instinctive than doctrinal. His roots, like Aulard's, were in the revolutionary tradition, informed by the Dreyfus Affair still raging around everyone. Mathiez was a member of the newly formed League of the Rights of Man, and of the Union of the Left. His admiration for Jaurès's *Histoire socialiste de la Révolution française* did not differ much from Aulard's, and he found there a straightforward Marxism which would remain the framework for his own exposition of the Revolution. The year 1789 was the victory of the **bourgeoisie**, but it had had to lean on the masses to succeed and the price to be paid was socialist concessions to their interests. The break with Aulard drove him further towards the left. He even turned to personal attacks on his former teacher as well as on Danton, nourishing his hatred of the republican bourgeoisie. One can almost sense a gleeful feeling on his part upon his discovering evidence to suggest that Danton was implicated in the **September Massacres**.[25]

The summer of 1914 turned the pacifist-socialist into an enthusiast for the war against German barbarity, as it did many like him. The professor of history from Besançon suggested to the lacklustre republicans in the government that the Convention of Year II was the best example for them to follow. He eagerly welcomed the Russian revolution of March 1917 as the daughter of 1789. But he saw Kerensky as a **Girondin**, and considered the coming to power of the Bolsheviks in October as the triumph of the **Mountain**. Nevertheless, he was disappointed when they concluded the treaty of Brest-Litovsk with Germany to bring them out of the war.

The disillusionment did not last because Mathiez saw the 'Blue Horizon' National Assembly of 1919, dominated by the right and centre-right, in terms of **counter-revolution**. He joined the Communist Party in 1920.

He saw Jacobinism and Bolshevism as dictatorships born in civil war and foreign conflict, both of them class dictatorships. They operated by the same methods: terror and taxation. They both proposed to transform universal society.[26] He had a small book published outlining all this. Lenin himself had said as much during the separation of Bolsheviks from Mensheviks in 1903.[27] Russia had replaced France as the avant-garde nation.

Lenin and Robespierre had the same conflict, Mathiez argued. But he did not stay long with the Comintern because he was temperamentally unsuited to its discipline, and he returned to the extreme left of independent socialism in 1922.[28] He left the party but remained within the intellectual scheme that brought it into being. He had, says Furet, moved Jacobinism from its natural place, the Third Republic, to the Soviet Union, thereby substituting another anachronism in which to manifest itself. In this way, he was still a devout follower of Robespierre. Aulard saw 1793 as great because of the promise made by its unadopted constitution. Mathiez held up the dictatorship that replaced it as an instrument of the war waged by the poor against the rich.[29] Furet saw in this a 'moralizing naivety mixed with partisan fanaticism, to make the awful springtime of 1794 into the fugitive triumph of fraternity around the **Laws of Ventôse** and the festival of the **Supreme Being**'.[30] But Mathiez's conclusion was a sad one, 'Alas! If Robespierre had been able to unite the majority of Frenchmen in the same patriotic feeling, that instant was short and his triumph without a tomorrow. Calumny, envy, fear and crime went to undermine his work and the Republic itself'.[31]

Furet, François, *Academic History of the Revolution,* in François Furet and Mona Ozouf (eds), *A Critical Dictionary of the French Revolution*, trans. Arthur Goldhammer (London: The Belknap Press of Harvard University Press, 1989), pp. 881ff. Notes above are from the French Edition.

Mathiez, Albert, *The French Revolution*, trans. Catherine Alison Phillips (London: Williams and Norgate, 1927).

Maury, Jean-Sifrein (1746–1817)

Maury was a shoemaker's son in the papal enclave of France, the Comtat-Venaissin, and was sent to the seminary of **Avignon**, where his teachers noticed his potential as a scholar and orator and sent him on to Paris. His speeches about Fénelon and Saint-Augustine were remarked upon. He was elected to the French Academy in 1785, and given the revenues of an abbey as the counsellor of Lamoignon, keeper of the seals, in 1788. He appeared to combine the Catholic faith with the **Enlightenment**, although his personal lifestyle was comparable with **Talleyrand**'s.

Maury made much of his oratorical skills once elected for the **clergy** of Peronne in the **Estates-General**, and was one of the most conspicuous debaters of the **Constituent Assembly**, often challenging **Mirabeau**. He did not pretend to be a constitutional monarchist, and he defended church property, an absolute veto for the king, and the Catholic Church as being the only one for the nation. He opposed the *assignats* and was the target for speeches by patriots in the assembly.

When the Constituent was wound up, he joined the *émigré* princes who welcomed him, and the pope nominated him in 1792 as his representative at the Diet of Frankfurt. By 1794, he was a cardinal archbishop, and Louis XVIII, as king in exile, made him his ambassador to the Holy See. Despite all that, he wrote to Napoleon in 1804, congratulating him on restoring the Catholic Church in France, and became his wholehearted supporter. Louis XVIII dismissed him at the **restoration**. Pope Pius VII imprisoned him in the Saint-Angelo in Rome for disobedience.[32]

Maximum, General, on Prices and Wages

The General Maximum on Prices and Wages was enacted by the **National Convention** on 27 September 1793 on the recommendation of the **Committee of Public Safety**. The **Law of Suspects** had been passed 12 days before. **Revolutionary Armies** of **sansculottes** were raised to act summarily against hoarding farmers who did not take their grain to market in the hope of a higher price later. Local committees of surveillance and the **Revolutionary Tribunal** were set up to enforce obedience. The Maximum, together with these measures, completed the apparatus of the régime of **Terror** that had become government policy.

The price of bread had been regulated since May 1793 at the same time as a forced loan from wealthy people. The purchasing power of the *assignat*, now regarded as paper currency, had fallen by 50 per cent. The

Jacobins in power, usually in favour of the natural equilibrium of market forces, reluctantly decided to systematize regulation on a national basis. The prices of all prime necessities were to be no higher than one-third more than local prices in 1790. Similarly, wages must not exceed the 1790 figures multiplied by half as much again. The system proved inefficient and attempts were made to modify it by a new version on 23 ventôse, year II (13 March 1794). Even so, the Subsistence Commission could not cope with the distribution of foodstuffs from areas of prosperity to places of scarcity.

After **Thermidor**, the severe penalties for disobeying the Maximum came to be disregarded. When the wind of liberalism was blowing, the **Thermidorean Convention** asked for a report on 4 November on the problems caused by the Maximum. Making it responsible for poverty, the Convention revoked it on 23 December.[33]

By the time the **Directory** forbade the use of *assignats*, broke the presses used for printing them, and returned to metal currency in February 1797, a free market economy had already reasserted itself.

Méhul, Etienne-Henri (1763–1817)

As a musician, Méhul's career was parallel to that of contemporary *militaires* such as **Hoche** and **Jourdan**. His parents had modest means (his father had a small wine-selling business), and his early musical education was at first informal, under the direction of a monastery organist near his birthplace at Givet in the Ardennes. He went to Paris at the age of 16, armed with a letter of introduction to Gluck from someone who had heard him play. Gluck fostered his education, and he produced works that were performed from 1783 onwards.

His first opera, *Euphrosine*, was put on in the *Comédie Italienne* (later *Opéra comique*) in Paris in 1790. It was warmly received, though his next was a failure. There were others which restored his reputation in the revolutionary decade. He also composed patriotic songs, such as the *Chant du départ* and the *Chant des victoires* written after the **Battle of Fleurus**.[34]

Méhul, **Gossec** and Cherubini were appointed inspectors of the Conservatoire de Musique when it was set up in 1795 and Méhul was nominated for the new French Institute in the same year. Méhul's work was the first to be called Romantic (in **Condorcet**'s review of *Le jeune sage et le vieux fou* in April 1793). Méhul was acquainted with **Bonaparte**, who later made him a member of the Legion of Honour and his work extended into the Empire, especially his orchestral output.

@ Words and music of *Chant du départ* are to be found online at:
http://musique-militaire.fr/tradition/patriotisme/le-chant-du-depart

Mercier, Louis-Sébastien (1740–1814)

Mercier was a first-rank writer before the revolutionary decade and a second-rank politician during it. His most prominent work known nowadays is his *L'An 2440, rêve s'il en fût jamais* (The Year 2440, a Dream if Ever There Was One). This was first published in 1770 and often revised with additional integral footnotes up until the fall of the monarchy in 1792. It was a Rip Van Winkle Utopia story of a 700-year-old man who wakes up in Paris and sees what changes have been made after the renunciation of despotism by the king and the setting-up of a deistic cult to which everyone consents. He finds himself in a harmonious, moral, egalitarian, Rousseauesque community set in a transformed and beautified city. Mercier anticipates many of the designs of the eventual revolutionaries. His book was forbidden, but many a *colporteur* risked being sent to the galleys to bring it to France from Amsterdam where it was published, and it became a bestseller on a European scale.

Mercier's father was a *marchand-fourbisseur* (he polished swords) and his maternal grandfather a master mason. He received a good education, however, at the College of Four Nations and afterwards became an habitué of the Café Procope, where many a revolutionary theme was discussed. He met Jean-Jacques **Rousseau** and absorbed his ideas for reuse in his own work. Between 1781 and 1788, he produced the 12 volumes of his *Tableau de Paris* (Picture of Paris), in which he popularized the ideas of **Enlightenment** writers. This was also censored and he went to Geneva as an exile in 1782, making personal contact with Jacques-Pierre **Brissot**, Etienne **Clavière** and **Mirabeau**. Back in Paris in 1786 he took to overtly political pamphleteering and, from October 1789, worked on a radical journal run by Jean-Louis **Carra**.

Mercier was elected a deputy for the Seine et Oise in the **National Convention**, but was more prominent as a journalist on **Girondin** newspapers. He was also a member of the **Social Circle**. He voted against the execution of the king, and in favour of prosecuting **Marat**. He was one of the 73 deputies who protested against the principal Girondins' exclusion on 2 June 1793. He was imprisoned during the **Terror** but not brought to trial, and resumed his place in the Convention in December 1794.

He sat on the council of 500 during the Directory until the partial elections of 1797. Then he taught history in the Ecole normale and was made a member of the Institut. This was the end of his active political involvement. He brought out *Le Nouveau Paris* in six volumes in 1798, a series of scenes and portraits from the Revolution. The French historian Marcel Dorigny quotes Mercier as saying of himself that he was equidistant from royal-noble despotism and from its popular counterpart.[35]

Mercier did not support **Bonaparte**, and died in obscurity at the end of the Empire.

 Darnton, Robert, *The Forbidden Best-Sellers of Pre-Revolutionary France* (London: Fontana Press, 1997). This book includes the complete text of the 1771 Edition of *L'An 2440*.

Mercy, Florimund, Comte d'Argenteau (1727–94)

Mercy d'Argentau had been Austrian ambassador in Paris since before the time of **Marie-Antoinette**'s marriage to the Dauphin Louis-Auguste in 1770, and remained as such until his transfer to Brussels in the Austrian Netherlands in 1790. His French name is accounted for by his birth in Liège.

He was the Empress Maria Teresa's source of information about her daughter's life at **Versailles** and a father-figure to the queen as she passed from her self-indulgent early years in France to her intelligent maturity after her thirtieth birthday. He remained a conscientious adviser to her in the reigns of Joseph II and Leopold II, but always represented the interests of Austria in the alliance that dated from 1756 and was waning in the eyes of French courtiers. He was one of the instigators of the **Brunswick Declaration**, and took refuge in Germany when the French took **Belgium**. He died soon after his appointment as Austrian ambassador in London.[36]

Merlin de Douai, Philippe-Antoine (1754–1838)

Merlin de Douai was an expert in the law from well before the Revolution and put his knowledge to good use after it began. He was a **Third Estate** deputy for Douai in the **Estates-General** and set to work in the committees concerned applying legal principles in the new conditions. He presented committee reports on redemption payments to free a tenant from feudal dues. These were embodied in the Law of 15 March 1790. A distinction was made between rights concerning persons and those concerning the land they occupied and worked. Persons were freed from feudal dues, but the land was not, and the occupier had to free himself from dues by a redemption payment of 25 times their value, which few could afford to pay, so the law was impracticable. The only ones able to free themselves were urban bourgeois or richer peasants who used the *assignat*'s falling value in 1792 to do so, otherwise landowners redeemed their own land in order to sell it.[37] On 15 July 1793, by decree of the **National Convention**, feudal dues were definitively abolished and the communes were ordered to burn the title deeds.[38]

Primogeniture was abolished under Merlin's guidance, as were torture and branding. The revision of laws on inheritance owed a good deal to him. He edited the Journal of Legislation to popularize the Legislative Assembly's decrees. Since, like all members of the **Constituent**, he could not be a member of the **Legislative Assembly**, he went home to Douai to be a judge in the criminal tribunal there.

He sat with the **Mountain** in the National Convention and voted for the king's death. He was on the Council of Legislation and presented the draft of the **Law of Suspects** accepted on 17 September 1793, although others such as **Couthon** and **Robespierre** were more forceful in gaining its acceptance. While a **representative on mission** in the Nord, he denounced **Dumouriez** as a traitor after the battle of Neerwinden.

Merlin was a member of the **Thermidorean Committee of Public Safety**. He was instrumental in closing the **Jacobin Club** on 19 November 1794. He took part in the negotiations for the **Treaties of Basle** which took Prussia out of the **War of the First Coalition** on 5 April 1795 and Spain on 22 July.

Elected to the Council of 500 in the **Directory**, he became Justice Minister and then Police Minister. After the **Fructidor coup**, he was chosen as a Director, only to be ousted at the **Prairial coup**. This was the end of his revolutionary career, but he held office under **Bonaparte**, becoming a Count of the Empire and a Grand Officer of the Legion of Honour.

Merlin de Thionville, Antoine-Christophe (1762–1833)

Merlin de Thionville had been training for the priesthood but changed to the law and, at the outset of the Revolution, was associated with the *parlement* of Metz. He was a municipal officer in his birthplace Thionville when local administrations were established in 1790, and was then elected a deputy for the Moselle in the **Legislative Assembly**.

He proposed the sequestration of *émigrés'* property, attacked the **'Austrian Committee'** and was prominent in the **'days' of 20 June** and **10 August 1792**. He played an important part in the northern war effort of September 1792. Elected to the **National Convention**, he was **representative on mission** at Mainz until it surrendered to the Duke of **Brunswick** on 23 July 1793. The Germans admired him and called him 'Fire-devil' (*Feuerteufel*).[39] He was on mission with the Army of the Coasts of La Rochelle at the time of **Louis XVI**'s trial, but he voted for his death. He favoured the institution of **surveillance committees**, but was not active in the **Terror**.

He joined **Robespierre**'s gainsayers at the **Thermidor coup** and was involved in the Thermidorian Reaction with a seat in the **Committee of General Security**. He harassed surviving Jacobins in company with the **Golden Youth**. In the **Directory** he was a member of the Council of 500 until replaced by the partial election of 1798. After **Brumaire**, Merlin retired from public life.

Metric System

As early as May 1790, a commission was appointed by the **Constituent Assembly** to examine the possibility of changing weights and measures, with all their *onces, gros* and *arpents*, to a nationally comprehensible metric system of *grammes, mètres* and *kilomètres*. The new measures would be natural and rational. However, other, apparently more important, concerns prevented the completion of this project. It had to wait until 7 April 1795 for its implementation by the **Thermidorean Convention**. There was, doubtless, a long overlap in the popular mind: thinking in *sétiers* and filling litre bottles in the *chais*.

Michelet, Jules (1798–1874)

Michelet wrote history coloured by vehemently anti-clerical republicanism for which his clear, aphoristic style is ideal. His commentary on the Revolution from the calling of the **Estates-General** to the fall of **Robespierre** is irresistibly forceful and well informed.

He was a history teacher at the Collège Sainte-Barbe in Paris in his middle twenties. It is a surprise to find him as tutor to Charles X's daughter-in-law. Then he was appointed in 1827 to a responsible post at the Ecole Normale Supérieure, training teachers and providing them with classroom material. The liberal monarchy set up by the 1830 Revolution was better suited to his temperament. He was Louis-Philippe's daughter's tutor until 1843. He deputized for Prime Minister François Guizot at the Sorbonne. More importantly, he was put in charge of the historical section of the National Archives and had free access to the necessary documents for writing the 19 volumes of his *History of France* as well as for his studies on the Revolution.

In 1838, Michelet was appointed to the chair of history at the Collège de France. His lectures were as popular, egalitarian, totally hostile to the Catholic priesthood (he was pantheistic in his beliefs), eloquent and nonconformist as his writing. He was never an authorized historian. These traits, and particularly his ear for a good story, pervade his *History of the French Revolution* which dates from 1847, the year before the replacement of the Liberal Monarchy with the Second Republic (1848–52). He did not take office in the Second Republic as other writers like Lamartine and de **Tocqueville** did.

Michelet opposed Prince Louis-Napoleon's 1851 *coup d'état* and was dismissed from the National Archives and his teaching post. He used the enforced leisure to complete his *History of France* in 1867. He wrote cogently about other, miscellaneous topics as well. When the Third Republic emerged out of the ruins of the Second Empire and the Paris Commune (1870–1) with Thiers as President, he was not restored to the Collège de France, and began a history of the nineteenth century which he did not have time to finish.

Michelet made his own the conviction that there had been a definite break with the past in 1789 and a new world had come into being, of which France was to be the figurehead.[40] At the outset, he defined the Revolution as 'the coming of the Law, the resurrection of Right, and the reactivation of Justice'. In the tension between 1789 and 1794, he preferred the former year but, even if the **National Convention** and the **Jacobins** had substituted dictatorship and **Terror** for the sovereignty of the people, he accepted that they had saved the *patrie*.[41]

Furet, François, 'Michelet', in François Furet and Mona Ozouf (eds), *A Critical Dictionary of the French Revolution*, trans. Arthur Goldhammer (London: The Belknap Press of Harvard University Press, 1989). References above are to the French version.

Michelet, Jules, *History of the French Revolution*, trans. C. Cocks (London: H.G. Bohn, 1847). Vols 1 and 2 are available online at: http://books.google.com/books.

Mirabeau, Gabriel-Honoré de Riqueti, Comte de (1749–91)

Mirabeau was the most colourful leader of the first part of the Revolution. He died with his project for a constitutional monarchy unrealized. Driven by enormous energy, he acquired a wide, enlightened education, but his turbulent, extravagant and unconventional life led to periods of prison and exile. He became a passionate writer against despotism after a visit to England in 1784, where he was impressed by free parliamentary debate and a free press. He had hopes of an alliance between the king and the people against the nobility, and was elected to the **Estates-General** as a **Third Estate** deputy for Aix-en-Provence, despite being more popular in **Marseille**. His fellow nobles rejected him. He rallied the Third Estate to himself, roaring at the Marquis de Dreux-Brèzé, 'We are here by the will of the people; we shall only leave by the force of bayonets!'

In the debate that led to the founding of the **Constituent Assembly** on 17 June 1789, when the question of a veto for the king was raised and a **Jansenist** clerical deputy called Camus tried to say it was not important, Mirabeau

abandoned all prudence, and lost his temper as far as saying:
I believe that the king's veto is so necessary that I would rather live in Constantinople than in France if he did not have it … Yes, I declare that I

can think of nothing more terrifying than the sovereign aristocracy of six hundred persons who, tomorrow, would make themselves irremovable, the next day, hereditary, and would end up, like aristocracies in every country of the world, by taking over everything.[42]

It would be only the wisdom of hindsight that could make that utterance prophetic, but in it Mirabeau expressed a feeling for the dangers to be feared if constitutional checks and balances were ever removed. He saw the king as a bulwark both against **counter-revolution** and the anarchy of a popular rising. In March 1790, he entered into secret negotiations with the royal family and the court paid him a retainer. At the time of his death on 2 April 1791, he was considered a national hero, given a state funeral and burial in the Pantheon. Perhaps the Constitutional Bishop of Saintes was not the only one to have his memorial bust carried in a cathedral procession before it was put in the town's **Jacobin Club**.[43]

After the overthrow of the **monarchy**, however, Mirabeau's secret letters were found in the king's strongbox (*armoire de fer*) and the payments he had received from the king became public knowledge. He was discredited then, and all images of him were destroyed. **Marat**'s remains replaced his in the Pantheon.

Luttrell, Barbara, *Mirabeau* (Chicago: Southern Illinois University Press, 2000).

Momoro, Antoine-François (1756–94)

Momoro was the printer to the Revolution in Paris, supporting **Hébert**, and secretary of the **Cordeliers Club**. He is attributed with having devised the slogan, 'Liberty, Equality and Fraternity'.

Antoine-François went to Paris in the early 1780s from Franche-Comté and had become a member of the guild of printers and booksellers by 1787. He had written a reference book on printing which had a long life. When press freedom came with the **Declaration of the Rights of Man and of the Citizen** in August 1789, he seized his opportunity. He bought presses and opened his printing shop at 171 rue de la Harpe. Orders for print came from the Paris Commune, and he published printed copies of public speeches. He was secretary of the Théâtre-Français section and of the Cordeliers Club, whose journal he printed. He signed the republican petition presented at the Champ de Mars on 17 July 1791, which provoked the massacre after martial law was proclaimed. He was put in prison for two months in the **Conciergerie** (not as dangerous then as it later became) and was released in a general amnesty decreed by the **Constituent** on 15 September. His section elected him to the council of the department of Paris, and he went to recruit volunteers to resist the Austro-Prussian invasion from the Eure and Calvados departments. Between May and October 1793, he was associated with events in the **Vendée**, present at the action against Saumur with General **Ronsin**, and was then reporting to the **Committee of Public Safety**, the **Jacobins** and the Cordeliers. He denounced **Westermann**'s conduct and upheld Ronsin's.

Associated with the de-Christianizers (it was his wife who played the Goddess of **Reason** in Notre Dame Cathedral in November 1793), he defended **Vincent** when he was arrested in December 1793 (he was released in February), and attacked the moderation (*indulgence*) of **Fabre d'Eglantine** and **Desmoulins** in the Cordeliers. He even criticized Hébert for taking too soft a line when **Collot d'Herbois** tried to effect a reconciliation between him and the Jacobins.

Momoro was arrested on the authority of the Committee of Public Safety with Hébert, Vincent and Ronsin (**Saint-Just** told **Fouquier-Tinville** to 'amalgamate' the charges against them), and condemned on 24 March 1794 without being able to offer any defence.

It appears that Mayor **Pache** had 'Liberty, Equality, Fraternity' incised on public buildings at Momoro's suggestion.[44]

Monge, Gaspard (1746–1818)

Already with a lengthy career as a mathematician and scientist behind him, Monge took part in the founding of the Republic and brought his technical expertise to the provision of war material and the development of the republican navy.[45]

His genius was noticed early in his life. An engineer officer saw a plan he had made of Beaune in Burgundy, his home town, and recommended him for a teaching post at the military school at Mézières, where his pupils included Lazare **Carnot** and Claude-Antoine **Prieur de la Côte d'Or**.

Turgot had founded a chair of hydrology in Paris, and he spent half a year in the chair while keeping his post at Mézières. He became a member of the Academy of Sciences in 1783. He struck up a close friendship with Claude-Louis Berthollet, also a scientist. He became an examiner of candidates for commissions in the navy. He travelled all over France in this function, and his reputation as a mathematician and scientist grew.

On 10 August 1792, when the monarchy was suspended, he was chosen by the Provisional Executive Council to be navy minister, alongside the **Girondin** ministers who were reappointed, and **Danton**. He agreed with **Louis XVI**'s execution – it is said he watched it from a balcony. He remained navy minister until the following April, activating his fellow scientists for the republic's defence and strengthening the fleet. He worked on the manufacture of steel and of cannon. He also had to be involved as naval minister in decisions concerning the deportation or not of **refractory clergy**.

Under the **Directory** he was elected to the Council of 500, and was prominent in the creation of the Ecole Polytechnique, but was sent to Italy to work with Berthollet. Here he was taken up by **Bonaparte**, who took both of them to Egypt and Syria with him as scientific members of his expedition. He returned with him in 1798 to be placed at the head of the Egyptian Commission and resume his work at the Ecole Polytechnique.

Napoleon made him a senator and a count of the Empire, but he lost all his honours during the **Restoration of the Monarchy**.

Mounier, Jean-Joseph (1758–1806)

Mounier emerged into national politics after the part he took in developments at **Grenoble** and Vizille in June and July 1788 with the assistance of Antoine **Barnave**. He drew up the **statement of grievances** in Grenoble where he was a judge. On the strength of this he was elected as a **Third Estate** deputy to the **Estates-General**.

It was Mounier who proposed that the **Tennis Court Oath** should be taken.[46] His outlook was that of a constitutional monarchist and he gathered like-thinking people around him who were known as the *monarchiens*. After the taking of the **Bastille** he was prominent among those who demanded the recall of **Necker**. The form of constitution he wanted was a bi-cameral legislative on the English model. The **Constitutional Assembly** rejected it. He resigned as a deputy and returned to Grenoble to ferment opposition there, but emigrated to Switzerland in May 1790. He kept out of the rest of the Revolution, apart from writing some essays, only returning to France in 1801.

First Consul **Bonaparte** appointed him prefect of the Ile-et-Vilaine in 1802, and in the Empire he was made a councillor of state, but died within a year.

Doyle, William, 'The Political Thought of Mounier', in *Officers, Nobles and Revolutionaries: Essays in Eighteenth-Century France* (London and Rio Grande: The Hambledon Press, 1995).

Mountain

When the **Constituent Assembly** followed the king to Paris in October 1789, it was reinstalled in the *Manège*, the former royal riding school alongside the **Tuileries Palace**. It was a long, oblong building, and the tribune, from which speeches were made, was in the centre of one side. The self-conscious **Jacobin** group sat in the higher tiers of the seats constructed to the left of the tribune and began to be called The Mountain. From where they sat they could look down on their antagonists, the **Girondins**, and the uncommitted deputies who were called the Plain or the Marsh. But there was something more. The Mountain had connotations of Sinai and the giving of the Law, of moral virtue and purity in the way romantics were beginning to speak.[47]

There were 250–300 Montagnards, conspicuous among them being Maximilien **Robespierre, Saint-Just, Collot-d'Herbois** and **Fouché**. They insisted on maintaining the One and Indivisible Republic by means of centralized control enforced by the **Terror**. It was they who dominated the later **National Convention** after the king's overthrow and packed the **Committee of Public Safety** which initiated the government's policy during the Terror.

The name persisted for a while even after the Convention moved on 21 May 1793 into the refurbished royal theatre in the palace itself. The Mountain went into abeyance after the fall of Robespierre in July 1794.

N

Nancy Mutiny

As War Minister, the Marquis de **La Tour du Pin** did what he could to re-establish the **army** after its loss of nerve in 1789, adopting the tricolour as the military banner. He had worked towards the re-establishment of discipline, but this backfired on him after troops mutinied at Nancy in August 1790 and punishments handed down by General the Marquis de **Bouillé** were as harsh as they had ever been before the Revolution.

Part of the Nancy garrison at the time was the Swiss Regiment of Châteauvieux, whose 1,400 men had been present at the **Festival of the Federation** in Paris in the preceding month. They complained that their officers withheld their pay and continued to use 'Prussian' disciplinary methods. The soldiers formed a military **Jacobin club**, but clubs such as these were suppressed nationwide by the **Constituent Assembly**'s decree of 6 August, at **Lafayette**'s instigation. When they protested, the Governor of Nancy proclaimed martial law and made two of them run the gauntlet of the garrison. The townspeople, backed by their municipality, rioted in support of the soldiers and this led to the governor making a public apology and the officers being ordered to pay 27,000 livres of back pay immediately.

Then the Constituent Assembly intervened to decree the death penalty for the leaders of the soldiers' protest. However, when the governor of Besançon was sent to Nancy to carry this out, he was arrested by the men of the Châteauvieux Regiment. General Bouillé arrived from Toul and the mutineers fought his 5,000 troops in the Place de Grève, leaving 300 dead or wounded. The Swiss were disarmed. On 1 and 2 September, Bouillé condemned 41 of them to 30 years in the galleys and sent 71 others for military punishment. The Constituent Assembly and War Minister La Tour du Pin praised Bouillé. The Nancy National Guardsmen were fêted in Paris for their loyalty.

In December 1790, there was a reaction and the king was asked to pardon the mutineers who had left for the Brest galleys. But it was not until 15 March 1792 that the Legislative Assembly voted for their being set free, largely at the instigation of **Collot d'Herbois**. The Jacobins successfully pressed for a festival to celebrate their liberation, which was held in Paris on 15 April with the men concerned parading before Mayor **Pétion** wearing **Phrygian bonnets** to the acclaim of the **sansculottes**. Six months later, after the proclamation of the Republic and the victory of its army at **Valmy** and Jemappes, there was a new kind of military discipline. Serving soldiers were soon regarded as **'active' citizens**.

Narbonne-Lara, Louis Comte de (1755–1813)

Narbonne was close to the royal family in the *ancien régime*, perhaps even being an illegitimate son of Louis XV, pursuing a military career typical for a noble, but embracing the idea of constitutional monarchy during the Revolution. He was elected colonel of the **National Guard** battalion at Doubs, dealing with several incidents with moderation. In 1791, he escorted **Louis XVI**'s aunts when they left for Rome. They were arrested by the municipality at Arnay-le-Duc, and he rushed back to Paris to obtain a decree to let them finish their journey.

In December 1791, he became war minister, largely because of the manipulations of his mistress Germaine de **Staël**. He realized that war was inevitable and made tours of inspection of the fortresses and sea-coasts. He laid his plans for the formation of new armies before the **Legislative Assembly**, **Girondins** and **Feuillants** who supported him. His political intrigues, and particularly the hostility of Bertrand de **Molleville**, led to his resignation on 10 March 1792.

Narbonne took up his military career again, but returned to Paris just before the **'Day' of 10 August 1792**. He was accused of financial misdemeanours while a minister, so he escaped to London with Germaine de Staël's help.[1] When **Louis XVI** was on trial, he asked for safe conduct back as a defence witness and was refused, though he sent a long memorandum. He made his way to Switzerland and then Vienna, returning to France after the **Brumaire** *coup d'état*. He served Napoleon as an ADC in the Russian campaign and died as governor of Torgau in Saxony.

National Convention

In the aftermath of the overthrow of the monarchy on 10 August 1792, the **Legislative Assembly** was dissolved and there were elections for the National Convention to replace it. This new body combined the legislative and executive functions of the new Republic, since the king was not replaced by a national president. The Convention met, as the Legislative had before it, in the old riding school (*Manège*) alongside the **Tuileries Palace** from September 1792 until its move on 21 May 1793 into the refurbished royal theatre in the palace itself. Its task was to draw up a new constitution. That was done, but it was not adopted because of the preoccupation with **Louis XVI**'s trial and war with the kings of Europe.

There was also civil war. During the period of the Convention, the 'One and Indivisible' Republic was at extreme risk of disintegration during the **federalist** risings in **Caen**, Bordeaux, **Lyon**, **Toulon** and **Marseille**, together with the continuing struggle against **counter-revolution** in the **Vendée**. Extreme measures and military force directed by **representatives on mission** were used to combat these.

The National Convention delegated responsibilities to 21 committees, of which the **Committee of Public Safety** (for executive decisions and policy forming) and of **General Security** (for internal policing) were the most prominent. Between April and July 1794, these committees seemed to have eliminated all opposition and reigned supreme. As long as the Convention lasted, there were no more ministers after April 1794. After the fall of **Robespierre** on 10 thermidor in the newly adopted **revolutionary calendar**, commentators speak of the **Thermidorean Convention**.

National Guard

When the '**Great Fear**' erupted in late July 1789, people in towns feared for their lives and property and turned the bourgeois militias of the old regime into units of the National Guard in imitation of what had happened in Paris on the eve of the fall of the **Bastille**. Uniformed battalions were soon formed also in villages once they had become the new *communes* and *notables* were elected as their commanders. Their parades on significant occasions, such as the **Festival of the Federation**, were meant to express national solidarity.

In Paris, the Marquis de **Lafayette** assumed command of the National Guard. In municipalities all over France *notables* put on uniforms and raised battalions which became a permanent feature of French provincial life. The lawyer **Bernard de Saintes**, who had never held military rank before, had himself appointed unquestioned colonel of the National Guard in his home town prior to his election as a deputy to the **Legislative Assembly**.

After the declaration of war against the kings of Europe, and the outbreak of civil war in the **Vendée**, the National Guard units from all the 84 departments (now including the Vaucluse) were amalgamated with regular troops under a unified national command as part of the strategy of the One and Indivisible Republic.

National Property (*Biens nationaux*)

Lands in the possession of the Catholic Church were thought to cover 10 per cent of French national territory in 1790, donated in *mortmain* and therefore not able to be disposed of or sold. Much of it was in the form of large estates owned by religious houses or large collegiate churches staffed by well-paid canons, or parcels of land on which rents were paid to bishops and other higher clergy. Some of the income from all this had already been secularized by means of the king appointing a lay courtier as a 'commendatory' abbot who financed himself with a large slice of an abbey's income.

Nationalization of church land had been considered frequently before the Revolution: **Talleyrand** had discussed it with **Calonne** as early as 1786. On 2 November 1789 the **Constituent Assembly** accepted the plan submitted by Talleyrand, now bishop of Autun.[2] Then, on 17 March 1790, the decision was made to sell the 'national properties' (*biens nationaux*) with the aid of bonds called *assignats* to the highest bidders.[3] The capital

249

from the sales and the income from unsold land were to be used to pay off the national deficit and regenerate the nation's finances. The Abbé de Montesquieu expressed the hope that increased property ownership would give more people a stake in the Revolution.[4]

Land was bought by richer members of the neighbouring peasantry (this was true even in the soon to be counter-revolutionary **Vendée**[5]) but mostly by wealthy town bourgeois who would become absentee landlords, causing friction with the tenant farmers who worked the estates. In the Vendée, the purchase of abbey lands by wealthy members of the **bourgeoisie** in places such as Nantes and Niort gave rise to the Catholic and royalist revolt, coupled with the war cry of 'Give us back our good priests' when the Oath to the **Civil Constitution of the Clergy** led to the exile or deportation of the refractory non-jurors and divided the nation. Contemporary with these decisions the Constituent undertook never to start a war of aggression. This policy would be changed under pressure from the **Girondins** in two years' time. Retrenchment might have succeeded, based on the sale of national property, if peace had been maintained.

At the **Restoration** after 1814, Louis XVIII returned only those lands that had not been sold. Those who had bought such estates, or lands confiscated from *émigré* nobles, were allowed to keep them.[6]

Naval Officers

Naval officers in the old regime were invariably nobles. Between December 1790 and January 1792, Jacobin ideas brought about mutinies of three ships' companies in the port of Rochefort alone. The officers everywhere were demoralized, with a good number of them resigning and withdrawing to their estates, later to be arrested as suspects. They were replaced with former pilots and sailing masters whom the revolutionary government had to accept on the grounds of their professional skills. They could not hope to gain the respect of their crews or overawe them, and the result was indiscipline.

The navy was reorganized on revolutionary lines by successive decrees of the **National Assembly** and **Convention**. Under the constitutional monarchy, the service was rebuilt without reference to nobility, though some noble officers retained their positions. Promotion was to be on the basis of merit. Young men were commissioned as ensigns on the basis of a competitive examination.

After the fall of the monarchy, the navy minister was in charge, and then, during the official **Terror**, there was a decree of purification (*épurement*) of the same kind as was applied to departmental, district and municipal councils, to weed out those not regarded as sufficiently enthusiastic for the Revolution. Republican virtue was as important as nautical skill. The names of the aspiring officers were posted up in their home *communes*, and denunciations were taken seriously. If officers were dismissed for lack of revolutionary zeal, the navy minister was responsible for finding replacements.

Noble officers maintained themselves in post if they took the Oath to the Constitution and had **certificates of civism**. The French commander at the battle of Ushant on 1 June 1794 was Admiral Villaret-Joyeuse, a nobleman who fought for the Revolution. Another naval officer, Charette, fought with the Vendéans.

Necker, Jacques (1732–1804)

Necker was comptroller of the finances three times despite being barred from membership of the king's council as a Protestant from Geneva. The first time was during France's involvement in the American War of Independence. His qualification for office was as an experienced banker, not an administrator. He paid 40 million livres of naval and military expenses by raising loans, by selling life annuities (**rentes**) at 8 per cent, and by a state lottery. In his published accounts (*compte rendu au Roi*) before his dismissal in 1781, Necker claimed that no additional taxation had been necessary and there was no deficit.

He returned to office in September 1788 with the national deficit publicly known and the price of flour increasingly out of control. When the decision to call the **Estates-General** had been made, a committee of the second Assembly of Notables presided over by **Provence** advised the king to double the number of **Third Estate** deputies from 300 to 600 to avoid them being defeated on every issue by a coalition of the nobles and the clergy. No changes were made in the method of the deputies casting their votes separately in their orders as opposed to a free vote in a plenary session (known as 'voting by head'). It has been suggested that this was a balancing act to preserve Necker's popularity with the **bourgeoisie** of the Third Estate and the nobles by giving each side what they wanted.[7] When the Estates-General opened, Necker and an assistant spoke inaudibly and failed to clarify the cause of the financial crisis. Pressure from the court and especially the royal family caused the king to order Necker's departure on 11 July 1789 and replace him with the Baron de **Breteuil** – a contributory factor to the taking of the **Bastille**. Necker had left quietly to go home to Switzerland when the events of 14 July forced the king to recall him and his former colleagues, since on that date the price of grain peaked and Necker's reputation as a provider of it swayed opinion. He was away for a fortnight, and by the time he had returned, **Mirabeau** and **Lafayette** had stolen the scene. He was no more than a finance minister in the constitutional monarchy.[8] He placed his trust in credit finance and tried again, unsuccessfully, to raise loans in August and then proposed the raising of a 'patriotic contribution' (and gave substantially himself) of 25 per cent of incomes over 400 livres per annum. He hoped for 200 millions, but took in no more than 20.[9]

Necker took no part in the decision to nationalize church property, but it was the discount bank with which he had links that issued the *assignats* and received revenue from the land sales. This deflated his popularity as a potential provider, and people looked to Mirabeau instead. From the spring of 1790, his financial schemes had the mark of desperation: an appeal to artists' wives to give their jewels to the state was one. When Mirabeau proposed increasing the issue of *assignats* in September, Necker resigned and left for Coppet, his home in Switzerland. He only managed to avoid being attacked on the way there because the Assembly gave him police protection.[10]

📖 Price, Munro, *The Fall of the French Monarchy: Louis XVI, Marie-Antoinette and the Baron de Breteuil* (London: Macmillan, 2002).

Night of 4 August 1789

Georges **Lefebvre** suggested that what happened at **Versailles** in the National **Constituent** Assembly on the night of 4 August 1789 was an endorsement of the popular revolution taking place all over France at the time.[11] Nobles and senior clergy in the National Assembly at Versailles orchestrated a feverish renunciation of their privileges.

The patriots of the **Third Estate**, particularly those who had associated with the Breton deputies in a café society, had been planning such a move ever since they arrived for the **Estates-General**. For them, the abandonment of privileges and the balancing of justice were essential to the regeneration of the nation's prosperity. They had already devised a programme, and the catalyst became evident when the Duc d'Aiguillon, one of the richest seigneurs in the kingdom, proposed the complete abolition of all feudal dues, as had been planned in preparation for the debate. The debate did have a momentum of its own and, if there had been a stricter agenda for it, it was obviously abandoned in 'a kind of magic', as Deputy Parisot called it.[12]

Some kind of Declaration of Rights was in the patriots' minds from early on.[13] In the last few days, some deputies had been proposing serious changes to the seigneurial system. This night gave them the opportunity to implement their intentions.[14] The Bishop of Chartres went to the tribunal to call for seigneurial hunting rights to be taken away and for country people to be allowed to eat pigeons and rabbits caught on noblemen's estates. The Duc du Châtelet made a counter-proposal to remove the tithe that was the only source of income for most of the parish clergy. More nobles and churchmen rose to their feet to vie with each other to defuse the national crisis without putting increased military or police powers into the king's hands. 'This great clearance sale' (*cette grande braderie*), as a French historian has called it, ended at three in the morning, and **Louis XVI** was associated in all this unexpected change by being proclaimed as 'the restorer of French liberty'.[15]

Intense days were spent in the National Assembly transforming what had been decided into new laws. The **Rights of Man and of the Citizen** were subsequently declared, seeming to establish freedom of thought, speech, belief, assembly and the press – as had been demanded in many noble and Third Estate lists of grievances six months earlier. The king accepted the Declaration in the Hall of Mirrors on 26 August.

It was argued that the nation was at one with itself. Nevertheless, the king's brother **Artois** and other princes of the blood royal had left France, followed immediately by a first emigration of those nobles who could not accept the crumbling of their alliance with the monarchy. Moreover, urban artisans could no longer afford to feed their families and were not satisfied with promises of improvements in some theoretical future.

Sutherland, D.M.S., *The French Revolution and Empire: The Quest for A Civic Order* (Malden, MA and Oxford: Blackwell, 2003), pp. 68–74.

Tackett, Timothy, *Becoming a Revolutionary* (University Park PA: Princeton University Press, 2006), pp. 169–75.

Nîmes, *'Bagarre'* de

Events in Nîmes can be seen as part of a **counter-revolutionary** movement in its early stages which affected a large area in southern France.[16]

Protestants in Nîmes had developed production of and trade in textiles and become the political leaders of the town. As a result, they were well represented among the **Third Estate** deputies of the place. In reaction to the **Great Fear**, they also dominated the **National Guard** when it was set up. When the local elections came round in spring 1790, there was a Catholic backlash which may have been related to a campaign in all the Midi towns stimulated from Turin by **Artois**, who took up a plan devised by an unemployed cathedral accountant from Toulouse.

In Nîmes itself, Protestants wanted to keep control of the National Guard and tried to exclude Catholic recruits. Brawls (*bagarres*) in the streets lasting for four days began on 13 June 1790. Protestant Guardsmen fired on Catholics in the run-up to the election of the Gard departmental officials. Protestants from the countryside came to help their urban co-religionists. Three hundred or so Catholics were killed, compared with penny numbers of Protestants.

The Protestants kept control of the town, and this meant they could dominate the departmental directory as well.[17] They organized all the changes demanded by the national government, including the ecclesiastical ones. The constitutional bishop would be elected by a majority of them, the intruded curés also. Catholics became counter-revolutionaries all through the Midi. They may have seen themselves as a national church before, but not now, when Protestants and atheists could elect a bishop for social control regardless of their tradition or the pope's decree.

Further disturbances broke out at Jalès in August and in Uzés in February 1791. There was a stream of incidents which are collectively called the camps of Jalès. These had largely dispersed by the time patriot National Guards arrived from as far away as **Marseille** and **Lyon**, although one of the organizers was found drowned in the Rhône after being imprisoned at Pont Saint-Esprit.

Nobility, Second Estate

There was a wide range of interests and outlook among the nobility. The spectrum spanned court nobles, military nobles (*noblesse d'épée*), through financial officials and magistrates ennobled by the offices they purchased and inherited (*noblesse de robe*), down to the *hobereaux* – the down-at-heel country squires. Many of the wealthier nobles took part in projects of imaginative capitalism on an equal footing with the elite of the **Third Estate**. Nobles drew part of their profits from the same sources as the merchants, involved themselves in Third Estate ventures, and shared the attitudes and behaviour of the wealthier **bourgeoisie**. They invested in commercial enterprises, mining, metallurgy, innovative textile production, colonial ventures such as French Guiana and Saint-Domingue. Others manufactured porcelain, glass, wire, chemicals, paper or cloth on their domains. Even **Artois** and **Orléans** adopted mechanized processes driven by steam power and incipient factory techniques.[18]

Culturally speaking, some nobles were avant-garde too. They read the work of the *philosophes*. Their culture was enlightenment culture. Magistrates in the provincial *parlements* dominated academies. Some were wealthy enough to afford the expensive volumes of the *Encyclopédie*, and many of them, such as d'Alembert and Jaucourt, had contributed articles.[19]

The myth of a ruling class of timeless origin keeping itself exclusive in relation to those recently ennobled from the Third Estate is exploded by the fact that the old nobility intermarried with the new on an equal footing. When the **statements of complaint** were drawn up by the provincial assemblies in early 1789, the majority of nobles called the whole social, economic and political organization of the old regime into question. **Enlightenment** ideas and the example of America – where many had served as officers – reduced any culture gap remaining between nobility and the bourgeois elite of the Third Estate.

The bureaucratic state was oppressive to nobility and bourgeoisie alike. The king was not criticized, but the ministers and the intendants in the provinces were. Opinions were expressed against the domination of responsible civil and military offices by court nobles and in favour of converting an absolutist state into an individualistic and liberal society. Nevertheless, influential orators among the 252 noble deputies elected to the **Estates-General** were courtiers who had not given their assent to these opinions. By the time the **Constituent Assembly** dispersed to give way to the elections for the **Legislative**, hopes for constitutional monarchy had been dashed by the king's flight to **Varennes** and many more nobles left France in the second emigration.

The elected noble deputies were largely wealthy and lived in towns, rather than in the country as squires. Only 22 *parlementaires* were sent to Versailles. The deputies were not representative of the nobility as a whole. Eight out of ten were from families ennobled before 1600 and were army or navy officers. That meant their educational standard was not up to the level of the clever Third Estate lawyers, while the lawyers resented their disdain which they regarded as snobbery. The liberal-minded nobles would have served in the American War of Independence, been to England, belonged to a local academy and had much in common with the bourgeois deputies in the way of their youth, their urban background and their dislike of privilege. [20]

Chaussinand-Nogaret, Guy, *The French Nobility in the Eighteenth Century. From Feudalism to Enlightenment*, trans. William Doyle (Cambridge: Cambridge University Press, repr. 1995).

Doyle, William, *Aristocracy and Its Enemies in the Age of Revolution* (Oxford: Oxford University Press, 2009).

○

October Days 1789

When the Flanders regiment came for a tour of duty to **Versailles** at the beginning of October 1789, the officers were provided with the usual welcoming supper and the king and queen were present. During the evening, a song was sung from **Grétry**'s opera *Richard Cœur de Lion* which had its debut in 1784, *O Richard, O mon Roi, l'univers t'abandonne* ('Richard, my king, the universe abandons you'), which soon became a royalist anthem. A revolutionary newspaper, the *Courier de Versailles*, reported that a tricolour cockade was trampled underfoot after dinner in the presence of the king and queen, and that the officers wore the queen's black one instead of it.[1] The rumour that it was an intentional insult was made worse when it was heard that there were shouts of 'Down with the assembly!' as the party broke up. The market women from Paris, after a demonstration at the Hôtel de Ville, set out in the rain on 5 October to walk the twelve miles to Versailles to protest against the shortage of food in the capital.

Put like that, it looks like a spontaneous march, but in fact it had been discussed by the patriots since August, and there had been a previous attempt at such an event. In the old regime, using women to lead a grain riot was common enough because troops sent to repress them did not shoot and there were few prosecutions. After the August decrees that translated the decision of the **Night of 4 August** into laws, the radicals did not have it all their own way. They won the debate about having a single-chamber legislature rather than a bi-cameral one on the English model, so the nobles were not to have a separate function or the ability to slow radical changes down. A suspensive veto, rather than an absolute one or none at all was allowed to the king, but even that gave him power because he would be able to hold decisions up for six years. The king refused to accept any of this. Nor had he accepted the August laws. The way to overcome his reluctance was to bring him away from his gilded isolation in Versailles and make him reside in the capital. **Necker** was back in office after his brief departure in July, but was powerless to resolve the economic crisis. Street orators continued to assert that the queen was an Austrian subversive, and that the king was planning to leave France (in fact, he had rejected the possibility – for the present). The **National Guardsmen** would be needed at Versailles should the loyal regular soldiers take action, and they were taunted into accompanying the women. **Lafayette** their commander was authorized by **Bailly**'s municipality to follow them, as he did after six hours' delay.[2] The women dragged cannon the whole twelve miles. Stanislas Maillard, the 'Captain of the Bastille', led the march and, on arrival, told the **Constituent Assembly** why it was happening.

The marchers passed a violent evening and night in the palace grounds. The king signed all the backlog of decrees, perhaps hoping the duress he was under would allow him to change his mind later. Lafayette had posted a very weak guard. The queen's bedroom was ransacked, after two of her bodyguards had been killed, but she had managed to reach the king with the children. In the morning, the king and queen appeared on the balcony and agreed to the demand that they would come to Paris and live in the **Tuileries**. The procession set out for Paris in the afternoon. There was a macabre element with the two murdered bodyguards' heads bobbing on pikes all along the way. The cry was that they were bringing 'the baker, the baker's wife and the baker's boy' to Paris, and wagons followed the royal family's carriages filled with flour from Versailles.

Louis XVI was now 'less a king than a hostage'.[3] The Tuileries Palace was cold and inhabited only by artists whom the king had permitted to have their studios there. Bringing the royal family there was seen as the capture of the monarch by the people of Paris who would not allow him independence. Nevertheless, the fact that money was made available for furniture and decorations suggests that what had been imposed was not entirely cynical. A few days later, the Constituent Assembly decided that it must hold its deliberations near the constitutional monarch, and the deputies came to Paris too. They occupied the former riding school alongside the Tuileries (*Manège*).

As for the king himself, he wrote a fair copy of a letter to his cousin, King Charles IV of Spain, which he had first drafted on the day after the fall of the **Bastille**. It said that he should not be held responsible for anything he may have to agree to from now on.[4]

Tackett, Timothy, *Becoming a Revolutionary* (University Park, PA: Princeton University Press, 1996), pp. 195–206.

Orléans, Philippe, Duc d' (1747–93)

Philippe, Duc d'Orléans, was the king's cousin and fourth in line to the throne. His income was reckoned at seven and a half million livres. He succeeded to the dukedom in 1785. He supported the Paris *parlement* and in November 1787, when government loans were to be approved in a royal session, the duke claimed that such a procedure was illegal. This elicited a rash reply from **Louis XVI**: 'That is of no importance to me … it is legal because I will it.'[5] The duke was exiled from Paris.

When he returned, he sided with liberal politicians like **Brissot** and subsidized them from his funds. The shops, restaurants and cafés that surrounded his Paris residence, the **Palais-Royal** near the **Tuileries**, were open to the public. Political pamphlets were available there, and one could hear the speeches of radical orators such as Camille **Desmoulins.** The duke was a Grand Lodge **Freemason** and a member of the **Society of Thirty**. **Marie-Antoinette** detested him, and he was accordingly refused the rank of Grand Admiral. Nevertheless, he had served as a subordinate at the Battle of Ushant in 1778.[6]

Orléans was elected by the *bailliage* of Crépy as a Second Estate deputy in 1789, and was among the first of the nobles to join with the Thirds in the National Assembly. He prudently refused the presidency of it in favour of the Bishop of Vienne in June.[7] After being accused of complicity in the **October Days**, he was sent on a diplomatic mission to England (organized by **Lafayette**) eight days later. He did not return until July 1790 when the accusation was lifted.[8] He was a member of the **Jacobin Club** but, after the king's flight to **Varennes**, was accused of having supported the **Cordeliers'** republican petition which led to the Champ de Mars massacre. He was certainly associated with **Danton**. He managed to resist a decree that would have made the princes of the blood ineligible for the **National Convention** after 10 August, and was given the name Philippe Egalité by the Paris Commune who elected him the 24th and last of its deputies on 15 September. He sat on the left, which drew the comment from **Le Peletier de Saint-Fargeau**, 'If you have an income of 600,000 from the *rentes*, you either have to be at Koblenz or sitting with the **Mountain**.'[9]

In December, the **Girondin Buzot** tried to have Orléans exiled. It was suggested that he went to the United States, to avoid involvement with the king's condemnation, but he stayed, and voted for Louis XVI's death, against suspension of the sentence and any appeal to the people as a challenge to those who attempted to exclude him. The Jacobins suspected him of hoping to replace Louis XVI on the throne and dissociated themselves from him. On 6 April 1793, however, he was arrested 'as a hostage for the Republic' when his son Chartres deserted to the Austrians with **Dumouriez**. The Palais-Royal became **national property**, but he was declared innocent by the criminal tribunal of the Bouches-du-Rhône. He was kept in the fortress of Saint-Jean at Marseille by the **Committee of Public Safety**, and then transferred to the Paris **revolutionary tribunal** where he was condemned and executed with the Girondins.[10]

P

Pache, Jean-Nicolas (1746–1823)
Pache was Mayor of Paris during the acceleration of the **Terror** and supported the **Mountain** in the expulsion of the **Girondins** from the **National Convention** in May–June 1793. Despite his connections with the **nobility** in the old regime, he allied with the cause of the Parisian **sansculottes**.

Before the Revolution, he had been educated at the expense of the Marshal de Castries at the same military school (Mézières) as Gaspard **Monge**. Castries made him his own children's tutor, and then gave him a responsible post in the Navy Ministry. Through the good offices of Jacques **Necker**, he became comptroller of the royal household.

Pache left France in 1784 to return to his native Switzerland but went back to Paris as the Revolution began. He was still attached to the reactionary Castries, but bought a good deal of nationalized church land. Jean-Marie **Roland** put Pache in charge of his office when he became a Girondin minister. Pache also assisted War Minister Servan. When the Girondin ministry fell in June 1792, he became war minister himself and was responsible for reorganizing the department.

He broke with the Girondins and turned to the **Mountain**. After all the Girondin attacks on him, he was forced to retire in February 1793 to be replaced by a Girondin supporter. He had received **Robespierre**'s support and that of **Marat**'s *Ami du Peuple* and **Hébert**'s *Le Père Duchesne* and became prominent in the Paris Sections as a radical. A week after leaving the war ministry he was elected mayor of Paris with 11,881 votes out of 15,191 voting.[1]

From the secure position of the Hôtel de Ville, he conducted a personal vendetta against the Girondins in revenge for his dismissal from the war ministry. Along with Hébert, he presented a petition from 35 of the 48 Paris Sections asking for 22 Girondin deputies to be excluded from the Convention. The Mountain balked at this at first, but then the Paris Commune brought another, much larger, petition three days later (18 April 1793), claiming the Girondins had formed a conspiracy against the sovereignty of the people. The acquittal of Marat on 27 April was the signal for the Jacobins to make a concerted effort against them.[2]

In the *journées* of 31 May to 2 June, Pache supported **Hanriot**, but was fearful of a repeat of the **September Massacres**[3] to the extent that on 5 June he presented a report to the **Committee of Public Safety** claiming not to have found any evidence of a conspiracy after all.[4] There was a strong alliance between the Commune and the Committee of Public Safety through Robespierre, so he avoided the fate of the Hébertists in March 1794. Even so, Robespierre and **Saint-Just** charged him with counter-revolutionary tendencies in May and a more biddable Robespierrist, Jean-Baptiste Fleuriot-Lescot, took his place as mayor, imposed by the Committee of Public Safety.[5] Pache may have remained under Robespierre's protection. Even **Fouquier-Tinville** – at his own trial later on – said he could find nothing to charge him with. However, he stayed in prison for a year and a half and was not prosecuted with the Robespierrists. The **Thermidorean Convention** tried hard to have him convicted, sending him for trial along with **Bouchotte** before the criminal tribunal of the Eure-et-Loire, but the public prosecutor there found nothing to charge him with and he was never brought to trial. He was released under the amnesty of 26 October 1795. Then he withdrew from political life altogether to live on a farm he had bought in the Ardennes. He wrote his memoirs, papers for an agricultural society, and a book about philosophy that was published after his death.[6]

Paine, Thomas (1737–1809)
Thomas Paine was English by birth, but moved to America in 1774, where he wrote *Common Sense* in justification of the American Revolution. In France, he was appreciated as an apologist by the **Girondins** on the basis of his authorship of *Rights of Man* the year before. After their fall on 2 June 1793, he

was arrested, but released after **Thermidor**. *The Age of Reason* was a literary product of that time, rejecting organized religion and Christian theology alike, and supporting deism. He went back to America in 1802 because he did not desire to stay in a France dominated by First Consul **Bonaparte**.

In England he had been a corset-maker and then an excise officer lobbying for better pay and conditions for his colleagues. He met Benjamin Franklin and decided to move to Philadelphia where the political climate was more to his liking. He went back to London in 1787, and visited France in 1790. After Edmund **Burke** had attacked events in France, Paine wrote his *Rights of Man* defending the Revolution's principles. The first part dates from 1791 and the second from the following year, as a result of which he was prosecuted in Britain for seditious libel.

He moved to France, where the **Legislative Assembly** made him an honorary French citizen. He stayed with **Condorcet** and was a member of the '**Social Circle**'. Paine allied himself with the Girondins. Elected to the **National Convention** by three departments and accepting the Pas de Calais, he argued for **Louis XVI** not to be executed but transported to America where he could observe how a free society functioned. He spoke no French, but he stood at the tribune while his speech was read for him. The **Mountain** singled him out for arrest in December 1793. He narrowly escaped the **guillotine**. James Monroe, the new American ambassador, gained his release in November 1794 after the Mountain had lost power. He was restored to the Convention with other Girondin survivors, and objected to the 1795 Constitution abandoning universal male suffrage.

He also complained that President Adams had turned away from the new government of France. Discussions with Bonaparte were warm at first but, when Paine recognized the extent of his personal ambition, he accepted President Jefferson's invitation to return to the United States.

Doyle, William, 'Thomas Paine and the Girondins', in *Officers, Nobles and Revolutionaries: Essays on Eighteenth-Century France* (London and Rio Grande: The Hambledon Press, 1995).

Paine, Thomas, *Rights of Man, Common Sense, and Other Political Writings*, ed. with an Introduction and Notes by Mark Philp (Oxford: Oxford World Classics, 2008).

Palais-Royal

Cardinal Richelieu built the first Palais-Royal in central Paris. He gave it to Louis XIII whose widow, Anne of Austria, brought up the Dauphin Louis XIV there. The palace was almost entirely rebuilt in the middle of the eighteenth century. It was the property of the Duc d'**Orléans** at the beginning of the Revolution and he had developed it with the money he made from selling his Saint-Cloud Palace to **Louis XVI**. This was part of the urban redevelopment that came in the wake of the stock market boom caused by **Calonne**'s policy of increasing government credit. Orléans benefited from it, so did **Provence**, who developed the Vaugirard quarter near what would later be the Pantheon but was then the Church of Sainte-Geneviève. **Artois**, on the other hand, lost 28 million livres on his developments.[7]

The arcades in the Palais-Royal, then as now, had shops and **restaurants** on the ground floor and the gardens were open to the public. The police were not allowed to patrol there. Prostitutes solicited their clients, pamphlets of all sorts were sold, and cafés and restaurants were opening. Anyone who wanted to attract a crowd to make a speech was not prevented from doing so. On 12 July 1789, Camille **Desmoulins** encouraged the crowd that went to storm the **Bastille**, standing on a table, taking a green branch to stick in his hat as a cockade only to realize later that green was Artois's colour.[8] This was the powerhouse of dissent against the constitutional monarchy, just as it had been before when the king was 12 miles away at **Versailles**.

Palloy, Pierre-François (1754–1835)

'Patriot' Palloy was an entrepreneur who took over the task of demolishing the **Bastille** after the events of 14 July 1789. The Paris Commune decided that this symbol of tyranny and oppression that towered over the **Faubourg Saint-Antoine** should be removed as soon as possible and Palloy's tender for demolishing the masonry was accepted, while others dealt with woodwork, metal objects, furniture and so on. Gangs of labourers recruited locally under his control took down the massive building, with its seven great machicolated towers, stone by stone and Palloy sold the stones. Little models of the Bastille were made out of some of them and sold as mementos. Displaced stones, which were of considerable size, were sent to the principal town (*chef-lieu*) of each department as proof of what had happened in the capital on that day so full of promise of better things for the nation. Palloy signed them himself.

Palloy was, in Simon Schama's phrase, a 'self-made bourgeois ... under the urban boom economy of the old regime'.[9] He went to a prestigious school along with noblemen's sons, and then gained an army commission which he soon gave up to become an apprentice stonemason. He married his master's daughter, and worked on projects such as the Wall of the Farmers-General for **Lavoisier** and his colleagues. By 1789, he had made a fortune. On 14 July, he rushed to the Bastille from the Ile de la Cité where he lived so as to qualify as one of its 900 *vainqueurs*.

On 11 August 1792, he was employed to make alterations to the tower in the Temple in the Marais quarter for it to be a prison for the royal family. Until 1814, he gave a banquet every 21 January to commemorate **Louis XVI**'s execution.

Palm, Etta Lubina Johanna d'Aelders (1743–99)

Etta Palm from Holland, like Mary Wollstonecraft in England, was a proponent of equality between the sexes when there was none. Etta Aelders was born in Groningen, was well educated and married Christiaan Palm in 1762, although her husband soon left on his own for the East Indies.

Palm moved to Paris in 1773 and lived near the **Palais-Royal**, the centre for opposition writers, and became a courtesan and a Dutch secret service agent. She set up a salon in her house and radicals such as **Marat**, **Chabot** and **Basire** (whose mistress she became) regularly attended it from late 1789 onwards. She also addressed the **Social Circle**, one of the few associations open to both men and women.[10] Then she became a French secret agent, and was accused of being a Prussian one, besides involving herself with feminist politicians and joining their societies, on the basis of which she gave her *Discourse on the Injustice of the Laws in Favour of Men, at the Expense of Women* before the French **National Convention**. She asked for the proper education of girls, to give them their majority at 21, and for divorce to be legalized.[11] She was heard with attention but politely ignored.

Palm moved to The Hague and spied on French *émigrés*. She was 'suspect' in the newly formed Batavian Republic set up in 1795, and was in prison until 1798. Deprivations had ruined her health and she died soon after her release.

Pantheon Club

While the participants of **Babeuf**'s plot were on trial in Vendôme, a group of Neo-Jacobins was permitted to open the Pantheon Club in the church of Sainte-Geneviève in Paris. The founder was a printer called Lebois, who was technically a **sansculotte**. There was a membership of between 900 and 1,500. They came to support Babeuf since, like the *enragés* before them, they wanted more extreme economic and social measures than the bourgeois republicans of the **Directory** were willing to countenance. The Directory ordered the club's closure on 26 February 1797.

Paris Sections

Paris had been divided into 60 administrative districts by royal regulation just before the Revolution, an arrangement that lasted until the **Constituent**'s decree of 21 May 1790 when the districts were replaced by 48, slightly larger, sections. They remained in this form until they were done away with at the outset of the **Directory**.

The political colour in their assemblies depended upon whether the **sansculottes** dominated them or not. The radicals of the Luxembourg section, under the presidency of **Danton**'s associate Louis **Legendre**, were particularly active in the arrest of nobles and **refractory clergy** after the overthrow of the monarchy and were implicated in the **September Massacres**. The **National Guard** unit of the Filles-Saint-Thomas Section, on the other hand, were on the side of the Swiss guards when they were massacred on 10 August, and the police in the section where Regnaud de Saint-Jean d'Angély lived as a royalist fugitive protected him.

It was representatives from the radical sections that took over the Paris Commune on the night of 9 August 1792 to prepare the attack on the **Tuileries** early the following morning. They kept Mayor **Pétion** in place, and became the **Insurrectionary Commune** until the establishment of the **National Convention** on 21 September.

Parlements

There was no such thing as a national parliament in France until June 1789 when the **Estates-General** were fused into the National **Constituent Assembly** by the hesitant **Louis XVI**. The old regime had functioned by means of 13 regional *parlements* sitting in Paris and provincial centres such as Grenoble, Rennes, Pau and Bordeaux – bodies of nominated magistrates with noble status they had purchased with very large sums of money, whose main functions were to register and promulgate the king's edicts and to be a regional high court.

In this respect, the Paris *parlement* had recently shown great docility. The magistrates had registered a double *vingtième* tax (twice 5 per cent) in 1780, a triple *vingtième* (three times 5 per cent) in 1782, loans of 125 million livres in 1784 and 8 million livres in the following year, despite there being only perfunctory economies on the part of the royal administration.[12]

The other *parlements* wanted to follow the example of the one at Rennes in Brittany, where there was a provincial assembly as well as a *parlement*. This would have given them extra clout in their opposition against what they saw as increasing monarchical despotism.[13]

The *Parlement* of Paris had jurisdiction over a third of France and had a little more authority than the 12 others only because it met in the Palais de Justice in the capital. Even so, since the seat of government was at **Versailles**, it was as limited in its power to protest as the provincial *parlements*. When the magistrates in the Paris *parlement* protested against **Calonne**'s designs to reform state revenues by raising a tax on land payable by nobles and commoners alike, with no exemptions, and agreed by provincial assemblies, Louis XVI exiled them to Troyes. (At the outset of his reign in 1774, Louis XVI had revived the *parlements* which Louis XV had quashed in 1770, hoping for their co-operation with him).

The king and Calonne called an **Assembly of Notables** in 1787 to side-step the Paris *parlement* in the hope of having reform adopted, only to find that this body of hand-picked men of substance held the same views as the magistrates. The *parlement* demanded the calling of the Estates-General as the only body that could pass financial legislation with legality according to the conventions of an unwritten constitution.

Once more in Paris, the magistrates in the *parlement* made the reactionary decision to have the three orders – nobles, clergy and **Third Estate** – voting separately from one another as they had done in 1614 when they had last been called. This led, after a period of ignoring the *parlements* as if they were perpetually on vacation, to their redundancy being declared by decree of the **Constituent Assembly** in October 1790, at a time when Louis XVI could still have been acceptable as a constitutional monarch.

A French historian concludes his remarks on the *parlements* in this way:

> The position of the *parlements* was in fact very ambiguous: instruments of royal power, they were at the same time a force for stopping it; obstinate defenders of privilege, at the same time they called upon the rule of law. They only served to let loose a Revolution to which they did not adhere and which crushed them.[14]

Doyle, William, *Origins of the French Revolution*, 3rd edn (Oxford: Oxford University Press, 1999), chap. 6.

Shennan, J.H., *The Parlement of Paris*, rev. edn (Stroud: Sutton Publishing, 1998), pp. 315–25.

Peasantry

Peasants (*paysans*) lived in the country (*paysage*) as opposed to the urban areas (even the built-up centres of villages are *bourgs*). In 1789, they made up 80 per cent of the total 28 million population of France.[15] The picture the word arouses is of grinding poverty in large families with anyone who was old enough to walk working in the fields in one way or another from scaring off the seigneur's pigeons to getting in the harvest and threshing it. Nevertheless, every commoner (*roturier*) who owned land, or who had access to it and worked it, was a peasant (*paysan*). Many peasants, in fact, owned large farms. Others, misleadingly called *laboureurs*, had enough land to enable them to be self-sufficient and, in good years, sell their surplus crops. Those who did not have enough land for more than poultry or a cow or two, had to be daily wage-labourers (*journaliers*) for wealthier farmers and eke out their income by weaving for urban cloth-manufacturers or working in other craft industries. Those who could not manage became beggars and vagrants.

Out of their income, the peasants had to find the money or crops for feudal dues, and had to accept the *banalités*: using their seigneur's mill for their grain, his oven for their dinners, his press for their grapes. They had to maintain the curé with the tithe, though often that was paid to an abbey or a layman commended as an abbot by the king, so that the priest received only a congruent portion (*portion congrue*) of it (about 800 livres a year, often compared with a hundred times that for the diocesan bishop who had had his share of the tithe too). There was also work service for bridges and roads, and peasants observed in their **statements of complaint** that they preferred to lose a few days' work on their holdings to paying cash instead, as was being suggested.

This hand-to-mouth existence was supportable if conditions passed for normal. But, in July 1788, the Paris basin experienced a hailstorm which destroyed the grain harvest that was nearly ripe in the Beauce and elsewhere, and there was very little seed-corn for the 1789 planting. This accounted for the panic caused all over the nation in the late summer by the **'Great Fear'** aroused by rumours of brigands paid by aristocrats to dismantle the Revolution so far by cutting crops before they were ripe. In the first half of 1789, the lives of people in the countryside were becoming more precarious than they usually were. The timescale between early and late summer meant that the insecurity that was growing was not identical with the panic caused by the Great Fear.[16]

Doyle, William, *Origins of the French Revolution*, 3rd edn (Oxford: Oxford University Press, 1999), chap. 15.

Pétion de Villeneuve, Jerome (1756–94)

Pétion was a radical mayor of Paris in the critical summer of 1792 when the monarchy was overthrown. He was close to the **sansculottes** in the sections whose representatives took over the Paris commune as a prelude to that event. He was subsequently elected as a deputy for the Eure-et-Loire in the **National Convention**.

He qualified as a lawyer in Chartres in 1778, and attempted to found a career as a writer of articles on current issues. He was a **Third Estate** deputy to the **Estates-General**, joined the **Jacobin Club**, continued into the **Constituent**, and was elected to the committee to draw up the 1791 Constitution. When the **Legislative** opened, he held legal office in the Paris Commune. As such, he was sent with **Barnave** to bring the royal family back from **Varennes**. After the Constituent closed, he visited London in the company of Madame de Genlis, governess to the Duc d'**Orléans**'s children.

On his return, Pétion was elected mayor of Paris, beating the now unpopular **Lafayette** in the election. The fiction that the king had been abducted in June 1791, despite having left an open letter behind in the **Tuileries** rejecting the Revolution, was not accepted by the radical sections of Paris. After the **'Day' of 20 June 1792**, Pétion was accused by the king and the departmental directory of the Department of Paris (his titular overlords) of having supported the riot and the incursion into the Tuileries. The directory suspended him from the post of mayor on 6 July, which increased his popularity among the Parisians themselves. The Legislative Assembly restored him to office. He was, after all, 'one of the heroes of 14 July 1789, in an atmosphere generally hostile towards the court'.[17]

On 3 August, after *fédéré* National Guards had arrived from many different places in France and the contents of the **Brunswick** Manifesto were known in the capital, Pétion, representing 47 of the 48 Paris Sections, went to the Legislative to demand the end of the Bourbon dynasty and the calling of a National Convention to draw up an appropriate constitution.[18] On 9 August in the evening, representatives of the radical sections took over the Hôtel de Ville and established the **Insurrectionary Commune**. They left Pétion in his post, but others made arrangements for the next day's violent attack on the Tuileries, and he seems to have had nothing to do with the **September Massacres**. Others, like **Marat** and **Danton**, had Girondin fingers pointed at them for those horrors, but it was Pétion who had to give an account of the Commune's implication in the Legislative.

Once elected to the Convention he resigned from the mayoralty of Paris, and was the first president of the new legislative and executive body. He broke with **Robespierre** and sided with the **Girondins**. He voted for the king's death, but also for the sentence to be suspended, and approved of the proposal for an appeal to the electors about it. He voted against putting Marat on trial.[19] He was arrested on 2 June as a Girondin sympathizer, when their leaders were expelled from the Convention. After hiding in Paris, he escaped to Caen, and raised an unsuccessful rebellion in Normandy. He escaped again, with Girondins Buzot and Barbaroux, to Bordeaux and hid. When he left his hiding-place he committed suicide together with Buzot in a wheat-field at Castillon. Real wolves had a good meal after that.

Phrygian Bonnet

The *bonnet rouge* became a **sansculotte** badge. In the ancient world it was the headdress of a freed slave, and that seemed an appropriate idea for the Revolution. Generals and politicians who wanted to show their association with the left occasionally wore it. It was of more use as an emblem, however. During the process of de-Christianization it was usual to take the Christian symbol down from the top of church towers and replace it with a red bonnet, adding others to the four corners of the towers as well.

Contemporary illustrations, like those of **Lesueur**, present the red bonnet as part of the sansculotte appearance: an open-necked shirt, a short '*carmagnole*' jacket and striped trousers, and a **revolutionary cockade** sewn on the bonnet, which fitted the head closely and had a pointed crown with earflaps hanging down over each ear. Lynn Hunt observes that the liberty cap was 'part of the standard repertoire of opposition and contestation.'[20]

Physiocrats

These were independent theorists concerned with the basis of a strong economy in France whose ideas began to be formulated in the middle of the eighteenth century by François de Quesnay and Pierre-Samuel du Pont de Nemours.[21] For them, land use was the most important consideration, and farming was the underpinning of the state. Agriculture produced the wealth to finance industrialists and merchants. Without it, their productivity was impossible, they asserted.

'*Laisser faire les hommes, laisser passer les marchandises*', was the key slogan they used (almost impossible to translate literally). Trade ought to be free, and internal customs barriers should be dismantled. France could feed herself and local scarcity of grain could be remedied from other areas. These ideas were usually resisted in government circles but **Calonne** tried to implement them in his far-reaching scheme to regenerate the French economy offered to the **Assembly of Notables** between February and May 1787, which was rejected. The trade treaty with Great Britain in 1786 had conditioned much contemporary economic thinking by the supposed effect of invading French internal commerce with cheap English manufactured goods.

The free market economy was also accepted by the **Jacobins**, until pressure from the Parisian **sansculottes** in the **Convention** on the **'Day' of 5 September 1793** forced them to compromise with the **Maximum on Prices and Wages**. After **Thermidor**, this soon dropped below the horizon, and the **Directory** returned to a metal currency.

Pichegru, Jean-Charles (1761–1804)

General Pichegru was a hero of the revolutionary wars who changed to being a royalist. He was born in humble circumstances but he was helped by a religious community to obtain a place in the military school at Brienne (the same one as **Bonaparte**). He gained his commission and served in the American War of Independence.

When the Revolution began, Pichegru joined the **Jacobin Club** of Besançon. A regiment of volunteers elected him their second-in-command. His competence was noticed and he was made a brigadier. He was discovered by **Saint-Just** while **representative on mission** to the Army of the Rhine and was promoted to be its commanding officer with orders to retake Alsace, which he accomplished alongside Lazare **Hoche** and the Army of the Moselle.

He succeeded **Jourdan** in command of the Army of the North and was involved in the operations which culminated in the victory at **Fleurus** on 27 June 1794. Pichegru took Nijmegen in the autumn, drove the Austrians beyond the Rhine and broke with custom to prepare a winter campaign to take Utrecht on 19 January 1794 and Amsterdam the day after. This involved taking the Dutch fleet frozen at anchor, and maintaining discipline to avoid pillage.

In the Thermidorian Reaction, he took action to suppress the **Germinal rising** in Paris in April 1795. Then, with three armies, he crossed the Rhine to take Mannheim in May. He became a royalist then, and began plotting for Louis XVIII. The **Directory** became aware of it, and accepted his resignation in October. He returned as a member of the Council of 500 at the partial elections of May 1797 as a royalist. For being involved in the **Fructidor coup** he was exiled to Guiana, but escaped arrest. He was in London in 1798, helping to plan the War of the Second Coalition.

Towards the end of the Consulate, he returned to France to help in Georges Cadoudal's rising against Bonaparte, was betrayed, arrested and found dead in his cell.[22]

Pillnitz, Declaration of (27 August 1792)

This Declaration was issued two months after the king's flight to **Varennes** by the Holy Roman Emperor Leopold II and King Frederick William II of Prussia from Pillnitz Castle, near Dresden in Saxony on 27 August 1791. Without committing himself to any course of action, Leopold called on European powers to intervene if the French king and his family were harmed in any way. Leopold hoped to preserve the general peace long enough to let the French Revolution settle down. Revolutionaries such as **Brissot** understood him to be threatening invasion. 'The patriot press … worked itself into a frenzy over the declaration.'[23]

The Emperor was at Pillnitz for a summit conference about political developments in Eastern Europe which led to the second partition of Poland in 1793, and about future relations with the Ottoman Empire. However, the prince-bishops of Mainz and Trier in the Rhineland (where French *émigrés* were organizing themselves) saw their territory threatened from Alsace and Lorraine, French noble *émigrés* wanted the Emperor's military support, and Gustavus III of Sweden was exerting pressure to save **Louis XVI**. Above all, Frederick William II had been in touch with the **Feuillants** and wanted Austria actively to intervene in France. Leopold knew, however, that the British ministers, Pitt and Dundas, were maintaining neutrality, and wanted to do the same.

The Pillnitz declaration was meant to calm the fears of Leopold's sister while curbing the zeal of the *émigrés* and reassuring the minor German rulers. A copy was given to **Provence** and **Artois** at Coblenz and they made it the basis of an open letter to Louis XVI asking him not to accept the 1791 Constitution. It was really a face-saving exercise on the part of Leopold II, a *comédie diplomatique*.[24] When Louis XVI had accepted the Constitution on 13 September, Leopold turned his attention to Poland again.

Polignac, Gabrielle de Polastron, Duchesse de (1749–93)

The duchess was **Marie-Antoinette**'s friend, and incurred popular disapproval for her reported extravagance – including what was expressed in pornographic pamphlets (*libelles*) that made the unfounded claim that she was the queen's lesbian lover.

Gabrielle was educated in a convent after her mother's death and married Comte Jules de Polignac on 7 July 1767, when she was 17. He was an army officer and, like her, not well-off. One of their sons was to be the right-wing prime minister at the end of the reign of Charles X.

She was presented to the new king and queen at **Versailles** in 1775 and was invited by the queen to live there permanently. When she said she could not afford it, the queen offered to pay her family's debts. She was befriended by the king and by **Artois**, which caused resentment among established courtiers, and was opposed by Comte **Mercy d'Argentau**.

Gabrielle was appointed governess to the royal children. Her husband was raised to a dukedom – making her a duchess, which increased the annoyance of the courtiers and the prurience of the gossip writers of the **Palais-Royal**. She had her own 13-room apartment for the better performance of her post as governess, and a cottage in the queen's hamlet in the grounds of the Petit Trianon.

The queen disliked Comte Vaudreuil, Gabrielle's friend and, after 1785, withdrew her friendship from her. Gabrielle went to stay in England with her friend Georgiana, Duchess of Devonshire. But by the time the Revolution came, she was back in favour, and party to the reactionary intrigues of Artois and of **Breteuil** against **Necker**. After Necker's dismissal on 11 July 1789, when Artois and Breteuil left, the Polignacs went to Switzerland, and the Marquise de Tourzel replaced Gabrielle as the royal governess. She died of natural causes in Austria in December 1793.

Politics and Politicians

The novelty of the French Revolution was that it was brought about by politicians who were a new phenomenon in themselves. As early as the time of the setting-up of the **Constituent Assembly**, a new sort of public man had appeared. He might be a lawyer from the lower courts in the provinces or a schoolmaster priest. He could be (and most likely was) a landowner, and might be a merchant, though probably not a 'capitalist' in the usual commercial sense, despite being wealthy. He could be an army officer who had never been allowed to rise above the rank of captain in the old regime because of not being noble.

Men like these became the new political class and shared responsibility with other politicians at all levels of French administration. When the Republic was declared in 1792, they were entirely responsible. A few ex-nobles – **Barras** and **Talleyrand** for example – would still be powerful, but the nation's government was directed by a cavalcade of new politicians, **Danton**, **Robespierre**, **Marat**, **Hébert**, **Fouché** and so on. They were in charge of the public rhetoric, the newspapers, the festivals, the imagery of government, and social control. They were also in charge of international relations, the treaties and the warfare, and the gearing of the national economy to support total warfare. They did all this on the basis of being elected by citizens above a decided level of affluence, and so could claim authority from a loosely defined entity called 'the people'.

Tackett, Timothy, *Becoming a Revolutionary* (University Park, PA: Princeton University Press, 2006).

Poor Relief

Revolutionaries claimed that church charity increased the problem of mendicity. Beggars were helped in the old regime but remained as beggars to beg another day. Repeatedly in **statements of complaint** there is mention of a large number of beggars. Early speeches in the **Constitutional Assembly** were concerned with policing the beggars. The **'Great Fear'** in the late summer of 1789 was about poor day-workers who had left their homes in search of work. Communities could not look after their own in conditions of such scarcity. A need for a secular and rational system of poor relief for the whole nation was frequently stated. The Committee of Mendicity set up on 21 January 1790 drew replies from 51 of the new departments to show that there were nearly 2 million beggars, an eighth of the population.[25]

Limited public assistance was instituted in 1791. There were rural work schemes for the poor to replace the old-regime work service: river dykes were strengthened, roads repaired, marshes began to be drained. Fifteen million livres were made available for this purpose by government, but there was increasing insistence that poverty was a problem to be treated locally as a charge on individual municipal councils in the communes. A decree of 25 May 1791 ordered local committees of welfare to be set up to administer assistance according to need.

The secularization of the Church caused increased unemployment with the redundancy of all the lay ancillary staff of cathedrals, collegiate churches and abbeys. A scheme to regard assistance payments as a 'national debt' was floated on 19 March 1793. Money was to be released at a department's daily wage-rate. The cantons were made responsible for its distribution. Abandoned children were to be provided for, along with children who were merely poor and people who were too old to support themselves by their work. As Peter McPhee points out, this could be no more than 'a statement of intent'.

Then, on 12 May 1794, there was the introduction of a 'Great Book of National Charity (*bienfaisance*)' to help with rural poverty, to be kept in each department. This would record the names of poor candidates to receive help. Begging was to become an offence. Foundlings were to be looked after by local councils too as 'natural children of the fatherland', with the religious stigma removed from unmarried mothers.

But in the end, the piecemeal poor relief by the now disbanded Church was no worse than these fits and starts that the nation could not afford. The national deficit had gone by 1797 when the sister republics were paying France's expenses and the republic's soldiers were living off their land. But the poor were still there in France, living on hope. Even the staple work of country women breast-feeding the babies of the urban wealthy had been cut by half by 1800 as a result of the new outlook on the subject stimulated by Jean-Jacques **Rousseau**.[26]

 📖 McPhee, Peter, *Living the French Revolution, 1789–99* (Basingstoke and New York: Palgrave Macmillan, 2009).

Pope Pius VI (1717–99, Pope from 1775)

Conte Giovanni Angelo Braschi was ordained priest in 1758 and was involved in the finances and diplomacy of the papal curia. He was raised to the cardinalate in 1773 and elected pope in 1775. He was known for his dilatoriness in policy-making, particularly in relation to the Jesuits (expelled from France in 1764). He took his time also over declaring himself opposed to the **Civil Constitution of the Clergy** on 10 March 1791.

In 1782, he made an unsuccessful visit to Joseph II and his minister Kaunitz who were adopting **enlightenment** policies in the Empire. He also had a dispute with the future Emperor Leopold II when the latter was Archduke of Tuscany. At the outbreak of the French Revolution, Pius VI gave little support to **Louis XVI** in his attempt to protect the Gallican clergy from the confiscation of their lands or, more importantly, from the Civil Constitution, his condemnation of which did not take place until it was a *fait accompli*. His officials were turned out of **Avignon** and Comtat-Venaissin in 1790 and a crowd in the **Palais-Royal** gardens burnt him in effigy.

He came more to the fore in the time of the **Directory**.[27] **Bonaparte** defeated his troops at Ancona and Loreto. He made peace at Tolentino on 19 February 1797. In a riot on 28 December, General Mathurin-Léonard Duphot, in Rome on the embassy staff with Joseph Bonaparte, was killed. In reprisal, General Berthier took Rome without opposition on 10 February 1798. The Roman Republic was set up, and demanded that the pope renounce his temporal authority. Pius VI refused, was taken prisoner by the French and removed from Rome. When France declared war on Tuscany, he was taken to Valence (Drôme) and died six weeks later. First Consul Bonaparte allowed him to be reburied in Rome as part of the negotiations for the 1801 Concordat with his successor.

Popular Images

Wood engravings, sold in frames for a few sous in print shops or by travelling salesmen, were put on the walls in modest households. The artisans who produced them and the pedlars who sold them played their part in the dissemination of the ideology of the Revolution.

Images of Liberty and Equality of several different kinds were sold as pictures or used as letterheads for administrative notepaper. Marianne took her turn as an image of the new society, but her femininity was suppressed. The father figure of the king had gone and it was the brothers in the **National Convention** and not the sisters in the public galleries who had taken control, so Hercules was a better image for a male-dominated society.[28] The figure of Hercules was used in the old regime for individual kings as a symbol of forceful power. Now the forceful power resided in the Nation and Hercules had a different function, whether in an engraving, a letterhead or a coat button.[29] Another theme was the sun rising on a new world. This was sometimes painted on church towers for all to see each morning. Bees and beehives appeared beside ploughs and garden implements for the industry that produced prosperity (if it rained on time). These images were the stock-in-trade of the artisans who produced them.

There is another class of wood engravings that relate to a surviving religious register. **David** painted the death of **Bara**, the 13-year-old republican martyr in the **Vendée**, but that was high art. Popular art dealt with such themes too. The republican struggle with the **Chouans** further north produced two young women martyrs whose stories virtually replicate each other. There is Perrine **Dugué** at Thorigné-en-Charnie and Marie Martin in the forest of Teillay, both earnest republicans who were abused and killed by Chouans with miracles claimed to take place at their graves. Cheap woodcuts of Perrine were readily available and republican piety reproduced what the de-Christianizers had supplanted.

Another type of feminine republican image produced and sold to inspire confidence was that of the republican heroine of Saint-Milhier defending her home and children in the **Vendée** when so many municipal officers had been killed there.

Hunt, Lynn, *Politics, Culture and Class in the French Revolution* (London, Berkeley and Los Angeles: University of California Press, 2004), chap. 3.

Prairial *Coup d'état* (18 June 1799)

When the Councils of 500 and of the Elders from the partial elections met in May 1799, the internal and external situation of the Republic was precarious. The **Second Coalition** had inflicted a series of military defeats. Naples and Milan had been lost. There was unrest in western France led by the *Chouannerie* and **Belgium** was in revolt. The Neo-Jacobins in the Council of 500 called the Directors to account for dismissing Jacobin generals and not supporting Jacobins in Switzerland, Italy and Germany. The Directors ignored the demands for change from the departments, began to repeat the steps they had taken before **Floréal** to organize the yearly elections.

Reubell left the **Directory** and **Sieyès** replaced him on his return from Berlin (where he had been French ambassador) on 8 June. Sieyès shared the views of the councils to some extent. He planned to modify the constitution, perhaps with the support of the Jacobin General Joubert, and to exclude, with **Barras**'s help, the other three directors, **Treilhard**, **Merlin de Douai**, and **La Révellière-Lépaux**. He had been assured of the support of Lucien Bonaparte who led the **Jacobin** deputies.

Treilhard was soon forced out, replaced by Grohier who had been a Jacobin judge in the **Terror**. Then La Révellière-Lépaux and Merlin were replaced by Roger **Ducos**, chosen by Sieyès, and General Moulin, nominated by Barras. **Talleyrand** and other ministers also left the government. These replacements constituted the *journée* of 30 prairial (18 June 1799). It was a pseudo-coup,[30] but it left Barras and Sieyès in control of the executive. Several generals benefited from it, however. **Bernadotte** became war minister, Joubert was put in command of the Army of Italy, and Championnet was given the new Alps Army to combat the Russian, Suvarov. Robert **Lindet** became finance minister. Newspapers reappeared, political clubs reopened. It was a coup, then, in the sense that Jacobins had power once more, and several measures were passed in the councils: on conscription, the **National Guard**, requisitioning, forced loans and the Law of Hostages to intern *émigrés* and rebels (24 messidor, 12 July 1799), all of which had the savour of **Robespierre**'s time.

Pre-Revolution

This term was used by a generation of French historians beginning with Jean Egret[31] in 1962, based upon the idea of Georges **Lefèbvre** that there was an 'aristocratic revolt' preceding the Revolution properly so called.[32] Lefèbvre's idea, published in France in 1951, was to some extent Anglicized by Albert Goodwin two years later and in subsequent revisions.[33]

More recently, in 2007, an American historian, Vivian R. Gruder, in her study of the **Assembly of Notables**,[34] has argued that the start of the Revolution ought to be pushed back to the time when **Calonne** summoned the Assembly to try to regenerate the French Monarchy and avoid a declaration that it was bankrupt. This argument gives a better continuity to the events than seeing the start of the Revolution as May or July 1789.

In terms of a contemporary assessment of the affair 'from below', a disgruntled lawyer called François-Guillaume Marillet in Saintes, a town in the south-west of France, kept a secret diary of the Revolution 'from the time that His Majesty called the **Estates-General**' (8 August 1788),[35] and this may suggest when the Revolution began in the minds of such of its contemporary opponents as he. This was the moment when the French monarchy acknowledged that it was no longer **absolute**.

Prieur de la Côte-d'Or, Claude-Antoine (1763–1832)

Like Lazare **Carnot**, Prieur was an *ancien régime* military officer who could not rise above the rank of captain, and brought technical and organizing ability to his membership of the **Committee of Public Safety**. He survived the **Terror** and **Thermidor**, and was a member of the Council of 500.

Prieur was very wealthy by the time he was elected to the **Legislative** in 1791. He found his niche in committee work from the outset. Re-elected for the Côte d'Or in the **National Convention**, he voted for the king's death and was **representative on mission** in Lorient and Dunkirk, making inspections of the port facilities. When the **Girondins** were expelled from the Convention, he was in Caen, and federalists held him hostage there until their little army was defeated at Vernon by the republicans.

Once back in Paris to a triumphal welcome,[36] he was elected to the Committee of Public Safety and to the National Food Commission. He was concerned most with the provision of munitions for the war against the

First Coalition, and set a target for production of 1,000 firearms a day. He organized the manufacture of saltpetre for gunpowder on a national scale – for some time every citizen was required as a patriotic duty to collect a sackful of weeds for this purpose. The munitions factories he set up in Paris and **Versailles** employed 5,000 people, required to produce 600–800 weapons each day.[37] He supervised experiments with air balloons and had one employed to observe Austrian movements at the battle of **Fleurus** on 26 June 1794, when Captain Coutelle stayed 500 feet above the action as an observer for 9 hours, pulled about by a rope. Prieur created a small company of specialist *aerostatiers*, much as Vauban a century before had formalized military engineers.

Prieur was appointed as government contact with all scientists. Along with Carnot, **Monge** and others, he set up the School of Public Works which was to become the Ecole Polytechnique. He was also most concerned that all citizens should learn and speak French. To allow Breton, Basque, German and Italian to continue as regional languages was in itself divisive, a sort of **federalism** expressed through language. He pressed for the adoption of **metric** weights and measures in May 1795.

At the time of passing the **Ventôse Decrees**, intended to give the resources of *émigrés* to poor patriots, he bravely reasoned with rioters. Politically, he agreed with **Danton**'s execution but, as Thermidor approached, he joined **Robespierre**'s opponents, and continued on the Committee of Public Safety until October 1794. He apposed the **Brumaire coup** in November 1799, and was not involved in public life during the Empire.

He founded a wallpaper factory, and kept up his scientific work. In 1811, he took a lieutenant-colonel's retirement pension. He was overlooked in the general exile of **regicides** in 1816. When he died in 1832, he was buried quietly since Louis-Philippe's government feared republican riots like those at General Lamarque's funeral in the same year (the ones which inspired Victor Hugo's *Les Misérables*).[38]

Prieur de la Marne, Pierre-Louis (1756–1827)

Prieur was a deputy from the Marne in the **Estates-General**, the **Constituent Assembly** and then the **National Convention**, for which he was a **representative on mission** while also being member of the

Committee of Public Safety. His nickname was '*Crieur de la Marne*' on account of his undoubted eloquence.

Like his father, he was a lawyer, working in Châlons-sur-Marne. In the Constituent Assembly he sat on committees, specializing in national finance and judicial organization. He sat with the left and supported radical measures. After the flight to **Varennes**, he proposed the removal of the king's name from the oath to the constitution, and demanded the Comte de **Provence** be put on trial. Ineligible for the **Legislative** he held important legal posts for a short time in the Marne, Versailles and Paris. In the Convention, he sat with the **Mountain** again, and went on mission to Châlons to supervise army recruitment along with **J.-L. Carra**. He conducted the enquiry into the loss of Verdun.

Back in the Convention he voted for the king's death, for 'a veil to be thrown over' the **September Massacres**, and for setting up **revolutionary tribunals**. More appointments as representative on mission followed from March until July 1793 and he never occupied his seat in the **Committee of General Security**. He was then appointed to the Committee of Public Safety, but still spent most of his time on mission, most significantly in the west. He was sent to revive patriotism in the fleet at Brest after mutinies, continuing then to Vannes, the Morbihan, Lorient, Rennes and Nantes, where he followed **Carrier**.[39] His words were ferocious, but he perpetrated nothing as excessive as many other representatives. He raised companies for the **National Guard**'s cadet force, the *Espérance de La Patrie*, for boys between 9 and 16.

At Lorient he made his anti-British peroration: 'London must be destroyed ... Let us rid the globe of the new Carthage,' built upon 'Pitt's despotism and gold'.[40] The Breton *levée en masse* was ineffective through desertions and poor equipment, so he could not send soldiers into the **Vendée**. The Breton troops went to join the Army of the North instead. At this point – November 1793 – a Vendéan force crossed the Loire and made for Granville in unfulfilled hope of British naval support. Prieur set up a military commission to punish the rebels, and followed republican troops to Nantes. In May 1794, he went to supervise the dockyard at Brest while Jeanbon Saint-André went to sea with the fleet to fight Admiral Howe's force off Ushant on 1 June. Prieur saw the ragged fleet return afterwards, but also welcomed in Van Stabel's convoy carrying essential Caribbean grain.[41]

The **Thermidorean Convention** did not allow representatives on mission to serve on the Committees any more. Prieur stayed in Brest until September. He took part in the **Germinal rising** in April 1795, escaped arrest and hid in Paris, and then at Chateau-Thierry until the general amnesty of 26 October 1795.[42] After **Brumaire**, he took up a private law practice in Paris, and was not involved with Napoleon until the 100 Days. Then he fled to Brussels where he died in poverty 11 years later.[43]

Privilege and Taxation in the Old Regime

There is a cartoon from the early days of the **Estates-General** at Versailles which Rebecca L. Spang reproduces in her book on **Restaurants**.[44] A clergyman, a noble and a bourgeois are sitting at a table in a café. The bourgeois says to the girl at the cash desk, 'That's right, separate checks (bills).' The significance of this was that the bourgeois was refusing to pay for the other two any more.

The **clergy** and the **nobility** were the privileged orders of the old regime. The greater burden of national taxation fell upon the **Third Estate**. Some members of the Third Estate were wealthy and living nobly, as was said of them. The majority were tenants working the estates of noble or bourgeois landowners. Taxes were collected by financial officials who had bought their offices, known as the Farmers-General, and they made a profitable living out of the surplus they acquired for themselves. The Parisian Farmers-General had recently built a ring of gates and walls around the city so that their taxes could be collected from country people bringing produce to market.

The diocesan and monastic clergy (including nuns) served the state by praying for it and their privilege was exemption from tax raised by the state. Instead, they met every five years and decided what voluntary donation (known as *don gratuit*) they would make towards the crown's expenses. This was all that was required from them.

Noble privilege had been acquired in the case of the ancient nobility of the sword down the centuries. They were exempt from the *taille* (the principal tax on land and individual wealth) as recompense in time past for having raised and officered the king's armies. The *robe* nobility had bought their hereditary offices for large sums of money, and this gave them privileged exemption also. Privileges were agreed at the time of ennoblement.

Nevertheless, since 1749, there had been the *vingtième* (5 per cent) tax levied on them, which had been doubled and trebled subsequently. This was a sum equivalent to a fifth of the value of all estates. This was due to end in 1786, and not receiving it any more was a major feature in the financial crisis declared by **Calonne** – a deficit of 112 million livres.

Privileges were abolished formally by the Constituent Assembly in April 1790.

Provence, Louis-Stanislas-Xavier, Comte de (1755–1824), King Louis XVIII (1814/15–24)

On the same evening as the flight to **Varennes** began, the Comte de Provence left France for the Austrian Netherlands. He told everyone that **Louis XVI** did not intend to stop at the border, but to go to Austria to find an army to return and overthrow the Revolution. He joined **Artois** in Koblenz – the prince-archbishop was his uncle too – and they, together with Condé at Mainz, formed the Army of the Princes with *émigré* nobles. He and Artois circulated the **Declaration of Pillnitz** in France as an open letter urging Louis XVI not to accept the 1791 Constitution. The princes disbanded their army two months after its ignominious defeat at **Valmy**.

Provence's movements illustrate the permanent leakage of *émigrés*.[45] After leaving Koblenz, he went to Liège in the Austrian Netherlands, then Hamm in Westphalia. Upon Louis XVI's execution in January 1793, Provence proclaimed himself regent for **Louis XVII**, the boy imprisoned in the Temple – although there were objections to him taking the place that might well have been given to his imprisoned mother. The '**federalist**' risings in the Midi in the summer of 1793 made him entertain hopes of appearing there, and when he heard of the surrender of **Toulon** to the British and Spanish fleet, he did go south but had only reached Verona in Venetian territory when Admiral Hood abandoned the venture. In his counter-revolutionary 'Declaration of Verona', he offered France little more than the resumption of the old regime with a few tax modifications, and an announcement that all **regicides** would be punished.[46] On Louis XVII's death in June 1795, he was declared Louis XVIII by the princes of the blood in exile. He gained the release of Louis XVI's daughter, Marie Thérèse, from the Temple in exchange for republican prisoners held in Austria, and she made her home with her mother's relations in Vienna. When General **Bonaparte** crossed the Alps with the Army of Italy, Louis XVIII left Verona to move to Blankenburg as the Duke of **Brunswick**'s guest, with a pension from Spain, then on to Mittau in Courland, as guest of Tsar Paul I.[47]

The constitutional royalists in the **Clichy Club** were considering Louis-Philippe, Duc d'**Orléans** (since his father Philippe Egalité had been executed) as an alternative to him. He moved to Brunswick and stayed there until, in 1788, Tsar Paul offered him the palace of Jelgava in modern Latvia and financial support (which was maintained for a while). Marie-Thérèse joined him there to marry Artois's son, the Duc d'Angoulême, in an arranged and loveless match.

After the Battle of Marengo in 1800, First Consul Bonaparte replied to a letter Louis had written earlier and said that he should hold out no hope of returning to France as king. Louis XVIII's wanderings did not cease until after Waterloo.

 Mansel, Philip, *Louis XVIII*, rev. edn (London: John Murray, 2005).

Prudhomme, Louis-Marie (1752–1830)

Prudhomme had been a Lyonnais bookseller who brought his business to Paris, then Meaux and then Paris again. He wrote lampoons and was arrested for doing so several times in the old regime. The three-volume collection of them which he published in 1789 was taken by the police. They included spoof **statements of complaint**.

From two days before the storming of the **Bastille** until the beginning of 1794, he issued a newspaper called *Révolutions de Paris*, with Pierre-Gaspard **Chaumette** and **Fabre d'Eglantine** among his contributors. By the time of the last issue, he had left Paris and the political arena.

He remained a political writer, however. In 1797, he published *The General and Impartial History of the Errors, the Faults and the Crimes*

Committed during the French Revolution in six volumes, which soon found its way to the police station. A new newspaper, *Le Voyageur*, saw the light of day between June and October 1799 at the tail end of the **Directory**.

Prudhomme was inactive in the Empire, but felt at home in the **Restoration Monarchy**. His last two volumes came out in 1825 with the title, *Europe Tormented by the French Revolution, Shaken by Eighteen Years of the Murderous Promenades of Napoleon Bonaparte*. He welcomed the restoration of the monarchy.[48]

Public Opinion on the Eve of the Revolution

Increased freedom of thought independent of government control was a startling feature of the 25 years up to 1789. The growth of literacy, the strength of the booksellers' trade, publication of lawyers' case briefs, proliferation of journals, and a flood of scurrilous pamphlets meant increased discussion of important concerns among the educated classes.

Nobles, businessmen, doctors, lawyers, government officials, military officers and Catholic priests read more, and expressed their ideas more than ever before. Salons run by the wives of notable men in their drawing rooms – like those of Madame **Necker** and her daughter after her, Germaine de **Staël** – provincial academies, libraries, reading rooms, and lodges of **freemasons** allowed for free discussion of the issues of the day, and this did not exclude politics or belief. The masonic lodges worked on the principle that all their members were of equal status during the meetings, whatever their rank in society outside, and were not restrained in expressing their ideas to each other. Once people were admitted to a salon, they were free to come to it and go from it, listen and speak as appropriate, and try to form the opinion of others present.

All the stages of the financial crisis resultant upon **Calonne**'s disclosure of his estimate of the national deficit (by no means a certain one[49]), when the king's secret became the nation's anxiety, were discussed. The scurrilous pamphlets accusing members of the royal family and their courtiers of immoral behaviour were freely available in the public domain despite the king's personal instructions to the Paris police to confiscate them. The calling of the **Estates-General** was not expected to turn into revolution. Nevertheless, public opinion in Paris and the provinces was attuned to revolution by the time it came, whether supportive or hostile towards it.

It was the translation in 1989 of a work by the German scholar, Jurgen Habermas, *The Structural Transformation of the Public Sphere*, that drew attention to the importance of this issue for historians writing in English.[50]

Blanning, T.C.W., *The Culture of Power and the Power of Culture: Old Regime Europe 1660–1789* (Oxford: Oxford University Press, 2002), chap. 8.

Doyle, William, *The Origins of the French Revolution* (3rd edn, Oxford: Oxford University Press, 1999), chap. 7.

Puisaye, Joseph-Geneviève, Comte de (1755–1827)

Puisaye was an old-regime army officer until he resigned in 1787. The **nobility** of the Perche in South Normandy elected him to the **Estates-General** and he was inconspicuous in the **Constituent Assembly**. When he could not stand for election to the **Legislative** in 1791, he returned to the army as a brigadier.[51]

Puisaye involved himself with the **federalist** rising in **Caen**, and led its little army which was defeated at Pacy-sur-Eure in July 1793. He then offered his services as a military leader to the **Chouans**. He had a plan to raise an army in Brittany and made a declaration on 29 October that he would help all who would opt for **Louis XVII**. He hoped to join with the Chouans and the **Vendéans** to defeat and take over the **National Convention**. He tried to take Rennes with 800 men, but was repulsed. He tried again but his army abandoned him. The Vendéan leaders persuaded him to go to London to enlist the support of the British cabinet. Once there, in October 1794, he was informed that **Artois** had appointed him General-in-Chief of the Royal and Catholic Army. Puisaye resisted the British desire to use the *émigrés* to fight in the West Indies, and this led him to a further defeat at **Quiberon** in July 1795.[52]

He returned to England. His next attempt to be of use was in Canada, where he tried – again without success – to found a Chouan expatriate settlement in Upper Canada in 1798. He returned to England for the rest of his life and published six volumes of his *Mémoires pour servir à l'histoire du parti royaliste* in 1808. His large archive was put in the British Museum after his death.[53]

Q

Quiberon

Emigrés in England persuaded Pitt and the British cabinet, despite having to deploy fleets and soldiers elsewhere against the French, to invade France itself. After the failure of their attempt to give military help to the rebels in the **Vendée** late in 1793, Pitt accepted **Artois** as the prince that the Vendéans and the **Chouans** would have at their head. Comte Joseph de **Puisaye**, who had organized the Chouan rebels after the defeat of the **federalists** in Normandy, was in London in September 1794. Artois was recalled from negotiations in Bremen and made Puisaye a general, but was too late to join the main expedition. Louis XVIII, who was in Verona organizing **counter-revolution** independently of his younger brother, had given alternative authority in London to the Comte de Hervilly.

In the spring of 1795, the **National Convention** had set up discussions with Vendéan and Chouan leaders at Rennes to try to end the civil war. In May, it was discovered from a captured Chouan courier that the rebel delegates at Rennes were duplicitous because they knew about the proposed landings of the *émigrés* on the Quiberon peninsula from British ships. The delegates were arrested.

On 17 June, Lord Bridport's fleet chased Vice-Admiral Villaret-Joyeuse away from the Ile de Groix, and fought a short action to clear the coast for landing. Then, four days afterwards, Admiral Warren landed 4,500 *émigrés* and republicans enrolled on the prison hulks[1] from British ships on the Quiberon peninsula in hopes of taking Rennes and inciting western France against the **Directory**. There were other landings also. Once ashore, Hervilly and Puisaye were in dispute about who was in command and delayed their move inland for eight days after landing, giving time for General **Hoche** to make his dispositions. The force from Quiberon linked up with Cadoudal's Chouans, but Puisaye had lost the initiative to Hoche.[2]

Hoche, with the Army of the Coasts of Brest, moved from Vannes with a much larger force. His main action was on the night of 20 July, taking the fort of Penthièvre which prevented further egress from the peninsula. Puisaye and 2,500 *émigrés* and Chouans escaped back to Warren's flagship, covered by Sombreuil's troops. Hervilly was fatally wounded. One and a half thousand *émigrés* died in action. Hoche took 6,000 prisoners, all the supplies that had been landed and the forged ***assignats*** that were to pay for the progress inland. Artois landed briefly on the Ile d'Yeu, but was too late and too far south to be of any help.[3]

The **representative on mission, Tallien**, arrived and set up a military commission. The Breton peasants who had joined with Hervilly's force were let go, but 751 prisoners, including 450 nobles, were shot. Nevertheless, a good many other prisoners escaped.[4]

Hoche then continued with his pacification policy; a negotiated peace was no longer possible.[5]

R

Rabaut de Saint-Etienne, Jean-Paul (1743–93)

Rabaut was one of the **Girondins** executed in the wake of their exclusion from the **National Convention**. He had been in hiding for some time after 2 June and went to the scaffold in December.

He came from Nîmes and had been a Protestant pastor before the Revolution, very active in gaining the recognition achieved by **Louis XVI**'s grant of civil identity in 1788. He was also a Greek scholar and gained a reputation for learning. He was elected for the **Third Estate** of Nîmes to the **Estates-General**, in which he was prominent in the devising of the Constitution for the **Legislative Assembly**, from which he was, like all his colleagues in the Constituent, excluded.

He allowed the king a suspensive veto and opposed the setting-up of the Republic. Unlike some of the Girondins, he did not support putting Louis XVI on trial. He was hunted down in the interests of Jacobin conformity to the One and Indivisible Republic and executed. The **Thermidorean Convention** rehabilitated his memory on 8 October 1795.[1]

Rastadt Conference

There was unfinished business from the Treaty of **Campo Formio** concluded the month before between France and the Empire. The German princes had not signed the treaty, and 90 small states were represented at Rastadt. They had lost territory on the left bank of the Rhine in the French desire for natural frontiers. They expected to be compensated with other portions of the Empire. Formal agreement to the loss of left bank territories was signed in March 1798.

Then the French delegation unsuccessfully demanded (the French verb *demander* – 'to ask' – has often caused difficulties) positions on the right bank to make the gains they had already made secure from attack. All this was against a background of French military gains in Switzerland and Italy.

Bonaparte left the conference early in December 1797 and the **Directory** was without a forceful presence at the conference to insist upon the surrender of the whole left bank of the Rhine. The Directory made General **Bernadotte** ambassador in Vienna. Austrian Chancellor Thugut refused to meet him. Austrian provocations to the French delegation at Rastadt were met with a like response. French and Austrian delegations then met in Alsace led by François de Neufchâteau and Cobenzl, which led only to a fresh outbreak of war.[2]

The Rastadt Conference was therefore at an end in April. The safety of the Austrian delegation could not be guaranteed as it left. Orders were given that only the French diplomats were to leave, and they did so as night fell. Their coach was attacked, and two of the three were killed. An enquiry held by Austria found French *émigrés* guilty of this outrage. It became a cause for denouncing 'the execrable House of Austria' in the 'tenth day' festivals all over France.

Reason, Cult of

Hébert and **Chaumette**, the leading de-Christianizers of 1793, proposed a replacement of the established Catholic religion with the cult of Reason which greatly differed from the cult of the **Supreme Being** advocated by **Robespierre**.

Chaumette organized a Festival of Liberty in the former Cathedral of Notre Dame de Paris on 10 November in which Thérèse Momoro, wife of the printer Antoine-François **Momoro**, played the Goddess of Reason. She was enthroned upon the high altar and was guest of honour at a public dinner afterwards. After the establishment of the **National Convention**, church buildings all over the country were renamed as Temples of Reason or of Truth, festooned with slogans like 'The French Republic recognizes the immortality of the soul' and, inconsistently, 'Death is but an eternal sleep'. As Christian churches, the buildings were closed in May 1793, and the Catholic Mass forbidden – even at the hands of constitutional priests – in November.[3] Obviously all state financial support was removed from the **refractory clergy** who by this time were either in 'voluntary' exile or suffering on the hulks of **Rochefort**. By then, there was no place for the constitutional clergy either, even if they had complied with what the revolutionary decrees required of them, even abandoning clerical celibacy in order, patriotically, to marry.

The Convention and its **representatives on mission** wanted to use the 'tenth day' festivals (provision for which was made in the **Revolutionary Calendar**) for community education. These occasions of church notices without the church encouraged hatred towards kings and 'the execrable House of Austria', respect for old people, especially parents of soldiers, and telling stories like that of **Bara**. They also were occasions for recruiting campaigns and the pursuit of army deserters. Understandably, there were complaints from officials that they were poorly attended. The churches by then were only halls since the bells (apart from the ones used on clocks that regulated working hours), plate and metal ornaments had all gone for the war effort.

Even after Hébert and Chaumette had been executed in March 1794, this cultural potential continued to be exploited right up to the end of the **Directory**.

Redouté, Pierre-Joseph (1759–1840)

Redouté was a botanical illustrator whose work spans the years from the old regime at **Versailles** until the reign of Louis-Philippe. Unlike **David**, he exhibited no interest in politics. His exquisite studies of plants and their blooms are in the tradition of the Renaissance illustrators of herbs for the use of pharmacists in winter, and Dutch flower painters.

Born in Luxembourg, he worked in the Austrian Netherlands (Belgium), and then arrived in Paris to join his brother. He was introduced to art dealers and booklovers, and was employed by **Marie-Antoinette** to record her plants in the garden she made for the Petit Trianon at Versailles. Then Redouté became her official artist at court. It is said that he visited the king and queen in the Temple prison because a rare cactus was in bloom and they wanted him to immortalize its flowering.

When the gardens became the property of the Nation, he was kept on by the republicans, and subsequently worked under the Empress Josephine's patronage in her gardens at Malmaison. After the **Restoration**, in 1822, he was appointed to the Museum of Natural History, still making scientific records, but extending his interest as a painter into scintillating flower compositions.

Blunt, Wilfrid, *The Art of Botanical Illustration* (London: Collins, 1950). Online at: www.octavo.com/editions/rdtrse/.

Michel, Marianne Roland, *The Floral Art of Pierre-Joseph Redouté* (London: Frances Lincoln, 2002).

Ridge, Antonia, *The Man Who Painted Roses: The Story of Pierrre-Joseph Redouté* (London: Faber & Faber, 1979).

Refractory Clergy

All over the country in early 1791 the same scene was repeated again and again: after the parish Mass on a Sunday morning, members of the municipality of the commune would wait for the *curé* (the parish priest) and the *vicaire* (his assistant, if he had one) and ask them to take the Oath to the **Civil Constitution of the Clergy** demanded by law, and they would reply. It has been calculated that, by September 1792, making allowance for those who retracted their oath after the pope condemned it, 45 per cent of the French clergy took the oath.[4] Then, a few days or weeks later, a constitutional priest would arrive, sent ostensibly by the constitutional bishop, but actually by the departmental directory, and take the parish over. These men were available because the Assembly decreed that there would only be a church for every 6,000 of population, so there were redundant churches. Soon, decrees of the **Legislative** and the **Convention** ordered the refractory clergy to leave France, and many of them went into exile in Spain, the Channel Islands or England. The death penalty was subsequently decreed for any still found on French soil and for anyone – even their relations – who harboured them.

Some of the refractory clergy stayed on (or, in the case of the **Vendée**, returned) and ministered in secret to their former congregations. These clergy were subjected to inhumane treatment if they were found. Six from the Vendée were hacked to pieces by a crowd on the quay at La Rochelle on 21–2 March 1793.[5] Some were summarily guillotined. Others were brought from all over France to Atlantic ports, ostensibly to be transported to French Guiana.

The navy minister Dalbarade had prepared a plan for them to work in a colony outside Cayenne to raise beef cattle, and a law was passed to implement it. A few were taken there. Most, however, were imprisoned and 'disappeared' in squalid former slave ships – the hulks of **Rochefort** – during the **Terror**. When de-Christianization took effect, many of the constitutional clergy suffered the same fate, although Henri **Gregoire** and a few others maintained their position as constitutional bishops and replacement curés.

 Aston, Nigel, *Religion and Revolution in France, 1780–1804* (Basingstoke: Macmillan Press, 2000).

Tackett, Timothy, *Religion, Revolution and Regional Culture in Eighteenth-Century France* (University Park, PA: Princeton University Press, 1986), chap. 3.

Regicides

Regicide, 'king-killer', was the word used by royalists for members of the **National Convention** who voted for the execution of King **Louis XVI** in January 1793.

The king's trial took place in the National Convention between 11 December 1792 and 17 January 1793, with his execution on 21 January. At the conclusion of the trial, the deputies had to vote three times: on whether the king were guilty or not of treason against the nation, whether there should be a national referendum on his sentence, and, when that was turned down, on the sentence itself. On the question of guilt, each deputy had to go to the tribune and declare his personal verdict. On the question of guilt, the decision was 691 affirmative votes out of 749. Twenty-seven expressed nuances equivalent to abstention, and thirty-one were absent. There were 424 votes against a referendum and 283 for it and there were 12 people who abstained. There were 366 votes for the king's immediate death, a majority of 6. For a suspended death penalty there were only 34 votes. There were 319 votes for imprisonment until the end of the war and then banishment.[6] The 366 deputies were the regicides.

In 1816, after the 'second' **Restoration**, King Louis XVIII's government excluded nearly all the regicides, and those who had supported Napoleon in the 100 Days, from political life and from French territory.

Renault, Aimée-Cécile (1778–94)

Maximilien **Robespierre** often stated that he feared assassination. On 24 May 1794, this fear seemed to be justified when a young woman called Cécile Renault persistently asked to see him at his lodgings in the rue Saint-Honoré and aroused suspicion. She was found to have brought a fruit knife in her basket.[7] Under questioning, she admitted to being a royalist and said she wanted to see what a tyrant looked like. She was kept in prison until guillotined on 17 June, under the Law of 22 prairial promulgated a week before. Her father, who was a craftsman in Paris, her brother and her aunt were executed with her, judged guilty by association. Like Charlotte **Corday**, **Marat**'s assassin, they were made to wear the red shirts traditionally worn by those executed as parricides.

Rentes, rentiers

The state, corporations and individuals in the French Monarchy depended a great deal on loans for the financing of their projects. Wealthy members of the **nobility** and the **bourgeoisie** were encouraged by finance ministers to lend large capital sums to the crown so as to be rewarded with a percentage interest on them each year in perpetuity, usually 8 per cent. **Necker** did this on a large scale to pay for French involvement in the American War of Independence from 1777 to 1781. Public indebtedness had become the basis of national finance.

The sums the lenders received were called *rentes*, and the recipients themselves *rentiers*. *Rentes* could be inherited. The beneficiaries of this system were collectively called the *rentier* classes. Four per cent of the members of **Jacobin Clubs** in a national sample were *rentiers* until 1791. In Dijon, the principal town of the Côte d'Or, there were 242 *rentiers*, 16.3 per cent of the population, in the tax year 1789–90.[8]

The need to keep up the interest payments on the loans was a major factor in the national deficit that **Calonne** made public knowledge in 1786. Reduction of the capital of the loan was beyond the scope of small-scale adjustments. The impossibly large deficit led to the summoning of the two Assemblies of Notables in 1787 and 1788. When they had failed to provide an agreed solution, the **Estates-General** were summoned for May 1789.

The French state cleared its debt in 1797 when France had conquered new sources of revenue. *Rentiers* remained, however, a feature of nineteenth-century economic life.

Representatives on Mission

The expulsion of the **Girondins** from the Convention with **sansculotte** support at the beginning of June 1793, left France governed by a 'rump' which did not represent large areas, like the large provincial cities – **Lyon**, **Marseille**, **Toulon**, Bordeaux. They were already determined in their opposition to centralized rule because the Paris Commune appeared to have more power than the elected **National Convention**. On 2 June 1793, the Convention had become virtually a Jacobin preserve. The Jacobins called their opponents' tendency **'federalism'**, took military action against it, and intensified the use of representatives (i.e. deputies) on mission from the Convention to control the disaffected departments. From July 1793 onwards, the orders made by these representatives were given the status of provisional laws, which meant that they had a totally free hand in their direction of local conditions. This status was embodied in the **Law of 14 frimaire**, year II (4 December 1793) which made the representatives answerable to the **Committee of Public Safety**.

Extremist representatives on mission applied a violent, sansculotte view of the Revolution which the Jacobin faction cultivated through the Committee of Public Safety, to which they were regularly to report on their activities. For example, **Carrier** drowned Vendéan rebels in the Loire, **Fouché** organized mass shootings (*mitraillades*) in Lyon, **Fréron** did the same in Toulon, and **Bernard de Saintes** was responsible for at least one judicial murder in Dijon.

These were exceptional, however. Eighty per cent of the representatives served the republic conscientiously. Joseph Lakanal brought basic literacy into the Dordogne. Jean-Baptiste Bo explained laws to illiterate mayors in the Cantal. Chaudron-Rousseau restricted taxation to people able to pay.[9] The representative could be mediator as well as enforcer. Members of the Committee of Public Safety were sometimes representatives themselves, like **Couthon** in the Puy de Dôme and then Lyon, **Prieur de la Marne** in Brittany, and **Collot d'Herbois** in Alsace and Lyon.

After the fall of **Robespierre** and the subsequent dismantling of the Committee of Public Safety, the remaining extremist representatives benefited from one of the last acts of the **National Convention**. The amnesty passed on 26 October 1795 drew a legal forgetfulness over all actions 'committed as a result of the Revolution', which meant that their incriminating papers were returned to them and they were set free.

Restaurants

Anecdotal evidence, taken up by the Goncourt brothers in the mid-nineteenth century, asserted that the principal reason for restaurants opening was the emigration of proprietors of noble households when the **Constituent Assembly** was wound down in 1791, leaving their staff behind. The redundant *chefs de cuisine* opened new establishments and began to cook for the public. With the abolition of guilds by the *Loi d'Allarde* in March 1791, it was possible for a caterer (*traiteur*) to set up a business on his own.

Utterances of revolutionaries such as **Barère** seemed to confirm that this happened, with their denunciations of people in Paris who could afford it becoming degenerate by eating like aristocrats. Indeed, revolutionaries were self-conscious about their new eating habits. Members of one of the revolutionary sections sent their caterer's itemized bill for their lunches when they were meeting daily in autumn 1793, which came to 2,539 livres, to the **Committee of General Security** for settlement saying it was for 'secret expenses'.

However, the grander nobles and bishops who emigrated obtained passports for their staff to emigrate as well. A truer picture of the origin of restaurants in Paris can be seen in the career of Antoine Beauvilliers, who was the Comte de **Provence**'s pastry chef. He had already set up a restaurant in the lodging house he opened in the rue Sainte-Anne in the early 1780s. Then, in 1787, when the Duc d'**Orléans** made a paying proposition of the new arcades in his **Palais-Royal**, Beauvilliers rented space in one of the arcades and opened a restaurant there. Jean-Baptiste La Barrière left private service in 1779 to be a caterer from his premises in the rue Saint-Honoré. He also rented a space in the Palais-Royal arcades for a restaurant. In 1787, he sold his *Café Militaire* to his former employees, the Véry brothers, who developed a famous business in the Empire.[10]

Fréron encountered his '**golden youth**' and the '*merveilleuses*' in a Paris restaurant. Louis-Michel **Le Peletier de Saint-Fargeau** was murdered in an establishment run by Dominique Février in the Palais-Royal. Eating in public, when not on a long journey, had become part of the public culture of the capital before the guilds were abolished.

Spang, Rebecca L., *The Invention of the Restaurant: Paris and Modern Gastronomic Culture* (London and Cambridge, MA: Harvard University Press, 2000), chap. 5.

Restoration of the Monarchy (1814–15)

After Tsar Alexander and King Frederick William III of Prussia had entered Paris on 31 March 1814, Napoleon abdicated and left for Elba. **Talleyrand** entertained the Tsar under his own roof, on the strength of a rumour that the Elysée Palace had been mined, and was instrumental in bringing Louis XVIII, formerly the Comte de **Provence**, from his exile in England to be king.[11] The allies decided to punish Napoleon, not the Nation, restored the frontiers of 1792, and allowed all the art treasures looted during the wars to remain in France. Louis XVIII promised to rule as a constitutional monarch. France was represented at the Congress of Vienna by none other than Talleyrand himself.

In March 1815, Napoleon returned from Elba, marched up through France and was welcomed by his soldiers, including Marshal Ney who had told Louis XVIII that he would bring him to Paris 'in an iron cage'. Louis XVIII fled to Ghent. Napoleon issued a constitution, his 'Additional Act', saying that he would have done so sooner or later in any case.

The allies at the Congress of Vienna ordered the Duke of Wellington and Field Marshal Blücher to be ready to intercept Napoleon when he marched towards Charleroi in Belgium in June 1815. The result of the Battle of Waterloo was that he lost his throne again. He crossed France to the Ile d'Aix near La Rochelle, and embarked for St Helena on H.M.S. Bellerophon.

Louis XVIII returned once more in July, 'in the baggage wagons of the allies'. The penalties exacted from the French were more severe than before. The art treasures went home, there was to be a huge war indemnity payment, and France was to be occupied by British, Prussian and Russian (always called 'Cossack') troops until it should be paid off.

Louis XVIII had the good sense not to provoke opposition by arranging a coronation, nor did he even consider ruling from Versailles. Like his elder brother after 1789, he was king of the French, not of France. Even so, there was an ultra-royalist revival in the elections for a Chamber of Deputies and they achieved a majority. The king called the new assembly '*La Chambre introuvable*'. Despite this, France entered a period of comparative economic prosperity, and the allied occupation army was withdrawn in 1819. There was a period of centrist government from 1816 until 1820, when the assassination of **Artois**'s second son, the Duc de Berry, caused another ultra-royalist backlash. Prime Minister Villèle granted compensation out of taxes to the noble *émigrés* of the Revolution. Artois followed his brother as Charles X in September 1824. His governments were increasingly rightist after 1828, which brought about the new revolution of July 1830, and the reappearance of **Lafayette**, who offered a republic for a few days, and then the Orleanist monarchy under Louis Philippe, who had been 'the soldier of **Jemappes**' in 1792.

📖 Tombs, Robert, *France 1814–1914* (London and New York: Longman, 1996), chap. 17.

Reubell, Jean-François (1747–1807)

Reubell was the second longest-serving member of the executive **Directory** (the first being **Barras**), from November 1795 to May 1799. He had aspirations as the Directory's foreign affairs expert, but was frustrated by the successes of General **Bonaparte** and the acumen of Charles-Maurice **Talleyrand**.

He came from Alsace, where his father was a royal notary in Colmar. After law studies at Strasbourg, he became a barrister there, and president of the Colmar bar before 1789. He won a case against the Duke of Wurttemberg, and became interested in his fief of Montbéliard and neighbouring Porrentruy, which became French annexations in 1793. He was elected to the **Estates-General**, and joined the Breton Club at **Versailles**, which became the **Jacobins** in Paris after the **October Days**. He was put on a committee to provide the capital with foodstuffs. He voted for measures against *émigrés* and the **refractory clergy**. He did not support **Robespierre**'s decree to prevent deputies to the **Constituent** being elected to the **Legislative**. Having lost the vote, he returned to Alsace as Procurator-General of the Haut-Rhin and, even at this early stage, proposed the Rhine as France's natural frontier in the east. He visited Basle and discussed a Swiss connection with the Francophile Peter Ochs. Meanwhile, he resented **Carnot**'s refusal to occupy more than a part of Montbéliard.

Reubell was elected first of the eight Haut-Rhin deputies to the **National Convention**, but he had no importance before the fall of Robespierre. He called himself a *Montagnard*, but was absent from Paris for more than a year and, elected with **Girondins** to diplomatic and military committees, he supported them against the Paris Commune, and was accused of wanting **Orléans** to replace **Louis XVI** as king. As a **representative on mission** (along with **Merlin de Douai**) he was caught at Mainz when the Duke of **Brunswick**'s siege was successful, and was defended by Robespierre from prosecution along with General **Custine**, for which **Hébert** was pressing. His only Convention speech in 1794 was to defend refugees from Mainz. He was kept out of committees until October when he served on the **Committee of General Security** for three months, and then on the **Thermidorean Committee of Public Safety** from March to July 1795. He had kept aloof at **Thermidor** and did not support the reinstatement of the surviving Girondins. He went with **Sieyès** to The Hague to set up the Batavian Republic, and visited the Army of the Rhine and Moselle, still keen on the natural frontier.

Reubell was elected to the Councils of the Directory by 18 departments, and was loyal to the Haut-Rhin, but was chosen as one of the 5 Directors. None of the other four was his political ally. After the **Fructidor coup** and the departure of **Carnot**, he directed the war along with Barras and **La Révellière-Lépeaux**. However, he had to accept what Bonaparte agreed with Austria at Leoben and at **Campo Formio**, thereby scrapping his design to use Italian gains as bargaining counters for the right bank of the Rhine, and the **Rastadt Conference** was a disaster. He had to accept **Talleyrand** as foreign minister because he was Barras's nominee but, when there was scandal over his insistence on large bribes for an American alliance, known as the XYZ affair from initials given to the US negotiators in the report made to President Adams, in September 1797, British resolve was reinvigorated and peace negotiations were cancelled.

Reubell suffered from bad health, took to going home to Arceuil every night, and even had August 1798 off for a cure at Plombières. He was toppled in May 1799 to be replaced by Sieyès, and was returned as a deputy for the Haut-Rhin in the partial elections. He was charged with misappropriation of funds by both neo-Jacobins and Bonaparte's supporters. He narrowly escaped conviction in a vote on 19 August 1799.

Reubell supported Bonaparte at Brumaire to help the military career of his elder son, and the rest of his life was spent trying to cope with his younger son's debts. There was no promotion for him in the Empire, and he resumed his private practice in Colmar.[12]

Réveillon, Jean-Baptiste (1725–1811)

Réveillon had been a haberdasher and stationer, importing wallpapers from England. After his marriage, he used his wife's dowry to expand his business and make his own stock in trade. He opened a wallpaper factory in the **Faubourg Saint-Antoine** in eastern Paris (in the shadow of the **Bastille**) and from 1759 onwards employed a workforce of 300. This was rare, because most employment was in small workshops of a master and a dozen or so journeymen – called *compagnons* in French. Saint-Antoine was where many craftsmen in the luxury furnishing trades worked side by side. His products were popular among the courtiers at **Versailles** and he became wealthy enough to buy a mansion at the side of his works, a shop in the **Tuileries Palace** and his own paper mill.

During the district electoral meetings prior to the opening of the **Estates-General** in April 1789, Réveillon was overheard discussing the economic crisis and tactlessly suggesting that the bread distribution should be deregulated to allow prices to fall. This was at the moment when nearly all a worker's wage (one estimate says 88 per cent) was spent on buying bread. In earshot of the people concerned, he remarked that, if the price of bread went down, wages could be lowered and sales increased. His hearers, and those whom they told, reacted immediately by destroying his mansion, burning all the wallpaper and other sales items in the factory, and liberating the contents of his wine cellar for immediate consumption.

There were some deaths in the riot, which involved burning effigies of Réveillon and his interlocutor, a saltpetre maker called Henriot.[13] There were more in its repression. Infantry and artillery arrived in the narrow streets of the faubourg to be met by rioters hurling tiles and chimney pots at them. They fired back. An element of increased politicization has been seen in this event. There were the usual calls for cheap bread and support for the king, but also expressions of approval for the Duc d'**Orléans** and **Necker**, regarded just then as popular heroes.[14]

Réveillon and his family escaped over a wall and sought refuge in the Bastille, with Necker's own help, and then moved to England.

Revolutionary Armies

Armées Révolutionnaires, or 'People's Armies', were **sansculotte** militia formed by municipalities dominated by **Jacobins** to take action against counter-revolution. The Parisian *armée*, created in September 1793, was the largest one. It had a bureaucracy of its own made up of military men, functionaries and radical politicians. Charles-Philippe **Ronsin** became its commander.

The armies' function was forcibly to gather food supplies from farmers who were waiting for a better market price for grain, whom they saw as counter-revolutionary hoarders. The troops had taken on **Hébert**'s de-Christianization as a motive too. If they had not been taken already, bells and plate disappeared from churches when they passed by. They usually took a **guillotine** with them on their marches. In their own eyes, they were the real patriots, the legitimate revolutionaries. After **Thermidor**, they were spoken of as 'drinkers of blood'.

The **Mountain** acquiesced in their presence after the **'Day' of 5 September**, but they denied the supremacy of the law by taking it into their own hands. Authority resided only in the nation through its elected representatives, which they were not. When the Mountain found itself more confident in early 1794, the enforcement of the **Law of 14 Frimaire** (4 December 1793), allowed the **Committee of Public Safety** to draw the teeth of these armies. Nevertheless, since all able-bodied men were by then considered to be soldiers, and the nation was 'revolutionary until victory', they represented the idea of total warfare.

Revolutionary Calendar

The revolutionary calendar was intended to announce a complete rupture with past time. The **National Convention** decreed its adoption throughout French territory on 5 October 1793. The Gregorian calendar, with its saints' days and Sundays bound the French people to the Crown and the Church. Time began anew on 22 September 1792 (1 vendémiaire, year I). The monarchy had been overthrown and the Nation was being de-Christianized.

1792 Anno Domini was replaced retrospectively by Year I of the French Republic (or of Liberty). Months were now to consist of 30 days each, leaving 5 or 6 days in early autumn spare. The calculations were the work of Gilbert **Romme**. The seven-day week gave way to the ten-day *décade* with every tenth day as a day of rest and an occasion for a festival in village churches, renamed as Temples of Reason or of Truth. The 24-hour day was replaced by division into 10, and each tenth was divided again by 10. The decision to replace clocks with decimal versions was, however, never implemented.

An additional plan was adopted after a second report presented by the dramatist Philippe **Fabre d'Eglantine** on 24 October. This gave names to the new months, instead of referring to them as first, second, third and so on, meaning to bring the French people back to their rural roots. The year was to begin now with the grape harvest, *vendémiaire*, followed by *brumaire* for fog, *frimaire* for mists, *nivôse* for snows, *pluviôse* for rain, and *ventôse* for wind. When spring came, meteorology gave way to growth, so there was *germinal*, for when buds appear, *floréal* for flowers, *prairial* for meadow grass, and then words indicating fruit and heat and harvest: *fructidor, thermidor* and *messidor*.

Days were no longer to bear the names of Christian saints, but things that were useful in daily life. André-Antoine **Bernard**, a deputy for the

Charente-Inférieure, adopted *Pioche-fer* (Iron pick-axe) as a first name when it replaced Saint-André in the calendar.

The Revolutionary Calendar lasted only 14 years. It had no usefulness after the *Concordat* with Pope Pius VII had been in operation for a while. Napoleon abolished it by imperial decree with effect from 1 January 1806.

Revolutionary Cockade

Men's hat brims at the time of the Revolution were secured in front by a circular cockade, and the revolutionary cockade (*cocarde révolutionnaire*) was adopted as a badge to denote adhesion. It was red, white and blue in colour. Red and blue were the colours of the city of Paris. When it was hoped that **Louis XVI** would comply with the Nation's will that he become a constitutional monarch, the white of the House of Bourbon separated the two other colours. The king actually accepted a cockade like this and wore it on his hat in Paris three days after the fall of the **Bastille**. As news of the king's apparent acceptance of change spread around provincial France, local revolutionaries offered cockades to establishment figures such as garrison commanders and bishops, many of whom accepted them, caught up in hopeful euphoria. The clergy wore them pinned to the front of their cassocks. Statues of the king were crowned with laurel.

When constitutional monarchy was abandoned, the cockade remained as a badge of adherence to the Republic, often worn sewn to a **Phrygian bonnet** to show enthusiasm for *sansculottisme*. The tricolore flag was adopted as the standard of the civil and military nation while the Comte de **La Tour du Pin** was War Minister. Already renowned as an artist, Jacques-Louis **David**, who was prominent in the **Jacobin Club**, insisted that it was more aesthetically pleasing to fly the flag with the blue next to the flagstaff with the red floating free.

Revolutionary Tribunal

On 10 March 1793, **Danton** and **Carrier** successfully proposed to the **National Convention** that political enemies of the newly established Republic should be tried by five judges in a special court that was called the Revolutionary Tribunal. Six months later. **Fouquier-Tinville** was appointed as public prosecutor when the man originally elected refused the post.

Two halls in the Palais de Justice on the Ile de La Cité were given over to the court, conveniently near the **Conciergerie**, which was regarded as the waiting room for the **guillotine**. Hearings began at the end of March and at first were conducted by the normal legal procedures. The **Committees of Public Safety** and of **General Security** were set up soon afterwards, and both of them provided lists of accused for the Tribunal. After the **Law of Suspects** had been passed on 17 September 1793, the official **Terror** began. **Robespierre** brought M.-J.-A. Herman, a fellow lawyer from Arras, to be the president of the Tribunal. It became the law's uncompromising instrument even against prominent members of the committees themselves such as **Hérault de Séchelles**. Another victim was the constitutional archbishop of Paris, Jean-Baptiste-Joseph **Gobel**, who had done all he could to side with the republicans. March and April 1794 saw the trials of the Hébertists and the Dantonists, and trials were now concerned with groups not individuals. Officials who had not satisfied Jacobin norms were sent for trial from the provinces by **representatives on mission**.

After the **Law of 22 prairial** (10 June 1794) was passed, neither defence counsel nor witnesses could be called. The only sentence the Tribunal could pass from then on was death. It continued in operation for a little while after the **Thermidor coup**, but it was enthusiastically dismantled in reaction against the 'tail of Robespierre' as the surviving Jacobins were called.

Robespierre, Augustin-Bon-Joseph de (1763–94)

Augustin Robespierre was usually referred to as '*le jeune*' in deference to Maximilien. It is amusing to note in passing that their name includes the nobiliary particle in spite of everything. He followed his brother into the law, and then into radical politics. He rose from being public prosecutor in Arras, where he was born, to being on the departmental directory of the Pas-de-Calais.

He was then elected to the **National Convention** as the nineteenth Paris deputy, to sit with the **Mountain**. He joined the **Jacobin Club**. He was **representative on mission** to the Army of Italy in 1794. On the way there, with his mistress, Madame de Sandraye, an academician's wife, he was allowed a roving commission to point out to other representatives on mission that, despite the execution of 'indulgents', the hard line of the **Terror** ought to be softened,[15] as his brother had told him privately.[16] He received respect in his own right and not just because of his incorruptible brother.

He insisted on being arrested with his brother in the National Convention on 9 **Thermidor**, saying, 'I am as guilty as he is; I share his virtues, I want to share his fate.' While the soldiers sent by the Convention came to arrest the Robespierrists in the Hôtel de Ville, Augustin jumped out of a window from the second floor and broke both legs.

He was carried to the scaffold in the morning.

Robespierre, Maximilien-François-Marie-Isidore de (1758–94)

The chief characteristic of 'the Incorruptible' was his single-minded devotion to the establishment of a Republic of Virtue: high-principled consistency, for which his recent biographer, Ruth Scurr, used the title 'Fatal Purity'.[17] Those who had voted for the king's death could not afford to lose the struggle with foreign enemies or with 'enemies of the people' at home. Fear of conspiracy and assassination made **Terror** the order of the day. Maximilien Robespierre came ever closer to the centre of information and control until, in what turned out to be the last year of his life, he was the ideologue of the **Committee of Public Safety**, with public platforms in the Convention and in the **Jacobin Club**. 'He arrived as a citizen in a Revolution where the others were still subjects.'[18] That is why he personified the Terror for contemporary Englishmen and for later French writers, though there were many as deeply involved in it as he was, some of whom he provoked to topple him in the **Thermidor** *coup d'état*.[19]

Robespierre's uncomfortable home life in Arras was marked by the death of his mother when he was six and by the repeated absence of his father. He was given a modest bursary by the Abbot of Saint-Vaast to be a boarder at the prestigious Lycée Louis-le-Grand in Paris. He was entrusted with a Latin oration to greet the newly crowned **Louis XVI** and **Marie-Antoinette** returning from the coronation in 1774. It rained. The king was late. Robespierre knelt in the rain to give his speech. The king listened from his carriage but left in the middle of it. Hostile biographers have given this more significance than it warrants.[20]

Once qualified, he returned home to be a provincial lawyer with a fastidiously austere way of life and a reputation for egalitarian justice. He joined the Academy at Arras. Perhaps on the strength of a pamphlet he wrote, he was elected as fifth deputy to the **Estates-General** from Artois. At **Versailles** he was one of the first members of the Breton Club that became the **Jacobin Club** after the move to Paris in October.[21]

He argued for man's natural rights in a state where the sovereign was to be the people, for everyone having the right to be in the **National Guard**, for **Avignon** being French, and for **Jews**, men 'of colour' and slaves being enfranchised. He opposed the royal veto, honours, martial law, the church's hierarchy and any distinction between 'passive' and **'active' citizens** as voters. On 18 May 1791, he gained acceptance for a decree that deputies who had served in the **Constituent Assembly** were not eligible for the new **Legislative** on the grounds that they had too much popular prestige and that they had let themselves be manipulated by the court faction.[22]

Entire passages in Robespierre's speeches recall **Rousseau**.[23] He saw the law in Rousseau's terms, as the expression of the General Will. This was to be the framework for the establishment of equality. He supported education proposals made on 13 July 1793, that schooling should be the same for all from age five to twelve to enable a peaceful revolution, without alarming property or offending justice. The Revolution was far from complete for him by then. He saw his own contribution as part of the great current that led from the **Enlightenment**: '... we are being watched by all nations; we are debating in the presence of the universe,' Robespierre said in February 1793.[24]

Despite his harsh voice and his Artois accent, the deputies listened to him. He became prominent, but not popular. There were several other presidents of the Jacobins before his turn came in April 1790 and he was kept off the Assembly's committees until July 1790. But he had gained enormous prestige by the autumn, after his *Adresse aux français*. Excluded himself from the Legislative, he made the Jacobin Club and his post as Public Prosecutor in Paris into his power bases, from which he criticized the manoeuvres of the court and the incompetence of the **Roland** ministry in its conduct of the war and provisioning the cities. His attacks on **Brissot** and **Vergniaud** were continuous. He made long tirades against **Dumouriez**. Along with **Marat**, he prepared the minds of the people for the overthrow of the monarchy on the **'Day' of 10 August 1792**, though he did not directly organize it. He was, however, elected to the **Insurrectionary Commune** by the Pikes section of the city on 9 August. He was not responsible for the **September Massacres**, but refused to denounce those who were. The Parisian response was to elect him the first of their deputies in the **National Convention** three days afterwards.[25]

Robespierre worked hard for the king's execution. His own comment after the king had been condemned on 14 January 1793 was:

I am inflexible in relation to oppressors because I am compassionate towards the oppressed; I do not recognize the humanity that butchers the people and pardons despots. The sentiment that led me to demand, in vain, in the National Assembly, the abolition of the death penalty, is the same that is forcing me today to demand that it is applied to the tyrant of my fatherland, and the king in person.[26]

The Jacobins had the hegemony in the Convention after the **Girondins** had been expelled on 2 June 1793 with the help of the Paris Commune and **Hanriot's sansculottes**. On 27 July, Robespierre became the theorist for his fellow members on the Convention's Committee of Public Safety, which administered the decrees enforcing the Terror – legal terror[27] – through a network of **representatives on mission**. He developed an idea of 'the people' by which he justified – to himself – his attitudes and actions in the One and Indivisible Republic of Virtue that could not tolerate opposing factions. These had to be denounced and sent to the scaffold. On 5 February 1794, he lectured the Convention's deputies that the first maxim of their policy must be to guide the people with reason and the people's enemies with Terror. Since Terror was nothing other than prompt, severe and inflexible justice, breaking the enemies of liberty with it would justify the *Conventionnels* as the Republic's founders and those who upheld liberty against tyranny.[28]

Originally against the death penalty, he supported the use of the guillotine against 'enemies of the people', even if they were his former associates, extremist Hébertists in March, and the 'indulgent' Dantonists in April 1794. Elected President of the Convention, he presided over the inaugural festival of his own cult of the **Supreme Being** on 8 June 1794, intensifying hostility against himself among the de-Christianizers who remained after **Hébert**'s execution, particularly **Fouché**. Robespierre wanted a deity, and promoted the Supreme Being above and beyond the goddess Reason (the printer **Momoro**'s wife) who had sat enthroned in Notre Dame Cathedral for an hour or so in November 1793 and gone to dinner with the organizers afterwards. As much as **Bonaparte** in his 1802 Concordat, Robespierre wanted religion as social cement. On 8 June, he appeared really to believe what he said about the Supreme Being as he presided at the Festival. 'Far from announcing the end of the Revolution, the new civic cult gave the Terror a lawful and moral basis.'[29] Then he was responsible for the Law of 22 prairial, year II (10 June 1794), known as the 'Great Terror', which ensured speedy judgements, without defence, in the Paris **revolutionary tribunal**.

Robespierre was beginning to realize that the excesses of terror had not delivered national unity, nor were they likely to. But it was too late. Other proponents of Terror, principally Fouché and **Tallien**, brought about the **Thermidor** *coup d'état* against him and his close associates in July.

Andress, David, *The Terror: Civil War in the French Revolution* (London: Little Brown, 2005).

Gueniffey, Patrice, *Robespierre*, in François Furet and Mona Ozouf (eds), *A Critical Dictionary of the French Revolution*, trans. Arthur Goldhammer (London: The Belknap Press of Harvard University Press, 1989). References here are from the French edition.

Mantel, Hilary, *A Place of Greater Safety* (London: Penguin, 1993). Novel.

Palmer, R.R., *Twelve Who Ruled: The Year of the Terror in the French Revolution* (University Park, PA: Princeton University Press, Bicentennial Edition, 1989).

Scurr, Ruth, *Fatal Purity: Robespierre and the French Revolution* (London: Chatto & Windus, 2006).

Wajda, Andrzej, *Danton* (Franco-Polish, 1983). Film.

@ http://www.marxists.org/history/france/revolution/robespierre/index.htm
provides texts of selected speeches of Robespierre.

Roland de la Platière, Jean-Marie (1734–93) and Roland de la Platière, Jeanne Manon (1754–93)

Before the revolution, Jean-Marie Roland held appointments in Picardy and **Lyon** as a factory inspector. He married Manon Philippon, the daughter of an artist and jeweller who carried out royal contracts in Paris. She was 20 years his junior and he accepted, despite the masculine-dominated times, that she was very clever. She was his ideal partner when it came to official correspondence: she wrote, he read and signed. This mattered a good deal when he was Minister of the Interior with other **Girondins** in the constitutional monarchy and in the early days of the Republic.

Roland distanced himself at first from the Lyon patriots when he was elected a notable in 1789, but a year later he was a municipal official and adopted much more of their position. He went to Paris as a *député extraordinaire* in 1791 to present the parlous state of the Lyon silk-weaving industry which, like other luxury trades, was in crisis after the adoption of new bourgeois styles. After a brief return to Lyon, the Rolands settled in Paris and entered the political arena. Jean-Marie joined the **Jacobin Club** at first, and Manon kept her salon in the rue Guénégaud, where they both encountered **Brissot**, **Vergniaud**, **Buzot** (all leading Girondins), **Robespierre** and **Pétion**.[30]

Roland was a member of the Girondin ministry formed in March 1792 in favour of war against the new Emperor Francis II. There was talk of an '**Austrian Committee**' under the queen's control. The king resisted plans to bring 20,000 provincial **National Guards** to Paris and delayed the acceptance of new laws against the **refractory clergy**. On 10 June, Roland and his colleagues publicly criticized the king for this in an open letter[31] drafted by Manon.[32] The king dismissed Roland, **Clavière** and Servan three days later to replace them with '**Feuillant** nonentities'.[33] The king faced a menacing incursion of **sansculottes** on 20 June and, when courtiers tried to dispense money to Paris officials to keep order, Manon wanted the king's immediate deposition. It seemed sure that the queen was disclosing military information to Vienna. **Brissot** and **Carra** became vociferous in their newspapers against the monarchy.

After the monarchy had been overthrown, its opponents remained disunited. The Rolands regarded **Danton** as a potential dictator after the **September Massacres**. He in turn despised Manon's influence on Roland, and they accused him of embezzling public funds. They had not realized that the pragmatist Danton could still have been an ally against the Jacobins, who launched a concerted attack on Brissot for conspiring against himself and Robespierre. The radical **Collot d'Herbois** joined in to have Brissot expelled from the Jacobin Club. **Marat** took his place there.

As evidence was being prepared for the king's trial, Roland was Minister of the Interior again. On 20 November, a locksmith told him about a secret iron strongbox in the **Tuileries**, which the king had ordered from him. Roland had it opened and noted – on his own – what papers were hidden in it before he took them to the **Convention**. Marat accused him of interfering with the papers or, perhaps, stealing valuable national property in the form of jewels. Robespierre suggested that Roland could have added documents to conceal Girondin perfidy and to incriminate Jacobins. A rumour was fed by Marat's newspaper that Roland had taken orders direct from the king. The **Paris Commune** ordered an investigation.[34]

Sufficient information was found to convict the king as the **Mountain** intended, and to destroy **Mirabeau**'s reputation. On the day after the king's execution, Roland resigned his ministry. Danton had denounced him in the Convention (of which, as a minister, he was not a member). He was replaced by a man whom Manon called 'a political eunuch'. This was D.-J. Garat who, as Danton's successor at the Ministry of Justice, had not investigated the **September Massacres** and appeared to have screened him from accusation concerning them.[35]

Roland stood in the elections for Mayor of Paris, but was defeated by his former protégé (but now a Jacobin), Jean-Nicolas **Pache**,[36] by 11,000 votes to 400. Mayor Pache was in full support of **Hanriot** and his sansculottes over the expulsion of the Girondins on the 'days' of 31 May to 2 June 1793. Manon was arrested on 1 June, having helped her husband to escape from the capital. She was released from the Abbaye prison, rearrested and taken to the Sainte-Pélagie, then the **Conciergerie**, where she wrote her memoirs. She went to the **guillotine** on 8 November 1793. She is credited with crying out, 'Oh, Liberty! What crimes are committed in your name!'[37]

When Jean-Marie heard about her death, he wandered out of Rouen where he had been hiding and ran himself through with his swordstick.[38]

📖 Shuckburgh, Evelyn (trans. and ed.), *The Memoirs of Madame Roland: A Heroine of the French Revolution* (London: Barrie & Jenkins, 1989).

Roman Republic

When the Cispadane Republic was set up in 1796, Bologna and Ferrara, until then papal cities, were incorporated into it, and this led to a demonstration and rioting in favour of French occupation of Rome itself in December 1797. The riot erupted into the French Embassy garden and the French General Duphot was shot dead by papal troops. The result was that, two months later, Rome was invaded, the pope was taken into captivity, and the Roman Republic was set up. General Berthier with the Army of Italy established it with resident Jacobins on 12 February 1798, and it gave itself a constitution six weeks later. The French asserted control by means of a commercial treaty signed on 28 March. **Pope Pius VI** did not co-operate in any of this. He was brought to France, where he died.[39]

During the warfare of the Second Coalition in 1799 the Republic collapsed.

Romme, Charles-Gilbert (1750–95)

Romme's skill as a mathematician was brought into use on the **National Convention**'s committees for the **revolutionary calendar** and for national education. He remained a **Jacobin** after the fall of **Robespierre** and was condemned by the **Thermidorean Convention**.

Before the Revolution, he had gone to Russia to be a private tutor to the Stroganoff family. He returned to Paris in 1788 in time to take part in the new politics and joined a lodge of **Freemasons**. He was not a deputy in the **Estates-General** or the **Constituent** but was elected to the **Legislative** and the Convention by the Puy-de-Dôme. He sat with the **Mountain**.

Romme voted for the king's death, and was **representative on mission** in Normandy, along with **Prieur de La Côte d'Or**, in April 1793. They were caught by **Girondins** in Caen and held prisoner by the **Federalists** until June. He remained out of Paris during July and had no part in the **Thermidor coup**. He pressed for equal education for all, having the prestigious girls' school at Saint-Cyr closed as 'a meeting place for aristocratic daughters', and closed the Ecole des Beaux-Arts for similar reasons. He was interested in military topics such as the manufacture of more efficient artillery pieces and the use of the semaphore. Romme presented the republican calendar to the Convention on 20 September 1793. He was attracted by **Hébert**'s de-Christianization, and proposed on 14 November 1793 that **Marat**'s remains be put in the Pantheon. He supported **Chaumette** with his festival of the Goddess of **Reason**. Romme was President of the Convention and Thérèse Momoro was his guest after the ceremony in Notre Dame Cathedral. He praised Archbishop **Gobel**'s renunciation of his priesthood. He was away on a long mission in the southwest at the time of Thermidor, but he had no sympathy with Robespierre's religious spirit. Even so, when he returned, he did not like the separation of church and state decreed by the Thermidorean Convention because he thought it would give the Catholics a toehold for their eventual return. He also disliked the Thermidoreans' lack of concern for the misery of the popular classes.

The **Germinal Rising** of early April 1795 was repeated in mid-May (1 prairial) and, as one of several persistent Jacobins who supported the rioters' demands for the release of those arrested in April, he had a decree passed that there should be only one type of bread baked for sale from then on: 'the bread of equality'. He also proposed that the section assemblies of year II should be allowed again. For this he was arrested. Tried by a military commission, since the **Revolutionary Tribunal** had been abolished on 31 May, he and the five deputies condemned with him agreed to commit suicide with a concealed knife if they were condemned to death, and they were. Romme succeeded in his attempt on the courtroom steps. The others were guillotined. All six became known as the Jacobin 'Martyrs of Prairial'.[40]

Ronsin, Charles-Philippe (1751–94)

Ronsin was an extremist in the Revolution, allied with **Hébert** and executed on 24 March 1793 along with him. He and François **Vincent** are typical of those members of the **bourgeoisie** who, despite their wealth (Ronsin was paid a general's salary of 40,000 livres), adopted what they took to be the manners and outlook of the **sansculotte** workers. The post-Thermidorean epithet of 'blood drinker' (*buveur de sang*) was, perhaps, more appropriate for him than for many other readers of Hébert's *Le Père Duchesne*.

Ronsin's father was a barrel-maker, and he joined the army as a boy, to be an NCO (the French term is *sous-officier*) after four years. He found his niche once elected as a captain in the Parisian National Guard in 1789. The patriotic plays he wrote were his introduction to the **Cordeliers Club**. Minister of War **Pache** sent him to **Belgium** where he criticized **Dumouriez**'s activities. When **Bouchotte** became war minister in April 1793, Ronsin was chosen as his assistant. He was sent to the **Vendée**, then in full rebellion, as his first military appointment. He was criticized by the Le Mans lawyer Pierre Philippeaux for his savage methods and extravagant expenditure. Then his political pull gained him general officer's rank in the Army of the Coasts of La Rochelle. His next appointment, as a result of the **'Day' of 5 September**, was as general commanding the Paris **Revolutionary Army**. By November, he and his men were in **Lyon** assisting **Fouché** in his brutal repression of the **federalists**, finishing off the victims of the *mitraillades*.

In mid-December 1793, **Fabre d'Eglantine** and **Couthon** demanded Ronsin's arrest for his excesses. He was in the Luxembourg prison until 2 February, when he and **Vincent** were released after pressure from the Cordeliers. On his own initiative in the Cordeliers, Ronsin called for a rising against the **Convention**. When **Fouquier-Tinville** was told by the **Committee of Public Safety** to prepare an indictment against Hébert, he made Ronsin out to be the centre of a huge conspiracy intending to replace the Convention with a military dictator, as the 'new Cromwell'. He was arrested at night on 14/15 March. At the trial of the Hébertists, guilt was established in the minds of the jury after three days for a conspiracy to starve Paris, open the prisons and overthrow the Convention. The verdict was given and the executions carried out on 24 March. On the 27th, the revolutionary army was disbanded.[41]

The Robespierrists had made their statement about Ronsin's sansculotte vulgarity, and against any official violence other than their own.

Rousseau, Jean-Jacques (1712–78)

Very few in the increasingly large educated French public in the decade of the Revolution could escape being influenced by Jean-Jacques Rousseau's ideas, either for or against them.

Although he had been a friend to the writers of the **Enlightenment**, he gradually distanced himself from them. In summer 1749, he was on his way to visit Diderot in his prison at Vincennes, and read a notice in the newspaper *Mercure de France* inviting entries for a prize-competition offered by the Dijon Academy. The subject set for an essay was whether the sciences and the arts had done more to corrupt or enhance morals. Reading this affected him profoundly, as he later related in his *Confessions*: 'I beheld another universe and became another man.'[42] Rousseau won first prize with his argument that science and art had given rise to the acquisitiveness that had corrupted man's simple innocence with a desire for luxury. The *Lumières* such as Diderot and d'Alembert, his friends and associates until then, had argued in the other direction. In a few years' time, Rousseau's writing had become an alternative to theirs. He publicly disowned his association with Diderot in 1758[43] in the preface to his *Letter to M. d'Alembert*, in which there were comments which also alienated Voltaire.[44]

Rousseau applied his argument for simplicity to his own life. His opera, *The Village Soothsayer* (*Le Devin du village*) was premiered at Fontainebleau on 18 October 1752 in the presence of Louis XV. After the performance, the king sent a duke to invite Rousseau to see him, offering him a pension. Rousseau refused the invitation and the pension on the grounds that he would lose his independence if he accepted them.[45]

Rousseau's *Contrat Social* is a study of the austere and virtuous way in which a country may govern itself. His language was on the lips of Maximilien **Robespierre** and his colleagues. He developed the ideas of 'civic virtue' and 'general will', and they provided a vehicle for Robespierre and **Saint-Just** to express their ideology during the Jacobin ascendancy. A classically educated (male) public would respond to examples drawn from the Greek and Roman world. Rousseau thought that women should have no place in intellectual life. This became the basis of Robespierrist misogyny and the rejection of women like **Olympe de Gouges** and **Théroigne de Méricourt**, and of **Bonaparte**'s rebuffs to Germaine de Staël.[46]

Rousseau was often considered by nineteenth-century commentators, such as Hippolyte Taine, Edgar Quinet, Louis Blanc and his successors in the socialist tradition, to have been the herald and guide of the Revolution. Quinet saw him as the 'legislator' and *Contrat Social* as the 'law-book'. For writers like these, Rousseau's ideas controlled developments between the overthrow of the monarchy and the fall of Robespierre: the Jacobin Republic became the high point of Rousseau's influence. Concepts like universal manhood suffrage, the nation as the source of sovereignty, direct democracy, managed economy, assistance for the poor, for Louis Blanc and his successors, grew from their reading of Rousseau. A political order that would not only protect individuals and society from arbitrary use of power, but also include positive action in favour of the dispossessed, was derived from Rousseau. In retrospect, Jean-Jacques was seen as the source of the will which seemed to animate revolutionary absolutism from August 1792 until after July 1794.[47]

Honour was accorded to Rousseau by the placing of his bust and a copy of the *Contrat social* in the *Manège*, where the Constituent Assembly met, in October 1790. Further votes to honour him were given in December 1790, and repeated in August 1791. The decision to transfer Rousseau's remains from the estate of his friend and patron, the Marquis de Girardin (after overcoming his obstruction) to the Pantheon in Paris was made at the height of the **Terror**. Robespierre invoked Rousseau's authority for the **Supreme Being** cult. But the transfer was not actually made until during the **Thermidorean Convention**, on 11 October 1794. After that, Rousseau's reputation was in decline. First Consul **Bonaparte** went to see rooms where Rousseau had lived at Ermenonville, and was reliably reported to have said, 'He was a fool, your Rousseau; he was the one that brought us where we are.' 'He who completed the Revolution pronounced the funeral oration over Rousseau's influence in a brutal formula; but in doing so, he recognized and seals, it seems, the identification between Rousseau and the Revolution,' was the comment of a French historian at the time of the bi-centenary in 1989.[48]

Until 1792, the anti-revolutionaries also adhered to Rousseau. Rousseau had a horror of violence: 'Liberty would be too dearly bought with the blood of even a single man,' he had said in his *Considerations on the Government of Poland*. After 1792, the Revolution's opponents made him responsible for its errors, and the revolutionaries claimed to be his true heirs. 'The Revolution guided the acceptance of Rousseau, rather than Rousseau inspiring the revolution.'[49] Robespierre and **Saint-Just** had praised Rousseau, but it was the Thermidoreans who overthrew the Jacobin tyranny and put his remains in the Pantheon with speeches and specially composed music. Successive waves of revolutionary leaders recognized their debt to him, but what they found useful in him varied. The principle that the deputies represent the people is not Rousseau's. From the moment when the representatives of the people decide things and not the people directly, the central principle of Rousseau's social contract was abandoned. In all **Sieyès**'s constitution-making, he is critical of Rousseau, remarking at one point that he was 'a philosopher as perfect in his sentiments as he was feeble in his opinions despite his eloquence.'[50] Sieyès came to regard the nobility as enemies of a just society, and there is nothing of that in Rousseau. Many of his friends were nobles and some of them were grandees. He kept the expression of his acrimony for the wealthy on behalf of the poor. 'Rousseau was not the legislator of the Revolution, but he exercised upon it what we could call a *magisterium* of opinion.'[51]

On a social rather than political level, Rousseau's novels were more important to the reading public than the *Social Contract*. In 1756, Rousseau left Paris for the Hermitage, a recently improved, isolated hunting-lodge, owned by his friend, Madame d'Epinay, near the valley of Montmorency to the north of Paris. It was hardly life in a cave: the house was warm and well appointed and he was looked after by his mistress and her mother.[52] He could develop his solitary instinct to some extent, however, and wrote the epistolary novel *Julie ou La Nouvelle Héloise* while he was there, removed from the dog-eat-dog conviviality of the salons or the court. This story is about love and virtue, full of what became known as sensitivity (*sensibilité*), where men and women both cry easily, and set against a backdrop of mountain scenery imagined by the Lake of Geneva.[53]

Another novel, *Emile,* taught its readers how to bring up their sons: no more wet-nurses, live in the country, give the children loose clothes, provide them with a tutor who would inculcate values such as respect for property, sometimes by crafty subterfuge.[54] That would train them in civic virtue, and the will of a people educated like that could assert itself in a form of government that would allow everyone to live with dignity. Rousseau felt how appropriate this was for an austere and virtuous Greek city-state like Sparta. The Jacobins tried to make it work for 28 million French citizens. They could not do it without imposing the Terror.

Rousseau supplied the idea of virtue to the Revolution. He allowed no distinction between private morality and public virtue and, in this respect, the most complete example during the Revolution of a disciple of Rousseau is Maximilien Robespierre, 'the incorruptible' himself. 'The *Social Contract* did not constitute the Revolution's programme because the revolutionaries did not follow its precise prescriptions, although they found images and general principles in it concerning the nature of man, of society and of history.'[55] Lakanal, one of those responsible for national provision of primary schools, made the speech when Rousseau's body was reinterred in the Pantheon. He observed that, rather than the *Social Contract* setting the tone of the Revolution, the Revolution explained the *Social Contract.*[56]

Robespierre's utterances were made on the basis of his own understanding of what he found in Rousseau's works, applied in a different set of circumstances from those of 'the noble savage'.[57]

Rousseau never *had* political authority. He could only *contemplate* it.

Cohen, J. (trans.), *The Confessions of Jean-Jacques Rousseau* (London: Penguin Press, 2005).

Cranston, Maurice, *Jean-Jacques: The Early Life and Works of Jean-Jacques Rousseau, 1712–1754* (London: Viking/Penguin, 1982).

——, *The Noble Savage: Jean-Jacques Rousseau 1754–1762* (London, Viking/Penguin, 1991).

——, *The Solitary Self: Jean-Jacques Rousseau in Exile and Adversity* (London: Viking/Penguin, 1997).

Rousseau, Jean-Jacques, *The Social Contract*, trans. Maurice Cranston (London: Penguin Press, 1968).

——, *A Discourse on Inequality*, trans. Maurice Cranston (London: Penguin Press, 2003).

——, *Emile*, trans. Barbara Coxley (London: J.M. Dent, 2000).

Roux, Jacques (1752–94)

Jacques Roux's importance is as a pre-Marxist socialist. He was very critical of the Revolution because it was not extreme enough from his point of view. He is known to posterity as the 'red priest of the good **sansculotte** Jesus-Christ'.

As assistant priest (*vicaire*) in the parish of Saint-Thomas de Conac in the Diocese of Saintes, he preached a sermon in April 1790 saying that Revolution was as much an act of God as the sending of Joan of Arc. Nevertheless, he asserted, nothing of significance had yet happened to improve the lives of tenant farmers, and they must not let up in the struggle.[58] A fortnight later, extensive rioting broke out in the villages around. By then, Roux had left for Paris, eventually to be elected *vicaire* of Saint-Nicolas-des-Champs, in the Gravilliers Section, the poorest area of the city. This became his base for urging extreme economic measures on the government.

Roux took the oath to the **Civil Constitution of the Clergy** in the Church of Saint-Sulpice, and made speeches using the same extremist idiom as Jean-Paul **Marat**. He became a member of the Paris Commune which sent him, as a constitutional priest, to escort the king to his execution. As **Louis XVI** was leaving the Temple prison, he presented his will to Jacques Roux to pass to the queen. Roux pushed the paper away saying, 'I am here to take you to execution, not to receive your notes.'[59]

The **Cordeliers Club** entrusted him with delivering the *enragés*' manifesto at the bar of the **National Convention**, demanding that hoarding food and speculation in grain prices should be crimes punishable by death. He claimed that the new constitution being drawn up in 1793 would be worthless for the poor if they were not. He said it would be like a pretty woman with one eye.[60] With his associates, Jean **Varlet** and Théophile **Leclerc**, he became an irritant to the Jacobins in their defence of property owners. **Robespierre** vehemently denounced Roux in the Jacobins from 28 June 1793 onwards. The Paris Commune suspended him from his post with them. On 30 June the Cordeliers expelled him after pressure from the Jacobins. The Paris Commune ordered him to 'improve his conduct'. On 4 July, **Marat** called him a 'false patriot' and a criminal on the run in *L'Ami du peuple*. When Marat was dead, claiming to succeed him, Roux issued 25 numbers of the journal, renamed *Le Publiciste de la République française par l'ombre de Marat, l'Ami du peuple*. In them he castigated the Convention's inactivity and the revolutionary tribunal's slowness. The **Mountain** reacted violently. On 5 August, Robespierre called him an enemy of the people in the Jacobins. The Cordeliers pressed for the Commune to arrest him on 22 August. He was freed on 27 August, with two Gravilliers section artisans standing bail for him. He was rearrested, at the request of the Jacobins, on 5 September. Roux continued to bring out his paper and denounce the government as repressive from the Saint-Pélagie prison, approving de-Christianization now at its height. He was transferred to greater security at the Bicêtre on 25 October and was brought before a police tribunal, which declared itself incompetent and transferred him to the **revolutionary tribunal**, where he stabbed himself during the hearing. Recovering in his cell, he stabbed himself again and died of his wounds.[61]

Royalists

There were those who wanted to put the clock back, like the rebels in the **Vendée** in the Catholic and Royalist Army, with their cry of 'Give us back our good priests!' The king's younger brother, **Artois**, represented such Frenchmen who would not compromise with the Revolution, nor with constitutional monarchists – those who had 'learned nothing and forgotten nothing', as **Talleyrand** is supposed to have said, since 1789. These were mostly found as *émigrés* in German states or in England, and a few, like the Duc de Richelieu, in Russia. It was their cause that was espoused by the reactionary writers de **Bonald** and de **Maistre** in the **Restoration Monarchy**, which earned them the epithet 'the prophets of the past'.

Pitt and Dundas were loth to commit Great Britain to supporting the Bourbons since they had taken the side of the Americans from 1778 until the British defeat at Yorktown in 1781. Only after Admiral Lord Hood's offer of support for counter-revolution in **Toulon** in return for a declaration in favour of **Louis XVII** in August 1793 did Pitt decide to support Bourbon restoration as a war aim.[62] Previously, even a modified republican system would have been acceptable to the British government.

Most of the re-emerging royalists in France after the **Terror** and during the **Directory**, such as were found in the **Clichy Club**, were constitutionalists, and had reacted adversely to Louis XVIII's Verona Declaration that he would restore the *ancien régime* and punish the **regicides**.

S

Saint-André, Jean Bon (1749–1813)

Jean Bon Saint-André was a member of the **Committee of Public Safety** who specialized in the organization of the French navy. He was a new type of Frenchman produced by the Revolution, an artisan's son who gathered executive power to himself as a **representative on mission**, even a proponent of religious freedom, inasmuch as that were possible, since he was also a Protestant minister at the outset of the changes.

He came from Montauban in the Tarn-et-Garonne, where his father was a cloth fuller. He trained as a Catholic priest, but reverted to his family's Protestantism. For a while, he was a merchant navy officer on long voyages, then he trained in Lausanne for the Calvinist ministry and worked in Castres and then Montauban, where he joined the local **Jacobin Club**. He adopted the Catholic name Saint-André as a cover.[1] He was elected to the **National Convention** for the Lot department. He sat with the **Mountain**, opposed **Buzot**, and supported the Paris Commune. He voted for the king's death, and went on mission to his own department. He was elected to the Committee of Public Safety in July 1793, being sent on mission to the armies at the eastern frontier. In between his missions, he occupied himself with reorganizing the navy, which was in a demoralized state. He was criticized for promoting Admiral Villaret Joyeuse, but he trusted him and revised the whole system of recruitment of officers and seamen alike, as well as the dockyard workers. Brest, after his reforms, became a democratic colony in the midst of a hostile Brittany full of **Chouans**.[2] He planned for a possible attack on Jersey, and for the reception of Van Stabel's grain fleet from the Caribbean. He undertook a great deal of warship construction and the Convention eventually agreed to meet the cost. He was actually at sea in Villaret-Joyeuse's flagship in 1794 when the French fleet protected the arrival of Van Stabel's convoy at a time of near famine – the action which the British call 'the Glorious First of June'. He was a moderate during the **Terror**, but was arrested afterwards and sent to the Four Nations College where Jacques-Louis **David** made a pen and ink portrait of him.

He was released in the amnesty of October 1795. He was sent as consul to Algiers and then Smyrna in 1798, but imprisoned by its Ottoman rulers until 1801 because of **Bonaparte**'s invasion of **Egypt**.[3] Upon Saint-André's release, First Consul Bonaparte made him a prefect in charge of three departments on the Rhine, where he remained until his death from typhus at Mainz. He was created a baron of the Empire in 1809.

Saint-Domingue (1789–93)

By the outset of the Revolution, France was losing hold on her colonies. Repeated conflicts and peace treaties with Great Britain and Spain had resulted in the loss of Canada and Louisiana (although it was back in French hands in time to enable First Consul **Bonaparte** to sell it to the United States in 1802), but there were still several French islands in the Caribbean, of which Saint-Domingue was the largest. However, the decline was illustrated by the closing of sugar refineries in the port of La Rochelle and many former colonial settlers returning home to add to economic distress in France.

In Saint-Domingue itself, white landowners – with a mixed-blood population (known as 'people of colour') demanding equal status – revolted against royal governors. In the **Constituent Assembly**, the *Amis des noirs* led by **Girondins** such as **Brissot** and the **Rolands**, and **Jacobins** such as **Robespierre**, aimed at abolishing the slave trade and freeing the slaves in a gradual process. Proprietors and traders, who met in the Hôtel Massiac and were represented in the Assembly by Antoine **Barnave**, pressed for things to remain as they were.

In March 1790, the Assembly allowed the French colonies a measure of self-government, but did not decide the race issue. So the people of colour in Saint-Domingue rose in unsuccessful revolt in December 1790. This led to a compromise in May 1791, when the Assembly enfranchized people of mixed race who could claim free birth. Léger Félicité Sonthonax, who had been to the colony before the Revolution, associated with **Brissot** to have a commission sent there by the **Legislative** in June 1792. He led the three-man commission himself and they declared the slaves free on their own initiative. A slave rebellion broke out in the northern province of Saint-Domingue resulting in the deaths of 2,000 white settlers and five times as many slaves.

After pressure from the Massiac Club, the Assembly decreed that the white settlers should decide issues of race relations, but the inter-racial struggle went on until French troops re-established order just before the overthrow of the monarchy. After that, there were pro-royalist revolts in Saint-Domingue, Martinique and Guadeloupe against republican administrators. The **Convention** declared the slaves free on 4 February 1794. White planters and landowners turned to the British for help. Sonthonax was accused by the white plantation owners of inciting the revolt. He was imprisoned as a Girondin on his return to France, but belatedly freed after a year by the **Thermidorean Convention** in July 1795.[4]

Sugar became as scarce as bread in metropolitan France while the slave rebellion gathered momentum under **Toussaint L'Ouverture**.

Saint-Just, Antoine-Louis (1767–94)

Saint-Just was the Revolution's child prodigy. He served for 14 months as one of the 12 members of what was effectively the ruling council of the sovereign nation.

His father had been a cavalry captain, and he was brought up by his widowed mother whose silver cutlery he stole to finance himself when he was 19. Nevertheless, she prevailed upon him to take a law course at Reims. For generations, his family had been comfortably off farmers in central France and, when he entered local politics as the revolution began, rural poverty and the lack of justice in the seigneurial system were his main preoccupations.[5] He moved to Paris in May 1789, to write scurrilous poems and pamphlets. Even so, an austere, single-minded streak soon emerged in him, and he wrote a very serious appraisal of the early stages of the Revolution, expressing satisfaction with the **Constituent Assembly**. He revised this opinion when his work was published and had coincided with the king's flight to **Varennes**, but his exaltation of natural virtue was still at the heart of his new-found republican ideals and he applied it to the conditions of revolutionary France.

Saint-Just was elected as a deputy for the department of the Aisne in the **National Convention** in 1792. His maiden speech before the king's trial attracted attention when he said, 'Royalty is an eternal crime' (a loose translation of '*on ne peut pas régner innocemment*'). From then on he was accepted, along with **Robespierre**, as a leading Jacobin republican theorist.

He was elected to the Convention's **Committee of Public Safety** in May 1793 and emerged in close mental accord with Robespierre during the official **Terror**. Saint-Just's speeches in the Convention were uncompromising. He had a horror of the factions – **Cordeliers**, **Girondins** and Dantonists were disastrous for national unity. 'Passion for national unity in the framework of a democratic republic was the motivation of Saint-Just's activity on the committee of Public Safety.'[6] In a report presented on 13 March 1794 on the factions he had this to say:

> Every faction is … criminal because it leads to a division of the citizens; every faction is criminal because it neutralizes the power of public virtue. The solidarity of our Republic is in the very nature of things. The sovereignty of the people wills that it shall be united; it is, then, the opposite of the factions, every faction is therefore an attack on sovereignty.[7]

His reproach against **Hébert**'s faction was that it had divided Paris against itself and, against **Danton**'s, that it had protected traitors. Both groups, in Saint-Just's view, had threatened France with **counter-revolution**.

Saint-Just instigated the **Ventôse decrees**, which were passed in the context of action against the Dantonists as 'indulgents'. Aristocrats were not to be pardoned, so patriots ought to be rewarded with property taken from aristocratic traitors, and even from those suspected of being 'recognized enemies of the Revolution'.[8]

In the face of conspiracies against the Revolution, Saint-Just justified the Terror as virtuous retributive action. He took part in the formulation of the **Law of 22 prairial, year II**. He shared Robespierre's conviction that there was always an 'aristocratic conspiracy' to fight against. But personal responsibility for individual deaths, claimed **Soboul**, was another matter. The arrest warrants issued by the Committee of Public Safety were collective, signed by all members present. Saint-Just shared the responsibility. The warrants were drawn up by subordinate functionaries and very likely police officers. The terrorist laws were applied in a bureaucratic fashion.[9]

As a **representative on mission** he was responsible for galvanizing the commanders on the northern front. He worked with Generals **Jourdan** and **Pichegru** to bring about victory over the Duc de Saxe-Coburg at **Fleurus**, the decisive battle which took the Austrians out of Belgium on 25 June 1794, and at which he was present himself. Victory was a partial justification for the Terror in the eyes of its perpetrators, and Saint-Just hurried back to Paris to announce it. The **Thermidor coup** followed a month later.

Saint-Just was only 27 when he went to the scaffold on 28 July 1794.

Hampson, Norman, *Saint-Just* (Oxford: Oxford University Press, 1991).

Palmer, R.R. , *Twelve Who Ruled: The Year of the Terror in the French Revolution* (University Park, PA: Princeton University Press, Bicentennial Edition, 1989).

Saliceti, Antoine Christophe (1757–1809)

Saliceti was born in Genoa, Italy. He studied law at Pisa and moved to France where he was elected to the **National Convention**. He was sent on mission to **Toulon** in 1792 and was still there when the town's moderates invited the Anglo-Spanish fleet into the harbour and declared themselves for **Louis XVII**. He met **Bonaparte**, then an artillery captain who produced the decisive strategy against the British, and held him in life-long respect.

Nevertheless, he opposed the **Brumaire coup** and his name was put by **Sieyès** on his list of known opponents. Bonaparte personally scratched it out.[10] Saliceti was appointed to Bonaparte's staff for the Army of Italy in 1796 performing the usual offices of a **representative on mission**. As

Bonaparte gathered momentum in Italy, Saliceti worked in partnership with him. He negotiated an armistice with the Papal States in 1797 and others in the Consulate and Empire.

Sansculottes

The French Revolution was largely the work of professional men, especially lawyers, but there were certain occasions between 1789 and 1794 when artisan sansculottes played a significant part in making political and social changes effective, especially in the capital and other major urban areas. Superficially, the French term denotes that they wore the trousers of tradesmen instead of the knee breeches (*culottes*) and stockings of nobles and professional men. The Parisian market women who went to fetch the king from **Versailles** in October 1789 were their female counterparts.

At a deeper level, however, Michael Sonenscher has pointed out that sansculotte is a neologism for people who did not have patrons and had a different culture from those who did. If you called yourself a sansculotte, you made a claim that social recognition was founded on your own merit not on someone else's patronage.[11]

The American historian Timothy Tackett identifies the emergence of the sansculottes as a 'self-conscious, well-organized political force' taking place on 23 June 1791, when Paris knew about the king's flight and recapture at **Varennes**. They joined other citizens in an enthusiastic procession into the **Legislative Assembly** to take the oath to the constitution with the wealthier citizens and the military, singing the **song** of revolution, '*Ça ira*'. It was a force armed with pikes.[12]

Some of the sansculottes were skilled craftsmen, sometimes in the luxury trades in Paris, who set themselves lower in social status than they actually were. One of these was Maurice **Duplay**, **Robespierre**'s landlord in the prosperous rue Saint-Honoré, who had a furniture business but, to be an accepted sansculotte, called himself a cabinet-maker. The **surveillance committee** in the port of La Rochelle included a clockmaker, Jean Parant,[13] and a bookbinder, Pierre Susbielle, both unquestioned sansculottes. A leader of violent activity, also in La Rochelle, was a wigmaker, Joseph-Honoré Darbelet, obviously literate, even eloquent as a demagogue, and the owner of his own business.

Others were 'passive' citizens, not qualified to vote as taxpayers, but not utterly poor either, such as coalmen, bakers, porters, fishwives or other market women, involved in the Revolution because they had something to lose.

Bourgeois leaders made use of them. For instance, when the **Girondins** were expelled from the **National Convention** in May–June 1793, they surrounded the building under the command of **Hanriot** and threatened violence against uncommitted deputies to make them comply with what the **Jacobins** – essentially bourgeois men – demanded.

Yet they were not simply complaisant. They had a cause of their own inasmuch as they objected to the Girondins claiming inviolability, which they saw as something belonging to the old regime. The 'people' had the right to recall their deputies.[14]

As a result of the **'Day' of 5 September 1793**, the Convention, despite most deputies preferring a free-market economy, compromised after sanculotte pressure on the regulation of prices and wages by the **General Maximum**. The **Revolutionary Army** was also set up with permission to move freely around the Ile de France region, under the command of **Ronsin**, to look for hoarders and impose summary punishment upon them with their travelling **guillotine**. However, the Convention soon reasserted its control by, for example, preventing the **Paris Sections** meeting in continual session and providing allowances to cover loss of work for no more than two meetings a week.

Many middle-class lawyers identified with their point of view, as did **Bernard de Saintes**, **representative on mission** in the Haute Saône and the Côte d'Or. The wealthy Parisian brewer, Antoine-Joseph **Santerre**, was conspicuous in the action that overthrew the monarchy, and then became a general in the **National Guard**. Jean-Baptiste Noël **Bouchotte**, for a time War Minister, continually identified himself with *sanculottisme*, although he had been a captain in the pre-revolutionary army. On a political level, **Hébert** (*Le Père Duchesne*) and Chaumette presented themselves in the guise of sanculottes.

In year II of the Revolution, sanculottes were hailed as reliable (*honnêtes gens*) and were accorded respect by their controllers. During the **Thermidor coup**, they were prevented from defending Robespierre and his associates. After it, they were denigrated in the property-based republic as 'drinkers of blood' (*buveurs de sang*), and they had to play down their former achievements. Whereas the Jacobins used the sansculottes to achieve some of their aims, the **Directory** used the **army** instead. They knew where they were with soldiers.

Cobb, Richard, *The Police and the People: French Popular Protest, 1789–1820* (Oxford: Oxford University Press, 1970).

Rudé, George, *The Crowd in the French Revolution* (Oxford: Oxford University Press, 1959).

Soboul, Albert, *The Sansculottes: The Popular Movement and Revolutionary Government 1793–1794*, trans. Rémy Inglis Hall (University Park, PA: Princeton University Press, 1980).

Santerre, Antoine-Joseph (1752–1809)

Santerre was a prosperous brewer in the **Faubourg Saint-Antoine** of Paris and identified with the ideals of his **sansculotte** workforce. He took part in the storming of the **Bastille** which was near his home, and was the acclaimed leader of the **National Guard** unit that went to attack the Château of Vincennes, for which he was reprimanded by General **Lafayette**.

He took a prominent part in the **'Day' of 20 June 1792**, which included the sansculottes' forced entry into the **Tuileries Palace** to corner the king and compel him to swear an oath to the Nation while wearing a **Phrygian bonnet**. He was also a member of the **Insurrectionary Commune** and aggressively present as a National Guard officer during the attack on the palace on 10 August, which led to the fall of the monarchy altogether. His unit was in combat with other National Guardsmen of the Filles de Saint-Thomas section who defended the Queen. Santerre was the officer who came to collect the king for execution from the Temple prison on 21 January 1793 with Jacques **Roux** in attendance. At the scaffold itself, it was he that ordered a drum roll to prevent the crowd hearing what the king wanted to say.

He was made a general when the *Amalgame* Law united the National Guard with units of the regular army. He had a command in the **Vendée**, but met with little success there.[15] He returned to private life and lived quietly under the **Directory**, the Consulate and the first five years of the Empire. In 1805, he bought a château in Normandy from the Prince of Monaco, but he lost his fortune in the litigation that went on around the purchase, and died in 1809, ruined and forgotten.[16]

Schools

Once the **refractory clergy** had left their parishes after 1790, there was a great gap in the system of country primary schools which taught reading for learning the church catechism. In the towns, the municipalities could carry on if there were enough constitutional clergy left to staff the colleges. A Law of 17 April 1791 said that nuns could continue running schools for girls, but this was cancelled in 1793 when nuns had to take the oath as well as well as priests. In any case, the constitutional church was very short-lived, and could not be counted on to fulfil an educational role in any full sense.

Most urban children had at least a smattering of reading and counting. In the country, children were extra farmhands and went to school at best intermittently in winter. Only large villages had a lay teacher. By 1793, departments were appointing untrained lay teachers chosen on the basis of **certificates of civism** issued by the **surveillance committees**. The Rights of Man, the constitution, republican feast days and martyrs were on the curriculum. School trips were encouraged to see how work was done and how the popular societies operated. There was physical and military training. Patois was avoided and a law passed in July 1793 to suit the requirements of the One and Indivisible Republic stipulated that there was to be a French language teacher in every commune.

Bouquier's Law in December 1793 set out republican education in terms of free elementary education for all children, with their parents being responsible for seeing they received it. There was also a cadet force for the **National Guard** called 'Hope of the Fatherland' (*Espérance de la Patrie*). Education in primary schools was to be free and compulsory from the age of six. In 1795, 150,000 copies of a book of exemplary heroic and civic behaviour were issued. This looked good on paper, but the **Jacobins** never had the time or resources to implement the scheme or to train teachers.

Representatives on mission often took over presbyteries for schools, and the salary of a (male) teacher called an *instituteur* – because everything was starting anew – was supposed to be 1,200 livres a year. This was the same sum as constitutional priests were to receive before they were abandoned. Women teachers (*institutrices*) were to receive 1,000 livres in theory. In rebellious areas like the **Vendée**, republican re-education was met with passive resistance and few pupils appeared.

The **Thermidorean Convention** inherited a dysfunctional system. By the Lakanal Law of 17 November 1794, only one school for 1,500 inhabitants was required and the districts reduced the numbers of schools. From November 1796, only the chief town (*chef-lieu*) of a district was to have a school. Even worse conditions faced the **Directory**. The Daunou Law (devised by a former Oratorian school chaplain) was passed on 25 October 1795. Teachers were to be paid from parents' fees. Girls were to be taught 'useful skills' in separate schools. Church schools started opening again, providing that the right oaths to the constitution had been taken. Two-thirds of all schools were private by 1798. Central secondary schools were to be set up in all departments, but the number of children receiving such education in 1799 was only a tenth of the 1789 figure.[17]

Seigneurial or Feudal Dues

The **statements of complaint** (*cahiers de doléance*), drawn up in rural communes in the spring of 1789, register many grievances about the various taxes and charges with which individual seigneurs so often burdened their tenants. Perhaps the most resented was the *champart*, which was a payment in kind demanded at harvest time, varying from a third to a twentieth of the grain crop. The *lods et ventes* had to be paid whenever tenants of the land sold their other property, and there were others. Other rights belonging to a seigneur were in the form of *banalités*: he had the right to make the tenants use his mill for their flour, his oven for their cooking, or his wine-press for their grapes, often at a charge which he himself set. There was also the *corvée seigneuriale*, or work-service: on several appointed days every year, the tenants had to leave their own rented fields to work on the seigneur's projects, even providing the draught animals. The *corvée royale* was also in operation for keeping roads and bridges in good order. The control of rented lands on an estate was total. The seigneur had the right to decree the date on which the grain or wine harvest should begin.

In March 1790, the **Constituent Assembly** received a report on the abolition of these dues, and the tenants' need to purchase redemption from them. It was not made clear whether this report had been acted upon or not until the **Legislative Assembly** suppressed all feudal dues as one of its final acts in September 1792. The **National Convention**, abolishing any possible feudal claims in July 1793, ordered all remaining seigneurial title deeds to be burnt in public all over the nation.

September Massacres

After the invasion of the **Tuileries** and the suspension of the monarchy on 10 August 1792, the **Insurrectionary Commune** ordered the 48 **Paris Sections** to be in perpetual session, and many nobles, bishops and clergy were rounded up and imprisoned on their orders.

Panic was caused by a rumour (helped along by **Marat**'s *Ami du peuple*) that these captives were planning to break out and murder the soldiers' families after the troops had left to oppose the Duke of **Brunswick**'s invading force on the eastern frontiers of France. So, on 2–3 September, bands of men massacred between 1,100 and 1,400 people at makeshift prisons in religious houses such as L'Abbaye, the Carmelites and the Salpetrière, and established ones such as La Force. The 'trials' the murderers held before beginning their action were in accordance with the **Cordeliers**' idea that the sovereign people had the right to enforce their own justice. Nearly three-quarters of the victims were not political prisoners at all, but half the prison population was killed.[18] A conspicuous victim was the queen's confidante, the Princesse de **Lamballe**, whose head was cut off to be carried on a pole under **Marie-Antoinette**'s window in the Temple prison. The **Girondins** accused **Jacobins** like **Danton**, **Tallien** and Marat of being implicated in these actions. They denied all responsibility, although Tallien sent circulars to provincial centres saying that they should do the same as the Parisians had, and Danton countersigned them. There were similar episodes in several provincial towns.

Hibbert, Christopher, *The French Revolution* (London: Penguin Books, 1980), pp. 169–80.

Price, Munro, *The Fall of the French Monarchy, Louis XVI, Marie-Antoinette and the Baron de Breteuil* (London: Macmillan, 2002), pp. 316–17.

Schama, Simon, *Citizens* (London: Viking, 1988), pp. 631–9.

@ For reaction from *The Times* newspaper in London see: http://www.english.ucsb. edu/faculty/ayliu/research/around-1800/FR/times-9-10-1792.html.

Sieyès, Emmanuel-Joseph (1748–1836)

Sieyès's career led him from being a Canon of Chartres Cathedral to the Consulate, via acting as a constitutional theorist all through the revolutionary decade. A French historian comments that he was 'admired much more … outside his own country than in France'.[19]

He was one of five children in the family of a struggling receiver of feudal dues in Fréjus. Noticed and educated by the Jesuits, he was ordained priest in 1772, after training at the Little Seminary of Saint-Sulpice (the Great Seminary was reserved for nobles). His father used contacts to gain him a secretary's post with a noble priest who took Sieyès with him to Chartres when he was made bishop there. For a while, Sieyès was chaplain to **Louis XVI**'s aunt. The Abbé Sieyès had taken in the whole ethos of the **Enlightenment**, from English as well as French writers, and was a **freemason**. He was the bishop's deputy (*grand-vicaire*) in the Diocese of Chartres, but only nobles could actually be bishops.

In the summer of 1788, the Duc d'**Orléans** asked him to look through a pamphlet by his secretary Choderlos de Laclos. He drew up his own on the same theme, published as an *Essay on Privileges* in November 1788, followed by *What is the Third Estate?* in January 1789. In slogan form, it said:

What is the Third Estate? Everything.
What has it been hitherto in the political order? Nothing.
What does it desire? To be something.

Despite his clerical status, Sieyès 'drew up the agenda of the **bourgeoisie** to which he belonged by birth and by aspiration'.[20] He argued that if the nobles claimed to be Franks who had conquered the Gauls, then the Third Estate could conquer the nobles in their turn. This was a consistent theme in Sieyès's political career.[21] The clergy did not elect him to the **Estates-**

General, but the Third Estate elections in Paris were held later than in other places, and he became the last of the capital's deputies who came late to **Versailles**. It was he who proposed on 16 June that the Thirds should designate themselves as the National Assembly. After the royal session on 23 June, though eclipsed by **Mirabeau's** talk of bayonets, Sieyès told the deputies who refused to leave the hall: 'You are still today what you were already yesterday.'[22]

After the **Night of 4 August**, Sieyès was much less in evidence. He tried to make the nationalization of church lands conditional upon the state paying the clergy a salary (as was offered) and the use of the rest of the money to provide schools and poor relief. He was the assembly's president in June 1790, and elected to the directory of the Paris *département* as well. He was a member of the **Social Circle**. Before **Gobel** was elected Archbishop of Paris, Sieyès refused to be a candidate for the post. So had **Loménie de Brienne** and **Talleyrand**.

He supported two chambers in the legislative, as in Great Britain, but this was attacked by **Danton** as if Sieyès had thought of it himself. He spoke rarely in the **Constituent** after that. He approved of **Bailly's** maintenance of order after the king's flight to **Varennes** in what became the Champ de Mars massacre. He took care not to be identified with either **Jacobins** or **Feuillants**, and his public credibility waned. At the end of the **Constituent**, he resigned his post in the Department as well, and went away to live quietly.

During the elections for the **National Convention** in September 1792, he was elected as a deputy in three departments and chose the Sarthe. He sat with the uncommitted deputies of the Plain, but voted for the king's death and against the **Girondins'** referendum on his sentence – surprising, because he had voted against the competence of the Convention to put the king on trial. His ideas about a new republican constitution were rejected as being too complicated. He kept silent while the Girondins were excluded from the Convention, and **Robespierre** called him 'the mole of the Revolution, never ceasing to work in the underground [passages] of the assembly'. He added with menace: 'He is more dangerous to Liberty than those who have faced the law's justice so far.'[23] In November 1793, Sieyès surrendered his certificate of ordination, saying that he recognized no other cult than that of liberty and equality, and no religion but love of humanity and his country. He did not attend the Convention during the **Terror**. There was a rumour that he had hidden in an attic, and when asked what he had done during that time, he replied, 'I survived (*J'ai vécu*)'.[24]

Sieyès returned to the Convention in December 1794 to serve on a committee to examine terrorists. In March 1795, he was on the **Committee of Public Safety**, and proposed measures against popular violence. He was on the Council of Eleven, to draw up the Constitution of Year III, but the Thermidoreans once more saw his plan as too complicated and set up the **Directory** instead. He resigned from the committee and was sent to The Hague, to sign the treaty with Holland. He told the Committee in his report that he was hoping for a general pacification.

He had been appointed as professor of economy at the Central School set up in Paris in the former College of Four Nations (recently a prison for perpetrators of the Terror), but in the elections at the start of the Directory he was elected by several departments and chose the Sarthe again. He had nothing to do with the **Vendémiaire coup**, and was elected as the fourth of the Directors on 31 October 1796. He refused the post, as well as that of minister of foreign affairs offered him on 4 November. For several months he was largely out of public life. He was nominated to the Institute, and did not reappear in the Council of 500 until he was elected its president on 26 November. He was perturbed by the revival of the royalists, and drew closer to the Directors. He opposed the **Clichy Club** and approved of the **Fructidor coup**.[25]

In 1798, Sieyès was re-elected as a deputy, but he could not take his seat as he was appointed ambassador to Berlin, where he kept Prussia neutral despite the blandishments of the British, but did not achieve a Franco-Prussian alliance against Austria as he had hoped because Prussia was content with the **Treaty of Basle** agreed in 1795.[26]

In April 1799, he was elected again to the councils and then to the Directory on 17 May. He was given an official welcome on his return from Berlin in June. It was known that he had accepted election to rearrange the constitution. The constitution had by law to stand as it was for nine years, so the **Prairial coup** on 18 June was the solution. One of the new directors, Roger **Ducos**, was Sieyès's ally. Another coup would be needed, and Sieyès said he was 'looking for a sword'. He, like **Barras**, saw the neo-Jacobins as a threat but was reassured by **Fouché** becoming police minister. **Bernadotte** became war minister.

The republic was seriously in danger again. Milan had been abandoned in April 1799. The Second Coalition had been activated. The Russian force sent by Paul I under Suvarov, with the Austrians, drove France out of Italy and Switzerland by the end of August. On receiving this news, General **Bonaparte** made his decision to leave Egypt and count on being regarded as a hero once he was back. He took until 9 October to reach Fréjus. By that time France had become victorious again after forced loans and a mass levy of troops. **Masséna** had repulsed the Russians and Austrians. The Anglo-Russian invasion of Holland had failed. But royalist risings in the Midi and further risings of **Chouans** led to the Messidor law empowering departments in tumult to take hostages of relatives of *émigrés* and Chouans in reprisal for assassinations of public officials or constitutional priests (not seriously carried out). The uncertainty of 1793 had returned.

Lucien Bonaparte was a political ally to Sieyès as he considered ideas for a fresh constitution to follow the Directory. He made approaches to General Joubert, now in command of the Army of Italy and then, after Joubert was killed at the battle of Novi on 15 August, thought of Moreau. When Bonaparte arrived and progressed to Paris with the acclamation of all who wanted stability after ten years of revolutionary expedients, there could be no other choice for Sieyès. He worked with Talleyrand and Fouché to bring him to power.

The **Brumaire** *coup d'état* was carried out a month after Bonaparte landed. Sieyès was one of the three consuls after that event, although after another month he was pushed aside to be president of the newly formed (and powerless) Senate.[27]

@ http://www.fordham.edu/halsall/mod/sieyes.html provides extracts from *What is the Third Estate?*

Soboul, Albert (1914–82)

Albert Soboul was a **Marxist historian** and a member of the French Communist Party in the critical years of the Second World War. His *Historical Dictionary*, completed under the direction of Jean-René Suratteau and François Gendron, typifies his emphasis on the challenge from the **bourgeoisie** to the **nobility** at the outset of the Revolution. In his latter years, he responded uncompromisingly to his revisionist critics.

He was called up for the French army in 1939, demobilized in 1940 and taught at the *lycée* (sixth form college) in Montpelier. This did not last long and he spent the remaining years of the Nazi occupation at the Museum of Popular Arts and Traditions. He went back to Montpelier after the occupation, and then quickly passed on to *lycées* in Paris. He became a close friend of Georges **Lefebvre**, who directed his doctoral thesis on the Parisian **sansculottes** in 1958.[28] As with Lefebvre, Soboul's interpretation of the Revolution concentrated on class struggle and history 'from underneath'.

His main work is his *Civilisation of the French Revolution*. Criticisms of the Marxist Orthodoxy, as it became known, began before he was at the Sorbonne, and he did all he could to maintain it during his lifetime He called it the 'classic' view. Readers, even of translations, are impressed by his detailed and informative presentation based on meticulous archival research.

Doyle, William, 'Reflections on the Classic Interpretation of the French Revolution', in William Doyle, *Officers, Nobles and Revolutionaries: Essays on Eighteenth-Century France* (London and Rio Grande: The Hambledon Press, 1995).

Soboul, Albert, *A Short History of the French Revolution 1789–1799*, trans. Geoffrey Symcox (London, Berkeley and Los Angeles: University of California Press, 1977).

——, *Sansculottes: The Popular Movement and Revolutionary Government 1793–1794*, trans. Rémy Inglis Hall (University Park, PA: Princeton University Press, 1980).

——, 'The French Revolution in the History of the Contemporary World', in Gary Kates (ed.), *The French Revolution: Recent Debates and New* (2nd edn, New York and London: Routledge, 2006), pp. 17–32.

Social Circle (*Cercle Social*)
This was a gathering of intellectuals in the early part of the Revolution which the **Marxist historians** regarded as progressive and radical. It had a newspaper called the *Iron Mouth* (*Bouche de Fer*) which came out against the division between 'active' and 'passive' citizens in the 1791 Constitution. The circle claimed to embody the ideas of the **Enlightenment** and of **Rousseau**. It was heavily imbued with the principles of **freemasonry** as well. The members welcomed **Paine** among them, as the author of *Common Sense* that had been so important in the American Revolution. He encapsulated its ideas for them in a placard put out in Paris on 1 July 1791 after the king's flight to **Varennes**.

The *Bouche de Fer* was thought to have disappeared, but it was turned into a publishing house after July 1791, no less radical, but the mouthpiece of the **Girondins** rather than of their opponents.[29] The *cercle social* concerned itself also with the rights of women. **Condorcet** published his endorsement of complete political rights for women in July 1790. Women such as Etta **Palm** joined the circle and argued for the legalization of divorce and reform of the laws of inheritance.

Songs of the Revolution
In 1789, songs were written to commemorate all the important events and became popular in the street. '*Il faut vaincre ou mourir*' (We must be victorious or die) was the conclusion of the song about the taking of the **Bastille** on 14 July. This developed into the slogan 'Liberty or death!' so often on the lips of the **sansculottes** as time passed until their suppression by the **Directory**.[30] A song against the clergy called the pope a turkey, and regarded the higher clergy in the same light as hoarders of grain later on.[31] Other songs celebrated the abolition of privileges on the **Night of 4 August** and the **Declaration of the Rights of Man and the Citizen** three weeks later.[32] After the **October Days**, when the king was brought to live in Paris, another song said he now lived where '*à la vue de nos canons, il devint doux comme un mouton*' (under the eyes of our cannon, he should become as docile as a sheep).[33]

These songs were ephemeral compared with the song of 1790, *Ah! Ça ira*. It was remembered in Paris that the American Benjamin Franklin

Songs of the Revolution

had often said of revolution on both sides of the Atlantic, 'Ah, it will happen, it will happen …'. When it was feared that the alteration of the Champ de Mars would not be finished for the **Festival of the Federation** by 14 July 1790, crowds turned out in their hundreds to move earth in wheelbarrows to excavate and build the huge amphitheatre. Taking a tune written recently by a theatre violinist called Bécourt known as 'The National Carillon', the street singer Ladré composed the original words of *Ça ira* for the occasion. They were often changed to suit new conditions, especially during the **Terror** when 'Aristocrats to the lamp post! We'll hang the aristocrats!' was added. 'It will happen,' sung three times, was the refrain to each verse. It was the song of the French Revolution on equal footing with *La Marseillaise*.[34] The Directors ordered it to be sung in theatres by a decree of 6 January 1796.[35]

The mayor of Strasbourg wanted a warlike song comparable to *Ça ira* to raise spirits in the face of probable invasion when war was declared in April 1792. An engineer officer, Captain Claude-Joseph Rouget de l'Isle, took up the challenge and provided the tune and the words for the battle song of the Army of the Rhine. It was renamed as *La Marseillaise* when **National Guardsmen** from Marseille came as *fédérés* to join the troops gathering in camps around Paris – despite the king's attempt at a veto – to march against the Duke of **Brunswick**'s invasion in August. It is, above all else, the song of resistance against invading slaves of monarchs, whose impure blood will soak into the furrows of the fields of France, as the refrain says. **Gossec** provided the tune with full orchestration, and other musicians developed variations upon it. It was also played at the scaffold during the **Terror**, which went along with the idea of foreign conspiracy justifying such a policy.[36] On 14 July 1795, it was decreed as the national anthem, but it did not really become such until the Third Republic in 1879. Napoleon I, the restored Bourbons, the Orleanist monarchy and Napoleon III all took it to be subversive and banned it.

La Carmagnole must also be mentioned. Its origin is uncertain. Perhaps it, too, came with the *fédérés* from Marseille, or perhaps it was sung in the military campaign in Piedmont at the town of Carmagnola. It was first heard on the **'Day' of 10 August** when the monarchy was violently overthrown, and was afterwards sung under the windows of the Temple intended to be heard by the king and queen imprisoned there:

> *Monsieur Veto avait promis,*
> *D'être fidèle à son pays,*
> *Mais il y a manqué,*
> *Ne faisons plus quartier.*

(Monsieur Veto had promised to be faithful to his country; but he wasn't, so let's show him no mercy). With the words changed, the *Carmagnole* remained the song of the left all through the nineteenth century.[37]

Staël-Holstein, Anne-Louise Germaine Necker, Baroness of (1766–1817)

Germaine de Staël was an impressively colourful personality of the revolutionary decade. She was **Necker**'s daughter, Swiss by nationality but born in Paris. Her father had arranged her marriage when she was 20 to Baron de Staël on condition that Gustavus III made him Swedish Ambassador to France. In her mother's salon she was an intellectual child prodigy impressing old regime savants like Buffon, **Voltaire** and La Harpe. She, likewise, maintained her salon for intellectuals and aspiring politicians and became the centre of a network of influential people before and in the early years of the Revolution. **Talleyrand** and **Condorcet** were adherents. She fell in love with the Comte de **Narbonne** and pulled strings to have him made war minister.

On the **'Day' of 10 August 1792**, she was alone in the Swedish Embassy since Gustavus III had recalled her husband to Stockholm for fraternizing with revolutionaries. Hearing that Narbonne, with whose child she was pregnant, had not perished in the king's defence at the **Tuileries**, she picked her way through the carnage, rescued and hid him in the embassy, even facing down a domiciliary visit by **sansculottes**.[38] Then she arranged for Narbonne's escape to England, where he joined the *émigré* colony at Juniper Hall in Surrey, and she paid his rent. She went to the Hôtel de Ville to see the procurator of the **Insurrectionary**

Commune, Manuel, to ask successfully for the release of two more of her royalist friends, **Lally-Tollendal** and Jaucourt, in time to save them from the **September Massacres** at the Abbaye prison.[39] Then she set out to leave Paris provocatively in a coach and six, which was stopped and brought to the Hôtel de Ville by a crowd. Once inside the building, she and her maid were kept safe by Manuel, in spite of his likely role in the massacres, and he drove her home when the streets were quieter. **Tallien**, the secretary of the Insurrectionary Commune, arrived in the morning with her passport and she went to stay with her parents at Coppet in the Vaud canton of Switzerland.

Just after the **Prairial** rising (May 1795), Germaine returned to Paris with Benjamin Constant in tow.[40] Baron de Staël was back in the Swedish embassy and her salons began again. Many royalist friends were involved in the **Vendémiaire** rising. She contacted **Barras** to gain Constant's release after his arrest. Then she left for Switzerland again after only six months. She was back in Paris again in May 1797 in her own accommodation in the rue du Bac, because de Staël was no longer Swedish Ambassador. Talleyrand was back from America and Germaine helped him to gain his appointment as Foreign Minister from Barras.[41]

She spent the last years of the revolutionary decade going back and forth between Paris and Coppet to be with her widowed father. Baron de Staël, from whom she separated in 1800,[42] died in 1802. She refused Constant's marriage proposal but they remained in their creative literary friendship. She met **Bonaparte** and, seeing how anti-feminist he was, opposed him from exile all through the Empire. Constant remained with her, but in 1811 she married a Genevan officer, Albert de Rocca, and returned to Paris to reopen her salon at the **restoration of the monarchy**.

Moore, Lucy, *Liberty: the Life and Times of Six Women in Revolutionary France* (London: Harper Press, 2006),

de Staël, Germaine, *Considerations on the Principal Events of the French Revolution* (Indianapolis: Liberty Fund Inc., 2009).

Statements of Complaint *(Cahiers de doléance)*

When the decision had been made to call the **Estates-General**, the king issued a decree on 24 January 1789 that each parish in the country must draw up its own statement of complaint (*cahier de doléance*) about the government of the country in order to aid the process of its regeneration. Then, all men over 25 whose names were on a list of taxpayers elected a representative of the parish at an assembly of the *bailliage* (or *sénéchaussée*) to reduce all the parish statements into a single one for the **Third Estate** for that *bailliage*. These assemblies also elected the deputies who would take the completed statements with them to **Versailles** as a basis for national action. The question then arose as to whether the deputies were bound by the contents of these statements in their collective regeneration of the state. Their conclusion was, usually, that they were not directly responsible to their primary assemblies.

All the parish **clergy (First Estate)** met at the same assemblies, and single representatives from each monastery and convent were also present. They drew up a statement of grievances for their order in their locality and elected their deputies. The **nobility (Second Estate)** of the *bailliage* did likewise.

There were models issued to follow for this process, but most of the lists departed from them when local issues were specified. Typical Third Estate complaints were about abuses in national taxation, resentment at **seigneurial dues** and tithes. The country nobles resented unfair allocations of military commands to officers who were courtiers and the practice of arbitrary arrest at royal command (*lettres de cachet*). Some nobles' lists wanted the luxury of well-endowed abbeys reduced and the parish clergy paid a reasonable stipend. The Catholic clergy defended their position against Protestants who had just received a measure of civil liberty, and asked for better educational facilities.

Across the three orders, provincial assemblies to assess taxation were requested, and some form of regular national parliament was desired. Criticisms expressed were against the instability caused by short-lived ministries, not the king. The poor looked to the king to alleviate their distress, and there was no hint of the coming rejection of monarchical government.

Stofflet, Jean-Nicolas (1751–96)

Stofflet was a miller's son from eastern France, who served for a long time as private soldier and then was gamekeeper to the Comte de Colbert-Maulévrier in Anjou. He joined the **Vendéans** in their Royal and Catholic Army with **Cathelineau** and **d'Elbée** at Fontenay-le-Comte, **Cholet** and Saumur, and in several other engagements.

Within a year, they made him a major-general and, after the death of Henri de **La Rochejaquelein** in March 1793, he became commander-in-chief. He most reluctantly accepted the peace made by **Charette** at La Jaunaye on 2 May 1795.[43] As the remaining Vendéan leader after Charette's execution, Stofflet soon violated this treaty and, at the instigation of Royalist agents, took up arms again in December of the same year on behalf of Louis XVIII. He was taken prisoner by the Republicans who put him before a firing squad at Angers.

Supreme Being

Proponents of the Supreme Being wanted all the moral support offered by religion to sanctify the application of the law, while tending to regard any other belief as fanaticism. The idea of the Supreme Being owed much to the 'Great Architect of the Universe' in **Freemasonry**, and was adopted by **Robespierre** as a substitute religion. He thought it would be useful in gaining adherents to the revolutionary ideal and as a sanction against those who opposed them. This cult was meant to supplant the worship of the Trinity.

Catholic priests released after 11 months from captivity in stinking **hulks** off the coast of **Rochefort** in western France in February 1795 found the slogan 'The French people recognizes the existence of the Supreme Being and the Immortality of the soul' painted over the west door of the village church at Port d'Envaux, where they spent a night on their way to further captivity. In the time since their place in the nation had been abolished and they had 'disappeared', official deism had replaced revealed religion.

Robespierre and **Saint-Just** did not go to the intended extremes of **Hébert** to de-Christianize France in the year of the **Terror**. They did not want to see the destruction of historic church buildings, but turned them into 'Temples of Truth' or 'of Reason' with revolutionary symbols replacing statues and crosses. Robespierre organized the Festival of the Supreme Being in Paris on 8 June 1794 and presided over the ceremonies of the day.[44] The slogan 'Death is an eternal sleep', put up by the de-Christianizers, was to be removed from cemeteries.

Other versions of deism followed the trend set by the new cult after Robespierre's execution. During the years of the **Directory**, an attempt was made to establish the extremely vague **Theophilanthropy** as a national cult with ceremonies in the Temples of Truth every tenth day according to the **Revolutionary Calendar**.

Bonaparte as First Consul, also motivated by social control, brought back the Catholic priests in 1801 under the *Concordat* with Pope Pius VII. He also allowed religious freedom to French Protestants and Jews.

Surveillance Committees

On 21 March 1793, the National Convention decreed that a surveillance committee should be elected in every municipality, even in the smallest rural communes. This was part of the apparatus of the official **Terror**, to make sure of the activity of any people denounced as suspects, and relations of *émigrés* or **refractory clergy**. The committee members were elected from among local patriots, who must not have been agents of deposed seigneurs.

The committees were responsible for the issuing of **certificates of civism** (*certificats de civisme*), the equivalent of an identity card. These carried a full description of the bearer's appearance and were a guarantee to the authorities of conformity with revolutionary principles. Nobody could hold a public office without one and records were meticulously kept of the ones that had been issued. The committees were ordered to draw up lists of suspects in their communes and impound their private papers at the same time as they ordered their arrest. Under such a system, the members of the committees of surveillance had every incentive to settle old scores and personal grievances.

T

Talleyrand-Perigord, Charles-Maurice de (1754–1838)

Combining aristocratic, self-interested charm with pragmatic insight, Talleyrand served the old regime, Revolution, Consulate, Empire, Restoration and July Monarchy. His club foot denied him a military career, but priesthood was a passport to Parisian high society and he became Bishop of Autun in 1788.

After being elected to the **Estates-General** by his diocesan clergy, he proposed the sale of the lands and property of the Catholic Church to restore France's financial security. He was one of the 7 bishops out of 136 who took the oath to uphold the **Civil Constitution of the Clergy**, and consecrated several of the newly elected 'constitutional' bishops. Talleyrand resigned his own bishopric to become foreign minister during the constitutional monarchy, but avoided the **Terror** by his removal to the United States.

He returned to France to be foreign minister again under the **Directory** in 1797, and was involved in tortuous negotiations with the United States about a treaty, through agents called X, Y and Z, in which American envoys were expected to pay him 50,000 *louis d'or* as a sweetener for what he was doing. **Chateaubriand** said of him: 'When he is not conspiring, he does deals' (*Quand il ne conspire pas, il trafique*).[1] Despite the scandal he had caused by this, his own disillusionment with the Directory led him to help bring about the **Brumaire coup** of November 1799 to establish General **Bonaparte** as First Consul.

Talleyrand was Foreign Minister in the Empire and Napoleon insulted him in January 1809 for not supporting the Spanish war: 'You're a shit in a silk stocking'[2] – more politely rendered in French as '*Vous êtes de la boue dans un bas de soie*.'[3] After that he was Imperial Grand Chamberlain. He welcomed the allies to Paris in 1814, and was plenipotentiary for France at the Congress of Vienna.

Talleyrand withdrew soon from the legitimate Bourbons and was in opposition to Charles X. He was involved when the Duc d'**Orléans** became King Louis Philippe I after the 1830 revolution, and served as ambassador to London until 1834. He had rejected Catholic morality and manipulated high office to become immensely rich, but was reconciled to the Church on his death-bed.

François Gendron concluded in 1989: 'He did not take fewer than thirteen oaths, more or less betrayed all the regimes he served, and took care to intrigue his contemporaries and to confuse posterity, in his life as much as in his memoirs, to give colour to his character more than to reveal it.'[4]

Harris, Robin, *Talleyrand: Betrayer and Saviour of France* (London: John Murray, 2007).

Tallien, Jean-Lambert (1767–1820)

Tallien was a colourful revolutionary, not least because he was for a while married to Thérèse **Cabarrus**, whom he rescued from prison when he was **representative on mission** in Bordeaux after its **federalist** rising in autumn 1793. He ruled the town by sticks and carrots, but the kind of harshness perpetrated in Nantes and **Lyon** did not touch Bordeaux. **Robespierre's** verbal attack on him in the **National Convention** led him to associate with **Fouché** in the **Thermidor coup**.

He had grown up in an aristocrat's house as the son of the *maître d'hôtel* and his father's employer had paid for his education. On the eve of the Revolution he was working for a printer employed by the king's brother, **Provence**. In 1791, he was secretary to Alexandre de **Lameth**. After **Varennes**, he invented the poster newspaper (*placard*) called *Ami des Citoyens*, financed by the **Jacobins**. Then he became secretary to the **Insurrectionary Commune**, signing arrest warrants, and was an active participant in the overthrow of the monarchy on the '**Day' of 10 August 1792**. The Jacobins later spread a rumour that he played a part in the

September Massacres, but he had freed prisoners so as to save them.[5] **Danton**'s patronage aided his election to the Convention, where he voted for **Louis XVI**'s death.

After the exclusion of the **Girondins** from the Convention, Tallien and Claude **Ysabeau** were sent on mission to settle federalist Bordeaux, with a **revolutionary army** of 2,000 under General Brume. They had local extremists to carry out their orders. A military commission was set up and there were 104 executions, a surprisingly small number in comparison with what happened in Nantes or Lyon. Thérèse Cabarrus gained his clemency for people she knew, such as Lucie de **La Tour du Pin**. It is no wonder that he was considered an indulgent and was attacked by Robespierre. Thérèse was imprisoned again, and Tallien threatened to assassinate Robespierre to save her. The intention was fulfilled in a way when he associated with Fouché in bringing Robespierre down.[6]

In the Thermidorean reaction he was on the **Committee of Public Safety**, being instrumental in the closing of the **Jacobin Club** and the repeal of the **Law of 22 prairial**. He was subject to an assassination attempt himself, and gave his support to his associate **Fréron**'s '**Golden Youth**' in their campaign against the Parisian **sansculottes** He was still a revolutionary, however: he was **representative on mission** in Brittany and incited General **Hoche** to execute the greater number of the *émigrés* landed by the British at **Quiberon** after their capture in 1795.

Under the **Directory** he was a member of the Council of 500 but had no role to play. First Consul **Bonaparte** sent him as an administrator to **Egypt**, but he returned to France in 1801 after disagreements with the governor. After an inactive time, he had a minor diplomatic career in the Empire. One of his postings was as consul in Alicante, where he caught yellow fever and had to resign. His sentence as a regicide in 1816 was suspended, and he died poor.[7]

Target, Guy-Jean-Baptiste (1733–1806)

Target's reputation is that of a moderate. He was a magistrate in the *parlement* of Paris before the Revolution and had served on a committee to revise the law. He was one of the defence counsel for the Cardinal of Rohan in the **Diamond Necklace Affair**. He became a member of the

Académie française in 1785. He also helped devise the Edict of Toleration for Protestants in 1787 and wrote pamphlets about the **Estates-General**. **Necker** consulted him about the doubling of the number of **Third Estate** deputies.[8]

With Dr **Guillotin** and Isaac **Le Chapelier**, he drew up the **statement of complaint** for Paris. He was elected to the Estates-General for the Third Estate and joined the Breton Club. Target was very active in devising the **Civil Constitution of the Clergy.**

Louis XVI chose him as one of his defence counsellors at his trial, but he refused on grounds of old age and illness. Nevertheless, he wrote and circulated a document in the king's defence. As a moderate, he did not participate in the **Terror** nor, surprisingly, was he a suspect. He supported the **Brumaire coup.**

In the Empire, he worked with other lawyers on the new *Code Criminel*, and was given public office in 1802.

Taxation

It was understandable that all the upheaval of 1789 resulted in massive avoidance of taxes. Among the first targets of July and August 1789 were the new gates and wall of the Farmers-General around Paris, which were not rebuilt and the tolls were not paid. Collectors were subjected to violence if they tried to enforce the payment of tax even to the extent of their houses being attacked. This was true all over the country, with petitions against even the idea of indirect taxation. A redundant feudal land-agent called François-Noël **Babeuf** was arrested in Picardy for organizing one there.

The **Physiocrats** had argued earlier that indirect taxes were actually harmful to national productivity, and the **statements of complaint** had been full of grievances about them.[9] On the **Night of 4 August 1789**, the principle of equal taxation was accepted and special tax rolls were drawn up to see that the formerly privileged now paid.[10] The **Constituent Assembly** passed many a decree in 1790 and 1791 which took away salt and tobacco monopolies, and all the divers tax-farms managed by private financiers, along with the congeries of taxes with names like *aides* and *octrois*. There was to be no more direct tax such as the twentieth on incomes (*vingtièmes*) or poll tax (*capitation*). A system was devised that would allow the taxpayer to be aware of how much he had to pay. Donald Sutherland points out how politically dangerous this was to become.[11]

How was the state to be financed, then? Decrees set up the land tax (*contribution foncière*), a tax on movable property (*contribution mobilière*) and a tax on the profits of business (*patente*). These were direct taxes, graded according to people's ability to pay. Deputies expected citizens to pay these because there were no privileges or apparent loopholes. But the pattern of payment had been broken. The deficit remained and was increasing. Declaring the nation bankrupt was not an option. **Necker** proposed a one-off 'patriotic contribution' in September from every citizen: a quarter of their income that could be paid in saleable valuables. He primed the pump with his own payment. The **Constituent** accepted this proposal and example, but had little hope of it being implemented. It was hoped that sale of **national property** would solve the long-term problem, but the *assignats* issued as bonds to buy them soon became paper money and lost their value.

Meanwhile, taxes actually increased between 20 and 40 per cent and then, when war started in 1792, to half as much again as they were before 1789. Donald Sutherland comments further: 'Those who hoped that the suppression of privilege would lighten their burdens must have been disillusioned.'[12]

Anything like prosperity on a national scale had to wait until taxes were raised in annexed and conquered territory by the Republic. Only then was the national deficit paid off.

Tennis Court Oath, Before and After …

The first task of the **Estates-General** was to verify the credentials of the deputies. This was to be done in their separate orders in the halls assigned to them at **Versailles**. The **Third Estate** wanted the registration to be done by all three orders together. A month was spent inactively while the thirds refused to verify their credentials without the presence of the **clergy** and the **nobility**. On 10 June, **Sieyès** persuaded the thirds to invite the other two houses to join them. The roll call began on 12 June. On 13 June, three curés from Bas-Poitou (soon to be the **Vendée**) joined the Third Estate in their hall and the thirds called themselves the National Assembly from 17 June onwards – again at Sieyès's urging. **Furet** comments that this title 'created a new power, independent of the king'. On 18 June, the assembly took decisions about taxation and accepted obligations towards the state's creditors. This told the Paris bourgeois *rentiers* that, even if kings in the past had declared state bankruptcy, the new sovereign assembly would protect their interests. Perhaps this was the true beginning of the Revolution.[13]

A majority of the clerical deputies now voted to join the thirds, as did a third of the nobles. However, the other nobles, including the bishops, went to Marly, where the king and queen were in mourning for the dauphin, and persuaded him to regain the initiative. He proposed a royal session to say what he thought.

On 20 June, the Salle des Menus-Plaisirs was being changed to allow for the session, although the thirds had not been told beforehand. They found notices posted up outside when they arrived which announced that it would happen on 22 June. They found they were locked out. It was pouring with rain and tempers were frayed because many thought that the royal session would announce the dissolution of the Estates-General. Dr Joseph-Ignace **Guillotin** suggested to their president Sylvain **Bailly** that they hold the day's session in an indoor tennis court in rue Saint-François nearby. They filed across to it, followed by the public who usually attended their sessions. There were only a few benches, and there was no agenda. **Michelet** made the point that in the Menus-Plaisirs the royal pomp had overawed the deputies at the opening session, but this 'miserable enclosure, completely modern, bare, unfurnished, had not a single recess where the thought of the past could still shelter', and they could take the initiative.[14] Sieyès and **Le Chapelier** proposed that they go to Paris, but they needed to be near the king. **Mounier** proposed they take a solemn oath, as he and his colleagues in the Estates of Dauphiné had done at Vizille the previous year. Bailly, **Barnave** (also from Dauphiné), and **Target** had the wording prepared, and it was voted for and signed unanimously except for deputy Joseph Martin-Dauch who, despite the shouts of disapproval, refused to do anything that might go against the king. The text of the oath stated that they would never separate and would meet anywhere that circumstances demanded until the constitution had been established and affirmed on solid foundations.

They had overstepped the limited powers given by their electors, but being a national assembly was more important. The king's assent would not be necessary because from now on it was the assembly that personified the nation and not the king. **Mirabeau**, Mounier and the patriots had won over nearly all the rest who did not realize the importance of their stance.[15]

The royal session took place on 23 June – a day later than announced – back in the Menu-Plaisirs. The king's decisions were read out. The queen and **Artois** had had the final say in what he ordered to be said. **Necker** stayed away. Taxes and loans voted upon already were approved. The wish that the privileged should accept equal taxes was expressed. The press and individuals should have their liberty. The administration should be decentralized. There were certain circumstances in which the three orders could deliberate together but they were restrictively defined. Then, speaking himself, the king added, 'If you abandon me in this great enterprise, I will work alone for the welfare of my peoples. I shall consider myself as their true representative.'[16] He then dismissed them to their separate meetings.

The nobles and most of the clergy left and the thirds, with a few clergy, stayed behind. The Grand Master of Ceremonies reminded them of the king's order. Sylvain Bailly replied, 'The Nation when assembled cannot be given orders.' Mirabeau roared out, 'We will not leave except by force of bayonets.' Sieyès added to the deputies, 'You are still today what you were yesterday.' Together, the deputies declared themselves inviolable, and stayed.[17] Soldiers were sent to move them, but liberal nobles sent them back. The king did not persist. On 27 June, the king 'invited' the nobility, the bishops and the clergy to join the thirds and the National Assembly was a constituent body.[18] The king and the assembly co-existed. Furet says that the decisions and discussions at court had 'left no trace', but concludes that 'Versailles was looking for revenge', and the king allowing the concentration of troops around the capital united 'the fears both of the Parisian mob and the deputies at Versailles'.[19]

Terror as Government Policy

'Terror is merely justice, prompt, severe, and inflexible,' said **Maximilien Robespierre** in the **National Convention** on 5 February 1794.[20] Prominent **Jacobins** who were also members of the Convention's **Committee of Public Safety** – **Saint-Just, Couthon, Collot d'Herbois, Billaud-Varenne** and **Barère**, as well as Robespierre – devised the Terror to frighten citizens into a unified effort in the war while France was being defeated.

Because they had voted for the execution of **Louis XVI**, excluded their **Girondin** opponents from the Convention, accepted the Paris Commune as a parallel centre of power and a civil war had been provoked alongside the foreign one, the Jacobins saw that they had to organize a double victory or suffer in their turn. They endorsed the culture of conspiracy that was deep in the revolutionary psyche. The Revolution had so many enemies that it must preserve itself by the momentum that repression would give it. So their Law of 10 October 1793 decreed that the government of France would be 'revolutionary until the peace'. This decision facilitated the increasing momentum of the Terror as the **representatives on mission** of the One and Indivisible Republic brought centres of **federalist** rebellion (**Lyon, Marseille** and **Toulon**) and the counter-revolutionary **Vendée** under control.

After the republican armies began to gain victories in the war against the First Coalition early in 1794, such intransigent justice seemed to have been justified. It was intensified against the 'factions' led by **Hébert** and **Danton** in March and April. The Jacobins in the Convention forced through the **Law of 22 prairial** on 10 June to deny any legal defence to those denounced as 'enemies of the Nation'. 'Moral certainty' was enough to obtain convictions and immediate death sentences in the **Revolutionary Tribunal**. The Jacobins tried to establish a golden age of liberty by means of denying it to their opponents. This was the so-called 'Great Terror'. The presence of English spies and assassination attempts by royalists against members of the Committee of Public Safety seemed further justification for having all prosecutions and executions thenceforth carried out in Paris.

Revolutionary violence was a different consideration from the Terror. It was not so much a question of 'body count'[21] as of deliberate intention that formed the Terror. The opposition of the Girondins to the Jacobin ascendance could not have been broken without action by the Parisian **sansculottes** from 31 May to 2 June 1793. Then the sansculottes, knowing their own potential, with scarcity continuing, entered the Convention on the **'Day' of 5 September** to make their demands, principally for a revolutionary army to proceed into the country to seize hoarded grain and punish the hoarders with their portable **guillotine**. Terror became 'the order of the day' (words used in the Convention by **Barère**). Two radicals, Billaud-Varenne and Collot d'Herbois, were elected to the Committee of Public Safety. The **revolutionary army**, the **Maximum** for grain and fodder, revolutionary tribunal reorganization, the **Law of Suspects** and **surveillance committees** were soon implemented as a result of sansculotte intimidation, but the Convention soon regained the initiative and permitted Jacobin dictatorship through the Committees. Revolutionary government was now in place, 'written into the logic of Montagnard policy'.[22] The second revolution that had occurred was embodied in the **Law of 14 Frimaire** on 4 December: government on the Convention's authority by the Committee of Public Safety through the representatives on mission on a national scale. This produced victories over external enemies, and ended the federalist rebellion against the Jacobin-dominated Convention.[23]

Terror continued after victory. The battle of **Fleurus** was won on 26 June 1794, and the prisons were fuller of suspects than ever by 27 July (8,000 people[24]) when the Robespierrists were overthrown – by other terrorists such as **Fouché** and **Tallien** – and the effectiveness of the sansculottes broken. The 'theory of circumstances'[25] would no longer work as a justification for it, but the **Thermidorian Convention** seemed in no hurry to end the 'bureaucratized Terror'.[26]

The Revolution had replaced the king with the people. This was an understanding of what **Rousseau** meant by the 'General Will'. The Revolution 'had survived since 1789 on the idea of a new absolute and indivisible sovereignty ... because it assumed the unity of the people. Since this unity did not exist ... the Terror had its constant re-establishment as its function'. The result is that 'nothing prevents the thought that, in the genesis of the bloody dictatorship of year II, the old regime and the Revolution had their cumulative effect'.[27]

📖 Andress, David, *The Terror: Civil War in the French Revolution* (London: Little Brown, 2005).

Furet, François, 'Terror', in François Furet and Mona Ozouf (eds), *A Critical Dictionary of the French Revolution*, trans. Arthur Goldhammer (London: The Belknap Press of Harvard University Press, 1989), pp. 137–50.

——, *Revolutionary France, 1770–1880*, trans. Antonia Nevill (Oxford: Blackwell, 1992), pp. 134–47.

Theophilanthropy

The **Supreme Being** was discredited along with **Robespierre** in July 1794. De-Christianizing had lost **Hébert**'s leadership in the previous March. Constitutional priests had a certain freedom, but the remaining Catholic laity saw them as schismatics, despite some degree of Catholic revival in the autumn of 1796. Other versions of deism came into use, but the only one fostered as an official religion was Theophilanthropy: Love of God and Mankind, and only one of the Directors, **La Révellière-Lépeaux**, really supported it.

It was a hybrid, made up from ideas of Thomas **Paine**, **Rousseau** and Robespierre set out in a *Manuel des théopanthropophiles* compiled by a Parisian bookseller, Jean-Baptiste Chemin Depontes. It was inaugurated in Saint-Catherine's Church in Paris in January 1797, and in other church buildings and college chapels all over France. Fathers of families were designated as 'Readers' as they officiated in appropriate robes. It sometimes combined its worship meetings with the tenth day (*decadi*) assemblies beloved of **representatives on mission** for imparting civic virtue.[28]

Theophilanthropy had opponents who were listened to. One was Henri **Grégoire**, constitutional bishop of the Eure et Loire, who called it a 'derisive institution'. The new pope Pius VII, spiritually from afar, banned Catholics from the use of all church buildings desecrated by it. First Consul **Bonaparte** clinched its disuse. He said to one of its proponents: 'What is your Theophilanthropy? Don't talk to me about a religion which only takes me for this life without telling me where I come from or where I'm going!'[29] The victor of Marengo was in a position to put the pope back and reconcile the French church's schismatics to provide himself with an instrument of social control.

The French historian Mona Ozouf has commented: 'Theophilanthropy was a collection of austere ceremonies which refused the help of the imagination and signified its own failure for that reason.'[30] It was far too reasonable to be accepted with enthusiasm, as real religion tends to be, by anybody. The ceremonies were boring. Theophilanthropy had already died on the vine before the Catholic clergy returned while the First Consul was negotiating his *Concordat* with Pius VII.

Théot, Catherine (1716–94)

In the old regime Catherine Théot had claimed to be the mother of God and was sent to the **Bastille**. During the **Terror**, people who held séances were sought after to give people some idea of permanence in all the turmoil, especially since more conventional reassurance about eternity was in abeyance. Théot held such séances, and she was said to have announced that **Robespierre** was the new Messiah. **Vadier** brought word of this to the **Committee of General Security** on 17 June 1794 (six weeks before the **Thermidor coup**). The story was used to discredit Robespierre as he was trying to gain acceptance for the cult of the **Supreme Being**.[31]

Thermidor, *coup d'état* of (27–28 July 1794)

The *coup d'état* of Thermidor overthrew Maximilien **Robespierre** and his associates. It allowed the **Thermidorean Convention** gradually to dismantle the apparatus of the **Terror** and end the supremacy of the **Committee of Public Safety**.

Robespierre had provoked resentment among members of the **National Convention** by his behaviour as he presided at the Festival of the **Supreme Being** on 8 June 1794. He walked on his own in his new blue coat in front of the other deputies who were exchanging derisory remarks about him, such as, 'What does he want now – to be God?'

He was responsible for the **Law of 22 prairial** on 10 June, denying any defence to those arraigned before the **Revolutionary Tribunal** in Paris. Nevertheless, he had become aware of the excessive cruelties administered by some of his fellow *conventionnels* in the provinces. **Fouché** had stayed on in **Lyon** after its brutal repression. Complaints about him from the supporters of the Jacobin martyr **Chalier**, who wanted their own

Revolution back, had reached Robespierre, and he had reproached Fouché with them.

Robespierre made a speech in the Convention, on 8 thermidor (26 July 1794), presenting himself as isolated and threatened, but he did not name his detractors.[32] Fouché, **Tallien, Barras, Fréron, Collot d'Herbois** and **Billaud-Varenne** recognized themselves in his speech. They were all members of the Convention and decided to turn his own Law of 22 prairial against him and have him executed before he could act against them.

In the Convention on the following day, Robespierre was prevented from speaking. Someone shouted that **Danton**'s blood was choking him. His close associate **Saint-Just** was pushed aside from the tribune in midspeech. The order was made for their arrest, along with **Couthon**, despite being members of the Committee of Public Safety. Maximilien's younger brother, **Augustin Robespierre**, chose to be arrested with him. **Le Bas**, from the **Committee of General Security**, chose to be arrested alongside Saint-Just. The Paris Commune, where Robespierre had great support, controlled the prisons, and none of their governors would take them in. They were accepted in the Hôtel de Ville, the seat of the Commune, and they had the support of thirteen **sansculottes** Paris Sections and the **Jacobin Club** in permanent session.

The Convention declared them outlaws, to be arrested on sight and executed without trial. Soldiers from the Convention rushed into the Hôtel de Ville. A shot shattered Robespierre's jaw (though it is sometimes said that he tried to commit suicide). Augustin broke both his thighs jumping from a parapet outside an upstairs window. Couthon was injured when he propelled his wheelchair down a flight of stairs. Le Bas shot himself. All four were brought as they were to the ante-chamber of the room where the Committee of Public Safety met in the **Tuileries Palace** until morning. Then they briefly appeared with 17 others (including eight members of the Paris Commune) regarded as their supporters before the Revolutionary Tribunal for the formalities of sentencing.

The Robespierrists went to the scaffold in the Place de La Révolution on the evening of 10 Thermidor, year II (28 July 1794). The power of the Commune over the prisons was broken, so the suspected 'enemies of the people' were set free, though it took a lengthy time to dismantle the machinery of the Terror itself.

Lefebvre, Georges, *The French Revolution*, vol. 2, *From 1793 to 1799*, trans. John Hall Stewart and James Frigugletti (New York: Columbia University Press, 1964), pp. 131–6.

Palmer, R.R., *Twelve Who Ruled: The Year of the Terror in the French Revolution* (University Park, PA: Princeton University Press, Bicentennial Edition, 1989).

Scurr, Ruth, *Fatal Purity: Robespierre and the French Revolution* (London: Chatto & Windus, 2006).

Thermidorean Convention

This is the name given to the **National Convention** after the *coup d'état* of **Thermidor** on 27 July 1794 (9 thermidor, year II in the **Revolutionary Calendar**). It lasted until 26 October 1795 (4 brumaire IV) when the **Directory** took over. It enforced the piecemeal dismantling of the apparatus of the Terror after the fall of the Robespierrist faction and, on 12 November 1794 (22 brumaire an III), closed the **Jacobin Club**.

The continuation of the war with the kings of Europe was largely successful. Austria and Prussia were preoccupied with their dispute over the third partition of Poland with Russia. The Austrians were driven back across the Rhine in October 1794. General **Pichegru** occupied Holland. Moves were made towards the pacification of the **Vendée** in February, and of the **Chouans** in April. General **Hoche** defeated the *émigré* force landed in **Quiberon** Bay from British ships in July 1795. By April 1795, France had achieved her natural frontiers. Peace terms were arranged successively with Prussia, with Holland (which became the **Batavian Republic**) and with Spain by July.

The other side of these successes was the eruption of the **'White Terror'** between December 1794 and May 1795. Murderous attacks on militant republicans and purchasers of **national property** were carried out by gangs linked to royalist organizations in the Lyonnais, the Rhône Valley and the Midi. This was the time of the wealthy **'golden youth'** (*jeunesse dorée*) who attacked groups of **sansculottes** in Parisian street fights. There was also the need to suppress a populist rising in Paris on **1 prairial** (21 May), and a royalist one on **13 vendémiaire** (5 October). Furthermore, it was against the backdrop of Catherine II of Russia joining Austria and Great Britain against France at the end of September that the new constitution of the Directory was drawn up.

Théroigne de Méricourt, Anne-Joseph (1762–1817)

Théroigne de Méricourt was a colourful feminist presence in the Revolution.

She came from Liège in the Austrian Netherlands, from a farming family. She was convent educated, but then became a courtesan in London, Paris and Genoa. She began her short political life on the first of the **October Days** in 1789 at **Versailles**, when she appeared in her distinctive clothing, a white riding coat, with pistols and a sabre, riding a black horse to meet the market women as they arrived there in the evening.

She associated with **Pétion** and Camille **Desmoulins**, and founded a political club with Gilbert **Romme**. She learned politics in the gallery of the National Assembly at Versailles and Paris, but could not dent the male revolutionary prejudice.[33] She left Paris to go home to Liège in February 1790, only to be abducted from there on Kaunitz's orders, suspected of planning to assassinate **Marie-Antoinette**. She was interrogated for a long time, and then was set free after an interview in Vienna with Leopold II himself.

Théroigne sided with the **Girondin** war party once back in Paris and was invited to address the **Jacobin Club** and the Minimes Society to recommend the formation of a women's battalion called the *Amazones* actually to fight. After her speech in the **faubourg Saint-Antoine**, Mayor **Pétion** awarded her a commemorative sword. There was an adverse reaction from Jacobins who shared **Robespierre**'s misogyny, particularly **Santerre**, who ordered her to stop her activities. Requests to the **Legislative** for women's equality and girls' education went unheeded.

Nevertheless, Théroigne played a part with **Collot d'Herbois** in the organization of the festival of liberty commemorating the soldiers of the **Nancy Mutiny**, and other patriotic festivals. Huge anti-feminist press coverage resulted.

Théroigne was with those who had been mobilizing the **sansculotte** sections up until **20 June**, when they menaced the king himself. On **10 August**, wearing her riding dress modelled on a **National Guard** uniform, she made a 'fatherland in danger' (*patrie en danger*) speech in front of the **Tuileries**, inciting the crowd to 'exterminate this race of vipers'. She was herself involved in a hand-to-hand sword fight.[34] A year later, she was regarded as an enemy of the nation. Members of **Léon**'s and **Lacombe**'s Society of Revolutionary Republican Women, dressed as sansculotte men, found her making a speech outside the Feuillants church. They stripped and thrashed her until **Marat** arrived to rescue her.[35]

After another year, she had lost her sanity from this experience. She was arrested on 27 June 1794 for making suspect remarks in public. She wrote to **Saint-Just** for help but the **Thermidor coup** intervened. She was pronounced insane in September, and did the sad rounds of the asylums. She was in La Salpêtrière – then a prison as well as a hospital – from 1807 until her death, muttering revolutionary slogans and denunciations and refusing to wear clothes.[36]

 Moore, Lucy, *Liberty: the Life and Times of Six Women in Revolutionary France* (London: Harper Press, 2006).

Third Estate in 1789

The Third Estate consisted of the male population of France who were neither nobles nor clergy (the French word for 'commoner' is *roturier*). Some of them were from the wealthier professional classes, others were members of the **bourgeoisie** living on as grand a scale as the leading nobles, but most were tenant farmers. Those least able to bear the burden of tax were nevertheless subject not only to royal taxation, but also to **seigneurial dues** imposed by their noble landlords or by an abbot or abbess if they lived on a monastic estate. Moreover, they had to pay at least a tenth of their annual income (tithe) to maintain their parish clergy. An appropriate image for this is the contemporary pair of cartoons of a tenant farmer carrying a nobleman and a bishop on his back, while his wife carries a noblewoman and an abbess on hers.

A significant contribution to **public opinion** at the time of the elections to the **Estates-General** in the spring of 1789 was a lengthy pamphlet by the Abbé **Sieyès** called 'What is the Third Estate?' The most important thing about it was its claim that in 1614, when the Estates-General had last met, the Third Estate was of very little significance, but on 27 December 1788, the number of Third Estate deputies was doubled (a decision attributed to **Necker**). The electors were required to find four deputies from each *sénéchaussée* or *bailliage*. The elected Third Estate deputies comprised 43 per cent office-holders, 25 per cent lawyers and 13 per cent traders, industrialists and bankers. There was only one tenant farmer and no artisans or workmen. There was another major question to be answered: whether voting in the Estates-General should be 'by head' or by estates. It was realized that this was something that the men they elected would have to confront immediately they met at **Versailles**.[37]

The dress regulations for the Third Estate stipulated a plain black suit and hat, as opposed to the elaborate costume prescribed for the nobles and the clerical finery seen on the bishops and priests. This was taken by many of them as a deliberately imposed statement of their inferiority by the Versailles courtiers.

Timothy, Tackett, *Becoming a Revolutionary* (University Park, PA: Princeton University Press, 2006), Pt I.

Tocqueville, Alexis-Charles-Henri Clérel de (1805–59)

As a politician and historian, de Tocqueville's thesis was that, with the growth in importance of the intendants as royal agents in the eighteenth century, the country nobility had been disempowered, and this had meant the end of local liberties. The Revolution was bound to happen in reaction against that tendency. As Hugh Brogan suggests, writing in the Second Empire which he detested, Tocqueville was asserting liberty by awakening the past.[38]

De Tocqueville was from an ancient family of the **nobility** of the sword with its roots in Normandy. He was not content with the liberal monarchy of Louis-Philippe (1830–48) but was politically active during it. He served as a deputy from the Manche department from 1830 until Prince Louis-Napoleon's *coup d'état* of 1851 when he withdrew to private life. His two volume study of Democracy in America appeared in 1835 and 1840 on the basis of a visit there to study prison conditions. He was a member of the Constituent Assembly after the 1848 revolution and on the constitutional committee of the Second Republic. As a member of the 'party of order,' he favoured universal suffrage as a means to assert the power of the countryside to restrain the leftist tendencies predominant in Paris. He supported General Cavaignac against Louis-Napoleon Bonaparte as presidential candidate. For four months in 1849 he was Foreign Minister.

He resisted Louis-Napoleon's seizure of power in 2 December 1851 and, like Thiers, was imprisoned for a short while. He withdrew from active politics to write *The Old Régime and the Revolution* as the first volume of an unfinished history of the 1789 Revolution as a whole. His historical scholarship was focused to write a political pamphlet. The old regime and the Revolution had continuity in his view, which surprised his readers who were used to seeing 1792 as a new start to history in the terms of the **revolutionary calendar**. As François **Furet** believed, the continuities between the long-term, previous developments in French society covered the discontinuities represented by the Revolution.[39] The old regime had achieved centralized government, and the Jacobin Republic developed the potential of it by means of **Terror**. Toqueville opposed centralization, especially in the form it took in the Second Empire at the time he was writing.
,

Brogan, Hugh, *Alexis de Tocqueville: Prophet of Democracy in the Age of Revolution. A Biography* (London: Profile Books, 2006), chap. 22, 'Writing Revolution'.

Furet, François, *Interpreting the French Revolution*, trans. Elborg Forster (Cambridge: Cambridge University Press: Editions de la Maisons des Sciences de l'Homme, 1981).

de Tocqueville, Alexis, *The Old Régime and the Revolution*, trans. John Bonner (New York: Harper & Brothers, 1856). Original, Paris, also 1856. Online at http://books.google.com/books.

Toulon: Federalist Rebellion (1793)

As there had been in **Lyon**, Bordeaux and **Marseille**, there was strife between local **Jacobins** and moderate revolutionaries in Toulon from the outset of the Revolution. This was intensified after the exclusion of the

Girondins from the **Convention** in June 1793. Jacobin dominance and the presence of the representatives on mission were particularly resented by the senior naval officers led by Jean-Honoré Trogoff-Kerlessy. The exclusion of the Marseille Jacobins in July weakened their counterparts in Toulon. The moderate sections set up a popular tribunal and closed the radical Saint-Jean Club. Thirty Jacobins were executed and the **representatives on mission**, Baille and Beauvais, were put in prison. **Barras** and **Fréron** ordered the departmental directory of the Var to be transferred from Toulon to Grasse.

On 29 August, the **Committee of Public Safety** heard that Toulon had opened its port to Admiral Hood's Anglo-Spanish fleet that had taken Fort Malgue. Antoine Christophe **Saliceti** and Thomas-Augustin Gasparin were representatives in charge of laying siege to Toulon. Barras and Fréron bought grain from Genoa to supply the besieging force. Carteaux's army from Marseille set up headquarters at Ollioules to the east of the port. General Doppet replaced Carteaux and accepted Artillery Captain **Bonaparte**'s plan of attack. The assault on 17 December was successful with the four representatives on mission (Saliceti, Augustin Robespierre, Barras and Fréron) each leading a column of 1,500 attackers in a sleet storm, taking the forts dominating the harbour.[40] When the attackers opened fire, the Anglo-Spanish fleet withdrew from the harbour taking up to 12,000 Toulonnais who feared retribution with them, and leaving French ships and the arsenal in flames. 'Patriots' emerged from hiding and took vengeance on **Federalist** sections. One of the captured representatives on mission, Beauvais, had committed suicide, and the other, Baille, died soon afterwards.

Barras and Fréron were the heroes. Plays were written about them and performed in Paris. The Committee of Public Safety called for Toulon to be destroyed and the site renamed Port de La Montagne. Fréron was put in charge of reprisals. Three hundred military officers and civilians were shot by firing squads. Most federalists had left in Hood's ships, but Fréron ordered 3,000 citizens to assemble in a public place, and the Toulonnais patriots who had been captives in the ship *Themistocles* were ordered to pick out the 'guilty', despite not having seen anyone for three months. Two hundred were chosen, and they were shot. By 30 December, the death-toll was 600, though Fréron claimed 800, and said there would have been more if he had had a **guillotine**. The Convention decreed the destruction of all the city's buildings but mines could not be used for fear of destroying the war *matériel* in the arsenal. Masons were summoned to Toulon from all around but, in the end, only the houses of the main federalist leaders were pulled down. Fréron and Barras left to complete their unfinished business in Marseille.

Crook, Malcolm, *Toulon in War and Revolution: From the Ancien Regime to the Restoration, 1750–1820,* (*War, Armed Forces & Society*) (Manchester: Manchester University Press, 1991), chap. 6.

Toussaint L'Ouverture (1743–1803)

Born into slavery in **Saint-Domingue**, Toussaint Bréda was set free at the age of 33 after receiving an education and became his former master's coachman. He joined the slave rising and achieved prominence as a military leader. The **Legislative Assembly**, prompted by **Brissot**, accorded full citizenship to all free men of mixed race on 28 March 1792 and sent three commissioners to pacify the colony. One of these, Léger-Félicité Sonthonax, on his own authority, declared the emancipation of all slaves of the colony in August 1793.

When news of the overthrow of the monarchy reached Saint-Domingue, the white settlers began a civil war in which Port au Prince was destroyed. The slaves were emancipated officially by the republican **National Convention** on 16 pluviôse, year II (4 February 1794). Commissioner Sonthonax, recalled to face trial in France as a **Girondin**, returned to Saint-Domingue in 1796 to find Toussaint L'Ouverture – he adopted this surname as 'the opener of the door' – in control of the north of Saint-Domingue with his black troops. Sonthonax made Toussaint L'Ouverture a brigadier-general.

L'Ouverture was admired for his integrity, and was insistent upon racial integration. So he argued with the unstable Sonthonax who proposed the massacre of the whites. After Sonthonax was forced out of the colony, Toussaint L'Ouverture was Governor-General from 1797 to 1802. He had fought in the Spanish army against France, and then for the French Republic against the British, with whom he made an agreement in 1797. However, First Consul **Bonaparte** sent a force of 60,000 men under Leclerc to restore French authority and slavery. Toussaint L'Ouverture finally surrendered and was brought to Fort de Joux in the French Alps, where the 'Black Napoleon of Haiti' died from pneumonia in his cell on 7 April 1803.[41]

His former subordinate, General Jean-Jacques Dessalines, declared the permanent independence of Haiti, after the Battle of Vertières, on 1 January 1804.

James, C.L.R., *The Black Jacobins' Toussaint L'Ouverture and the San Domingo Revolution* (London: Penguin History, 2001).

Online at:

http://www.amazon.co.uk/Black-Jacobins-Toussaint-Louverture-Revolution/dp/0140299815/ref=sr_1_1?s=books&ie=UTF8&qid=1290878822&sr=1-1.
http://thelouvertureproject.org/index.php?

Treilhard, Jean-Baptiste (1742–1810)

Treilhard was not among the front rank personalities of the Revolution, but he had legal and administrative experience in the Paris *parlement* beforehand which made him suitable as a deputy for Paris to the **Estates-General**. He was put on the ecclesiastical committee and dealt with the small print of the suppression of contemplative orders of monks and nuns in December 1789, and the taking over of their property by the Nation in the subsequent year. He was one of the instigators of the transference of the remains of **Voltaire** to the Pantheon on 8 May 1791.

During the Legislative Assembly, Treilhard was president of the criminal tribunal of Paris. The Seine et Oise department elected him to the **Convention** and he sat with the **Mountain** but showed moderate tendencies, apart from being a **regicide**, and was an associate of **Danton**. He was on the Committee of Defence from April to June 1793. When the **federalist** revolt in Bordeaux began he was on mission in the southwest and is said to have prevented the Dordogne and the Lot-et-Garonne from joining the rebellion. During the intensity of the **Terror**, he kept a low profile on the Committee of Legislation, and had no part in the **Thermidor coup**. Immediately after it, however, he became a member of the **Committee of Public Safety**. He became attached to **Reubell** as a diplomat and was involved in the discussions with Prussia for the treaty of **Basle** in April 1795, and then with the exchange of **Louis XVI's** daughter (Madame Royale) for revolutionaries held by Austria on 30 June (among them was Drouet, the man in charge of the post-horses who had recognized the king at Saint-Ménéhoude during his flight in 1791).

Treilhard was elected as a member of the Council of 500 by the Corrèze. During his tenure of its presidency coinciding with the 'festival of the just punishment of the last king of the French', he proposed an oath to be taken for hatred for royalty and the death penalty for anyone who proposed the **restoration of the monarchy**.[42] He was also intransigent towards the parents of *émigrés* and the **refractory clergy** found on French territory. This led to his not being returned in partial elections for the council,

He was chosen to replace Letourneur as president of the French delegation for the abortive peace talks with Britain at Lille. He was then sent by Reubell to the Congress of **Rastadt** and became president of the delegation when **Bonaparte** left it. He was re-elected to the 500 in April 1798. Although the elections were declared invalid by the **Floréal coup**, he had been chosen to replace the excluded Neufchâteau as a Director on 5 May. He remained as such until June 1799 but, subjected to criticism as an '*intru*', he resigned. He became a loyal Bonapartist after **Brumaire**, and was a member of the body that devised large sections of the civil Code in the Empire, for which he was made a member of the senate and a Count of the Empire.

Tuileries Palace

This Parisian collection of pavilions and squares beside the Seine was begun by Catherine de Medici in 1563 and developed until **Louis XIV** abandoned the works in favour of **Versailles**. It takes its name from the tile factory that previously occupied the site. Its importance at the time of the Revolutionary upheaval is that it became in effect the only royal palace – others like Saint-Cloud that Louis XVI had recently acquired were denied to him. After the end of the monarchy, the palace was restyled as the centre of government for the One and Indivisible Republic.

When the market women brought 'the baker, the baker's wife and the baker's boy' back to Paris from Versailles in October 1789, the cold, uncomfortable rooms were adapted to accommodate the royal family and reclaimed from the artists who were allowed to use them as their studios. The nearby church of the Feuillants became the royal chapel. When the **Constituent Assembly** followed the king to the capital, its meetings were held at first in the Archbishop's palace and then in the former royal riding school (*Manège*) nearby.

Guards were posted under the command of **Lafayette**, and the royal family sensed that they were prisoners from then on. After the so-called 'Flight to **Varennes**', the royal family spent a further 14 months in the Tuileries, before they were taken to the Temple, the former palace of the Knights of Malta. This was their prison in reality until the deaths of the king, the queen and the dauphin, who had become Louis XVII. Madame Royale, their daughter, was exchanged with French prisoners from Austria, and later married her cousin, **Artois**'s son, the Duc d'Angoulême.

The National Convention moved into the former royal theatre in the palace since the *Manège* was too long and it was virtually impossible to hear speakers, especially with the noisy public filling the galleries and no means of silencing them. The rest of the rooms became offices of one kind or another. The king's former private office was used by the **Committee of Public Safety**.

V

Vadier, Marc-Guillaume-Alexis (1736–1828)
Vadier had been an army officer in the *ancien régime* and then a magistrate. He kept a low profile in the **Estates-General** and in the **Constituent Assembly**. But in the **National Convention**, he became a devoted opponent of everything and everybody **Girondin**. The **Jacobins** put him on the **Committee of General Security**. He attacked **Danton** as an indulgent who wanted to end the war and the **Terror**, trading insults with him that he meant and Danton regarded as a joke. One of the insults Vadier offered was: 'The great stuffed turbot must be emptied out!' (*Il faut vider le gros turbot farci*).[1]

Then Vadier aligned himself with the anti-Robespierrists to bring the **Thermidor coup** about. This did not prevent him being arraigned as a terrorist himself. Together with **Billaud-Varenne**, **Collot d'Herbois** and Barère he was condemned to be deported to Guiana. Vadier escaped and successfully hid. He was amnestied on 26 October 1795. He did not abandon his leftist views, but allied with **Babeuf**. He was put in prison for this, and then freed under surveillance.

Valmy, Battle of (20 September 1792)
This unexpected but decisive victory for the new French Republic gave it confidence to rally against the invasion by the kings of Europe.

The Duke of **Brunswick** led his army of 34,000 Prussians and French *émigrés* into eastern France in August and they took Longwy and the fortress of Verdun.[2] The *fédérés* gathered in Paris from all over France, intending to march east to repel the invader. After the massacres on 1–3 September, these volunteer troops, sensing there was no danger to their families left behind them, were formed, with existing regulars, into a fighting force under the overall command of **Dumouriez** assisted by **Kellermann**.

Just west of Chalons in the Marne Department, they encountered Brunswick's force which they outnumbered by 2000. The Prussians and the *émigrés* advanced in the mist of early morning in their disciplined ranks to be surprised by the accuracy of the superior French artillery at Valmy, which was followed up by musket fire. The invaders broke ranks and retreated eastwards, while the French advanced singing the *Marseillaise*. Dumouriez was criticized for allowing the Prussians to leave the field of battle with their equipment, but he went north to secure the Belgian border by means of the battle of **Jemappes**.

Goethe had been invited to be present with the Prussian army by the Duke of Weimar. He commented, 'Here and today a new epoch in the history of the world has begun'. The encounter was a vindication of Danton's war-cry that all the volunteers would need was 'Audacity, audacity, and then more audacity and then France is saved!'

Varennes, Louis XVI's Flight to (20–21 June 1791)

Forced to abandon **Versailles** on 6 October 1789, Louis XVI and his family were virtually prisoners in the **Tuileries Palace** in Paris. They were prevented by a popular demonstration and the **National Guard**, commanded by **Lafayette**, from going to Saint-Cloud for Easter 1791 to receive communion from a **refractory priest** they knew to be there. The king then agreed to a plan suggested by Comte Axel **Fersen** and the Baron de **Breteuil**. He would leave Paris secretly and go to the citadel at Montmédy on the north-eastern frontier of France. Once there, a royalist general, the Marquis de **Bouillé**, would protect him while he declared himself independent of the **Constituent Assembly**. The queen had made independent plans to go to **Belgium** via Montmédy, and Bouillé fused the two designs.[3]

The Tsarina Catherine II had ordered her minister in Paris to provide passports for them as Russian nationals, so the dauphin's governess,

Madame Tourzel, posed as a Russian baroness with the royal children as her own. The king and queen and the king's sister were her butler and maids. The king left a memorandum explaining why he could no longer support the limitations imposed upon him.

Successfully out of Paris at night, they made their journey in a conspicuous black and yellow carriage as far as an overnight stop at Saint-Ménéhoude, but failed to rendezvous with the loyal troops. The man in charge of the post-horses there (sometimes misleadingly called the postmaster), whose name was Drouet, claimed afterwards to have recognized the king from his portrait on the *assignat* and announced his presence. (Drouet went on to become a hero of the Revolution. He was elected to the Convention, sent on mission to the Army of the North, captured at Mauberge, exchanged with others for the Princess Royal, took part in Babeuf's conspiracy, and escaped imprisonment. There was much more after the revolutionary years.)

When it was known in Paris that the royal family had been found and were being brought back, the Corpus Christi procession was transformed into a celebration of the *Patrie*, with group after group coming into the Constituent Assembly to swear an oath to the nation, including the artisans and their wives who were beginning to call themselves the **sansculottes**.[4]

Representatives of the National Assembly caught up with the royal family at Varennes, a few miles further on, and they were brought back to Paris with **Barnave**, the deputy from **Grenoble**, sitting with them in the carriage. They were received in complete silence by the Parisian crowd, and returned to the Tuileries. When the news reached regional centres, there was a panic reminiscent of the **Great Fear** two years earlier: rumours of an army of nobles and refractory clergy assembling north of Paris, of plots of prisoners about to break out and murder, and of mines already laid in the sewers ready to be let off.[5] This was not confined to Paris, but was felt in almost every region of the eastern side of the country.[6]

The Constituent Assembly chose to believe the convenient fiction that the royal family had been 'abducted', and persisted with the attempt at constitutional monarchy. This was assisted by General Bouillé having written to the Constituent taking the responsibility for the king's flight upon himself. Those who had become, or were becoming, republicans saw the king's journey as desertion. The **Cordeliers Club** drew up their republican petition for 17 July on the Champ de Mars, but with disastrous results when Mayor **Bailly** declared martial law and Lafayette's troops fired into the crowd. Barnave, **Lameth** and **Duport** left the **Jacobins** to form the **Feuillant Club** to try to preserve what they could of monarchy. The sansculottes were now overtly in existence as a politically conscious group, and they menaced the king in the Tuileries on 20 June 1792. Finally, the monarchy was suspended after the violence of 10 August 1792, and then replaced with the republic on 22 September by the **National Convention**.

A significant subsidiary result was that a new oath was required to be taken by all army officers not, this time, to the king but to the Nation. Many noble officers refused, and went to join the Army of the Princes, already established by **Artois** and the Duc d'Condé in cities across the Rhine. The Nation was becoming polarized between the patriots on the one hand, and their apparently conspiratorial enemies on the other. Although the reaction in the Clubs all over the country was slow in being complete, fewer people could trust the king. Accepting the fiction that he had been abducted discredited the Assembly.[7]

Tackett, Timothy, *When the King Took Flight* (Cambridge, MA and London: Harvard University Press, 2003).

Varlet, Jean-François (1764–1837)

Varlet was a member of the group known as the *enragés* ('madmen', or 'rabids') in the **Cordeliers Club** who wanted the constitution being devised in 1793 to be more radical than the **Jacobins** were prepared to allow. Like his associates Jacques **Roux** and Théophile **Leclerc**, his concern was for the poorest people in the capital who were spending on bread all of what money they might (or might not) have. Varlet and Roux wanted the death penalty for grain hoarders and speculators.

Paris was his home, and his family was quite well off. He went to the prestigious Collège d'Harcourt. When the Revolution started, he wrote songs in praise of it. He made speeches in the **Palais-Royal** and drew up petitions. He went out to **Versailles** to hear the adoption of the **Declaration**

of the Rights of Man, and was involved in preparing for the **Festival of the Federation** in July 1790. After the Flight to **Varennes**, he made speeches about 'the perjured king'. He hated **Lafayette** after the massacre on the Champ de Mars and spoke in the Jacobins almost a year later to vent his anger against financiers and ministers alike. He gave a warning that a new kind of aristocracy was replacing the one that had been overthrown. The Jacobins expelled him.

His main assertion, unlike Roux and Leclerc, was that election of a deputy meant that he was accountable to his electors in the primary assemblies. The deputy was not free to make his own decisions in the **Legislative** or the **Convention**, but should be subject to the people's will, the electors' mandate. Two stage elections were nonsense in terms of Liberty. He accused the deputies in the Convention of becoming as tyrannical as the king they had replaced. His insurrectionary Central Revolutionary Committee of nine men was instrumental in the exclusion of the **Girondins**. His statement that direct democracy meant that the people could resort to force seemed vindicated when **Hanriot**'s **sansculottes** acted against **Brissot**, **Vergniaud** and the other Girondins on 2 June 1793.

Varlet then turned his guns on the **Mountain** 12 days after the **'Day' of 5 September**, when they decreed that the sections could not meet more than twice a week. He spurned the 40 sous offered for an attendance allowance. They arrested him as a counter-revolutionary! The sections – and **Hébert** – protested and he was released in November, but he made no moves in March and April 1794 to help the Hébertists or Dantonists. He even wrote the address brought to the Convention from his section to congratulate **Collot d'Herbois** after an assassination attempt had failed.[8]

The **Thermidorean Convention** arrested him on 5 September 1794. He was kept in various prisons until 31 October 1795. By then he had had enough and took no part in **Babeuf**'s Conspiracy of Equals. After the **Brumaire coup** he became a convinced Bonapartist. He kept quiet until the 1830 Revolution, and there was no more rage …

Slavin, Morris, *Jean Varlet as Defender of Direct Democracy*. Available online at: http://www.athene.antenna.nl/ARCHIEF/NR03–Parijs/SLAVIN%20–%20Jean%20Varlet%20as.htm.

Venal Offices

Since the sixteenth century, the crown had sold offices. They were not sold cheap, so substantial revenue was made available. In 1789, the going rate was 120,000 livres. The offices that were sold carried **nobility** with them: that was what made them attractive to their purchasers.

The people concerned were judges and magistrates in the *parlements* and the financial courts. Mayors of some large towns also bought nobility. Once nobility had been acquired, it was hereditary, and there was no real exclusiveness on the part of the old nobility against the new ones whose sons married into money. Even so, in the noble **statements of complaint** prior to the **Estates-General** there were many objections from the military nobles (*noblesse de l'épée*) to the dilution of their order by excessive purchase. Royal intendants in charge of the generalities of the kingdom were often descendants of those who had bought offices carrying nobility in the past.

On the **night of 4 August** 1789, venal offices were abolished. A great number of deputies present had benefited from the system, but they still did away with it with delight as the record of the occasion says. William Doyle has shown that almost no one was willing to defend the system of venal offices by the time the Revolution came, and produces the comments of an office-holder called Faulcon who, after the abolition had occurred, wrote that he was glad that poor men's gold would not be passing into extortioners' hands any more.[9]

Bossenga, Gail, 'Society', in *Old Regime France*, ed. William Doyle (Oxford: Oxford University Press, 2001).

Vendée Rebellion

In western France – from the river Loire southwards to the Sèvre – a great number of acts of collective rage occurred from 1792 onwards, with crowds of country people converging on towns to murder republican officials with cries of, 'Give us back our good priests!' and '*Vive le Roi!*' For the people of the rural Vendée, the republicans who opened fire on them were responsible for stealing and selling off church and noble lands, persecuting lawful priests and killing the king. Reconciliation was impossible after events like these.

A horror story was beginning which has been presented by one French historian for 20 years as 'Franco-French genocide', a claim recently repeated without modification in an American translation.[10] Critics of this view have regarded it as anachronistic to bring in a term from so much later in European history, and prefer to refer to these events as a civil war.[11] With armed outbreaks like that at Machecoul on 10 March 1793, and provocation by the soon to be organized 'Whites' against the **National Guard** and the constitutional *curé*,[12] it is hard to maintain the idea of a one-sided action on the part of the republicans, even if the language of 'extermination' they used was deliberate. The arrival of widows and orphans seeking refuge in La Rochelle after the massacre of their husbands and fathers by the Vendéan rebels brought forth a concerted, national response to the *brigandage* in the Vendée. The **National Convention** set up the **Committee of Public Safety** in April 1793 to implement an uncompromising response towards the rebels in the Royalist and Catholic Army. All British subjects found in France were arrested to prevent them dispensing financial help to the rebels. All departmental, district and municipal authorities were purged to replace suspect officials with known patriots.

For a while, successive Vendéan leaders, the carter **Cathelineau**, the Marquis d'**Elbée**, the junior naval officer **Charette**, kept up military pressure on republican forces but, in October 1793, the Vendéans suffered a serious setback at **Cholet**. The British cabinet sent an agent to offer help to the Vendéans if they could reach a channel port. The young nobleman **Larochejacquelein** took his force across the Loire and besieged Granville, a port facing Jersey, on 13–14 November, but could not sustain his attack. Lord Moira's British squadron arrived off Cherbourg too late and too far away to find Larochejacquelein.[13]

The Vendéans were defeated by the republicans at Angers and Le Mans and Larochejacquelein was shot. General **Westermann** claimed utterly to have defeated the Royal and Catholic Army at Savenay on 23 December. This was accepted as an exaggeration (**Robespierre**'s word). Then General Louis-Marie Turreau was appointed commander of the Army of the West, and presented his plan for what became known as **'infernal columns'** which the **Committee of Public Safety** swiftly authorized. The **representative**

on mission, Jean-Baptiste **Carrier**, organized the barbaric mass drowning of captured rebels in the Loire at Nantes. On paper, hostilities ceased when Charette made peace under duress at La Jaunaye in February 1795. Nicolas **Stofflet** carried the struggle on, but he was executed a year later. Charette was executed after supporting the *émigrés'* defeated action at **Quiberon**.

Vendémiaire *coup d'état* (5 October 1795)

By October 1795, three months after the fall of **Robespierre**, there were running fights in the streets of Paris between well-off, extravagantly dressed young men called *Muscadins* and the remnant of the **sansculotte Jacobins**. There was talk of spies in the pay of England disguised as Americans. There were anti-republicans everywhere. The **Thermidorean Convention** had run out of steam. The Constitution of year III was about to be adopted.

Most of the remaining members of the **National Convention** had voted for the king's death in January 1793. They voted through the '**Law of Two Thirds**' whereby it was decreed that two thirds of the new legislative body were to be from the old Convention. To face down the unpopularity of this measure, the Convention called the army into Paris. On 2 October, the moderate sections of the capital sounded a call to arms which produced 20,000 men to protest.

The Army of the Interior and the police could not match that number. Two days later, drums and the tocsin sounded in the rain. The supreme command of the Convention's armed forces was entrusted to **Barras**, with orders to defend the deputies in the **Tuileries** where many had brought their families for safety. He sent for **Bonaparte**, although he had not seen him since the heady days of the retaking of **Toulon** after Admiral Hood's withdrawal.

During the night of 4–5 October, 20,000 insurgents surrounded the Tuileries and Lieutenant-Colonel Joachim Murat was sent to find cannon. Bonaparte drew them up facing out from the Tuileries along the rue Saint-Honoré. In the morning, the rebels were waiting for the rain to stop. This gave Bonaparte time to finish making his dispositions, while Barras explained what was happening to the members of the Convention. Towards five o'clock in the afternoon of 13 vendémiaire, the rebels advanced on the Tuileries and Bonaparte opened fire, driving them back to reassemble in front of the church of Saint-Roch.

His 'whiff of grapeshot' cleared the street and, by nightfall, there were no rebels left.[14]

Venice

Venice tried to preserve her neutrality in the War of the **First Coalition**, even to the extent of asking Louis XVIII (**Provence**) not to stay on her territory at Verona – he complied. This neutrality was not allowed to last. After his victory at Lodi on 10 May 1796, and with Lombardy about to become the **Cisalpine Republic, Bonaparte** left Mantua besieged and crossed into Venetian territory in pursuit of Johann Beaulieu's Austrians. He wanted to reach the frontier of the Empire, but that meant crossing neutral Venetian territory. The Venetians permitted Beaulieu to occupy Peschiera on Lake Garda with 50 men, but he took the place over altogether. Bonaparte decided on Venice's humiliation. The Serene Republic sent Foscarini to Verona from where, on 31 May 1796, he sent Bonaparte a bill for damage done to Venetian territory. Bonaparte threatened to destroy Verona. Foscarini believed him and agreed to give him free passage over the Adige on three bridges and even to provision the French army. While he was away, there were anti-French outbursts in Verona which caused Bonaparte to issue threats against the Venetian Signoria through Junot.

Leaving token forces, Bonaparte left Verona and crossed the Brenner Pass to offer peace terms – claiming that the **Directory** had authorized him to do so – at Leoben on 18 April 1797. Austria was to receive Venetian territory, Dalmatia and Istria, besides the Venetian mainland. The French would have a free hand in **Belgium**. Venice would be compensated in a niggardly way by lands seized from the Pope, Romagna, Ferrara and Bologna. All this would be confirmed at **Campo Formio**.

Then there was the incident when three French luggers entered the lagoon on 1 May and were fired upon from the castle, killing Ensign Laugier who had already hove to. This convinced Bonaparte that the Signoria would prefer to remain hostile to France. 'I shall be an Attila to Venice,' he told two Venetian envoys who had caught up with him.[15]

The newly elected Doge of Venice, Ludovico Manin, realized his military weakness and that his navy was reduced to a token force, but he did not expect the Venetian state to disappear. Bonaparte declared war. The French had imposed their type of municipal government in the cities of the Venetian mainland. Eleven days later, the Great Council of Venice voted to accept French ways for the city itself and, on 16 May, a provisional municipal government was in being. Nevertheless, in the treaty of Campo Formio, Venice and the Veneto went to Austria. On 18 October 1797 the agreement was signed at Passariano, Manin's own villa.[16]

French troops briefly occupied Venice itself. The Horses of Saint Mark were taken down from the Cathedral and sent to Paris.

📖 Norwich, John Julius, *A History of Venice* (London: Allen Lane, 1982), chap. 46.

Ventôse Decrees, 8 and 13 ventôse, year II (26 February, 3 March 1794)

The old regime had not been able to cope with beggars in the street. The Revolution had **poor relief** in mind from the outset but could do little about it. With de-Christianization and the end of the abbeys and convents, what sustained charitable giving there had been was dismantled.

Saint-Just gave a good deal of thought to this, and devised the Ventôse Decrees as a member of the **Committee of Public Safety**. His intention was that property confiscated from enemies of the Revolution – *émigrés* – should be redistributed to patriots in distress. The **National Convention** approved the decrees in order to gain support from the popular classes, but the problem was too great to be solved in this way. After **Thermidor**, five months later, the short-lived social experiment was abandoned. The Thermidoreans considered it was more likely that they could control the 'dangerous classes' than win supporters by supporting the poorest patriots.[17]

Vergniaud, Pierre-Victurnien (1753–93)

Because Vergniaud was a deputy for the Gironde in the **Legislative Assembly** the name **Girondins** attached itself to the group of his associates, although they had no other connection with the area around Bordeaux.

They were originally called Brissotins because of Jacques-Pierre **Brissot** who emerged as the most prominent among them.

As a native of Limoges, the young Vergniaud was under the patronage of Turgot – later **Louis XVI**'s first finance minister – at that time intendant of Limousin province, who offered him an education in Paris. He was appointed secretary to the president of the Bordeaux *parlement*, and qualified as a lawyer in 1782. He gained a reputation for sporadic brilliance. As soon as the new departments were set up, Vergniaud was elected a councillor in the Gironde, and was recognized as a persuasive orator.

He was in the **Legislative** from 1791 onwards, and impressed his fellow deputies by his maiden speech in favour of confiscating the property of *émigrés*. On 18 January 1792 he called for an aggressive foreign policy and it was the Girondins who most actively supported the **declaration of war** on the Holy Roman Empire on 20 April. He issued bellicose exhortations parallel to those of Brissot. On 10 March he denounced court intrigues and identified them with counter-revolution, which led to another Girondin, Jean-Marie **Roland**, being appointed minister of the interior. In other speeches Vergniaud accused the king himself of betraying the constitution of 1791. Yet it was only after the king's flight to **Varennes** that he become a convinced republican. Popular antagonism intensified, supported by the Jacobins, and led to the invasion of the Tuileries on the **'Day' of 20 June**. Vergniaud was president of the Legislative Assembly on the **'Day' of 10 August** 1792, and it was he who proposed the suspension of the king from office.[18]

He pointed the finger at leading **Jacobins** as organizers of the **September Massacres**. It was his proposal to hold a national referendum on the king's sentence on the last day of 1792, which the Jacobin **Garnier de Saintes** eloquently prevented. Vergniaud and the other Girondins voted for the king's execution. It fell to him, once again president, to announce the verdict on 17 January 1793.

Vergniaud was totally opposed to the introduction of the **Revolutionary Tribunal** and the Girondins were accused of lukewarm support for the Republic by **Robespierre** on 10 April, using the fact that Vergniaud had offered his services as a minister and the idea of the referendum on the king's sentence as evidence. Vergniaud's reply to the charge in the Convention staved off the Jacobin attack, but the Girondins found themselves in danger. The crisis came between 31 May and 2 June. After that, they were excluded from the Convention.

Vergniaud was placed under house arrest, and then sent to La Force Prison in July. He and 21 others were tried by the revolutionary tribunal over three days from 27 October and guillotined on 31 October.

Versailles Palace

Louis XIII's hunting lodge underwent a fantastic transformation under his son once he had become of age and freed himself from his regents. Louis Le Vaux and Jules Hardouin-Mansart began the enlargement of the house, and Le Nôtre started on the gardens, with 30,000 craftsmen and labourers. It became the seat of government in 1682 in preference over Paris. It had developed a great deal by 1789, but Louis XIV's vision still governed it. The courtiers lived in the attics, leaving the royal family, a fair number of people, to have first and second floor apartments.

It was a wonderland far remote from the experience of the majority of French men and women, existing as an instrument to deprive the country nobles of power so that they, like everybody else, had to accept the rule of royal intendants, one for each generality in the provinces, and military governors appointed by the king. Royal power thus undercut seigneurial power. This led to lingering resentment such as was shown in the nobles' **statements of complaint** in 1789.

Versailles on the eve of the Revolution is well presented in Patrice Leconte's film *Ridicule* (1995), where a country seigneur wants to gain the king's authority for a project to drain his marshland so that his tenants can be cultivators, not just living on fish caught by hand and subjected to plagues of malaria-bearing mosquitoes. Established court nobles hinder him at every point in the convoluted process of approaching the king, and nothing can be done for his people. A note at the end tells us that the marshes were drained by order of the National Convention in 1793 with the former seigneur as the civil engineer.

Third Estate deputies were put in their place at the opening of the **Estates-General** by having to wear sombre black as opposed to the

378

peacock costumes of the clergy and the nobility. The pecking order was everything at Versailles as the young **Marie-Antoinette** found in 1774. Little had changed by 1789.

After the '**October Days**', when **Louis XVI** was brought to Paris, Versailles was left empty. At the **Restoration of the Monarchy**, it remained so, and Louis Philippe, who reigned between further revolutions of 1830 and 1848, designated it as a focus of national collective experience, dedicated 'to all the glories of France'.

Vigée Le Brun, Elisabeth Louise (1755–1842)

Vigée Le Brun painted portraits of **Marie-Antoinette** and her circle of friends at **Versailles**. Then she worked as an exile in St Petersburg and London before returning to the France of the Empire. Her portrait of the queen and her three children for the 1787 salon was controversial because she showed the queen as a mother without the more obvious trappings of royalty, and a hairstyle modest by comparison with how she was usually seen. It was meant to make a statement that the queen was not the superficial '*Madame Deficit*', but a dutiful parent. The large jewel cabinet beside the cradle was meant as an allusion to the Roman matron Cornelia who called her children her jewels.[19] Yet it was impossible for those who went to the salon not to associate the portrait with the **Diamond Necklace Affair** of two years before.

The painting has a sad, prophetic quality in hindsight: the Dauphin points towards the cradle left empty by his recently dead sister, and he himself died in May 1789 at the time the deputies gathered for the **Estates-General**. His brother, shown on his mother's knee, became **Louis XVII** who died as a prisoner in the Temple after the execution of his parents. Only Madame Royale survived to re-enter Paris in deepest mourning alongside her uncle, Louis XVIII, at the Restoration of 1814, married to her cousin, the Duc d'Angoulême.

Goodden, Angelica, *The Sweetness of Life: A Biography of Elisabeth Louise Vigée Le Brun* (London: André Deutsch, 1997).

Vincent, François-Nicolas (1767–94)

Vincent was associated with **Hébert** in the early stages of the Revolution, treading a tightrope between the **Mountain** and the *enragés*. He had two power bases: the **Cordeliers Club** and his post as general secretary of **Bouchotte's** war ministry which was being **sansculottized**. In the latter, he worked very closely with **National Guard** General **Ronsin**, another extremist, and the printer **Momoro**. All three were executed on 24 March 1793 as Hébertists.[20]

He was the son of a Paris jailer, and eked out a living as a clerk in a law firm until the overthrow of the monarchy in August 1792. The Cordeliers elected him their Orator and he followed Hébert in his campaign against the **Committee of Public Safety** which he considered too soft towards the opponents of the Republic. Vincent also agreed, against **Robespierre**, with Hébert's de-Christianization.

Robespierre reacted with the charge that they were trying to undermine the Committee and, even, restore the monarchy for which they conspired with foreigners. Vincent and Ronsin pleaded with the **Revolutionary Tribunal** to be allowed defence witnesses, but the jury had taken their three days to have a 'moral certainty' of their guilt and sent them all to the scaffold immediately after judgement.

Voltaire, François-Marie Arouet (1694–1778)

Voltaire was an independent spirit who was always having brushes with authority in the regency before, and during, the reign of Louis XV, even to the extent of being exiled to England for two years and doing time (11 months) in the **Bastille**. He became a celebrity at the age of 24 after the success of a play called *Oedipus* in 1718.[21] There was a sense of joyful release in 1734 when Voltaire found that in England you could go to heaven by whichever route you chose, and that 'commerce, by enriching the people has increased their freedom'.[22] He associated himself with the **Enlightenment**, wrote plays, poems, novels, essays, history books and translated some of Isaac Newton's works into French in company with Madame de Chatelet, his mistress, at the Château de Ciray.

On 1 November 1756, Lisbon was shaken by an earthquake and tidal waves in which an estimated 15,000 people died, many attending churches which fell in on them. This put an end, as far as Voltaire was concerned, to any optimistic idea that all is for the best in the best of all possible worlds, as he was to say later in his witty fantasy story *Candide* in parody of Liebniz and the pope.[23] In the summer of 1757, he wrote a sceptical poem about the disaster in which he abandoned the idea he had held hitherto that the best evidence for a benevolent deity is the systematic design of the universe. He had the poem sent to his friend **Rousseau**, and that was the beginning of the rupture of their friendship, because Rousseau responded to it in defence of divine providence in a letter he meant to publish. Providence had not neglected to prevent the disaster, but the Portuguese had built 20,000 houses five and six stories tall in a place where it was likely to happen. Rousseau 'insisted that man, not God, is the author of human suffering'.[24]

He became most antagonistic towards the power of the Catholic Church. When he heard of the Calas affair, he fizzed into action. In October 1761, Calas's son, Marc-Antoine, brought up as a Protestant, embraced the Catholic religion in order to obtain the required certificate to qualify as a lawyer, and committed suicide during a subsequent crisis of conscience. His elderly father was charged before the Toulouse *parlement* with murdering his son, was tortured and then broken on the wheel by the public executioner.[25] After the case had been given international proportions by Voltaire in his 12 pamphlets and his *Treatise on Toleration* (1764), Calas was posthumously reinstated by Louis XV, and compensation paid to his widow in 1765. That was not his only campaign against contemporary injustice.[26]

When Madame de Chatelet had died, he went to Potsdam to be an intellectual at the court of Frederick the Great, who paid him a generous salary until it all went sour. The outward sign of this was his argument with the president of the Berlin Academy of Science. Louis XV would not let him return to Paris in 1753 and he went to the Swiss frontier, near Geneva. He soon went back into France to buy his estate at Ferney, near enough to the border for him to escape if he had to. He was there from 1759 for nearly all of the rest of his life, and distinguished people came to see him. He published his *Philosophical Dictionary* there in 1764 but, like Bonaparte, seeing the value of Catholicism as social control, built a chapel at Ferney and expected his domestics to go to Mass there. He had been to the same Jesuit school as Maximilian **Robespierre** and Camille **Desmoulins** (only the Jesuits were still running it in his time there).

Voltaire's friends had taken his body from Paris very quickly upon his death to escape the Church's prohibition of Christian burial. The **Constituent Assembly** decided in 1791 to bring his remains from Champagne, and rebury him in the church of Sainte-Géneviève, taken over as the Pantheon, with great ceremony supported by an enormous crowd outside. In the early days of the Revolution, he could be regarded as a prophet of the Liberty which seemed to have been achieved. He was the first of the Revolution's great men to be given that honour.[27]

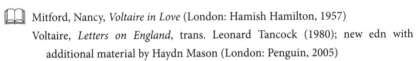

Mitford, Nancy, *Voltaire in Love* (London: Hamish Hamilton, 1957)

Voltaire, *Letters on England*, trans. Leonard Tancock (1980); new edn with additional material by Haydn Mason (London: Penguin, 2005)

——, *Candide and Other Stories*, trans. Roger Pearson (Oxford: Oxford University Press, 2008).

War of the First Coalition

After **Louis XVI** had been executed, the Republic rejected compromise with the other kings of Europe. The **National Convention** adopted the doctrine of natural frontiers for France on the Rhine, at the Pyrenees and at the Alps. The basis of Britain's European policy was that the Low Countries should not be dominated by a hostile power and had mobilized for action by the time France declared war on 1 February 1793. William Pitt organized and subsidized the First Coalition by the end of the summer. It included the Dutch Republic, Spain, Portugal, Austria, Prussia, Naples and some of the German states. It also had the moral support of Sweden and Catherine II of Russia. Austria took **Belgium** back, and the Spaniards crossed into Roussillon. The Republic reacted with conscription, provoking the intensity of the **Vendée Rebellion**.

Then there were the **federalist** rebellions in the summer. By spring 1794, however, the Jacobin government, by means of the **Terror**, the **Committee of Public Safety** and **representatives on mission**, was in full working order.

While **Carnot** was organizing victories, the coalition was not in such efficient order. Austria and Prussia were still involved in partitioning Poland. In June 1794, the French expelled the Austrians from Belgium by the battle of **Fleurus**, invaded the Rhineland and crossed the Alps and the Pyrenees. In January 1795, cannon were dragged across the frozen Rhine to attack the Dutch Republic. This caused William V to leave and allowed the 'patriots' driven out eight years before to return. Prussia concluded a separate peace with the Directory in May 1795, leaving France a free hand on the left bank of the Rhine and not objecting to the occupation of Dutch provinces.

After that, the First Coalition was in name only. The Dutch patriots formed the **Batavian Republic** allied to the French, paying an indemnity and maintaining their troops. Spain made peace in July, ceding her half of Hispaniola to France. Britain put out peace feelers, but negotiations failed over the French annexation of Belgium in October. Austria remained at war for the same reason also.

France attacked British trade with privateers – often captured coalition ships sold to private individuals manned by commissioned officers – but sent land forces against Austria. In the campaigning season of 1796, a huge pincer movement was arranged: from the north through Bavaria led by **Jourdan** and from the south through Lombardy under **Bonaparte**. Early in 1797, Bonaparte drove the Austrians out of Italy and paid the troops with plunder. He was initiating policy and the Directors in Paris were acquiescing in it, though their intention had been to extend France to her natural frontiers and use Bonaparte's Italian conquests as bargaining tokens at a subsequent peace conference. But Bonaparte installed protectorates (though he called them 'sister republics') and ended the war with the preliminaries of Leoben. This was extended into the treaty of **Campo Formio** in October. Austria gave up Belgium for the Dalmatian coast and **Venice**, and France took the Ionian Islands. The Rhineland settlement was left to the **Rastadt Conference** which dragged on until 1799.

Blanning, T.C.W., *The Origins of the French Revolutionary Wars* (London and New York: Longman, 1986).

Schroeder, Paul W. , *The Transformation of European Politics 1763–1848* (Oxford: Oxford University Press, 1994), chap. 3.

Stone, Bailey, *Re-interpreting the French Revolution: A Global-Historical Perspective* (Cambridge: Cambridge University Press, 2002).

War of the Second Coalition

In late 1798, Britain and France were still at war and Austria wanted to recover the Italian possessions lost to **Bonaparte**. War at sea had not stopped with the end of the **First Coalition**, and land war began again with the French occupation of the Papal States in February 1798 and a sister republic in Switzerland in March. Tsar Paul I looked askance at French occupation of the Ionian Islands, and at Bonaparte in Egypt and Syria. With the French Mediterranean fleet destroyed at Aboukir Bay in August, Paul made an alliance with the Ottoman Empire and began action to take the Ionian Islands in October. Then Naples attacked the French in the Papal States in November with Nelson supporting Ferdinand IV at sea. Russia and Naples made an alliance, and Pitt offered Paul I the leadership of the Second Coalition.

Frederick William III offered no more than benevolent Prussian neutrality. An alliance was made right at the end of the year between Russia and Austria, the Vatican, Portugal and some German states, all subsidized by Britain. Francis II wanted to make progress in Italy, but held back from a formal alliance until June 1799. There was no agreement on not making separate peace treaties with France. The French established the Parthenopean republic in Naples early in 1799.

The year 1799 saw French armies being forced into defensive positions: **Masséna** in Switzerland by the Archduke Charles, Schérer and then Moreau in Italy by the Russians under Suvarov. A French fleet under **Bruix** tried to contact the Army of Egypt. The **Directory** tried to organize another mass mobilization without much success to attack in Italy and on the Rhine.

Meanwhile Austria was alarmed when Suvarov took Turin and re-established the Piedmontese monarchy. Sweeping movements of armies in all theatres of war were going on when Bonaparte reappeared in Paris and overthrew the Directory by the **Brumaire coup** in November. After his fortunate success at Marengo on 14 June 1800, moves were made towards the Peace of Amiens with Pitt's replacement, Addington, and of Lunéville with Austria.

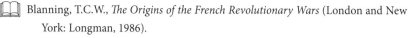

Blanning, T.C.W., *The Origins of the French Revolutionary Wars* (London and New York: Longman, 1986).

Schroeder, Paul W. , *The Transformation of European Politics 1763–1848* (Oxford: Oxford University Press, 1994), chap. 4.

Stone, Bailey, *Re-interpreting the French Revolution: A Global-Historical Perspective* (Cambridge: Cambridge University Press, 2002).

Westermann, François Joseph (1751–94)

In his youth, Westermann had been a cavalryman, but left the army to live in Paris. He was in Hagenau at the outset of the Revolution, and was secretary to the municipality there, though he was put in prison for inciting riots. Then he went back to Paris and associated himself with **Danton**. He was involved in the **'Day' of 10 August 1792**.

He was an assistant to **Dumouriez** in the Army of the North, and was arrested as his accomplice after he defected to the Austrians. Westermann was released and, promoted to brigadier, sent into the **Vendée**. He suffered one defeat but went on to win other engagements with the rebel forces and become 'the butcher of the Vendée'.[1] In December 1793, he was victorious at Le Mans and Savenay, after which he announced 'the Vendée is no more'. **Robespierre** considered that to be an exaggeration. He was recalled to Paris. Turreau sent in his **'infernal columns'**.

In April 1794, Westermann was implicated with the Dantonists and executed along with them.

'White Terror'

With the fall of **Robespierre** and the end of **Jacobin** domination of the governmental machine a reaction set in known as 'White Terror' or 'anti-terrorism'. This was particularly a feature in the south-east, a third of the territory of France, beginning in September 1794 and going on with intense momentum until September 1799. Nearly every town between Châlons-sur-Saône and Marseille experienced it, and former terrorists who fled from centres like **Lyon** were pursued wherever they went.[2]

At the outset, the killings began against a background of economic hardship as the terrible winter of 1794–5 took hold. They were, as Richard Cobb pointed out, 'neither blind, nor anarchical, nor spontaneous'.[3] The nature of the organization was essentially secret, but the murder gangs were under direction, and they had specific targets. The murderers (*égorgeurs* or *sabreurs*) wore a sort of uniform, and were sometimes on the official lists of *émigrés*, small-time squires who had lost everything but had, nevertheless, come home.

Their targets were **sansculotte** militants, sometimes associated with the **revolutionary armies** that had scoured the countryside looking for hoarders in 1793–4. Members of the disbanded **surveillance committees** who had denounced suspects were often set upon, so were national agents appointed to administer the **Terror** (or threat of it) under the authority of **representatives on mission**. Former Jacobin officials were assassinated, often stabbed or shot when caught on their own and, in some cases, their corpses were left on their colleagues' doorsteps. The *sabreurs* had a regular toll of people who had purchased church or *émigré* property, Protestant farmers, urban artisans and **Jews**. Many other victims were poor, tied to where they lived by debts and unable to escape vengeance.

In the Bouches-du-Rhône especially, returned *émigrés* and other anti-republicans imitating the **Golden Youth** in Paris, were organized into the Companies of Jesus and of the Sun who carried out wholesale massacres of Jacobins in the prisons of Tarascon and Marseille. Current representatives on mission ignored or openly encouraged these actions. This was by no means an urban phenomenon. In small communes it was often a matter of people taking revenge on those whom they knew personally. Whole families perished, and women and children were not spared. The judges, including the new **justices of the peace**, helped the assassins, so they had no fear of the law, and the former terrorists had no protection. In addition, the **National Guards** of Marseille, who had helped overthrow the monarchy, chased **refractory clergy** and put down anti-revolution in Arles and **Avignon**, were no longer available to defend their own since the guardsmen had volunteered for or been conscripted into the army and were no longer there to defend their fellow Jacobins.[4]

Y

Young, Arthur (1741–1820)

Arthur Young was an English writer who specialized in farming topics and travelled in France at the outset of the Revolution. He recorded the state of agriculture in several areas and reported the conversations he had. Some of his entries deal with the rural poverty that was the background of the political events of 1789.[1]

Young was from a Suffolk gentry family, who worked on experiments in scientific farming. Yet he was more a chronicler of developments than an active participant. He was appointed secretary to the Board of Agriculture in 1793 and remained as such until his death in 1820.

 Extracts from Arthur Young's journal are available online at: http://history.hanover.edu/early/young.html.

Ysabeau, Claude-Alexandre (1754–1831)

Before 1789, Ysabeau had been a priest in the Oratorian order and a teacher in Tours. He accepted the whole apparatus of the constitutional church in 1790 and took the Oath to the **Civil Constitution**, being elected curé of Saint-Martin de Tours. Then he was appointed episcopal vicar (i.e. assistant) to the constitutional bishop of Indre-et-Loire. He soon decided to marry and give up the priesthood altogether.

He was elected to the **National Convention** for Indre-et-Loire and was a **regicide**. As a **representative on mission** to repress the **federalists** in Bordeaux along with Jean-Lambert **Tallien** in 1793, he showed a particular animosity towards **refractory clergy** who had remained in France against the law. Nevertheless he was recalled to Paris in May 1784 by the **Committee of Public Safety** on account of being too moderate, though he avoided **Danton**'s fate as an indulgent. He took no part in the **Thermidor coup** which brought **Robespierre** down in July 1794,[2] but was elected to the post-Thermidorean **Committee of General Security** and to the Council of 500 under the **Directory** until his resignation in 1798.

After **Bonaparte**'s **Brumaire coup** he became and remained a member of the bureaucracy as an inspector of the Post Office.

Reference Notes

Preface

1 Perhaps taken from Victor Hugo, *Quatrevingt-Treize, Introduction et notes par Bernard Leuilliot* (*Le Livre de Poche Classiques, Edition* 06, 2010), p. 250.

A

1 Michèle Fogel, in Albert Soboul, *Dictionnaire historique de la Révolution française*, ed. Jean-René Suratteau and François Gendron (Paris: Quadrige/Presses Universitaires de France, *2ème tirage*, 2006), p. 2.

2 Munro Price, *Politics: Louis XVI*, in William Doyle (ed.), *Old Regime France* (Oxford: Oxford University Press, 2001), p. 248.

3 D.M.S. Sutherland, *French Revolution and Empire: The Quest for a Civic Order* (Malden, MA and Oxford: Blackwell, 2003), pp. 26–7.

4 Ibid., p. 27.

5 Michel Pertué, *Dictionnaire historique*, pp. 1001–2.

6 Sutherland, *French Revolution*, p. 83.

7 Pertué, *Dictionnaire historique,* p. 1002,

8 Jean-Jacques Clère, *Dictionnaire historique*, pp. 5–10.

9 Sutherland, *French Revolution*, p. 82.

10 Emmanuel Le Roy Ladurie, *The Ancien Régime: A History of France 1610–1774*, trans. Mark Greengrass (Oxford: Blackwell, 1998), p. 151.

11 Nigel Aston, *Religion and Revolution in France 1780–1804* (Washington, DC: The Catholic University of America Press, 2000), p. 140.

12 Jean-René Suratteau, *Dictionnaire historique*, p. 18.

13 Ibid.

14 David Andress, *The Terror: Civil War in the French Revolution* (London: Little Brown, 2005), p. 233, and Lucy Moore, *Liberty: The Lives and Times of Six Women in Revolutionary France* (London: Harper Press, 2006), pp. 236–8.

15 Jean-René Suratteau, *Dictionnaire historique*, p. 19.

16 Ibid.

17 Ibid.

18 Marcel Dorigny, *Dictionnaire historique*, p. 22.

Reference Notes

19 Ibid., p. 23.
20 Ibid.
21 Ibid., p. 24.
22 Ibid., p. 25.
23 C. Lucas, 'Résistances populaires à la Révolution dans le sud-est', in J. Nicolas (ed.), *Mouvements populaires et conscience sociale* (Paris, 1985), pp. 473–85, quoted in William Doyle, *Officers, Nobles and Revolutionaries: Essays on Eighteenth-century France* (London and Rio Grande: The Hambledon Press, 1995), p. 204.
24 Alan Forrest, in François Furet and Mona Ozouf, *Dictionnaire Critique de la Révolution française* (Paris: Flammarion, 1988), p. 443.
25 Ibid.
26 Ibid.
27 Ibid., p. 444.
28 Ibid., p. 445.
29 Ibid., p. 446.
30 Jules Michelet, *Histoire de la Révolution française, Tome VIII* (Paris: C. Marpon et E. Flammarion, 1887), p. 62. Author's translation.
31 Forrest, Ibid., 448.
32 Ibid.
33 Ibid., p. 449.
34 Ibid., p. 451.
35 Ibid., p. 452.
36 Ibid.
37 Philippe Bordes, *Dictionnaire historique*, p. 830.
38 *The Anti-Jacobin Review and Magazine*, vol. 26 (London: J. Whittle, 1807), p. 44.
39 Bordes, Ibid., p. 831.
40 Ibid., p. 776.
41 Eleanor P. DeLorme, *Garden Pavilions and the 18th-Century French Court* (Woodbridge: Antique Collectors' Club, 1996), p. 263.
42 Philip Mansel, *Louis XVIII* (London: John Murray, 2005), chap. 4.
43 Emile Gabory, *L'Angleterre et la Vendée d'après documents inédits, Tome I, Granville, Quiberon, L'île de Yeu* (Paris: Librairie Académique Perrin, 1931), chaps 8 and 9.
44 Ibid., chap. 11.
45 Ibid., *Tome II*, pp. 270ff.
46 D.M.S. Sutherland, *French Revolution and Empire*, p. 21.
47 Ibid., p. 22.
48 Vivian R. Gruder, *The Notables and the Nation: The Political Schooling of the French 1787–88* (London and Cambridge, MA: Harvard University Press, 2007), p. 31.
49 John Hardman, *Louis XVI* (New Haven and London: Yale University Press), 1993, p. 126.
50 Gruder, *Notables and Nation*, p. 30.
51 Ibid., p. 31.
52 Ibid., p. 1.
53 Robin Harris, *Talleyrand: Betrayer and Saviour of France* (London: John Murray, 2007), p. 49.
54 D.M.S. Sutherland, *French Revolution*, p. 85.
55 Ibid.
56 Ibid.
57 François Furet, *Revolutionary France 1770–1880*, trans. Antonia Nevill (Oxford and Cambridge, MA: Blackwell, 1992), p. 81.
58 François Furet, in François Furet and Mona Ozouf (eds), *Dictionnaire Critique de la Révolution française* (Paris: Flammarion, 1988), p. 979.
59 Ibid., p. 980.

60 Ibid., p. 981.
61 Ibid., p. 985.
62 Ibid.
63 Ibid., p. 986.
64 Ibid., p. 987.
65 Emile Ducoudray, *Dictionnaire historique*, p. 252.
66 Olivier Blanc, *L'Eminence grise de Napoléon, Regnaud de Saint-Jean d'Angély* (Paris: Pygmalion, Gérard Watelet, 2002), p. 52.
67 Ducoudray, Ibid.
68 Ibid., p. 253.
69 Antoine-François Bertrand de Moleville, *Private Memoirs relative to the Last Year of the Reign of Lewis XVI*, vol. 2, anonymous translation (London: Strahan, Cadell and Davies, 1797), p. 142.
70 Michel Vovelle, *Dictionnaire historique*, p. 60.
71 Ibid.
72 Ibid., p. 61.
73 Anne-Marie Duport, *Dictionnaire historique*, p. 507.
74 Michel Vovelle, *Dictionnaire historique*, p. 61.

B

1 Georges Lefèbvre, *The French Revolution from 1793 to 1799*, trans. John Hall Stewart and James Friguglietti (New York: Columbia University Press, 1964), pp. 175–6.
2 François Wartelle, *Dictionnaire historique*, p. 63.
3 Ibid., p. 64.
4 Ibid., p. 65.
5 Michèle Fogel, *Dictionnaire historique*, p. 67.
6 François Gendron, *Dictionnaire historique*, p. 67.
7 Sutherland, *French Revolution*, p. 120.
8 Gendron, *Dictionnaire historique*, p. 68.
9 Claudy Valin, *La Rochelle – La Vendée 1793* (Paris: Le Croît vif, 1997), p. 324.
10 Jean-René Suratteau, *Dictionnaire historique*, pp. 74–7.
11 Sutherland, *French Revolution*, pp. 124–5.
12 Robert Chagny, *Dictionnaire historique*, p. 79.
13 Colin Jones, *The Great Nation, France from Louis XIV to Napoleon* (London: Penguin Books, 2002), p. 508.
14 Claudine Wolikov, *Dictionnaire historique*, p. 89.
15 Paul W. Schroeder, *The Transformation of European Politics, 1763–1848* (Oxford: Oxford University Press, 1994), pp. 151–2.
16 Jean-René Suratteau, *Dictionnaire historique*, p. 69.
17 Raymonde Monnier, *Dictionnaire historique*, p. 93.
18 François Wartelle, *Dictionnaire historique*, pp. 94–6.
19 T.C.W. Blanning, *The Culture of Power and the Power of Culture: Old Regime Europe 1660–1789* (Oxford: Oxford University Press, 2003), pp. 432–5.
20 Ibid.
21 François Gendron, *Dictionnaire historique*, p. 102.
22 Blanning, Ibid.
23 Paul W. Schroeder, *Transformation*, p. 66.
24 François Wartelle, *Dictionnaire historique*, pp. 103–5.
25 Stephen Pope, *The Cassell Dictionary of the Napoleonic Wars* (London: Cassell, 1999), p. 100.
26 Simon Schama, *Citizens* (London: Viking, 1989), p. 447.

27 Jean-Christian Petitfils, *Louis XVI* (Paris: Perrin, 2005), p. 700.
28 Schama, *Citizens*, p. 809.
29 R.R. Palmer, *Twelve Who Ruled*, p. 376.
30 Ibid., pp. 388–9.
31 Michel Dorigny, *Dictionnaire historique*, p. 128.
32 Ibid.
33 Elisabeth G.-Sledziewski, *Dictionnaire historique*, pp. 128–9.
34 John Julius Norwich, *A History of Venice* (Harmondsworth: Penguin Books, 1983), p. 610.
35 Jean-Paul Bertaud, *Dictionnaire historique*, p. 132.
36 Harris, *Talleyrand*, pp. 99–102.
37 Andress, *Terror*, p. 207.
38 Raymonde Monnier, *Dictionnaire historique*, p. 140.
39 Munro Price, *The Fall of the French Monarchy*, pp. 113–14, 119–20.
40 Timothy Tackett, *When the King Took Flight* (Cambridge, MA and London: Harvard University Press), pp. 68–71.
41 Ibid., pp. 134,137.
42 Mona Ozouf, *Varennes, La mort de la royauté* (Paris, Gallimard, 2005), p. 206.
43 Jean-Paul Bertaud, *Dictionnaire historique*, p. 141.
44 William Doyle, *The Oxford History of the French Revolution* (Oxford: Oxford University Press, 1989), p.22.
45 Timothy Tackett, *Becoming a Revolutionary: The Deputies of the French National Assembly and the Emergence of a Revolutionary Culture 1789–1790* (University Park, PA: Pennsylvania State University Press, 2006), p. 78. Edmund Burke, *Reflections on the Revolution in France*, ed. with Notes and introduction by L.G. Mitchell (Oxford: Oxford World's Classics, 1999), p. 42.
46 Colin Jones, *The Great Nation, France from Louis XV to Napoleon* (London: Allen Lane, 2002) p. 546.
47 Claudy Valin, *La Rochelle – La Vendée 1793* (Paris: Le Croît vif, 1997), pp. 68–9.
48 Guy Chaussinand-Nogaret, *The French Nobility in the Eighteenth Century: From Feudalism to Enlightenment*, trans. William Doyle (Cambridge: Cambridge University Press, 1985), chap. 5.
49 Munro Price, *Fall*, p. 51.
50 Ibid., p. 75.
51 Marcel Dorigny, *Dictionnaire historique*, pp. 153–4.
52 Ibid., p. 155.
53 Stephen Pope, *Cassell Dictionary*, p. 120.
54 François Furet, *Revolutionary France 1770–1880*, trans. Antonia Nevill (Oxford: Basil Blackwell, 1992), p. 209.
55 Werner Giesselmann, cited in Lynn Hunt, *Politics, Culture and Class in the French Revolution* (London, Berkeley and Los Angeles: University of California Press, 2004), p. 233.
56 Patrice Gueniffey, *Le Dix-huit Brumaire, L'épilogue de la Révolution française* (Paris: Gallimard, 2008), p. 388.
57 Jean-René Suratteau, *Dictionnaire historique*, p. 160.
58 Ibid., p. 162.
59 Sutherland, *French Revolution*, p. 135.
60 François Wartelle, *Dictionnaire historique*, pp. 163–5.
61 Robert and Isabelle Tombs, *That Sweet Enemy: The French and the British from the Sun King to the Present* (London: William Heinemann, 2006), p. 194.
62 Edmund Burke, *Reflections on the Revolution in France*, ed. with Introduction by L.G. Mitchell (Oxford: Oxford University Press, 1993, repr., 2009), p. 42.
63 Thomas Paine, *The Rights of Man* (Indianapolis: Hackett Publishing, 1992), p. 22.
64 Marcel Dorigny, *Dictionnaire historique*, p. 168.

65 Ibid.
66 Ibid.
67 Ibid.
68 Ibid., pp. 168–9.

C

1 Lucy Moore, *Liberty, The Lives and Times of Six Women in Revolutionary France* (London: Harper Press, 2006) p. 263.
2 Caroline Moorehead, *Dancing to the Precipice, Lucie de La Tour du Pin and the French Revolution* (London: Chatto & Windus, 2009), pp. 184ff.
3 Moore, *Liberty*, p. 273.
4 Ibid., p. 312.
5 Ibid., pp. 379–80.
6 Andress, *Terror*, p. 184.
7 Sutherland, *French Revolution*, p. 21.
8 Jean-René Suratteau, *Dictionnaire historique*, pp. 181–3.
9 Paul W. Schroeder, *The Transformation of European Politics 1763–1848* (Oxford: Oxford University Press, 1994), pp. 171–3.
10 Jean-Paul Bertaud, *Dictionnaire historique*, p. 189.
11 Ibid., p. 190.
12 Ibid., p. 191.
13 Ibid.
14 Marcel Dorigny, *Dictionnaire historique*, pp. 192–3.
15 Serge Bianchi, *Dictionnaire historique*, p. 194.
16 Claude Petitfrère, *Dictionnaire historique*, pp. 195–6.
17 Departmental Archives, *Charente-Maritime*: L 458.
18 Claudine Wolikow, *Dictionnaire historique*, pp. 199–200.
19 Ibid.
20 Ibid.
21 John Adolphus, *Biographical Memoires of the French Revolution* (London: Cadell and Davies, 1799), vol. 1, p. 287.
22 Wolikow, Ibid.
23 Andress, *Terror*, p. 188.
24 Wolikow, Ibid.
25 Sutherland, *French Revolution*, pp. 205–6.
26 François Wartelle, *Dictionnaire historique*, pp. 200–1.
27 Anne Bernet, *Charette* (Paris: Perrin, 2006). pp. 71–4.
28 'La Sentinelle', 9 April 1796, in Emile Gabory, *L'Angleterre et La Vendée, Tome I*, pp. 7–13.
29 William Doyle, *Aristocracy and Its Enemies in the Age of Revolution* (Oxford: Oxford University Press, 2009), p. 17, and François-René de Chateaubriand, *Mémoires de l'outre-tombe*, ed. Edmond Biré (Paris: Garnier Frères, 1880), vol. 1, pp. 26–7.
30 Chateaubriand, Ibid., Introduction by Edmond Biré, pp. ix–xii.
31 Serge Bianchi, *Dictionnnaire historique*, p. 213.
32 *Œuvres Poétiques d'André de Chénier, Avec une notice et des notes par M Gabriel de Chénier* (Paris: Alphonse Lemerre, n.d.), *Tome III*, p. 216.
33 Ibid., Gabriel de Chenier's *Notice et Mémoire*, in *Tome I*, p. cxxxiv.
34 Claude Petitfrère, *Dictionnaire historique*, p. 217.
35 Roger Dupuy, *Dictionnaire historique*, pp. 217–20.
36 Jean-René Suratteau, *Dictionnaire historique*, pp. 221–3.
37 Sutherland, *French Revolution*, p. 91.

Reference Notes

38 Timothy Tackett, *Becoming*, pp. 289–91.

39 Nigel Aston, *Religion and Revolution in France, 1780–1804* (London: Macmillan Press, 2000), p. 175.

40 Sutherland, *French Revolution*, p. 96.

41 William Doyle, *The Oxford History of the French Revolution* (Oxford: Oxford University Press), 1989, pp. 136–46.

42 Sutherland, *French Revolution*, pp. 188–9.

43 Ibid., p. 189.

44 Marcel Dorigny, *Dictionnaire historique*, pp. 226–8.

45 Vivien R. Gruder, *The Notables and the Nation*, pp. 19–22.

46 Jean-René Suratteau, *Dictionnaire historique*, p. 232.

47 Guy-Robert Ikni, *Dictionnaire historique*, p. 233.

48 William Doyle, *Aristocracy and Its Enemies*, pp. 1–8.

49 Guy-Robert Ikni, Ibid.

50 Françoise Brunel, *Dictionnaire historique*, p. 247.

51 Ibid., p. 248.

52 Françoise Brunel, *Dictionnaire historique*, p. 256.

53 Ibid., p. 254.

54 Georges Lefèbvre, *The French Revolution, Volume I: From Its Origin to 1793*, trans. Elizabeth Moss Evanson (New York: Columbia University Press, 1962), p. 102f.

55 Sutherland, *French Revolution*, p. 28.

56 François Hincker, *Dictionnaire historique*, p. 272.

57 Raymonde Monnier, *Dictionnaire historique*, p. 274.

58 Elizabeth and Robert Badinter, *Condorcet, Un intellectual en politique* (Paris: Arthème Fayard, 1988), p. 593 and n. 2.

59 Tackett, *Becoming*, pp. 157–65.

60 Tackett, *Becoming*, pp. 197–202.

61 Michel Pertué, *Dictionnaire historique*, pp. 292–3.

62 Sutherland, *French Revolution*, pp. 111–13.

63 Ibid., pp. 115 and 120.

64 Sutherland, *French Revolution*, p. 99.

65 Ibid., pp. 99–100.

66 D.M.S. Sutherland, *France 1789–1815: Revolution and Counterrevolution* (London: Fontana Press, 1985), p. 14.

67 Sutherland, *French Revolution*, pp. 103–4.

68 Martine Braconnier, *Dictionnaire historique*, p. 310.

69 Jean-Paul Bertaud, *Dictionnaire historique*, pp. 316–17.

D

1 Sutherland, *French Revolution*, p. 120.

2 Albert Mathiez, *La Révolution française*, vol. 2, *La Gironde et la Montagne* (Paris: Editions Denoël, 1985), pp. 33–4.

3 Jules Michelet, *Histoire de la Révolution française*, vol. 9 (Paris: C. Marpon et E. Flammarion, 1868), p. 82.

4 Jean Starobinski, *1789, Les Emblèmes de la Raison* (Paris: Flammarion, 1979), p. 70.

5 Sutherland, *French Revolution*, p. 13.

6 Antoine-François Bertrand de Moleville, *Private Memoirs relative of the Last Year of the Reign of Lewis the Sixteenth*, vol. 2 (London: Strahan, Cadell & Davies, 1797), p. 24.

7 Sutherland, *French Revolution*, p. 132.

8 Ibid.

9 Sylvia Neely, *A Concise History of the French Revolution* (Lanham, MA and Plymouth: Rowman & Littlefield, 2007), p. 158.

10 Ibid.

11 Sutherland, *French Revolution*, pp. 133–4.

12 Jean-René Suratteau, *Dictionnaire historique*, p. 162.

13 Neely, *Concise History*, pp. 160–1.

14 Neely, *Concise History*, p. 191.

15 Denis Richet, 'Journées révolutionnaires', in Furet and Ozouf, *Dictionnaire critique*, p. 122.

16 Ibid., pp. 122–3.

17 Richard Cobb, *The Police and the People: French Popular Protest 1789–1820* (Oxford: Oxford University Press, 1970), p. 153.

18 Tackett, *Becoming*, pp. 183–8.

19 Marc Seguin, *Jonzac pendant la Révolution* (Jonzac: Université Francophone d'Eté, 1986), pp. 43–8.

20 Paul W. Schroeder, *Transformation*, p. 94.

21 Ibid., pp. 94–5.

22 R.R. Palmer, *Twelve Who Ruled*, p. 258.

23 Claudine Wolikow, *Dictionnaire historique*, p. 348.

24 Palmer, Ibid., pp. 259–60.

25 Jules Michelet, *Histoire de France* (Paris: C. Marpon & E. Flammarion, 1867), vol. 19, chaps 17 and 18.

26 Schama, *Citizens*, pp. 203–10.

27 Blanning, *Culture of Power*, pp. 413–14.

28 Sutherland, *French Revolution*, p. 258.

29 Jean-René Suratteau, *Dictionnaire historique*, p. 300.

30 *Dictionnaire historique*, p. 286.

31 Jean-Paul Bertaud, *Dictionnaire historique*, p. 371.

32 Ibid.

33 Ibid., p. 372.

34 Madeleine-Anna Charmelot, 'Perinne Dugué, la "saint aux ailes tricolores"', *Annales historiques de la Révolution française*, no. 253 (1983): pp. 453–65.

35 Jean-Paul Bertaud, *Dictionnaire historique*, p. 379.

36 Raymonde Monnier, *Dictionnaire historique*, pp. 279–380.

37 Tackett, *Becoming*, p. 157.

E

1 Jean-René Suratteau, *Dictionnaire historique*, p. 406–10.

2 Claude Petitfrère, *Dictionnaire historique*, p. 410.

3 Roger Dupuy, *Dictionnaire historique*, p. 412.

4 Ibid.

5 Robert Tombs, *France 1814–1914* (Harlow: Addison Wesley Longman, 1996), pp. 342–3.

6 William Doyle, *The Old European Order 1660–1800* (Oxford: Oxford University Press, 1984 edn), p. 195.

7 Tackett, *Becoming*, p. 182.

8 Sutherland, *French Revolution*, p. 28.

9 Furet, *Revolutionary France 1770–1880*, trans. Antonia Nevill, pp. 52ff.

F

1 Andress, *The Terror*, pp. 253 and 263.

2 Jean-Christian Petitfils, *Louis XVI* (Paris: Perrin, 2005), pp. 746–8.

3 Relevant comments are provided by Antonia Fraser, *Marie-Antoinette, The Journey* (New York: Anchor Books, 2001), p. 364.
4 Timothy Tackett, *When the King Took Flight* (Cambridge, MA and London: 2003), pp. 58 and others.
5 William Doyle, *Oxford History*, p. 171.
6 Antonia Fraser, *Marie-Antoinette*, p. 443.
7 Robin Harris, *Talleyrand*, p. 52.
8 Departmental Archives Charente-Maritime L 458, author's translation and italics.
9 Andress, *Terror*, p. 54.
10 Sutherland, *French Revolution*, pp. 120–1.
11 Stephen Pope, *Cassell Dictionary*, p. 191.
12 Georges Lefèbvre, *The French Revolution, Volume II, from 1793 to 1799*, trans. John Hall Stewart and James Friguglietti (New York: Columbia University Press, 1964), pp. 127–9.
13 Sutherland, *French Revolution*, p. 291.
14 Ibid.
15 T.C.W. Blanning, *The Origins of The French Revolutionary Wars* (London: Longman, 1986), p. 75.
16 Neely, *Concise History*, p. 199.
17 Sutherland, *French Revolution*, p. 189.
18 Ibid., p. 206.
19 François-René de Chateaubriand, *Mémoires de l'outre-tombe*, vol. 4, p. 57. Author's translation.
20 Tackett, *Becoming*, p. 53.
21 William Doyle, *Origins of the French Revolution* (3rd edn, Oxford: Oxford University Press, 1999), p. 40 and n. 24.
22 François Gendron, *Dictionnaire historique*, p. 484.
23 Neely, *Concise History*, pp. 229–230.
24 Jean-René Suratteau, *Dictionnaire historique*, p. 301.
25 Sutherland, *French Revolution*, pp. 285–6.
26 Suratteau, Ibid.
27 François Furet, *Interpreting the French Revolution*, trans. Elborg Forster (Cambridge: Cambridge University Press, 1981), pp. 1–79.
28 William Doyle, *Origins of the French Revolution*, p. 36.
29 François Furet, *Revolutionary France, 1770–1880*, trans. Alison Nevill, p. 537.
30 François Furet and Mona Ozouf (eds), *A Critical Dictionary of the French Revolution*, trans. Arthur Goldhammer (London: The Belknap Press of Harvard University Press, 1989).

G

1 Denis Richet, 'Journées révolutionnaires', in Furet and Ozouf, *Dictionnaire Critique*, p. 123.
2 Ibid., pp. 123–4.
3 Neely, *Concise History*, p. 224.
4 William Doyle, 'Thomas Paine and the Girondins', in *Officers, Nobles and Revolutionaries; Essays on Eighteenth-Century France* (London: The Hambledon Press, 1995).
5 Serge Bianchi, *Dictionnaire historique*, pp. 507–8.
6 Sutherland, *French Revolution*, p. 254.
7 Michel Vovelle, *Dictionnaire historique*, pp. 600–1
8 Lucy Moore, *Liberty: The Life and Times of Six Women in Revolutionary France* (London: Harper Press, 2006), p. 309.
9 Jean Starobinski, *1789, Les Emblèmes*, p. 170.
10 Frédérique Robert, *Dictionnaire historique*, p. 511.
11 Moore, *Liberty*, pp. 105–5.
12 Ibid., p. 254.

13 Tackett, *Becoming*, p. 163.
14 Tackett, *Becoming*, p. 172n.
15 Tackett, *Becoming*, p. 286n.
16 Doyle, *Oxford History*, p. 83.
17 Jean-Christian Petitfils, *Louis XVI*, p. 605.
18 Ibid.
19 Doyle, *Oxford History*, p. 85.
20 Blanning, *Culture of Power*, pp. 357–74.
21 Frédérique Robert, *Dictionnaire historique*, p. 523.
22 Walter F. Friedlander, *David to Delacroix* (Cambridge, MA: Harvard University Press, 1952), p. 60.
23 Ibid.
24 Daniel Arasse, *The Guillotine and the Terror*, trans. Christopher Miller (London: Penguin Books, 1991), p. 8.
25 Petitfils, *Louis XVI*, p. 664.
26 Emile Ducoudray, *Dictionnaire historique*, p. 528.
27 Arasse, *The Guillotine*, pp. 19–25.
28 Ibid., pp. 26–8.
29 Ibid., p. 28.

H

1 Raymonde Monnier, *Dictionnaire historique*, p. 531.
2 Ibid.
3 Ibid.
4 Ibid.
5 Ibid.
6 Jacques Guilhaumou, *Dictionnaire historique*, p. 537.
7 Andress, *Terror*, p. 268.
8 Jean-René Suratteau, *Dictionnaire historique*, p. 543.
9 Stephen Pope, *The Cassell Dictionary of Napoleonic Wars* (London: Cassell, 1999), p. 469.
10 Claudine Wolikov, *Dictionnaire historique*, pp. 547–8.
11 Ibid., p. 549.
12 Annie Crépin, *Dictionnaire historique*, p. 553.
13 R.R. Palmer, *Twelve Who Ruled, the Year of the Terror in the French Revolution* (University Park, PA: Princeton University Press, Bicentennial Edition, 1989), pp. 91–6.
14 Annie Crépin, *Dictionnaire historique*, p. 557.
15 Richard Ballard, *The Unseen Terror, The French Revolution in the Provinces* (London and New York: I.B.Tauris, 2010), chaps 12 and 13.

I

1 Sutherland, *French Revolution*, pp. 222–3.
2 Claudy Valin, *La Rochelle – La Vendée 1793* (Paris: Le Croît vif, 1997), p. 363f.
3 Philippe Bordes, *Dictionnaire historique*, pp. 268–9.
4 Sutherland, *French Revolution*, p. 136.
5 Ibid.
6 Munro Price, *The Fall of the French Monarchy: Louis XVI, Marie-Antoinette and the Baron de Breteuil* (London: Macmillan, 2002), pp. 299–301.
7 Philippe Bordes, Ibid.
8 Ibid.

Reference Notes

9   Gregory Fremont-Barnes (ed.), *Encyclopedia of the Age of Political Revolutions and New Ideologies, 1760–1815* (Westport, CT: Greenwood Press, 2007), p. 355.
10 Marcel Dorigny, *Dictionnaire historique*, p. 583.
11 Stephen Pope, *The Cassell Dictionary of the Napoleonic Wars* (London: Cassell, 1999), pp. 271–4.

J

1   Sutherland, *French Revolution*, p. 27.
2   Tackett, *Becoming*, pp. 206–7.
3   Ibid., p. 254.
4   Ibid., p. 253.
5   William Doyle, *Jansenism* (Basingstoke: Macmillan Press, 2000), p. 83.
6   Sutherland, *French Revolution*, p. 10.
7   William Doyle, *Jansenism*, p. 84.
8   Stephen Pope, *Cassell Dictionary*, p. 279.
9   Rina Neher-Bernheim, *Les Juifs en France sous la Révolution française et l'Empire* (Le site du Judaïsme d'Alsace et de Lorraine), pp. 1–6. Available online at: http://judaisme.sdv.fr/histoire/historiq/consisto/rneher.htm.
10 Frances Malino, *Dictionnaire historique*, p. 607.
11 Jean-Paul Bertaud, *Dictionnaire historique*, p. 601.
12 François Wartelle, *Dictionnaire historique*, p. 610.
13 Anthony Crubaugh, *Balancing the Scales of Justice: Local Courts and Rural Society in Southwest France, 1750–1800* (University Park, PA: Pennsylvania State University Press, 2001), pp. 100–1.
14 Sutherland, *French Revolution*, p. 64.
15 Ibid., p. 87.

L

1   Lucy Moore, *Liberty*, p. 225.
2   Dominique Godenau, *Dictionnaire historique*, pp. 622–3.
3   François Gendron, *Dictionnaire historique*, p. 624.
4   Patrice Gueniffey, in François Furet and Mona Ozouf (eds), *Dictionnaire Critique de La Révolution française* (Paris: Flammarion, 1988), p. 260.
5   Ibid., p. 262.
6   Ibid.
7   Ibid., p. 263.
8   Ibid.
9   Ibid., p. 264.
10 Ibid.
11 Leonie Frieda, *Catherine de Medici: A Biography* (London: Weidenfield & Nicolson, 2004), p. 266.
12 Ibid., p. 265.
13 Sutherland, *French Revolution*, p. 120.
14 Gueniffey, in *Dictionnaire critique*, Ibid.
15 Gueniffey, Ibid., p. 258.
16 François Gendron, *Dictionnaire historique*, p. 626.
17 Ibid.
18 Maurice Genty, *Dictionnaire historique*, p. 635.
19 Caroline Moorehead, *Dancing to the Precipice: Lucie de La Tour du Pin and the French Revolution* (London: Chatto & Windus, 2009), p. 265.
20 Andress, *Terror*, pp. 93–5.

21 Marcel Dorigny, *Dictionnaire historique*, p. 638.
22 Jean-René Suratteau, *Dictionnaire historique*, pp. 644–6.
23 Claude Petitfrère, *Dictionnaire historique*, pp. 648–9.
24 Ibid.
25 François Hincker, *Dictionnaire historique*, p. 653.
26 François Hincker, *Dictionnaire historique*, p. 447.
27 Ibid.
28 R.R. Palmer, *Twelve Who Ruled: The Year of the Terror in the French Revolution* (University Park, PA: Princeton University Press, 1970; 1989), p. 127.
29 Andress, *Terror*, p. 311.
30 Ibid., pp. 211–12.
31 François Wartelle, *Dictionnaire historique*, p. 655.
32 Doyle, *Oxford History*, p. 149.
33 Sutherland, *French Revolution*, p. 31.
34 Ibid., p. 38.
35 Roland Gotlib, *Dictionnaire historique*, pp. 658–9.
36 Albert Soboul, *The Sans-Culottes*, trans. Rémy Inglis-Hall (University Park, PA: Princeton University Press, 1980), Foreword.
37 François Furet, *Histoire Universitaire de la Révolution*, in Furet and Ozouf, *Dictionnaire Critique*, p. 992.
38 Ibid.
39 Ibid., p. 995.
40 Sutherland, *French Revolution*, pp. 121–2.
41 Albert Mathiez, *La Révolution française, Tome 2, La Gironde et la Montagne* (Paris: Denoël, [1922] 1985), pp. 8–46.
42 Moore, *Liberty*, p. 31.
43 Dominique Godineau, *Dictionnaire historique*, pp. 664–5.
44 Michel Pertué, *Dictionnaire historique*, p. 667.
45 Ibid.
46 Richard Ballard, *The Unseen Terror* (London and New York: I.B. Tauris, 2010), pp. 100–8.
47 Henri, Marquis de Grailly, *Histoire de Famille*, completed by Jean de Grailly, 1986 (privately printed. Original edn, no. 7), pp. 193–5.
48 Philippe de Carbonnières, 'Les gouaches révolutionnaires de Lesueur au musée Carnavalet', *Annales historiques de la Révolution française*, vol. 343 (January–March 2006, available online from 1 March 2009, consulted 28 October 2010, at: http://ahrf.revues.org/9882.
49 Harry Hearder, *Italy in the Age of the Risorgimento 1790–1870* (London: Longman, 1983), pp. 49–50.
50 Palmer, *Twelve*, p. 297.
51 François Wartelle, *Dictionnaire historique*, pp. 677–8.
52 Gruder, *Notables*, pp. 14–19.
53 Sutherland, *French Revolution*, pp. 26–7.
54 François Gendron, *Dictionnaire historique*, p. 684.
55 Ibid.
56 Tackett, *Becoming*, p. 157.
57 Sutherland, *French Revolution*, p. 73.
58 Petitfils, *Louis XVI*, p. 734.
59 Timothy Tackett, *When the King Took Flight* (Cambridge, MA: Harvard University Press, 2003), chap. 5.
60 Hardman, *Louis XVI*, p. 149.
61 Stephan Zweig, *Marie-Antoinette, The Portrait of an Average Woman*, trans. Eden and Cedar Paul (New York: The Viking Press, 1933; repr. Grove Press, 2002), p. 438.

Reference Notes

62 Deborah Cadbury, *The Lost King of France: The Tragic Story of Marie-Antoinette's Favourite Son* (London and New York: Fourth Estate, 2003), pp. 156–7.

63 Jean-René Suratteau, *Dictionnaire historique*, p. 689.

64 Sutherland, *French Revolution*, pp. 205–7.

65 Suratteau, Ibid., pp. 690–6.

66 Sutherland, *French Revolution*, pp. 247–53.

M

1 A term first borrowed from Friedrich Schlegel by Germaine de Staël, according to Joyce O. Lowrie, *The Violent Mystique: Thematics of Retribution and Expiation in Balzac, Barbey d'Aurevilly, Bloy and Huysmans* (Geneva: Droz, 1974), p. 18. Jules Amedée Barbey d'Aurévilly used it as a title for his 1851 discussion of de Maistre and de Bonald.

2 Massimo Boffa, 'Maistre', in Furet and Ozouf (eds), *Dictionnaire critique*, p. 1016.

3 Ibid. Author's translation.

4 Jean-René Suratteau, *Dictionnaire historique*, pp. 703–4.

5 Madeleine Fabre, *Dictionnaire historique*, p. 704.

6 Mona Ozouf, in Furet and Ozouf (eds), *Dictionnaire Critique*, p. 279.

7 Michel Vovelle, *Dictionnaire historique*, p. 711.

8 Ibid.

9 Ibid.

10 Andress, *Terror*, p. 122.

11 Ozouf, in *Dictionnaire Critique*, p. 278.

12 Andress, *Terror*, p. 164.

13 *Andress, Terror*, pp. 165–7.

14 Antonia Fraser, *Marie-Antoinette*, p. 364.

15 Stefan Zweig, *Marie-Antoinette*, p. 206.

16 Michel Vovelle, *Dictionnaire historique*, pp. 720–2.

17 Gary Kates (ed.), *The French Revolution, Recent Debates and Controversies* (New York and London: Routledge, 1998), *Introduction*, p. 3 (in 2007 reprint).

18 Guy Chaussinand-Nogand, *French Nobility*, p. 167.

19 Jean-Paul Bertaud, *Dictionnaire historique*, p. 726.

20 Schroeder, *Transformation*, pp. 204–5.

21 François Furet, in Furet and Ozouf (eds), *Dictionnaire Critique*, p. 988.

22 Ibid.

23 Ibid.

24 Ibid., p. 989.

25 Albert Mathiez, *La Révolution française*, vol. 2, *La Gironde et la Montagne* (Paris: Editions Denoël, 1985), pp. 33–4.

26 François Furet, *Interpreting the French Revolution*, trans. Elborg Forster (Cambridge: Cambridge University Press, 1981), p. 85, and n. 7.

27 Ibid., p. 86.

28 Furet, in *Dictionnaire critique*, p. 990.

29 Ibid.

30 Ibid., p. 991.

31 Albert Mathiez, *Etudes sur Robespierre 1758–1794* (Paris: Messidor, Société des études robespierristes, 1988), cited in Furet, Ibid.

32 Serge Bianchi, *Dictionnaire historique*, p. 728.

33 G. Lemarchand, *Dictionnaire historique*, p. 730.

34 F. Robert, *Dictionnaire historique*, p. 734.

35 *Dictionnaire historique*, pp. 735–7.

36 François Gendron, *Dictionnaire historique*, p. 737.
37 Sutherland, *French Revolution*, p. 87.
38 Ibid., p. 88.
39 Jean-René Suratteau, *Dictionnaire historique*, p. 741.
40 Furet, in Furet and Ozouf (eds), *Dictionnaire Critique*, p. 1033.
41 Ibid., p. 1037.
42 Jules Michelet, *Histoire de la Révolution française*, vol. 1, pp. 169–70. Author's translation.
43 Ballard, *Unseen Terror*, p. 151.
44 R. Gotlib, *Dictionnaire historique*, pp. 752–3.
45 Jean-René Suratteau, *Dictionnaire historique*, pp. 763–4.
46 Marcel Dorigny, *Dictionnaire historique*, p. 770.
47 Andress, *Terror,* p. 131.

N

1 Jean-René Suratteau, *Dictionnaire historique*, p. 780.
2 Harris, *Talleyrand,* pp. 45–8.
3 Sutherland, *French Revolution*, p. 85.
4 François Furet, *French Revolution 1770–1880*, p. 81.
5 Sutherland, *French Revolution*, p. 86.
6 Alfred Cobban, *A History of Modern France*, vol. 2: *From the First Empire to the Second Empire 1799–1871* (Harmondsworth: Penguin Books, 1961), pp. 73–4.
7 François Hincker, *Dictionnaire historique*, p. 783.
8 Ibid., p. 784.
9 Ibid.
10 Ibid.
11 Georges Lefèbvre, *The French Revolution, Volume 1,* p. 129.
12 Tackett, *Becoming,* p. 172, n. 108.
13 Sutherland, *French Revolution*, pp. 68–73.
14 Tackett, *Becoming,* pp. 171–5.
15 Jean-Christian Petitfils, *Louis XVI* (Paris: Perrin, 2005), p. 706.
16 Sutherland, *French Revolution*, pp. 100–3.
17 William Doyle, *The Oxford History of the French Revolution* (Oxford: Oxford University Press, 1989), p. 138.
18 Guy Chaussinand-Nogaret, *French Nobility*, chap. 5.
19 Sutherland, *French Revolution*, p. 27.
20 Ibid., p. 34.

O

1 Petitfils, *Louis XVI*, pp. 717–18.
2 Sutherland, *French Revolution*, pp. 74–8.
3 François Furet, in Furet and Ozouf (eds), *Dictionnaire Critique*, p. 156.
4 Sutherland, *French Revolution,* p. 115.
5 Sutherland, *French Revolution*, p. 26.
6 François Gendron, *Dictionnaire historique*, p. 800.
7 Ibid.
8 Ibid.
9 Ibid.
10 Ibid, p. 801. Munro Price, *The Perilous Crown, France between Revolutions 1814–1848* (London: Macmillan, 2007) pp. 35–6.

Reference Notes

P

1 Raymonde Monnier, *Dictionnaire historique*, p. 806.
2 Andress, *Terror*, pp. 166–7.
3 Ibid., p. 174.
4 Ibid., p. 181.
5 Ibid., p. 293.
6 Monnier, Ibid.
7 Sutherland, *French Revolution*, p. 21.
8 Simon Schama, *Citizens* (London: Viking, 1989), p. 379.
9 Schama, *Citizens*, pp. 409–16.
10 Lucy Moore, *Liberty*, p. 61.
11 Ibid., p. 120.
12 Sutherland, *French Revolution*, p. 20.
13 Ibid.
14 Michel Pertué, *Dictionnaire historique*, p. 818. Author's translation.
15 Doyle, *Oxford History*, p. 16.
16 Sutherland, *French Revolution*, p. 68.
17 Marcel Dorigny, *Dictionnaire historique*, p. 839.
18 Sutherland, *French Revolution*, p. 135.
19 Dorigny, Ibid.
20 Lynn Hunt, *Politics, Culture and Class in the French Revolution* (Berkeley: University of California Press, 2004), p. 86.
21 Doyle, *Oxford History*, pp. 57–8.
22 Annie Crépin, *Dictionnaire historique*, p. 842.
23 Sutherland, *French Revolution*, p. 124.
24 Annie Crépin, *Dictionnaire historique*, p. 844.
25 Peter McPhee, *Living the French Revolution 1789–99* (New York: Palgrave Macmillan, 2009), p. 67.
26 Ibid., p. 217.
27 Jean-René Suratteau, *Dictionnaire historique*, pp. 843–4.
28 Lynn Hunt, *Politics*, p. 104.
29 Ibid., 102–14.
30 Jean-René Suratteau, *Dictionnaire historique*, p. 157.
31 Jean Egret, *La Pré-Révolution française: 1787–1788* (Paris: Presses Universitaires de France Vendôme, 1962).
32 Georges Lefebvre, *The French Revolution from Its Origins to 1793*, trans. Elizabeth Moss Evanson (New York: Columbia University Press, 1962), p. 97.
33 Albert Goodwin, *The French Revolution* (London: Hutchinson, 1953), pp. 25–38.
34 Gruder, *Notables*, p. 1.
35 Ballard, *Unseen Terror*, p. 229 n.1.
36 Jean-René Suratteau, *Dictionnaire historique*, pp. 861–3.
37 Ibid.
38 R.R. Palmer, *Twelve*, p. 393.
39 Jean-René Suratteau, *Dictionnaire historique*, pp. 860–1.
40 R.R. Palmer, *Twelve*, p. 211.
41 Ibid., p. 343.
42 Suratteau, Ibid.
43 Ibid.
44 Rebecca L. Spang, *The Invention of the Restaurant: Paris and Modern Gastronomic Culture* (Cambridge, MA and London: Harvard University Press, 2000), p. 120.

45 Roger Dupuy, *Dictionnaire historique*, pp. 412–13.
46 Ibid., p. 413.
47 François Gendron, *Dictionnaire historique*, p. 873.
48 Hervé Guénot, *Dictionnaire historique*, p. 874.
49 Sutherland, *French Revolution*, p. 21.
50 Blanning, *Culture of Power*, pp. 5–14.
51 François Gendron, *Dictionnaire historique*, p. 875.
52 Emile Gabory, *L'Angleterre et la Vendée,* vol. 1, pp. 133–51.
53 Ibid.

Q

1 Roger Dupuy, *Dictionnaire historique*, p. 877.
2 Gabory, *L'Angleterre*, pp. 218ff.
3 Ibid., pp. 261ff.
4 Ibid., pp. 307ff.
5 Dupuy, Ibid., p. 878.

R

1 Anne-Marie Duport, *Dictionnaire historique*, p. 881.
2 Schroeder, *Transformation*, pp. 189–90.
3 Serge Bianchi, *Dictionnaire historique*, pp. 312–15.
4 Nigel Aston, *Religion and Revolution in France 1780–1804* (Washington, DC: The Catholic University of America Press, 2000), p. 176.
5 Ballard, *Unseen Terror*, pp. 74–83.
6 Petitfils, *Louis XVI*, pp. 929–30.
7 Scurr, *Fatal Purity*, pp. 293–4.
8 Colin Jones, *Longman Companion to the French Revolution* (London and New York, 1990), pp. 186, 280.
9 Alan Forrest, *Paris, the Provinces and the French Revolution* (London: Arnold, 2004), p. 172.
10 Spang, *Invention of the Restaurant*, pp. 140–1.
11 Harris, *Talleyrand*, p. 219.
12 Jean-René Suratteau, *Dictionnaire historique*, pp. 898–903.
13 Raymonde Monnier, *Dictionnaire historique*, p. 904.
14 Sutherland, *French Revolution*, p. 54.
15 Claude Mazauric, *Dictionnaire historique*, p. 913.
16 Armand Lods, *Un Conventionnel en mission, Bernard de Saintes et la Réunion de la Principauté de Montbéliard* (Paris, 1888), chap. 8.
17 London: Chatto & Windus, 2006.
18 Patrice Gueniffey, in Furet and Ozouf (eds), *Dictionnaire Critique*, p. 319.
19 Jean-Clément Martin, *La Révolution française* (Paris : Cavalier Bleu, 2008), pp. 45–9.
20 Scurr, *Fatal Purity*, pp. 29–30
21 Claude Mazauric, *Dictionnaire historique*, pp. 915–16.
22 Ibid., p. 916.
23 Ibid., p. 917.
24 Ibid.
25 Ibid.
26 Maximilien Robespierre, *Œuvres complètes*, ed. E. Hamel (Paris: Société des Etudes Robespierristes, Ernest Leroux, 1910–67), vol. 9, p. 228, quoted in Scurr, *Fatal Purity*, p. 227.
27 Mazauric, *Dictionnaire historique*, p. 919.

28 Scurr, *Fatal Purity*, pp. 274–5.
29 Gueniffey, *Dictionnaire critique*, p. 332.
30 Marcel Dorigny, *Dictionnaire historique*, pp. 926 and 928.
31 Ibid., p. 926
32 Ibid., p. 929.
33 Andress, *Terror*, p. 74.
34 Ibid., pp. 138–9.
35 Ibid., p. 150.
36 Ibid., p. 151.
37 Dorigny, Ibid.
38 Ibid., p. 927.
39 Schroeder, *Transformation*, pp. 183–4.
40 Jean-René Suratteau, *Dictionnaire historique*, pp. 933–5.
41 Raymonde Monnier, *Dictionnaire historique*, p. 936.
42 Blanning, *Culture of Power*, pp. 361–2.
43 Maurice Cranston, *The Noble Savage: Jean-Jacques Rousseau 1754–1762* (London: Penguin, 1991), pp. 134–5.
44 Ibid., p. 137.
45 Blanning, Ibid., p. 363.
46 Colin Jones, *Great Nation*, pp. 195–6.
47 Bernard Manin, *Dictionnaire critique*, p. 872.
48 Ibid., p. 873.
49 Ibid., p. 874.
50 Ibid., p. 875.
51 Ibid., p. 881.
52 Cranston, *Noble Savage*, pp. 16–21.
53 Ibid., pp. 32–5.
54 Ibid., pp. 175–89.
55 Manin, Ibid., p. 885.
56 Ibid., p. 883.
57 The title of Maurice Cranston's second book in his definitive biography of Rousseau.
58 Printed in Paris later as *Le Triomphe des braves Parisiens sur les ennemis du bien public* (Bibliothèque Nationale, P87, 1172). Dominique Rousseau, *Saint-Thomas de Conac: Une histoire en bord d'estuaire* (privately printed), 2008.
59 Augustin-Alexis Taillet, *Eglise de Saintes 1789–1796*, ed. P. Lemonnier (Saintes: *Bulletin des Archives Historique de la Saintonge et de l'Aunis XXI*, 1902), pp. 333–4.
60 John Hardman, *The French Revolution: The Fall of the Ancien Régime to the Thermidorean reaction 1785–1795* (London: Arnold, 1981), p. 171.
61 Roland Gotlib, *Dictionnaire historique*, pp. 939–40.
62 Schroeder, *Transformation*, p. 134.

S

1 Daniel Ligou, *Dictionnaire historique,* p. 595.
2 Ibid., p. 596.
3 Ibid., p. 597.
4 Jean-René Suratteau, *Dictionnaire historique*, p. 991.
5 Albert Soboul, *Saint Just, Discours et Rapports* (Paris: Messidor/Editions sociales, 1988), *Introduction*, p. 13.
6 Ibid., p. 16.
7 Ibid., p. 17.

8   Ibid., p. 20.
9   Ibid., p. 18.
10 Ange Rovère, *Dictionnaire historique*, p. 956.
11 Michael Sonenscher, *Sans-Culottes: An Eighteenth-Century Emblem in the French Revolution* (University Park, PA: Princeton University Press, 2008), p. 133.
12 *When the King Took Flight*, p. 108.
13 Claudy Valin, in François Julien-Labruyère (ed.), *Dictionnaire Biographique des Charentais* (Paris: Le Croît vif, 2005), p. 1000.
14 Soboul, *Sans-Culottes*, pp. 111–12.
15 Raymonde Monnier, *Dictionnaire historique*, p. 965.
16 Ibid.
17 Jean-René Suratteau, *Dictionnaire historique*, p. 144 and Dominique Julia, Ibid., pp. 632–3. See also, Colin Jones, *Longman Companion*, pp. 271–4.
18 Sutherland, *French Revolution*, p. 140.
19 Jean-René Suratteau, *Dictionnaire historique*, pp. 982.
20 Ibid.
21 Ibid., pp. 982–3.
22 Ibid.
23 Ibid., p. 984.
24 Ibid.
25 Ibid.
26 Ibid., p. 985.
27 Ibid.
28 Albert Soboul, *The Sans-culottes, The Popular Movement and Revolutionary Government 1793–1794*, trans. Rémy Inglis Hall (University Park, PA: Princeton University Press, 1980).
29 William Doyle, *Thomas Paine and the Girondins*, in *Officers, Nobles and Revolutionaries* (London and Rio Grande: Hambledon Press, 1995), pp. 211–13.
30 Ginette et Georges Marty, *Chansons de la Révolution* (Paris: Tallandier, 1988), pp. 71–3.
31 Ibid., p. 77.
32 Ibid., pp. 79–80.
33 Ibid., p. 81.
34 Ibid., pp. 97–9.
35 Robert Brécy, *Dictionnaire historique*, p. 178.
36 Marty, Ibid., pp. 9–10.
37 Ibid., pp. 146–7.
38 Lucy Moore, *Liberty*, pp. 137–8.
39 Ibid., pp. 142, 146.
40 Ibid., p. 331.
41 Ibid., p. 344.
42 Elisabeth G.-Sledziewski, *Dictionnaire historique*, p. 994.
43 Claude Petitfrère, *Dictionnaire historique*, p. 996.
44 Scurr, *Fatal Purity*, pp. 295–6, 314–15.

T

1   François Gendron, *Dictionnaire historique*, p. 1014.
2   David Lawday, *Napoleon's Master, A Life of Prince Talleyrand* (London: Jonathan Cape, 2006), p. 2.
3   François Gendron, *Dictionnaire historique*, p. 1014.
4   Ibid., p. 1015. Author's translation.

Reference Notes

5 Michèle Belle-Labat, *Dictionnaire historique*, p. 1015.
6 Ibid., p. 1016.
7 Ibid.
8 Jean-René Suratteau, *Dictionnaire historique*, pp. 1016–17.
9 Sutherland, *French Revolution*, p. 96.
10 Ibid.
11 Ibid., p. 97.
12 Ibid., p. 98.
13 Furet, *Revolutionary France 1770–1880*, trans. Antonia Nevill, pp. 63–6.
14 Jules Michelet, *Histoire de la Révolution française*, vol. 1, p. 181. Author's translation.
15 Jean-Christian Petitfils, *Louis XVI* (Paris: Perrin, 2005), pp. 663–5.
16 Michelet, Ibid., p. 191.
17 Furet, *Revolutionary France 1770–1880*, trans. Antonia Nevill, p. 64.
18 Ibid., p. 65.
19 Ibid., p. 66.
20 Scurr, *Fatal Purity*, p. 275.
21 Schama, *Citizens*, p. 447.
22 Furet, *Revolutionary France 1770–1880*, trans. Antonia Nevill, p. 134.
23 Ibid.
24 Ibid., p 147.
25 For a view critical of Furet's, see Sutherland, *French Revolution*, pp. 175ff.
26 Furet, Ibid.
27 François Furet, 'Terreur', in Furet and Ozouf, *Dictionnaire Critique*, pp. 168–9. Author's translation.
28 Serge Bianchi, *Dictionnaire Historique*, pp. 1029-30.
29 J. Holland Rose, *The Life of Napoleon I* (London: Bell, 1910), vol. 1, p. 274.
30 Mona Ozouf, in Furet and Ozouf (eds), *Dictionnaire critique*, p. 611.
31 Ruth Scurr, *Fatal Purity*, pp. 303–4.
32 Scurr, *Fatal Purity*, pp. 311–25.
33 Dominique Godineau, *Dictionnaire historique*, pp. 1032–3.
34 Moore, *Liberty*, pp. 111–33.
35 Ibid., pp. 192–3.
36 Ibid., pp. 387.
37 Doyle, *Oxford History*, pp. 101, 93.
38 Hugh Brogan, *Alexis de Tocqueville, Prophet of Democracy in the Age of Revolution, A Biography* (London: Profile Books, 2006), p. 575.
39 Furet, *Interpreting*, p. 135.
40 Michel Vovelle, *Dictionnaire historique*, pp. 1040–3.
41 Marcel Dorigny, *Dictionnaire historique*, pp. 1043–4.
42 Jean-René Suratteau, *Dictionnaire historique*, p. 1045.

1 Jean-René Suratteau, *Dictionnaire historique*, p. 1064.
2 Stephen Pope, *Cassell Dictionary*, p. 496.
3 François Gendron, *Dictionnaire historique*, p. 1071.
4 Timothy Tackett, *When the King Took Flight* (Cambridge, MA and London: Harvard University Press, 2003), pp. 104–8.
5 Sutherland, *French Revolution*, p. 117.
6 Tackett, *When the King*, pp. 162–78.
7 Mona Ozouf, *Varennes, La Mort de la royauté* (Paris: Gallimard, 2005), p. 408.

8   Morris Slavin, *The Left and the French Revolution* (Atlantic Highlands: Humanity Press, 1995), pp. 58–80, *Jean Varlet as Defender of Direct Democracy*. Available online at: http://www.athene.antenna.nl/ARCHIEF/NR03–Parijs/SLAVIN%20–%20Jean%20Varlet%20as.htm.

9   William Doyle, *4 August 1789, The Intellectual Background to the Abolition of Venality of Offices*, in *Officers, Nobles and Revolutionaries, Essays on Eighteenth-Century France* (London and Rio Grande: The Hambledon Press, 1995), pp. 152–3.

10 Reynald Secher, *A French Genocide*, trans. George Holoch (Notre Dame, IN: University of Notre Dame Press, 2003).

11 Peter McPhee, *H-France Review*, vol. 4, no. 26 (March 2004). Available online at: www.h-france.net/vol4reviews/mcphee3.html.

12 Anne Bernet, *Charette* (Paris: Perrin, 2005), pp. 61–3.

13 Emile Gabory, *L'Angleterre et la Vendée*, pp. 94–112.

14 Doyle, *Oxford History*, pp. 320–1.

15 John Julius Norwich, *A History of Venice* (Harmondsworth: Penguin Books, 1983), pp. 623–31.

16 Schroeder, *Transformation*, p. 171.

17 Françoise Brunel, *Dictionnaire historique*, p. 1083.

18 Marcel Dorigny, *Dictionnaire historique*, p. 1084.

19 Angelica Goodden, *The Sweetness of Life: A Biography of Elisabeth Vigée-Le Brun* (London: André Deutsch, 1997), pp. 77–8.

20 Jacques Guilhaumou, *Dictionnaire historique*, p. 1092.

21 Colin Jones, *Great Nation*, p. 188.

22 Quoted in Colin Jones, *Great Nation*, p. 189.

23 Doyle, *Old European Order*, p. 199.

24 Cranston, *Noble Savage*, p. 30.

25 Jones, *Great Nation*, p. 270.

26 Doyle, *Old European Order*, p. 203.

27 Jones, *Great Nation*, p. 530.

W

1   Annie Crépin, *Dictionnaire historique*, pp. 1101–2.

2   Richard Cobb, *The Police and the People, French Popular Protest, 1789–1820* (Oxford: Oxford University Press, 1970), pp. 131–50.

3   Ibid., p. 140.

4   Sutherland, *French Revolution*, p. 109.

Y

1   Jean-René Suratteau, *Dictionnaire historique*, pp. 1104–5.

2   Jean-René Suratteau, *Dictionnaire historique*, p. 1106.

Bibliography

Andress, David, *The Terror, Civil War in the French Revolution* (London: Little Brown, 2005).

Arasse, Daniel, *The Guillotine and the Terror*, trans. Christopher Miller (London: Penguin Books, 1991).

Asprey, Robert, *The Rise and Fall of Napoleon Bonaparte*, 2 vols (London: Little Brown 2000, 2001).

Aston, Nigel, *Religion and Revolution in France, 1780–1804* (London: Macmillan, 2000).

Ballard, Richard, *The Unseen Terror: The French Revolution in the Provinces* (London and New York: I.B.Tauris, 2010), pp. 43–57.

Bertrand de Moleville, Antoine-François (Marquis de), *Private memoirs relative to the last year of the reign of Lewis the Sixteenth, late king of France*, vol. 2 (London: A. Strahan, 1797). Available online at http://books.google.com/.

Birch, Una, *Secret Societies, Illuminati, Freemasons, and the French Revolution*, ed. James Wassermann (Lake Worth, FL: Ibis Books, 1911 and 2007).

Birchall, Ian H., *The Spectre of Babeuf* (Basingstoke: Macmillan, 1997).

Blanning, T.C.W., *The Origins of the French Revolutionary Wars* (London and New York: Oxford University Press, 1983).

—— (ed.), *The Rise and Fall of the French Revolution* (London and Chicago: The University of Chicago Press, 1996).

——, *The Culture of Power and the Power of Culture, Old Regime Europe 1660–1789* (Oxford: Oxford University Press, 2002).

——, *The Culture of Power and the Power of Culture: Old Regime Europe 1660–1789* (Oxford: Oxford University Press, 2003), pp. 432–5.

Blaufarb, Rafe, *The French Army, 1750–1820: Careers, Talent, Merit* (Manchester: Manchester University Press, 2002).

Blunt, Wilfrid, *The Art of Botanical Illustration* (London: Collins, 1950). Online at: www.octavo.com/editions/rdtrse/.

Boyd, Malcolm (ed.), *Music and the French Revolution* (Cambridge: Cambridge University Press, 1992).

Bruce, Evangeline, *Napoleon and Josephine: An Improbable Marriage* (London: Weidenfeld & Nicolson, 1995).

Burke, Edmund, *Reflections on the Revolution in France*, ed., with Introduction, L.G. Mitchell (Oxford: Oxford University Press; repr. 2009).

Cadbury, Deborah, *The Lost King of France: The Tragic Story of Marie-Antoinette's Favourite Son* (London and New York: Fourth Estate, 2002).

Censer, Jack H., and Hunt, Lynn, *Liberty-Equality, Fraternity; Exploring the French Revolution* (University Park, PA: Pennsylvania State University Press, 2001).

Bibliography

Charlton, David, *Grétry and the Growth of Opéra-comique* (Cambridge: Cambridge University Press, 1986).

Chaussinand-Nogaret, Guy, *The French Nobility in the Eighteenth Century: From Feudalism to Enlightenment*, trans. William Doyle (Cambridge: Cambridge University Press, 1985).

Cobb, Richard, *The Police and the People: French Popular Protest 1789–1820* (Oxford: Oxford University Press, 1970).

Cohen, J. (trans.), *The Confessions of Jean-Jacques Rousseau* (London: Penguin Press, 2005).

Cranston, Maurice, *Jean-Jacques, The Early Life and Works of Jean-Jacques Rousseau, 1712–1754* (London: Viking/Penguin, 1982).

——, *The Noble Savage, Jean-Jacques Rousseau 1754–1762* (London, Viking/Penguin, 1991).

——, *The Solitary Self: Jean-Jacques Rousseau in Exile and Adversity* (London: Viking/Penguin, 1997).

Crook, Malcolm, *Toulon in War and Revolution: From the Ancien Regime to the Restoration, 1750–1820 (War, Armed Forces and Society)* (Manchester: Manchester University Press, 1991).

Crubaugh, Anthony, *Balancing the Scales of Justice: Local Courts and Rural Society in Southwest France, 1750–1800* (University Park, PA: Pennsylvania State University Press, 2001).

Darnton, Robert, *The Forbidden Best-Sellers of Pre-Revolutionary France* (London: Fontana Press, 1997).

Devlin, F. Roger, *Bonald's Theory of the Nobility*, *The Occidental Quarterly Online*, available online at: http://www.toqonline.com/2009/12/bonalds-theory-of-the-nobility/.

Doyle, William, *The Oxford History of the French Revolution* (Oxford: Oxford University Press, 1989).

——, *Origins of the French Revolution* (Oxford: Oxford University Press, 2nd edn, 1988; 3rd edn, 1999)

——, *Officers, Nobles and Revolutionaries: Essays on Eighteenth-Century France* (London and Rio Grande: Hambledon Press, 1995).

——, *Jansenism* (Basingstoke: Macmillan, 2000).

——, *The French Revolution: A Very Short Introduction* (Oxford: Oxford University Press, 2001).

—— (ed.), *Old Regime France* (Oxford: Oxford University Press, 2001).

——, *Aristocracy and Its Enemies: In the Age of Revolution* (Oxford: Oxford University Press, 2009).

Forrest, Alan, *Soldiers of the French Revolution* (Durham, NC and London: Duke University Press, 1990).

——, *Paris, The Provinces and The French Revolution* (London: Arnold, 2004).

Fraser, Antonia, *Marie-Antoinette: The Journey* (London: Weidenfeld and Nicolson, 2001).

Furet, François, *Interpreting the French Revolution*, trans. Elborg Forster (Cambridge: Cambridge University Press, 1981).

——, *Revolutionary France 1770–1880*, trans. Alison Nevill (Oxford: Basil Blackwell, 1988).

——, and Ozouf, Mona (eds), *A Critical Dictionary of the French Revolution*, trans. Arthur Goldhammer (London: The Belknap Press of Harvard University Press, 1989).

Goldstein Sepinwall, Alyssa, *The Abbé Grégoire and the French Revolution: The Making of Modern Universalism* (Berkeley: University of California Press, 2005).

Goodden, Angela, *The Sweetness of Life: A Biography of Elisabeth Louise Vigée Le Brun* (London: André Deutsch, 1997).

Goodwin, Albert, *The Friends of Liberty: The English Democratic Movement in the Age of the French Revolution* (London: Hutchinson, 1979).

Gruder, Vivian R., *The Notables and the Nation: The Political Schooling of the French 1787–1788* (London and Cambridge, MA: Harvard University Press, 2007).

Hampson, Norman, *Danton* (Oxford: Basil Blackwell, 1974).

——, *Saint-Just* (Oxford: Oxford University Press, 1991).

Hardman, John, *The French Revolution; The Fall of the Ancien Régime to the Thermidorean Reaction 1785–1796* (London: Edward Arnold, 1981).

——, *Louis XVI* (New Haven, CT and London: Yale University Presss, 1993).

Harris, Robin, *Talleyrand: Betrayer and Saviour of France* (London: John Murray, 2007).

Hibbert, Christopher, *The French Revolution* (London: Penguin Books, 1980).

Hunt, Lynn, *Politics, Culture and Class in the French Revolution* (London, Berkeley and Los Angeles: University of California Press, 2004).

Hyman, Paula, *The Jews of Modern France* (London and Berkeley, CA: University of California Press, 1998).

James, C.L.R., *The Black Jacobins' Toussaint L'Ouverture and the San Domingo Revolution* (London: Penguin History, 2001). Available online at: http://thelouvertureproject.org/index.php.

Jones, Colin, *The Longman Companion to the French Revolution* (London and New York: Longman, 1988).

——, *The Great Nation, France from Louis XV to Napoleon* (London: Allen Lane, The Penguin Press, 2002).

Kates, Gary (ed.), *The French Revolution: Recent Debates and New Controversies* (2nd edn, New York and Abingdon: Routledge, 2006).

Kohl, Hubertus, and Reichardt, Rolf, *Visualizing the Revolution: Politics and Pictorial Arts in Late Eighteenth-Century France* (London: Reaktion Books, 2008).

Lawday, David, *The Giant of the French Revolution: Danton, A Life* (New York: Grove Press, 2009).

Lefebvre, Georges, *The Great Fear of 1789: Rural Panic in Revolutionary France*, trans. Joan White (New York: Schocken Books, 1973).

Luttrell, Barbara, *Mirabeau* (Chicago: Southern Illinois University Press, 2000).

McLynn, Frank, *Napoleon* (London: Jonathan Cape, 1997).

McManners, John, *Church and Society in Eighteenth-Century France*, vol. 2 (Oxford: Oxford University Press, 1998).

McPhee, Peter, *Living the French Revolution, 1789–99* (Basingstoke and New York: Palgrave Macmillan, 2009).

Maistre, Joseph de, *Considerations on France,* ed. Richard A. Lebrun with an Introduction by Isaiah Berlin (Cambridge: Cambridge University Press, 1974 and 1994).

Mansell, Philip, *Louis XVIII* (London: John Murray, 2005).

Mantel, Hilary, *A Place of Greater Safety* (London: Viking, 1992; Fourth Estate, 2010). Novel.

Mathiez, Albert, *The French Revolution*, trans. Catherine Alison Phillips (London: Williams and Norgate, 1927).

Michelet, Jules, *History of the French Revolution*, trans. C. Cocks (London: H.G. Bohn, 1847). Vols 1 and 2 are available online at: http://books.google.com/books.

Mitford, Nancy, *Voltaire in Love* (London: Hamish Hamilton, 1957).

Moore, Lucy, *Liberty: The Lives and Times of Six Women in Revolutionary France* (London, Harper Press, 2006).

Moorhead, Caroline, *Dancing to the Precipice: Lucie de La Tour du Pin and the French Revolution* (London: Chatto & Windus, 2009).

Neely, Sylvia, *A Concise History of the French Revolution* (Lanham, MA, and Plymouth: Rowman & Littlefield, 2008).

Norwich, John Julius, *A History of Venice* (London: Allen Lane, 1982).

Paine, Thomas, *Rights of Man, Common Sense, and Other Political Writings*, ed. with an Introduction and Notes by Mark Philp (Oxford: Oxford World Classics, 2008).

Palmer, R.R., *Twelve Who Ruled, The Year of the Terror in the French Revolution* (University Park, PA: Princeton University Press, Bicentennial Edition, 1989). Online at: http://www-history.mcs.st-and.ac.uk/Biographies/Carnot.html.

Pope, Stephen, *The Cassell Dictionary of the Napoleonic Wars* (London: Cassell, 1999).

Price, Munro, *The Fall of the French Monarchy: Louis XVI, Marie-Antoinette and the Baron de Breteuil* (London: Macmillan, 2002).

Ridge, Antonia, *The Man Who Painted Roses: The Story of Pierre-Joseph Redouté* (London: Faber & Faber, 1979).

Roland Michel, Marianne, *The Floral Art of Pierre-Joseph Redouté* (London: Frances Lincoln, 2002).

Rousseau, Jean-Jacques, *The Social Contract*, trans. Maurice Cranston (London: Penguin Press, 1968).

——, *A Discourse on Inequality*, trans. Maurice Cranston (London: Penguin Press, 2003).

——, *Emile*, trans. Barbara Coxley (London: J. M. Dent, 2000).

Rudé, George, *The Crowd in the French Revolution* (Oxford: Oxford University Press, 1959).

Schama, Simon, *Citizens: A Chronicle of the French Revolution* (London: Viking, 1989).

Schom, Alan, *Napoleon Bonaparte* (New York: HarperCollins, 1997).

Schroeder, Paul W., *The Transformation of European Politics 1763–1848* (Oxford: Oxford University Press, 1994).

Scurr, Ruth, *Fatal Purity: Robespierre and the French Revolution* (London: Chatto & Windus, 2006).

Shennan, J.H., *The Parlement of Paris* (rev. edn, Stroud: Sutton Publishing, 1998).

Shuckburgh, Evelyn (trans. and ed.), *The Memoirs of Madame Roland, A Heroine of the French Revolution* (London: Barrie & Jenkins, 1989).

Slavin, Morris, *Jean Varlet as Defender of Direct Democracy*. Available online at: http://www.athene.antenna.nl/ARCHIEF/NR03–Parijs/SLAVIN%20–%20Jean%20Varlet%20as.htm.

Soboul, Albert, *The Sansculottes: The Popular Movement and Revolutionary Government 1793–1794*, trans. Rémy Inglis Hall (University Park, PA: Princeton University Press, 1980).

——, *Dictionnaire historique de la Révolution française*, ed. J.-R. Suratteau and F. Gendron (Paris: Quadrige/Presses Universitaires de France, 2nd edn, 2006).

Sonencher, Michael, *Sansculottes: An Eighteenth-Century Emblem in the French Revolution* (University Park, PA: Princeton University Press, 2008).

Spang, Rebecca L., *The Invention of the Restaurant, Paris and Modern Gastronomic Culture* (London and Cambridge, MA: Harvard University Press, 2000).

Staël, Germaine de, *Considerations on the Principal Events of the French Revolution* (Indianapolis: Liberty Fund Inc., 2009).

Stone, Bailey, *Reinterpreting the French Revolution: A Global Historical Perspective* (Cambridge: Cambridge University Press, 2002).

Sutherland, D.M.G., *France 1789–1815: Revolution and Counterrevolution* (London: Fontana, 1990).

——, *The French Revolution and Empire: The Quest for a Civic Order* (Oxford: Blackwell, 2003).

——, *Liberty and Its Price: Understanding the French Revolution*. Unabridged audiobook, narrated by the author (Recorded Books LLC, 2008).

Tackett, Timothy, *Religion, Revolution and Regional Culture in Eighteenth-Century France: The Ecclesiastical Oath of 1791* (University Park, PA: Princeton University Press, 1996).

——, *When the King Took Flight* (Cambridge, MA and London: Harvard University Press, 2003).

——, *Becoming a Revolutionary* (University Park, PA: Princeton University Press, 2006).

Thomas, Chantal, *The Wicked Queen: The Origins of the Myth of Marie Antoinette*, trans. Julie Ross (New York: Zone Books, 1999).

Tocqueville, Alexis de, *The Old Régime and the Revolution*, trans. John Bonner (New York: Harper & Brothers, 1856). Original edn, Paris, 1856. Available online at: http://books.google.com/books.

Tombs, Robert, *France 1814–1914* (London and New York: Longman, 1996), chap. 17.

Tombs, Robert, and Tombs, Isabelle, *That Sweet Enemy: The French and the English from the Sun King to the Present* (London: Heinemann, 2006).

Voltaire, *Letters on England*, trans. Leonard Tancock (1980; new edn with additional material by Haydn Mason, London: Penguin, 2005).

——, *Candide and Other Stories*, trans. Roger Pearson (Oxford: Oxford University Press, 2008).

Zweig, Stefan, *Marie-Antoinette: The Portrait of an Average Woman*, trans. Eden and Cedar Paul (New York: The Viking Press, 1933; repr. Grove Press, 2002).

General Index

Entries in the Dictionary are not included in this index.

Aachen (Aix La Chapelle) 133
Abbaye de Saint-Denis 216
Abbaye Prison 41, 68, 92, 111, 312, 332, 341
Abercrombie, Sir Ralph, British General (1734–1801) 123
Abolition of hereditary titles xvii, 84
Academy of Sciences 90, 194, 244
Acre 45, 123
Act of Mediation 164
Addington, Henry, Vicomte Sidmouth (1757–1844) 385
Aerostatiers 281
Agriculture 61, 271, 388
Aiguillon, Armand II de Vignerot du Plessis de Richelieu, Duc d' (1750–1800) 89, 253
Air balloons 136, 281
Alexander I, Tsar of Russia (1801–24) 298
Alexandria 122
Alps 64, 116, 138, 198, 218, 279, 285, 364, 383
Alsace 138
Amalgame Law 116, 330
Amazones 359
American War of Independence 47, 52, 61, 98, 133, 180, 185, 190, 251, 256, 272, 295
Ami du peuple 93, 94, 98, 142, 199, 222, 223, 261, 320, 332
Amiens, Peace of 52, 123, 385
Amnesty of 26 October 1795 6, 64, 205, 208, 262, 283, 297, 323
Anacreon 28
Anarcharsis 83
Anexagoras 72

Angoulême, Marie-Thérèse de France, Duchesse d' (1778–1851) 210, 216, 226, 285, 366, 379
Annales Patriotiques 65
Antiboul, Charles-Louis (1752–93) 227
Apollon 204
Arcola xxii, 157, 175
Armoire de Fer (The king's secret strongbox) 311
Army of Italy xxiv, 12, 31, 35, 45, 115, 171, 231, 279, 285, 306, 312, 326, 336
Army of the Alps 116, 198, 218, 279
Army of the Coasts of La Rochelle 239
Army of the Moselle 166
Army of the Princes 13, 19, 92, 125, 201, 210, 284
Army of the Sambre and Meuse 135–6, 144, 167, 180
Army of the Rhine and Moselle 300
Army of the Vosges 98
Arras 24, 139, 306
Augereau, Charles-Pierre-François (1757–1816) 31, 65, 144
Austria, Austrian xviii, xix, xxii, xxv, 1, 19, 32, 33, 36, 37, 40, 45, 50, 54, 62, 63, 65, 67, 68, 75, 76, 77, 95, 103, 110, 113, 119, 125, 132, 135, 137, 138, 139, 142, 144, 156, 164, 166, 167, 173, 174, 175, 178, 180, 188, 189, 190, 196, 202, 210, 222, 225, 226, 237, 239, 258, 260, 264, 272, 273, 274, 281, 284, 285, 291, 292, 301, 310, 326, 335, 336, 357, 358, 365, 366, 375, 376, 383, 384, 385, 386
Autun 16, 63, 82, 134, 249, 345

Avignon xvii, 4, 20, 21, 22, 79, 132, 137, 138, 179, 206, 227, 234, 277, 307, 387

Balzac, Honoré de (1799–1850) 404
Barry, Jeanne Bécu, Comtesse du (1743–93) 102, 112, 160
Barthélémy, Balthazar-François, Marquis de (1747–1830) xxiv, 33, 83, 145
Beaulieu de Marconnay, Johann Peter 174, 375
Bellegarde, Adèle de 165
Berne 222
Berthollet, Claude-Louis (1748–1822) 123, 244
Besançon 132, 231, 232, 246, 272
Beurnonville, Pierre de Ruel, Marquis de (1752–1821) 119
Bicêtre 161, 320
Bishoprics 78, 79
Bo, Jean-Baptiste (1743–1814) 227, 297
Boisgelin de Cicé, Jean de Dieu-Raimond (1732–1804) 82
Bologna 76, 312
Bonaparte, Joseph (1768–1844) 277
Bonaparte, Lucien (1775–1840) 53, 56, 279, 336
Bonaparte, Pauline (1780–1825) 143
Boucher, François (1703–70) 101
Boulogne 52, 122
Bourbon, Louis Henri, Duc de (1756–1830) 124
Bourgeois militia 33, 248
Brest xxii, 52, 85, 88, 102, 117, 247, 282, 283, 289, 322
Breton Club 154, 176, 198, 300, 307
Brigandage 2, 373
Brissotins 50, 103, 377
Brittany 40, 75, 131, 192, 287, 322, 347
Brouage 169
Brune, Guillaume-Marie-Anne, Comte de (1763–1815) 35, 77, 164
Brussels 32, 37, 103, 133, 136, 157, 178, 237, 283
Bungay 72
Burgundy 39

Ça ira 327, 339
Cadoudal, Georges (1771–1804) 75, 76, 273, 289
Cairo 122, 123
Camps of Jalès 255
Cantal 297
Cape of Good Hope 89

Carmagnole 271, 339, 340
Carmelites 332
Carteaux, Jean-Baptiste-François (1751–1813) 22, 44, 132, 143, 227, 362
Casoni, Filippo (1733–1811) 21
Castiglione 175
Catherine II, Tsarina of Russia (1762–96) 13, 14, 358, 368, 383
Catholic and Royal Army 75, 80, 124, 170
Cavaignac, Louis-Eugène (1802–57) 361
Cayenne 86, 294
Championnet (so-called), Jean Étienne Vachier (1762–1800) 279
Champ de Mars xvi, 26, 27, 83, 99, 105, 110, 133, 163, 166, 186, 187, 202, 223, 243, 260, 334, 339, 370, 371
Champollion, Jean-François (1790–1832) 123
Charente 134, 158
Charleroi 37, 136, 299
Charles, Archduke of Austria (1771–1847) 175, 180, 181, 231, 385
Charles IV of Spain 95, 212, 259
Charles X 13, 44, 124, 126, 188, 240, 274, 299, 346
Chartres, Louis-Philippe, Duc de, future Louis Philippe I 100, 119, 178, 260
Châtelet 165
Châtelet, Louis-Marie-Florent de Lomont d'Haraucourt, Duc du (1727–93) 253
Chaudron-Rousseau, Gillaume (1752–1816) 297
Chemin-Depontes, Jean-Baptiste (1761–1852) 354
Chénier, Marie Joseph (1764–1811) 74
Cherubini, Luigi (1760–1842) 235
Choiseul 1
Cispadine Republic xxiv, 45, 175
Clermont-Tonnerre, Charles-Henri-Jules, Duc de (1720–94) 155, 218
Cobb, Richard 200, 386
Cobban, Alfred (1901–68) 200, 229
Cobenzl, Johann Ludwig Joseph Graf von (1753–1809) 62, 291
Coburg, Frederick Josias, Prince of (1737–1815) 135, 136, 166, 180, 326
Collenot d'Angremont, Louis-David (1748–92) 159
Commission of Monuments 12
Committee of General Defence 62, 87, 116
Communism 23
Communist Party 232, 337

Comtat-Venaissin xvii, 4, 131, 138, 179, 233, 277
Comte, Auguste (1798–1857) 18
Concordat 4, 76, 126, 154, 169, 277, 304, 309, 344, 355
Condé, Louis Joseph, Prince de (1736–1818) 13, 55, 63, 95, 124, 284, 370
Conscription xxv, 38, 116, 151, 180
Conspiracy of Equals 24, 56, 120, 181, 208, 371
Constant de Rebecque, Henri-Benjamin (1767–1830) 136, 341
Constantinople 123, 242
Constitution of 1791 3, 134, 213, 226, 270, 274, 284, 338, 377
Constitution of 1793 xxi, 18, 24, 42, 46, 147, 148
Constitution of 1795 (Year III) 31, 115, 263
Constitutional Guard 191
Constitutional Monarchy xix, 40, 50, 134, 135, 137, 149, 152, 173, 180, 188, 190, 193, 201, 203, 206, 212, 213, 215, 241, 247, 250, 252, 256, 264, 304, 310, 345, 369,
Consulate xxv, 8, 38, 42, 44, 53, 76, 117, 120, 182, 189, 197, 208, 273, 327, 330, 333, 345
Coppet 220, 252, 341
Corsica 44, 56
Council of 500 24, 31, 43, 53, 62, 117, 143, 154, 174, 180, 205, 208, 237, 238, 239, 244, 273, 279, 280, 335, 347, 365, 389
Council of Elders 53, 64, 191
Créoles 6, 35

Dalbarade, Jean (1743–1819) 168, 294
D'Alembert, Jean le Rond (1717–83) 90, 126, 255, 315
Daunou, Pierre-Claude-François (1761–1840) 331
Davidovich, Paul, Baron (1737–1814) 175
'Day of the Daggers' xvii, 187
'Day of the Tiles' xvi, 29
Dechézeux, Gustave (1760–93) 204
De-Christianization 62, 73, 80, 85, 97, 140, 154, 163, 178, 190, 204, 218, 271, 294, 302, 313, 320, 326, 380
Declaration of Verona 83
Deficit 14, 16, 17, 60, 112, 127, 208, 225, 250, 251, 276, 284, 286, 296, 349, 379
Départements xvii, 4, 9, 37, 58, 60, 64, 65, 84, 116, 137, 173, 228, 249, 263, 276, 323, 330, 334, 335, 336, 377
Desaix, Louis Charles Antoine (1768–1800) 123

Diderot, Denis (1713–84) 6, 65, 126, 221, 315
Dillon, Arthur (1750–94) 111, 112
DNA Testing 216
Dorigny, Marcel 237
'Doubling the Third' xvi, 128
Doyle, William (1942–) 127, 141, 149, 210, 229, 372
Drouet, Jean-Baptiste (1763–1824) 24, 25, 365, 369
'Dry Guillotine' 29, 145
Ducos (or Roger-Ducos), Pierre-Roger (1747–1816) 53, 279, 336
Dugommier (real name Coquille), Jacques, General (1738–94) 45
Dundas, Henry 1st Vicomte Melville (1742–1811) 192, 273, 321
Dunkirk 166
Duphot, Mathurin-Léonard (1769–97) 277, 312

Egret, Jean 280
Elections xiv, 3, 4, 7, 18, 22, 31, 44, 69, 79, 86, 88, 92, 136, 137, 138, 143, 144, 145, 148, 156, 191, 201, 222, 237, 248, 254, 256, 273, 279, 299, 301, 311, 334, 335, 360, 365, 371
Emilia 76
Enragés 5, 11, 73, 94, 184, 185, 198, 202, 266, 319, 370, 380

Farmers-General 23, 194, 195, 265, 283, 348
Faubourg de Saint-Marcel 161
Féraud, Jean Bertrand (1759–95) 42, 148
Flanders Regiment 257
Flesselles, Jacques de (1721–89) 33, 39
'Flour War' 40, 210
Foulon de Doué, Joseph-François (1715–89) 39
Fouquier-Tinville, Antoine Quentin (1746–95) xxi, 51, 89, 90, 112, 120, 163, 193, 226, 243, 262, 304, 314
Fox, Charles James (1749–1806) 100
Francis II, Emperor of Austria xviii, xix, 50, 109, 135, 138, 226, 310, 385
Frankfurt 98, 180, 221, 234
Franklin, Benjamin (1706–90) 263, 339
Frederick William II, King of Prussia (1786–97) 32, 50, 51, 273
Frederick William III, King of Prussia (1797–1840) 298, 385
Fréjus 45
Frey Brothers 32, 69

Gasparin, Thomas-Augustin (1754–93) 44,
    228, 362
George III, King of England (1760–1820) 14,
    96, 125
Glacièristes 22
Granville 117, 192, 282
Grenelle 64
Gueniffey, Patrice (1955–) 54, 186
Gustavus III of Sweden (1771–92) 50, 133,
    273, 340

Haxo, François-Nicolas-Benoît (1774–1838)
    74, 170
Herman, Martial-Joseph-Armand (1749–95)
    226, 305
Hervilly, Louis-Charles, Comte d' (1756–95)
    76, 288–9
Hoarders 73, 94, 106, 195, 302, 328, 338
Holland xix, xxiii, xxv, 34, 37, 136, 336,
    357
Holy Roman Empire xviii, xix, 54, 109, 290,
    375, 377
Hondschoote xxi, 167
Hood, Samuel, Vice-Admiral Lord
    (1724–1816) 31, 106, 132, 143, 204, 215,
    228, 284, 321, 362, 374
Hugo, Victor (1802–85) 281, 391
'Hundred Days' 43

India 122
Ireland 52, 80, 167
Isabey, Jean-Baptiste (1767–1855) 59
Istanbul 73

Jacobin Misogyny 5, 358
Jacobin Republic 144, 316, 361
Jaffa 123, 157
Jaucourt, Arnail-François, Marquis de
    (1757–1852) 255, 341
Jaurès, Jean (1859–1914) 3, 199, 228, 232
Jersey 67, 72
Jesuits 277, 382
Jones, Colin 31
Joseph II, Emperor of Austria 15, 37, 210, 237,
    277
Joubert, Barthélemy-Catherine (1769–99) 35,
    77, 279, 336
Juniper Hall 189, 340

Kaiserslautern 166
Kates, Gary 228

Kaunitz, Wenzel Anton Graf (1711–94) 166,
    277, 358
Kellermann, François-Christophe (1735–1820)
    98, 116, 140, 218, 368
Kersaint, Armand-Guy-Simon, Comte de
    (1742–93) 87
Kléber, Jean-Baptiste (1753–1800) 45, 52, 74,
    123, 192
Koblenz 13, 19, 54, 55, 71, 92, 95, 125, 260, 284

La Jaunaye, Peace of xxiii, 71, 167, 343, 374
La Rochefoucauld-Bayers, Pierre Louis de
    (1744–92) 82, 91
Lakanal, Joseph (1762–1845) 296, 318, 331
Larochefoucauld-Liancourt, François-
    Alexandre-Frédéric, Duc de (1747–1827)
    89, 212
Launay, Bernard René Jourdan, Marquis de
    (1740–89) 21
Law of Hostages xxv, 279
Law of Two Thirds 374
Le Vieux Cordelier 112
Leconte, Patrice 378
Legendre, Louis (1752–97) 93, 266
Leoben 62, 301
Leopold II, Emperor of Austria 109, 226, 273,
    274, 358
Letourneur, Etienne-François (1751–1817) 83
Levée en masse xxi, 3, 10
Lodi 174
Loi d'Allarde 297
Louis XIV 1, 4
Louis XV 1, 118, 142, 160, 209, 210, 221, 247,
    380, 381
Louis XVIII 83, 125, 126, 131, 143, 284
Lucas, Colin 7

Madeira 39
Madrid 59
Maillard, Marie-Julian-Stanislas (1763–94) 33,
    91, 258
Mainz 98, 109, 136, 239, 273, 284, 300, 323
Malouet, Pierre Victor, Baron (1740–1814) 110
Manège xxi, 176, 366
Mantua xxiv, 175, 375
Manuel, Pierre-Louis (1751–93) 341, 354
Marengo 77, 285, 354, 385
Marillet de La Courboisière, François-
    Guillaume (1742–1800) 280
Marseillaise 132, 146, 151, 339, 368
Marsh (or Plain) 42, 62, 162, 224, 245, 334

Martin-Dauch, Joseph (1741–1801) 350
Martineau, Louis-Simon (1733–1800) 78
Massiac Club 6, 323, 324
May Edicts 155, 209
Mazauric, Claude (1932–) 230
McPhee, Peter 276
Merveilleuses 150
Mesmer, Anton (1734–1815) 121, 158
Metz 47, 154
Mézières Engineering School 63
Midi 4, 14, 20, 143, 174, 218, 227, 228, 254, 284, 336, 357
Milan xxv, 76, 77, 157, 174, 231, 279, 336
Minimes Society 358
'Ministry of a Hundred Hours' 50
Mitraillades 219
Modena 76
Moira, Francis Rawdon-Hastings, Lord (1754–1826) 192
Momoro, Thérèse 72, 243, 291, 309
Monarchiens 82, 114, 188, 215, 244
Montauban 152, 322
Montbéliard 39, 300
Montesquieu, Charles-Louis de Secondat, Baron de (1689–1755) 6, 250
Montmorin de Saint Herem, Armand-Marc, Comte de (1745–92) 20, 100, 225
Montpensier, Antoine-Philippe d'Orleans, Duc de (1775–1807) 119
Morbihan 198
Moreau, Jean Victor Marie, General (1763–1813) 144, 174, 180, 336, 385
Mortagne-au-Perche 75
Motte, Jeanne de Valois, Comtesse de (1756–91) 113
Moulin, Jean-François-Auguste (1752–1810) 53, 279
Murat, Joachim (1767–1815) 53, 374
Musée Carnavalet, Paris 142, 205, 206

Nantes xxi, xxii, 4, 27, 66, 71, 80, 117, 124, 139, 181, 185, 250, 346, 347
Neerwinden xviii, 34, 37, 87, 119, 135, 166, 179, 238
Nelson, Horatio, Vice-Admiral Lord (1758–1805) 122
Neo-Jacobins 141, 145, 266, 279
Neufchâteau, François de (1750–1828) 12, 137, 145, 291, 365
Neuwied 167
Nivière-Chol, Antoine (1744–1817) 70, 217

Nolay 63
Normandy 66, 92, 287, 330

Oath to the Civil Constitution 150, 209, 250, 293
Ochs, Peter (1752–1821) 164, 300
Oléron, Ile d' 38, 56, 145, 169
One and Indivisible 2, 28, 73, 87, 149, 152, 195, 245, 248, 249, 290, 308, 330, 352, 365
Oratorians 41, 99, 139, 165, 331, 388
Ozouf, Mona (1931–) 146, 355

Paris Commune of 1871 18, 240
Pâris, Philippe de 203
Parisot, Jean-Nicolas-Jacques 253
Passive citizens 3, 93, 172, 173, 177, 307, 328, 338
Patrie en danger xix, 9, 32, 104, 106, 107, 111, 165, 195, 206, 336, 359
Paul I, Tsar of Russia (1796–1801) 123, 285, 336, 385
Pertué, Michel 115
Philosophes 83, 126–7, 255
Picardy 23, 24, 310, 348
Piedmont xxiv, 55, 174, 207, 340
Pitt, William (1759–1806) 14, 75, 122, 137, 138, 192, 273, 282, 288, 321, 383, 385
Pius VII (Pope, 1800–23) 76, 126, 169, 304, 344, 355
Plain: see Marsh
Porrentruy 150, 300
Princes of the Blood 15, 209, 210, 221, 253, 260, 285
Prussia xviii, xxiii, 32, 37, 50, 51, 54, 65, 109, 113, 137, 139, 202, 222, 238, 273, 298, 335, 357, 365, 383
Puy-de-Dôme 96, 97, 329
Pyramids, battle of 45, 122
Pyrenees 28, 33, 64, 38, 383

Quesnay, François (1694–1774) 272
Quimper 75

Raynal, Guillaume Thomas, Abbé (1711–96) 6
Referendum on the king's sentence 214
Republic xix, xxiii, xxiv, xxv, 2, 3, 28, 31, 33, 34, 41, 50, 55, 63, 70, 76, 77, 98, 102, 106, 111, 122, 140, 144, 146, 163, 164, 168, 177, 181, 184, 203, 206, 207, 222, 233, 240, 243, 245, 247, 248, 266, 275, 277, 279, 290, 291, 303, 304, 306, 308, 312,

316, 325, 330, 339, 352, 361, 364, 367, 375, 377, 383, 384
Révolutions de France et de Brabant 110
Révolutions de Paris 69, 285
Rhine 38, 62, 76, 98, 136, 144, 167, 174, 198, 201, 272, 273, 290, 300, 357, 383, 384
Rivoli xiv, 175
'Robespierre's Tail' 150
Roederer, Pierre-Louis (1751–1835) 13, 159
Rohan, Louis-René-Edouard, Cardinal (1734–1803) 36, 112, 113, 124, 348
Rossignol, Jean Antoine (1759–1802) 24
Royer-Collard, Pierre-Paul (1763–1845) 82
Russia 14, 109, 119, 137, 220, 228, 233, 312, 358, 385

Saint-Cloud Palace 53, 113, 187, 213, 225, 226, 264, 365, 368
Saint-Ménéhoude 47, 365, 369
Saint-Roch, Church of 31, 375
Saintes 38, 82, 91, 158, 169, 193, 242, 280, 319
Sambre 135
Sardinia xviii
Savenay, Battle of xxii, 170, 192, 386
Savona 174
Schérer Louis-Joseph (1747–1804) 385
Scurr, Ruth 306
Second Empire (1852–70) 18, 240, 360, 361
Second Republic (1848–52) 240, 361
Ségur, Louis-Philippe, Comte de (1753–1830) 8
Sens 209
Servan, Joseph-Marie (1741–1808) 103, 105, 149, 261, 310
Seven Years' War 19, 49, 98, 118, 192
Smith, Sir Sidney (1764–1840) 123
Social Contract 102, 108, 317, 318
Society of 1789 186, 195
Sonenscher, Michael 327
Sonthonax, Léger-Félicité (1763–1813) 324, 363
Spain xx, xxi, xxiii, xxiv, 6, 14, 33, 37, 64, 95, 113, 125, 181, 201, 212, 238, 259, 285, 293, 323, 357, 383, 384
Spang, Rebecca L. 283
Sutherland, D.M.G. 94, 96, 102, 349
Suvarov, Alexander Vasilyevich (1729–1800) xxv, 77, 279, 336, 385
Syria 45, 244

Tackett, Timothy 176, 327
Tarbes 28, 29
Temple Prison xix, xx, xxiii, 30, 62, 105, 143, 189, 210, 214, 215, 226, 265, 284, 285, 293, 319, 329, 332, 340, 379
The Hague 34, 141, 266, 300
Thionville 71, 239
Third Republic 3, 18, 19, 28, 146, 233, 240, 339
Thorigné-en-Charnie 117, 278
Thugut, Johann-Amadeus-Franz von (1736–1818) 139, 291
Tipu Sultan (1750–99) 31
Tone, Wolf (1763–98) 167
Toulouse xxv, 28, 129, 203, 254, 381
Tribune des Patriotes 111
Tricolore 193, 246, 257
Trier 109, 273
Trogoff-Kerlessy, Jean-Honoré, Vice-Admiral (1751–94) 362
Turgot, Anne-Robert-Jacques, Baron de Laune (1727–81) 6, 90, 194, 244, 377
Turin 13, 50, 95, 174, 254, 385
Turreau, Louis-Marie (1756–1816) 71, 74, 75, 124, 170, 171, 181, 373, 386

United States of America 51, 71, 80, 81, 90, 107, 115, 194, 260, 263, 323, 345
Universal Male Suffrage 3, 18, 35, 105, 114, 197, 263, 316, 361

Veto 94, 104, 125, 114, 132, 241, 258
Vieux Cordelier 112
Villaret-Joyeuse, Louis-Thomas, Comte de (1748–1812) 251, 288, 322, 323
Vizille 155–6

Warren, Sir John Borlase (1753–1822) 288–9, 299
Waterloo 141, 181, 188, 285
Willot, Amédée (1755–1823) 82
Wimpffen, Georges Felix de (1744–1814) 60
Wissembourg 167
Women 5, 12, 93, 103, 148, 184, 185, 198, 199, 202, 265, 331, 338, 359
Wörms 98, 125
Würmser, Dagobert Sigismund Graf (1724–97) 166, 175

'X', 'Y', and 'Z' 345